F V

CHANGE IN
SOCIETAL INSTITUTIONS

CHANGE IN
SOCIETAL INSTITUTIONS

Edited by

Maureen T. Hallinan
David M. Klein
and
Jennifer Glass
University of Notre Dame
Notre Dame, Indiana

PLENUM PRESS • NEW YORK AND LONDON

Library of Congress Cataloging in Publication Data

Change in societal institutions / edited by Maureen T. Hallinan, David M. Klein, and Jennifer Glass.
    p.   cm.
    Includes bibliographical references and index.
    ISBN 0-306-43541-1
    1. Social institutions—United States. 2. Social structure—United States. 3. United States—Social conditions—1980–   .I. Hallinan, Maureen T. II. Klein, David M., 1943–   . III. Glass, Jennifer.
HN65.C46   1990   90-7464
306$^\backslash$.0973—dc20$^{\backslash\backslash}$ CIP

© 1990 Plenum Press, New York
A Division of Plenum Publishing Corporation
233 Spring Street, New York, N.Y. 10013

Printed in the United States of America

To Art, Jennifer,
and Bruce with appreciation

Contributors

JAMES R. BENIGER, Annenberg School of Communications, University of Southern California, Los Angeles, California 90089-0281

CHRISTOPHER BOTSKO, Department of Sociology, Indiana University, Bloomington, Indiana 47405

JOYCE L. EPSTEIN, Center for Research on Elementary and Middle Schools, The Johns Hopkins University, Baltimore, Maryland 21218

WILLIAM FORM, Department of Sociology, Ohio State University, Columbus, Ohio 43210

JENNIFER GLASS, Department of Sociology, University of Notre Dame, Notre Dame, Indiana 46556

LARRY J. GRIFFIN, Department of Sociology, Indiana University, Bloomington, Indiana 47405

JOHN HAGAN, Faculty of Law, University of Toronto, Toronto M5S 2C5, Ontario, Canada

SUSAN HERBST, Department of Communication Studies, Northwestern University, Evanston, Illinois 60208

BARBARA HEYNS, Department of Sociology, New York University, New York, New York 10003

DAVID M. KLEIN, Department of Sociology, University of Notre Dame, Notre Dame, Indiana 46556

CORA BAGLEY MARRETT, Department of Sociology, University of Wisconsin–Madison, Madison, Wisconsin 53706

HOLLY J. MCCAMMON, Department of Sociology, Vanderbilt University, Nashville, Tennessee 37235

JOHN MIROWSKY, Department of Sociology, University of Illinois at Urbana–Champaign, Urbana, Illinois 61801

CATHERINE E. ROSS, Department of Sociology, University of Illinois at Urbana–Champaign, Urbana, Illinois 61801

RICHARD A. SCHOENHERR, Department of Sociology, University of Wisconsin–Madison, Madison, Wisconsin 53706

TERESA A. SULLIVAN, Department of Sociology, University of Texas at Austin, Austin, Texas 78712-1088

RUY A. TEIXEIRA, Economic Research Service–ARED, 1301 New York Avenue, NW, Washington, DC 20005-4788

LAWRENCE A. YOUNG, Department of Sociology, Brigham Young University, Provo, Utah 84601

ROBERT ZUSSMAN, Department of Sociology, State University of New York–Stony Brook, Stony Brook, New York 11794, and Center for the Study of Medicine and Society, Columbia University, New York, New York 10032

Preface

In the second half of the twentieth century, a number of researchers have conceptualized modern society as a social system composed of differentiated yet interrelated institutional spheres. Commonly identified institutional spheres are the family, religion, the economy, the polity or state, medicine or health care, religion, law, and education. The institutional perspective has sometimes been linked to a structural–functional framework; it has often been asserted that institutions must be understood as parts of a larger whole operating at the societal level.

Equally important have been recent institutional theory and research focusing on the more microscopic dynamics of intrainstitutional change. The concern here has been processes governing the institutionalization of rules and practices and the formation and decline of particular social structures.

Although valid and useful, neither of these perspectives has yielded a systematic comparative assessment of societal institutions. The aim of this edited volume is to meet this critical need. It brings together recent theoretical and empirical research on societal institutions in a time of rapid change. The chapters focus on how these institutions adapt to societal change and what the outcomes of these changes are.

In addressing these concerns, three central questions arise:

What are the major changes that have taken place over the past decade in the institution under consideration?

What are the structural, organizational, and other antecedents or determinants of these changes?

What are the consequences of these changes for other institutions and for individuals in American society and abroad?

Each of the authors in this volume addresses these questions explicitly, and they form the unifying theme of the book. In addition, three secondary questions are considered:

Does current theory developed within an institutional sphere generalize across spheres, and with what modifications?

What are the implications of intrainstitutional dynamics for interinstitutional linkages, that is, are changes mutually reinforcing or countervailing?

Which theoretical perspectives on comparative institutional change offer the greatest promise for understanding society in the years ahead?

Five of the chapters in this volume were presented at a conference entitled "Change in Societal Institutions" held at the University of Notre Dame on March 28–29, 1988. These are the papers by Griffin, Hagan, Heyns, Ross, and Sullivan. In order to expand the comparative institutional perspective discussed at the conference, six additional authors were invited to contribute to the volume. Finally, William Form wrote the summary chapter, once again addressing the questions that guided the authors' work. This volume, then, represents the most recent contemporary thinking on comparative institutional change.

The book is aimed at a wide audience of social scientists. It should also be useful to graduate students in various disciplines who are interested in the study of institutions. It is hoped that the chapters presented will stimulate new theoretical and empirical research in order to advance our understanding of the interconnectedness of societal institutions.

The editors express gratitude to the Institute for Scholarship in the Liberal Arts at the University of Notre Dame and to the Exxon Foundation for sponsoring the conference that led to this book. We are also grateful to Loretta Budzinski, Julie O'Block, and Sylvia Phillips for their assistance with the conference and with the preparation of the volume for publication. Mostly, we thank the authors of the chapters for the significant contribution each of them made to the success of this project and, indeed, to social science in general.

MAUREEN T. HALLINAN

Contents

Introduction   1

Jennifer Glass and David M. Klein

Chapter 1. The Decline of Occupations: Redefining the Labor Force . .   13

Teresa A. Sullivan

Occupation and a New Workplace Revolution   14
The Traditional Significance of Occupations   15
    Occupations as Trouble.   15
    Occupations as a Social Problem   16
    Occupations as a Sociological Problem   17
Recent Labor Force Developments   19
    Products.   19
    Technology   20
    Organization.   21
    Supply-Side Changes   23
    Summary.   26
The Declining Significance of Occupation   26
Conclusion.   28
References   30

Chapter 2. Women, Work, and Family: Changing Gender Roles and
           Psychological Well-Being   33

Catherine E. Ross and John Mirowsky

Introduction   33
Employment and Marriage   34

Employment and Children   39
Women's Work   44
Conclusion.   44
References   46

Chapter 3. Gender and the Structural Transformation of the Legal
             Profession in the United States and Canada   49

John Hagan

Introduction   49
The Demographics of Professional Growth in the
     United States and Canada   50
The Segmentation and Stratification of Legal Practice   54
Partnership, Profit, and Pleasure in Practice   56
Power in Practice   58
Lawyers' Lives and the Structural Transformation of Legal Practice . .   65
References   66

Chapter 4. The Changing Composition of Schools: Implications for
             School Organization   71

Cora Bagley Marrett

Changes in the Makeup of Schools   71
Effective Schools Research.   74
The Organization of American Schools   76
     On Loosely Coupled Systems.   76
     Rethinking the Model   77
     Beyond the Coupling of Roles   79
On the Significance of Social Ties   80
On Networks and Learning.   81
     In-School Networks.   81
     School–Community Networks   81
     On Effective Social Networks   82
     Networks and School Achievement   84
     Networks and Social Capital.   84
Networks and Culture   86
The Tasks Ahead   87
References   88

Chapter 5. Single Parents and the Schools: Effects of Marital Status
            on Parent and Teacher Interactions 91

Joyce L. Epstein

Introduction 91
Theoretical Perspectives.. 92
Sample, Variables, and Approaches................................... 96
    Characteristics of Parents...................................... 97
Results: Parents' Reports of Teachers' Practices of
    Parent Involvement 99
Teachers' Reports of Single and Married Parents' Helpfulness and
    Followthrough 103
Teachers' Reports of the Quality of Homework by Children from
    One- and Two-Parent Homes 107
Parents' Awareness, Knowledge, and Evaluations of Teachers 112
Other Reports about School from Single and Married Parents 112
Summary and Discussion 114
References 118

Chapter 6. The Changing Contours of the Teaching Profession 123

Barbara Heyns

Trends in Attrition... 125
Attrition Rates in the National Longitudinal Study................. 127
Who Left Teaching and Who Wants to Return? 130
Teacher Attrition and Teacher Qualifications....................... 132
Schools and Patterns of Attrition among Teachers.................. 135
Conclusions.. 138
References 139

Chapter 7. Contradiction and Change in Organized Religion: Roman
            Catholicism in the United States and Spain............. 143

Lawrence A. Young and Richard A. Schoenherr

Organizational Demography and the Catholic Church 146
Population Change and the Demographic Transition 148
Data and Methods 151
Analysis... 151
    Trends in Growth Rates, 1966–1984 151

Estimates and Projections of Size and Age Distribution,
  1966–2045 154
Discussion 162
References 165

Chapter 8. The "Unmaking" of a Movement? The Crisis of U.S. Trade
            Unions in Comparative Perspective 169

Larry J. Griffin, Holly J. McCammon, and Christopher Botsko

Introduction 169
Unionization before and during the Decline 173
Theoretical Explanations of the Decline 176
Analyzing the Decline 181
   Regression Diagnostics 182
   "Implied" Union Growth and Decline 184
"Explaining" the U.S. Density Reduction 185
Conclusion and Implications 187
Data Appendix 191
References 192

Chapter 9. Medicine, the Medical Profession, and the Welfare State . . 195

Robert Zussman

Medicine's Professional Project 196
Medicine and the Welfare State 199
Costs and Controls 202
The Rise of Bioethics 203
Professions and Proprietors 205
The Limits of Professionalism 207
References 209

Chapter 10. Mass Media and Public Opinion: Emergence of an
             Institution 211

James R. Beniger and Susan Herbst

Mass Society Revisited 213
The Emergence of a Public Opinion 214
Convergence of Mass Media and Public Opinion 216
Emergence of an Institution 219
New Mass Media 221
Conflict with Other Institutions 222

Conflict with the Family.. 223
Conflict with Education 225
Conflict with Religion.. 226
Conflict with the Polity.. 227
The New Institutional Paradigm 230
Summary... 231
References 231

Chapter 11. Things Fall Apart: Americans and Their Political
            Institutions, 1960–1988............................. 239

Ruy A. Teixeira

Introduction 239
Decline of Political Participation............................... 241
Decline of Political Parties 246
Decline of Traditional Forms of Political Consciousness............ 249
Conclusion... 252
References 254

Chapter 12. Institutional Analysis: An Organizational Approach 257

William Form

Early Conceptions 257
Introductory Textbooks 261
Critique of Institutional Theory 262
Organizational Institutional Analysis.......................... 265
The Structure of Institutional Complexes...................... 267
Conclusions.. 270
References 271

Index... 273

Introduction

JENNIFER GLASS AND DAVID M. KLEIN

The subject matter of this book, changing social institutions, is intended to familiarize scholars with the breadth and depth of changes in the American institutions that meet most of our major social needs. Almost all of the human endeavors that require structured social cooperation are touched on here—how we as a society form and maintain familial bonds, educate our children, produce and distribute material resources, treat the sick and infirm, disseminate information to the populace, define and promote national interests through government, and seek spiritual comfort and solace. All too often, the individual components of social systems are studied in isolation rather than as parts of an intricate whole, a tendency exacerbated by the trend toward specialization within sociology and the social sciences generally. The sheer amount of information to be absorbed and the magnitude and complexity of the social problems we face discourage most scholars from venturing far outside their own narrow domain. We hope this book will prove to be an antidote. This volume attempts to familiarize readers with the most important and most enduring changes in our social institutions as we enter the next century.

As we all know, however, integrating knowledge from a wide array of sources is a difficult matter. Our intent in preparing this book, therefore, is to focus on the interrelationships between social institutions as well; to look at the ways in which institutional changes are interlocking. Some far-reaching changes in different institutions are in fact responses to the same underlying dilemma, whether it comes from demographic, environmental, or technological challenges. Other changes stem more directly from one institution's alteration of form or content; for example, when schools are

JENNIFER GLASS AND DAVID M. KLEIN • Department of Sociology, University of Notre Dame, Notre Dame, Indiana 46556.

1

forced to adjust to changing family structures or medical practice is altered in response to government intervention in health care funding.

Although not wanting to deny the complexity of social change, careful examination of the chapters in this volume shows that several of the same driving forces are mentioned repeatedly as the source of institutional change. Three in particular are worth noting: (1) economic challenges from global competition and technological advances, (2) demographic shifts in population composition stemming from both cultural and technological process, and (3) changes in the values and behavior of American women that have eroded traditional definitions of public and private life. These three underlying sources of change both impact institutions directly by altering their purpose or client population and indirectly by setting in motion conflicts between institutions that must work in close harmony with one another. Each will be briefly elaborated upon later.

Tremendous changes in the American economy have occurred in the last 20 years as American dominance in the world economy has declined. The internationalization of labor and the growth of global capitalism through multinational corporations have displaced American workers in favor of cheaper labor elsewhere and eroded the power of organized labor. The growing technological sophistication of developing countries, particularly in the Asian rim, has given the American economy serious competition for world markets. Technological advances have affected the economy in other ways as well. Most prominently, technology has eliminated many unskilled and semiskilled jobs in manufacturing, while increasing the demand for educated workers and service industries. In general, these economic changes have decreased the value of population growth, increased the costs of childbearing, destabilized the monetary base for family formation, and, in turn, the fiscal base for government expenditures on social goods. The reverberations can be felt in our educational, health care, and religious institutions.

The second dynamic source of institutional change is demographic. Improvements in nutrition, life-style changes, and medical technology have produced dramatic increases in longevity over the twentieth century. As Americans live longer, the number of older Americans has risen sharply, particularly in contrast to the declining proportion of youth in the population stemming from the long-term decline in fertility. However, fertility decline has not been uniform, and ethnic minorities continue to have higher than average fertility rates. That, combined with increased immigration from economically unstable Asian and Latin American countries, has produced a shift of epic proportions in the size of the nonwhite population in the United States. By the end of this century, the American population will be significantly older and less white than it has ever been before. Once again, our educational system must address the needs of new kinds of students, our economic system must incorporate new kinds of workers and new kinds of consumers, and our cultural definitions of appropriate family forms, religious practices, and forms of government assistance must be realigned.

Finally, the increased participation of women in the labor force and decreased participation in childbearing and child rearing has forced a major redefinition of the goals and purposes of family life, government, and the provision of goods and services from the economy. The private provisions of household goods and services to individuals is less assured as women find it more costly to remain out of the paid labor force. As women are pushed into the public economy both by necessity and choice, so too must economic organizations change to incorporate the provision of services to the populace once provided in the private household for free. This includes pressures for change in the treatment of workers within organizations as well as pressures for the economy to market new services such as child and elder care, prepared meals, housecleaning, and the like.

These three major sources of change are not analytically distinct, of course. Changes in women's roles and obligations are fueled by declining fertility, growth in service sectors of the economy, increased longevity, and cultural norms promoting equality. The differential access of women of color to economic opportunities fuels differential rates of fertility decline. Demographic change is also encouraged by immigration from developing nations plagued with economic and political instability. Taken together, these social forces form a powerful and interlocking impetus for change.

Teresa Sullivan begins our look at how these major forces have shaped institutional change by arguing that occupational classification, once the bulwark of our stratification system and an almost infallible indicator of social class, is losing its significance in a changed economy. Sullivan reviews the ways in which the fortunes of different industries have risen or fallen with increased global competition or technological innovation. Similarly, she shows how firm size and internal organizations have drastically altered the wages and working conditions of workers ostensibly working in the same occupation. Sullivan notes that this is particularly true for female-dominated occupations such as secretary, nurse, social worker, and so forth. Because industry and firm size often determine the technical requirements for jobs as diverse as managers, sales, clerical, and service staff, these new variables deserve closer attention in the study of stratification and perhaps should supplant the study of occupations *per se*.

Catherine Ross looks at how the dramatic increase in women's labor force participation is affecting the institution of marriage, the domestic division of labor among married couples, and subsequent psychological well-being. Ross shows that although demands on wives' time are increasing, husbands are moving much more slowly toward increased participation in housework and child care. The resulting stress in these transitional marriages affects both, particularly in those families where wives must cope with fragile or unsatisfactory child care arrangements. The movement from traditional to egalitarian conceptions of marital roles requires adjustments in individual beliefs about women's and men's primary responsibilities, the nature of marriage and family life, and appropriate forms of child care. Couples in the midst of this difficult reorientation are most likely to be psychologically distressed.

Turning to another consequence of women's increased representation in the labor force, John Hagan studies the transformation of the legal profession. As the number of lawyers has dramatically increased, fueled mostly by the upsurge in women entering the field, competition and stratification within the profession have increased as well. The effects of the growth of huge legal conglomerates on both the practice of law and the careers of new entrants to the profession, particularly women, have not always been salutary. The growth of a two-tiered legal profession has left most women out of partnerships and into temporary, part-time, or lower status legal employment as they struggle to balance family obligations with the fast-paced demands of the legal profession. The effects of expansion and competition extend to the larger society as well through the increased use of expensive litigation.

Cora Marrett's work on the need for effective intervention in the education of minority children turns our attention to the educational system. Minority children, particularly black and Hispanic, represent a growing share of the nation's school-age population but score lower on standardized achievement tests and are often concentrated in decaying urban areas. These children comprise a high-risk population whose schools require particular attention given the shrinking population of American schools and the increased need for trained workers. Marrett, rather than echoing the cry for tighter centralized management in innercity schools (which some fear will erode the autonomy and professionalism of classroom teachers), reinterprets both the problems and intervention strategies that hold promise for such schools. Noting the fragmentation of contacts and lack of consensus on educational goals in problem schools, Marrett suggests renewed emphasis on strengthening interpersonal contacts and social networks among teaching staff, administrators, parents, and students.

Joyce Epstein, writing on parent–teacher interactions and their influences on student achievement, looks at differences in the experiences of single and married parents. Echoing the need for better teacher–parent communication in problem schools, Epstein finds that initially less positive perceptions among single parents are primarily due to other home and school conditions. The children of single parents, although growing in number, are more often nonwhite, live in less affluent circumstances, and attend schools with less interpersonal contact between teachers and parents. Although many critics of single-parent families feel that single parents are less likely to be involved and concerned about their children's education, Epstein reports that it is primarily teacher leadership and teacher involvement practices that influence any parent's interest in and connection to the school. Interestingly, both Marrett and Epstein point out that it is the interpersonal networks of students that need enrichment to enhance student achievement, rather than focusing on curriculum or disciplinary issues.

Turning to an analysis of the teaching profession itself, Barbara Heyns argues that, contrary to popular myth, teacher quality is not declining and the best teachers are not most likely to leave teaching. Further, teacher attrition is actually decreasing over time, due to the dramatic increase in the continuous labor force participation of women in general. Moreover, Heyns's research indicates that retention is higher in relatively poor schools, suggesting that teachers primarily leave because of better economic alternatives in affluent areas rather than because of job dissatisfaction. Scarce evidence exists to support the claim that teachers are less prepared now than previously; however, expectations for teacher performance have clearly increased as our dependence on an educated work force intensifies. Future teacher shortages, especially in technical subjects where alternative employment exists, will only magnify the problem.

Richard Schoenherr and his associates write of a different personnel shortage—the decline in the number of active Catholic priests. Using demographic data from dioceses in the United States and Spain, Schoenherr assesses the change in the size and age composition of the priest population over the last two decades. Results show significant erosion and aging of the population as recruitment and retention have slowed down. Projections using a variety of assumptions show continued rapid decline even under optimistic conditions. Such changes in manpower will soon force the Church as an organization to take drastic measures if it is to retain its sacramental function. The unfortunate paradox is that declining recruitment has selectively produced smaller but more conservative cohorts of new entrants. Thus as a decision-making body, the priesthood is becoming more traditional as it faces intensified pressures for change.

Although economic reorganization has reached into all sectors of our stratification system, nowhere have the reverberations been more dramatic than within organized labor. Larry Griffin and his colleagues, looking at data on union membership and activity in the United States and Europe, find that the United States has experienced the sharpest erosion in both union coverage and influence. Although most observers conclude this is the result of intensified competition and decline in manufacturing employment where American unions are strongest, Griffin suggests other sources of decline. Pointing out the low rates of strike activity and other displays of collective resistance, Griffin advances the view that American unions have become too focused on wage agreements, too collaborative with management in efforts to control union membership, and have failed to understand or protect the interests of their members during this economic transition. Given the costs associated with union membership, it is not surprising that working-class participation in unions has cooled.

Next, Robert Zussman explores the changes in American medicine caused by growing reliance on government expenditures to fund health care and medical research. As health care costs escalate, the state has begun to intervene in dramatic and unprecedented ways both to define appropriate treatment and appropriate reimbursement costs for services. Although the state had previously benefited the medical profession by expanding health care coverage to underserved populations, the current fiscal crisis has prompted government action that threatens to seriously erode the professional autonomy of physicians.

While many institutions face challenges from technological innovation, James Beniger and Susan Herbst argue in the following chapter that modern communications technology has created an entirely new social institution—mass information processing and communication. The combination of sophisticated public opinion polling and mass dissemination of the resulting information through media has created an institutionalized information industry. This new convergence has the potential to challenge community-based cultural and familial norms and values by promoting its own version of objectively measured majority views. By ordering and selecting information to particular target audiences, survey researchers and their media outlets can generate new forms of social control.

In his chapter, Ruy Teixeira tackles the problem of decline in political participation among the American electorate. Tracing the problem back to the erosion of partisanship and the decline of the New Deal partnership among southerners, blacks, and blue-collar workers, Teixeira shows how emerging political interests among women, baby-boomers, people of color, and so forth, have spawned disinterest in the traditional political parties and apathy toward the outcomes of elections. He questions whether the fragmentation of the American electorate can be halted within the existing political framework.

Although the chapters differ significantly in form and content, all emphasize the dependencies of institutions on one another. Although causes and consequences are sometimes institution-specific, rarely do we see institutional changes in these pages that are solely attributable to internal problems or conflicts. Rather, institutions are pushing and chafing against each other, competing for legitimacy and social functions as the economic, cultural, and demographic bases of our social fabric change into the twenty-first century.

The final chapter in the book, by William Form, offers a revitalized perspective for institutional analysis, designed to be useful regardless of the institutional complex taken as the starting point. Form begins by tracing key aspects of the history of institutional theory and research in sociology. Although not highlighted in the chapter, an institutional perspective can be found among the earliest works of well-known social theorists such as Sumner (1906) and Spencer (1910). Later important contributions not summarized by Form would include the treatments by Chapin (1935) and Parsons (1951). Chapin's perspective was unconventional because it went beyond ideational and social structural elements. For Chapin (1935, p. 15), institutions encompassed "material culture traits" or symbols such as the Bible (in the religious institution), homes (in the family institution), and money (in the economic institution). Parsons (1951, pp. 39–40) was more conventional in his approach, emphasizing social roles or "action expectations and value patterns." In a fashion not often associated with Parsons, however, the verb form of the term played an important part in his scheme. To *institutionalize* meant to establish or make regular and predictable a set of action possibilities. This concern with process remains important in Form's more contemporary approach.

Empirical studies guided by an institutional framework during the twentieth century are too numerous to catalogue here, but they would include projects such as Smelser's (1959) study of social change in the industrial revolution and others reviewed by Kantor (1977). Both of these monographs happen to explore the linkages between family and occupational systems, a focus that remains popular as we enter the 1990s.

Recent developments in institutional theory seem to be uneven, depending upon substantive specialty. For example, more than a quarter-century ago, Sirjamaki (1964) declared that a distinct institutional perspective on family life was no longer viable and had dissolved into comparative and historical research methodology. Although subsequent family research occasionally may have employed ideas based on institutional and especially interinstitutional thinking, Sirjamaki's epitaph has gone unchallenged, and metatheoretical surveys in the family field no longer mention an institutional framework as an active one (cf. Thomas & Wilcox, 1987). By contrast, the specialty of complex organizational studies has recently experienced a surge of interest in the institutional framework (e.g., Zucker, 1988). As Hall (1989) notes, the perspective has advanced to the point where "East Coast" and "West Coast" versions have emerged as rivals.

As an interesting twist of jargon, we note that although Form treats his contribution as an organizational view of institutional analysis, Zucker and her colleagues view their work as an institutional view of organizational analysis. These are perhaps quite different emphases, but we are unsure about the significance of the distinction.

Although exceptions can be found in selected subfields, Form makes a good case that *institution* is normally used in an abstract and ambiguous way by sociologists, intended to carve up societies into functionally distinct subsystems, but without an observable anchorage in organizational structures and patterns of social interaction (cf., Smith, 1964). At best, Form suggests, the term refers to established sets of norms, values, and/or procedures that regulate social life. Among other problems, sociologists have seldom analyzed these elements in requisite depth, and Form proceeds to outline and illustrate a more appropriate strategy.

Form's approach emphasizes observable features of institutions by embedding them in concrete organizational settings. Although he does not characterize them in the same words, Form's approach also takes seriously two important analytic principles that seem to us to be basic to all institutional theories. The *generalization principle* argues that key structural and dynamic features of social institutions are replicated across institutional contexts or spheres. Hence, for example, changing power structures in the manufacturing industry are expected to follow a similar course as do changing power structures in marriage or in educational institutions. It is the parallel operation of processes and structurally equivalent patterns of social relations across institutional spheres that permit generalization to higher order theoretical premises. Without the ability to generalize in this way, we would have to develop separate theories for each institutional complex, and an integrated theory of society would be impossible. Of course, and Form recognizes this, our ability to generalize to institutions in the abstract depends heavily on the accumulation of empirical evidence and even on the availability of comparable data about the operation of various institutions. So far this ability is limited by the infrequency with which appropriate studies have been conducted. The generalization principle is therefore more like an assumption or an hypothesis than an established law of society, but it remains a core idea in most institutional analyses nevertheless.

The second principle stressed by Form is the *interconnectedness principle*. Following a line of reasoning central to virtually all images of society as a social system or as a nested set of interaction networks, a theory of institutions must posit some linkages among institutional units. Although interinstitutional linkages may vary in frequency, density, emotional intensity, and so on, they must exist and take some determinate form for the system as a whole to exist.

A heavy dose of new studies on interinstitutional linkages is on Form's agenda for the field, and we heartily concur with that opinion. It may turn out that changes in one institutional sphere consistently, at least under specific boundary conditions, have causal priority over changes in another institutional sphere. To some significant degree, the great theoretical debates in sociology have been debates about which institution controls social change in the other institutions. Because, in our opinion at least, no convincing victor has been declared by a panel of legitimate judges, we would opt for a conservative approach at this time and simply suggest that the existence of interinstitutional linkages is much more certain than the causal direction of those linkages.

Generalizing and connecting are the two cardinal methods of integration, regardless of the field of study. It is not surprising, therefore, that they constitute fundamental ideas in the arena of institutional analysis.

Two other principles of institutional analysis seem important enough to discuss briefly here. They are not explicitly covered in Form's concluding chapter, but they appear to us to be consistent with his approach. One of these is the *differentiation principle*. Emphasized even in the earliest of institutional analyses such as Spencer's, this idea refers to the proposition that as social systems grow in size and complexity, they give birth to new and specialized social structures. So "modern" societies have more institutions than do "primitive" societies.

Differentiation implies that there is at least some degree of autonomy for each institution. If there is too much blurring or overlap between a pair of institutions, it makes little sense to treat them as separate social forms at all. Interestingly, the differentiation principle may be thought of as operating in opposition to the interconnectedness principle. The former separates, and the latter pulls together. Investigations of the relative importance of these two forces in a defensible sample of cases warrants a high priority on our own agenda for future institutional studies.

The differentiation principle operates within institutions as well as between them. With bitter irony, this idea may help account for the historic failure of the institutional perspective to gain more rapidly in sophistication and stature within sociology. The discipline itself has undergone structural differentiation over the years (Collins, McCarthy, Meyer, Oliver, & Turner, 1989), the number of sections alone having jumped from 14 to 26 in the dozen years ending with 1988. Many of the older and newer sections are devoted to particular institutional complexes (family, medicine, education, political, etc.). When the study of institutions is itself institutionalized into relatively distinct specialties, one institution at a time, sharing knowledge about the various institutions is impeded. An overarching theoretical perspective that effectively addresses multiple institutions is very difficult to develop when knowledge and its social aspects are fragmented in this manner. It remains to be seen whether or not this assessment is overly pessimistic, but several possible remedies are discussed by Collins and his colleagues (1989).

The fourth and final fundamental idea in institutional analysis is the *deinstitutionalization principle*. Perhaps better called the *noninstitution concept*, we have in mind the notion that social structuration is a continuous variable. At one extreme is the complete or total institution, with a high degree of regularity, order, and predictability. At the other extreme is the totally uncertain, ambiguous, or chaotic social situation. One example of a noninstitution is remarriage, analyzed by Cherlin (1981) as such because of its structural variety and complexity and the absence of widely shared social norms about how to act toward ex-relatives, noncustodial children, step-sibs, and so on.

It is emphatically not essential within an institutional perspective to argue that all movement historically is toward the increasing institutionalization of social life. A variety of processes of social change is possible, and movements both toward and away from institutional forms may be incorporated in sinusoidal models, dialectical models, and several other types of models.

It is important to keep in mind that the authors of the chapters in this book did not have an opportunity to read earlier drafts of each others' chapters. Several were conferees at a symposium and orally presented earlier drafts to an audience including some of the other authors. Form has not derived his arguments from a critical examination of the other authors' contributions, however, nor did any of the other authors read in advance about Form's perspective or about the four principles we have just discussed. It remains an interesting issue, therefore, as to how faithfully the other authors have coincidentally followed the suggestions proposed by Form or have employed the principles we have introduced. Our impression is that the fit is fairly good, but his needs to be confirmed by a systematic content analysis or some alternative type of study.

Although our guidelines to the authors were quite flexible, it was clear to all that the book was about changing societal institutions and that they each were chosen to represent an institutional complex or set of such complexes. Such guidance is essential for a book of this kind, even though it makes the collection unrepresentative of the literature on institutions as a whole. We are not eager to be typical and would rather cultivate new ground.

It seems likely that the book would have looked somewhat different had there been a much greater exchange of ideas among the authors before the final drafts of each chapter were written. If what we argued about differentiation within sociology is correct, however, it seems unlikely that there would have been much reason to find these works within the same cover, except insofar as they can be rendered coherent by something like an institutional framework. The authors and editors of this volume have provided some illustrative material along with core ideas for advancing the institutional framework. We are not under the illusion that the task is finished. This is hopefully a new beginning rather than the celebration of an achievement.

REFERENCES

Chapin, F. S. (1935). *Contemporary American institutions*. New York: Harper.
Cherlin, A. (1981). *Marriage, divorce, remarriage*. Cambridge: Harvard University Press.

Collins, R., McCarthy, J., Meyer, M., Oliver, P., & Turner, J. (1989). Future organizational trends of the ASA. *Footnotes, 17,* 1–5, 9.

Hall, R. H. (1989). Review of *Institutional patterns and organizations. Contemporary Sociology, 18,* 54–56.

Kantor, R. M. (1977). *Work and family in the United States: A critical review and agenda for research and policy.* New York: Russell Sage.

Parsons, T. (1951). *The social system.* New York: The Free Press of Glencoe.

Sirjamaki, J. (1964). The institutional approach. In H. T. Christensen (Ed.), *Handbook of marriage and the family* (pp. 33–50). Chicago: Rand McNally.

Smelser, N. (1959). *Social change in the industrial revolution: An application of theory to the Lancashire cotton industry, 1770–1840.* Chicago: University of Chicago Press.

Smith, H. E. (1964). Toward a clarification of the concept of social institution. *Sociology and Social Research, 48,* 197–206.

Spencer, H. (1910). *First principles.* New York: Appleton-Century-Crofts. (Originally published in 1862)

Sumner, W. G. (1906). *Folkways.* Boston: Ginn.

Thomas, D. L., & Wilcox, J. E. (1987). The rise of family theory: A historical and critical analysis. In M. B. Sussman & S. K. Steinmetz (Eds.), *Handbook of marriage and the family* (pp. 81–102). New York: Plenum Press.

Zucker, L. G. (Ed.). (1988). *Institutional patterns and organizations: Culture and environment.* Cambridge: Ballinger.

CHAPTER ONE

The Decline of Occupations
Redefining the Labor Force

TERESA A. SULLIVAN

"Black Monday," October 19, 1987, shocked one of the fastest-growing industries in the United States. When the Dow-Jones average plummeted over 500 points, millions of workers on three continents were affected through their companies' losses or through the investments of their pension plans and personal savings. Workers on Wall Street were affected directly: within a few months, an estimated 15,000 of them were looking for new jobs (Reflett, 1988). Black Monday and its aftermath demonstrated the vulnerability even of prestigious jobs filled by the well educated and well compensated. The nagging fear of the past decade became more openly voiced: Is no occupation safe?

Black Monday illustrates in boldface the major changes affecting the labor force: new technology, internationalization, corporate reorganization, and failed government regulation. Each of these changes has affected the rapidly growing finance industry. Its products are generated by the new technology and marketed through it. Although the various options and indexes are collectively referred to as *paper*, even the metaphor is more tangible than its electronic reality. The paper is marketed using advanced technology that links brokers to worldwide markets. By conquering both time and space, the technology creates arbitrage possibilities around the clock and across the planet for the insomniac New York broker. Perhaps the technology, in the form of portfolio-managing computer programs, even intensified the crisis during the days following Black Monday. Furthermore, the industry is a corporate battleground. When E. F. Hutton talks, no

TERESA A. SULLIVAN • Department of Sociology, University of Texas at Austin, Austin, Texas 78712-1088.

one listens—Hutton's acquisition was another event of autumn 1987 on Wall Street. Finally, Black Monday occurred despite government regulation that was comparatively stringent given the deregulatory climate.

Every one of these changes undercuts the long-standing significance of the division of labor as enunciated by Adam Ferguson, Adam Smith, and Emile Durkheim. At the level of individual workers, the division of labor really meant occupational specialization. Yet when technology changes jobs rapidly, when international and government restrictions are ineffective, and when firms merge and grow larger, then the division of labor at the individual level becomes mutable. Occupational preparation and identity become less important both to corporate planners and to individual workers. The future of the workers depends not so much on what they do but on where and how they do it.

Black Monday is a dramatic incident of lost jobs, more dramatic perhaps because it occurred within a glamorous industry in the media capital of the world. But thousands of other jobs have been lost in the United States in recent years, more slowly and quietly and in smaller towns and cities. Occupation, long the mainstay of labor force analysis because of its close link to social class, fails as an explanatory variable for these job losses. Moreover, virtually no other recent labor force development hinges on occupation. The rapid growth of female employment cannot be understood by examining occupation because the women are still segregated into only half a dozen occupations. Important changes in the content of work, such as those implied by the seemingly contradictory processes, *deskilling* and *occupational upgrading*, cut across occupational boundaries and blur the distinctions once made between adjacent occupational groups (e.g., sales and clerical work). Other factors must explain why, for example, the occupation of secretary can have widely different job content, with varying levels of autonomy and skill, depending on site.

OCCUPATION AND A NEW WORKPLACE REVOLUTION

Sociologists sense a sea change in the world of work. It is the thesis of this chapter that occupation, the concept on which sociologists have lavished so much research, will be of much less significance for understanding this new revolution than will industry and firm. Rapid and relatively unpredictable changes are the hallmarks of this new revolution in work. Given our foreshortened perspective, we may be no better off in understanding the change than were observers in the midst of the Industrial Revolution. We nevertheless seek the best means to analyze the change. Because the measurement tools are in place to study occupation, we may find ourselves studying occupation through these changes *faute de mieux* of studying anything else.

This does not imply that we should ignore occupation; on the contrary, charting the decline of occupation is a tribute to its significance. But occupation has become so much a part of the conventional tool kit of sociologists that its meaning is taken for granted. Occupation is unreflectively used as an independent variable or a control variable. Its relative rarity as a dependent variable occurs because occupational sociology is not a "hot" area of the discipline, and that in turn is true because occupation is seen as a concept that is "settled." I am thus placed in the paradoxical position of defending a thesis of declining significance by scrutinizing occupation even more carefully.

This essay consists of three sections. The first section describes the traditional significance that sociologists ascribe to occupation. The second section reviews important recent developments in the labor markets of the industrialized countries to show why occupation may no longer fulfill its traditional significance. The final section argues that greater attention to industry and firm as variables would be helpful, despite the paucity of measurement tools currently available for examining them.

THE TRADITIONAL SIGNIFICANCE OF OCCUPATIONS

OCCUPATIONS AS TROUBLE

At the end of the twentieth century in America, occupations are the convergence of a personal "trouble," a social problem, and a sociological problem (Mills, 1959). As a source of *trouble*, occupations interest everyone, not merely the specialist. Both sociologists and laypersons rely on occupation as a short-hand indicator of life-style, income, and social standing. It is a commonsense approach that has reliably predicted behavior. We identify cartoonists' caricatures of occupations because of our common understandings. But it is hard to make sense of the world if the old shibboleths are daily contradicted. If investment bankers are laid off, who is safe? Occupations become a greater "trouble" because of their rising uncertainty, an uncertainty that parallels the spread of economic volatility and personal vulnerability into occupational groups once defined as "safe."

As a result of this uncertainty, workers face greater difficulty in preparing for an occupation or in persevering in one with any security. Parents and teachers can no longer provide young people with specific advice on occupational preparation. Choosing an occupation becomes a "trouble" for students, career switchers, labor market reentrants, the technologically obsolete, the dislocated, and the unemployed. Indeed, even the notion of occupational choice may be misleading if the occupation is blundered upon or fortuitously achieved. In the absence of an orderly career, occupational changes become synonymous with job changes.

The second source of uncertainty is related to the first. Occupations are changing rapidly. Choice of occupations is complicated by the rapid adoption of technology. Women workers, in particular, were once advised to choose "safe" occupations such as nursing or secretarial work that could be reentered later. Unless she has been absent for a very brief period, however, no nurse or secretary can reenter the labor force today without some retraining. New machinery has made many skills obsolete and has made others (e.g., typing) only the entry-level skill in a hierarchy of technologically sensitive skills.

Furthermore, the rapid growth of technology leads managers to create new occupational titles that convey little meaning about job content to outsiders or perhaps even to the incumbents. Not only are children uncertain about "what Mommy and Daddy do," but so are the neighbors and the adult kin. Word processors in some firms are still called *secretaries* in other firms or "data entry personnel" in still other firms. Even more common, perhaps, is the development of firm-specific job titles along the order of "widget attendant." As occupation moves into that area of life marked by greater uncertainty, it comes to be perceived as a cause of trouble for more people and during longer periods of their lives.

OCCUPATIONS AS A SOCIAL PROBLEM

Social problems are the collective and aggregated results of pervasive, structurally induced "troubles." Because the social problem is structural in origin, its solution is beyond the efforts of an individual or even of groups of individuals. This fact alone makes social problems difficult to remedy, but in addition, there are always powerful actors who benefit from the existing structure and who resist changes. The cross cutting effects of costs and benefits create many potential interest groups who coalesce as allies or as adversaries.

Work-related social problems rank among the most significant and most intractable problems of a society. Widespread occupational shifts and dislocations become social problems because of their impact on personal identity and income. Much of the individual dislocation that accompanied the Industrial Revolution could be traced to the effects of economic transformation. If, as I have suggested, we are in the midst of a new revolution, then its accompanying economic transformations may leave their traces in cross-sectional changes in occupational distributions and in longitudinal career disruptions.

The conventional solution to this social problem, retraining to help workers avoid unemployment, implicitly analyzes the problem as an *occupational* problem that is best attacked at the level of the *individual*. All too often the training programs have prepared workers for occupational specialties that are rapidly being phased out or are really dead-end jobs. A good example was the training program that produced keypunch operators, many of them minority-group women, only a few years before remote data entry made keypunch machines obsolete. *Analyses predicated on workers' having the wrong occupations will always miss the mark if occupation is not the right variable.* But these analyses will continue to be popular because it seems possible to ameliorate the situation of individuals and impossible to deal with the larger, intractable causes of the problems.

OCCUPATIONS AS A SOCIOLOGICAL PROBLEM

Occupation becomes a sociological problem if our theories and measurement techniques continue to emphasize it even if other concepts are more valuable. Occupation has been an important variable in sociological theories, and this section reviews the reasons for that importance. The issue is not whether occupation has been important in the past; it is occupation's future significance.

Sociologists study occupation because it is a foundation of stratification that is assumed to persist in time and space. "Do your job and I shall know you," wrote Emerson. In the same vein, sociologists have identified occupation as a key indicator of class and one closely associated with the other indicators. Occupation, education, and income are highly correlated with one another; this empirical fact is the basis of the Duncan Socioeconomic Index (Duncan, 1961). There are discrepant categories—high-paid entertainers, or entrepreneurs with little education, or well-educated professionals serving the nonprofit agencies—but they are noted principally as exceptions to the general rule. Along with education and income, occupation is further linked to the stratification system through occupational subcultures and life-styles.

Occupation is the basis for understanding historical changes in the stratification system. Occupational mobility studies examine the occupational statuses across generations, postulating that the meaning of an occupation in one generation will be approximately the same in the next generation. Even within a generation, the movement from a first job to eventual status attainment is usually examined in terms of occupation. The "opportunity structure" is, at its root, the distribution of occupations within an economy. When we tell our students that the opportunity structure changed within the United States, allowing for more structural social mobility, we mean that the relative proportions have shifted from predominantly farm occupations to other manual occupations and finally to white-collar jobs (Blau & Duncan, 1967; Hauser & Featherman, 1977). We do not pretend that the shift in occupation was somehow exogenous to the process, but rather we measure the process by measuring the changes in occupation.

Nor is occupation's role as an identifier in the stratification system known only to the ivory tower types. Occupational prestige studies have repeatedly replicated prestige hierarchies in the same country and even across countries (although with some variations) (Treiman, 1977). The claim is made that even new occupations will be easily fit within the existing prestige structures.

Finally, social cohesion and action among those who pursue the same occupation can be a notable source of collective power. Professionalization is an effort to raise the collective prestige of an occupation by pursuing collective power—in this case, by adopting the characteristics of the most powerful occupations, the professions. Unionization among those in the same occupation provides a second route to seeking collective power. Guildhalls, registries, referral networks, common training curricula, journals, conventions, and occupational associations are all sources of individual benefit derived from common identification with an occupation. Even negative identifications, such as popular stereotypes, jokes, and the occupational tax (still levied in Pennsylvania), tend to emphasize one's identification with the occupation, and ultimately, to emphasize one's position within the stratification hierarchy.

The significance of occupation is magnified by the number of tools available for its measurement. Before 1940, the U.S. Census measured the labor force through the occupational identification of "gainful workers." This approach was eventually abandoned because it required social and personal occupational identities to be identical. There were too many unemployed workers and new entrants without socially recognized occupational identities, and too many retired and "visibly underemployed" workers (Robinson, 1936) with misleading (i.e., not contemporaneous) personal occupational identities (Hauser, 1949). Nevertheless, the census occupational coding scheme was claimed to capture the stratification hierarchy implicit in occupational identities (Edwards, 1943), and later surveys confirmed a national consensus on prestige (Hodge, Siegel, & Rossi, 1964; North & Hatt, 1947; Treiman, 1977).

The Census Bureau's major occupational categories were used as a rough ordinal measure of prestige. Later work developed prestige scores for a large number of occupations, and still later, multiple regression techniques were used to "interpolate" socioeconomic status scores for other occupations. Prestige scores are at least ordinal-level variables, and they are often used as interval-level variables.

Further efforts at finer occupational codes were accompanied by more detailed measures. The *Dictionary of Occupational Titles (DOT)* classified over 20,000 occupations by title, although frequently the titles were merely the name of a machine the incumbent operated. Analysts studied actual job performance of each *DOT* job to provide measures of how much the incumbents worked with data, people, and things and estimates of the

specific vocational preparation and general education required were added. Still later, the occupations were rated in terms of how dangerous they
were, whether the work was indoors or outdoors, and how long it would
take to be trained for the job. DOT jobs were classified using a 9-digit code
that permitted aggregation to larger, grosser categories. Designers of large
databases could then incorporate DOT information for the occupations of
their respondents (Cain & Treiman, 1981). The General Social Survey is an
example of a database that includes this information.

These developments meant that occupations could be ranked not only
in terms of average characteristics of their incumbents but also in terms of
the jobs themselves. Not surprisingly, occupation became routinely required in social science questionnaires, but it also became standard information required by creditors and government agencies—even the IRS. This
widespread use alone would make an argument against using occupation a
foolish one. But we may also be affected by "the law of the hammer." (This
law states that a child with a hammer will find that everything requires
hammering.) It is worth considering whether events have overtaken such
widespread use of occupation as an indicator.

RECENT LABOR FORCE DEVELOPMENTS

Labor markets around the world are in a state of flux. Some changes
stem from labor supply, and they will be discussed later. Other changes
arise from the shifting demand for labor, and they are more difficult to
analyze because they arise from so many different sources. Three de-
mand-side sources of change I will consider are products, technology, and
organization. The interplay of labor supply and labor demand determines
what proportion of the labor force is employed and, among the employed,
their occupational distribution. (Unemployed persons are also members of
the labor force but do not have a current occupation to report.)

PRODUCTS

The well-known "tertiarization," or shift to service production, has
occurred in both the advanced and the developing countries. In the advanced countries, the service sector is disproportionately composed of
professional and business services (Bell, 1973). This sector grows through
the specialization of professional services (as with medical or legal specialties), through new markets accompanying the shift of payment to third
parties (as with professional services provided in fringe benefit packages),
and with new services (as with information or telecommunication services). State action also affects product mix; much of the recent growth in

the finance industry has resulted from the development of new financial products. In the developing countries, tertiarization is more likely to take place in the personal and distributive services: household service, retail trade, transportation, prepared food, and so on.

Tertiarization refers to the industrial distribution of a labor force and only derivatively to its occupational distribution. On the other hand, tertiarization has an important impact on occupational distribution. Personal and distributive services tend to be relatively unskilled, and it is easy for these workers to change "occupations" every time they change "jobs." Their occupational identification is ephemeral. Professional and business services are more likely to require specific training and skills. This increases the likelihood that professionals and technicians have a long-term identification with their occupations, but it does not increase the likelihood that there will be a long-term demand for their specialties. Indeed, within the high-skill service sector, technological and informational obsolescence are greater dangers than they are in the personal service sector.

TECHNOLOGY

Perhaps no development has more potential to alter the labor market than the new electronic technologies. Technology could change the *level* of demand, resulting in a reduction in labor when capital replaces labor. In the longer run, labor demand could increase if product demand rises. For example, the increased size and bureaucratization of work sites led to a rapid expansion in the number of clerical workers needed. But the application of electronic technology to the production, distribution, and storing of information has the potential to change drastically the requirements for clerical workers versus other types of workers.

Whatever happens to the level of demand, technology will almost certainly change the *composition* of the demand. One possibility is that the highest skills of workers will be underutilized and eventually unneeded. Just as the mechanization of factory work led to the replacement of skilled machinists with semiskilled operatives, so the advent of computers has the potential to replace skilled workers with machine tenders. Even the judgment of professionals may soon be supplemented with on-line diagnostics and recommendations. One difference is that the tenders of newer vintage machines tend to be called *technicians* (and hence thought to be white-collar), whereas the tenders of older vintage machines tend to be called *operatives* (and hence blue-collar).

Another possibility is that jobs will be enlarged and combined. "Smart" cash registers have already led to a blurring of the distinctions between clerical and sales workers in retail trade. At the checkout counter, the cashier simultaneously serves a customer, decrements the inventory, keeps tabs on the cash flow, and so on. Job enlargement results whenever the new technology permits consideration and redefinition of more events as "routine." In banking and insurance, workers who were formerly clerical workers now perform specialized functions that the professional staff once performed. Technology diminishes the realm of uncertainty, the domain of the highly trained workers, because it can access an alternative source of relevant knowledge (Hodson & Sullivan, 1990). At the other end of the occupational ladder, the new technology may require workers who are able to use, maintain, and repair their own equipment. Especially when the work sites are also decentralized, this may eliminate centralized repair and maintenance staffs.

All of this implies that technology has the potential to change job content and job distribution in ways that will profoundly affect our concept of "occupation." Technology has the power to make occupations obsolete because their occupational identity is predicated on acquiring the unique lore and knowledge of an occupation, a process that is most advanced in the professional occupations. As the technology itself proliferates and mutates, even the technicians will quickly become obsolete. This process will not proceed of its own accord, however: Its pace and impact will depend to a large extent on when, where, and how the technology is implemented. This is not a decision that will be made by members of occupational groups but one that will be made by firms and perhaps that will be affected by industrywide considerations. And the final factor affecting demand, organization, is critically important in determining technology adoption.

ORGANIZATION

Organization affects the demand for various occupations principally through effects on specialization and skill level. The characteristics of the organizations that create these effects are size, complexity, and innovation.

The size of the work site is a critical determinant of the types of workers required. In general, the size of the firm is inversely related to the "size" of the job. Small work sites and small firms typically have lower levels of specialization; jobs are "larger," and an occupational title may be a misleading indicator of all the tasks the workers do. For example, the secretary in a small law firm may do the tasks of law librarians, paralegals, messengers, word processors, legal secretaries, bookkeepers, and other specialized personnel within the large law firm. In the large law firm, *secretary* may well be a designation distinct from *legal secretary* and much narrower in focus (Murphree, 1981). Perhaps for this reason, the workers in small firms are more likely to report that their skills are adequately utilized and to report that they are satisfied with their jobs (Hodson & Sullivan, 1985). In most sociological research, however, this distinction will be lost.

Aggregated occupational data will not distinguish between the two "secretaries." The point is more general: The job content conveyed by an occupational title is likely to vary by size of work site.

Size and complexity of work site need to be distinguished from the size and complexity of the firm, especially with the development of multi-establishment firms. Mergers, acquisitions, and other corporate reorganizations have greatly complicated the structure of firms without necessarily complicating the work sites in the same way. Franchised fast food outlets, for example, may look quite similar and uncomplicated if one examines only the local outlets. Every site will need a fry cook and a cashier for each shift. The number of jobs created for fry cooks will depend at least partly on the success of each outlet, but it will also depend upon the number of outlets that are developed. The number of managerial jobs, however, may depend not only on the number of outlets but also on their organization into regions and divisions, the size of national headquarters, their international expansion, relationships with a parent company, and so on.

Organizational complexity usually creates needs for coordination and supervision, and this in turn leads to the creation of cadres of managers and clerical workers. Part of the reason for the rapid recent growth in both occupational fields was the growth of complex organizations as employers. It is difficult to foresee, however, whether the adoption of new technologies may replace some layers of supervision and some forms of coordination. If this were to happen, then the relative demand for, say, clerical workers versus technicians might change; alternatively, workers whose jobs are basically technical in nature might still be called (and paid as) *clerical workers*.

The final variable is the rate and extent of organizational innovation, both in technology and in organization. Organizational environments, both internal and external, are complicated, and there are many considerations aside from the mere availability of the innovation. Competition with other firms, international competition, substitutability of other products, government regulation, and the creativity of management are among the many variables that can affect how fast a workplace changes. One simple form of organizational innovation, reclassifying and reanalyzing job descriptions, may not be done even though there may have been great changes in job content. Old job titles may be retained because of tradition, because of the preferences of existing personnel, for convenience in negotiating labor contracts, and for a whole host of other reasons. For example, today's "typographer" has a far different job than did the "typographer" of only 20 years ago.

Organizational innovation may also affect the conditions of work for occupational members, facilitating or hindering the chances for solidarity and identity among them. The organization and the occupation may form opposing bases of identification for workers. A worker with a strong occupational identity may pursue a career of lateral moves. A worker who is more interested in vertical movement within a firm may be forced to change occupations in the interest of the organizational career. For example, university administrators may gradually shift their external reference group from disciplinary associations to associations of university administrators, and their internal reference group from disciplinary colleagues to other administrators. This phenomenon has been most intensely studied among professionals employed in organizations.

One of the strongest arguments for the use of occupation has been its relationship to income. But organizations may employ a number of tactics that reduce the correlation between occupation and pay. The two-tiered pay systems adopted in some industries (e.g., the airlines) have the effect of rewarding quite differently two groups of employees pursuing the same occupation. A second tactic is extended probationary periods. A third is contracting work outside the firm. This may permit quite different rates to be paid to occupational members outside the firm than are paid inside the firm. In manufacturing, this may mean that subcontractors handle overflow work while paying their operatives much less than operatives doing the same job for the general contractor. In professional services, by contrast, outside contractors (say, law firms) may command premium prices compared with in-house workers.

To a large extent, it is the organization and not the worker that determines the worker's occupation. We turn now to the labor supply issues that may affect occupation.

SUPPLY-SIDE CHANGES

Gender

The labor market is also affected by changes in the types of persons offering their services in the market. There is likely to be a change over time, for example, in the racial or ethnic composition of the population. Immigration or differential fertility among racial and ethnic groups will lead to varying ethnic compositions among the cohorts presenting themselves for the first time as workers. More important, however, changes occur in labor supply because the rate of participation among population groups changes. During this century, the most important change in participation has been the rapid increase in female labor force participation. Not only has this participation risen, but it has risen for virtually all groups of women, even the mothers of young children.

This development has enormous importance for occupation because of the occupational segregation of women workers. Although there has been some decrease in occupational segregation during the past decade, women are still greatly overrepresented in six or seven occupational categories

(Reskin, 1984; Reskin & Hartmann, 1986). There are many theories and explanations of this phenomenon, but they may be dichotomized as *voluntary* and *structural* explanations. Voluntary explanations assume that occupation is an achieved status freely chosen by the worker. According to the various voluntary explanations, women choose occupations that permit easy exit and entry if the woman must move to another city, leave the labor force, or work part-time for family reasons. Women choose to invest less in their human capital, according to such explanations, because they are discounting for the time spent out of the labor force. Aside from their ideological appeal to some observers, these explanations imply that occupation is an important, relatively immutable characteristic of workers. It is freely chosen, and it is either prepared for, or the lack of preparation becomes part of a "discount" factor. The problem of occupational segregation is turned on its head and becomes the phenomenon of occupational concentration. Just as minority groups are assumed to want residential segregation to "be with their own kind," so the segregation of women into a few occupations is seen as a peculiar feminine bonding that is best left to psychologists.

Although detailed treatments of voluntary explanations are left to others, a few relevant facts suffice to illustrate the poverty of such explanations. First, because of technological requirements, many fewer occupations permit easy reentrance. Second, women are spending very little time out of the labor force. Third, women's human capital investment, at least as measured by years of schooling, parallels or exceeds that of men except in postgraduate work. Even there, the proportion of women students has risen sharply in recent years. For example, in the previously all-male preserves of medicine, dentistry, law, ministry, and management professional schools, roughly one-third of the seats are now occupied by women students.

Structural explanations of sex segregation rely on the stereotyping of jobs. Because many Americans receive no specific occupational training, the content of their first job becomes the description of their "occupation." If they change jobs, they change occupations. Although sex-based assignment of jobs can no longer be legally advertised, except where it is a bona fide occupational qualification, the stereotyping of jobs is pervasive, and it is widely understood in which gender's "turf" a particular job is (Bielby & Baron, 1984). Employers, counselors, agencies, and others who steer the new workers to their first jobs tend to think of some jobs as "female" and others as "male." Many experiments done with resumes identical except for the gender have found the women sent to clerical and service jobs and the men to management trainee or skilled jobs. This stereotyping may be briefly disrupted by new technology. For example, when the typewriter was introduced, there was some concern as to whether women would be able or should be allowed to use it. For a while, it seemed that the progress of women into clerical jobs might be halted because of concerns that machinery was a "man's realm." But soon the machinery itself became sex stereotyped and so did the occupations that arose to service the machines (Davies, 1982). If occupations are sex stereotyped by this external process and not by the choice of the workers, then there must be some characteristic other than occupation that is significant.

An extra twist on this argument is provided by Oppenheimer (1970), who argues that the demand for (stereotypical) female work led the rise in women's labor force participation and led to the crowding of certain jobs. Unlike many "male" jobs, many "female" jobs require credentials from an educational institution. This permits the employer to transfer the costs of training to female employees, although the training costs for males might be borne at least partly by the employer. Thus women prepare themselves by acquiring certification in teaching, social work, library sciences, nursing, and similar paraprofessional jobs. Women are also the great majority of the enrollment in proprietary business schools. What is interesting about this pattern is the way it casts into bold relief the process of occupational preparation among *men*, a subject to which we now turn.

Education

In both the advanced and the developing countries, there is a growing segment of workers who are very well educated. In the advanced countries in particular, rates of attendance in institutions of higher education have been rising, and there are now many more credentialed young workers than at any time in the past. One effect of this rising education level has been a reduction in the association between levels of education and occupation. The "mismatch" between occupations and jobs, measured by the increasing heterogeneity of education within detailed occupational groups, has risen steadily for about 20 years in the United States (Clogg & Sullivan, 1983; Clogg & Shockey, 1984; Clogg, Sullivan, & Mutchler, 1986; Sullivan, 1978).

Mismatch reflects an effort by workers to compete for entry-level jobs *because occupational preparation is so diffuse.* Most occupations in the labor force have no specific preparation required; the specific training will be provided on the job. So for most workers, the issue is being selected from among multiple applicants for the entry-level position and the opportunity for specific training. If the initial job is in a bank, the eventual occupation will have a different name than if the initial job is in an insurance company. What is common to the situation is that it is the hiring firm and not the worker's choice that will eventually determine the occupational title.

The professions, semiprofessions, and skilled trades require specific preparation, but they are not necessarily exceptions to this generalization. In these cases, persons compete for training slots in the professional schools. Higher quality or more extensive schooling are ways to compete for the limited positions in the top professional schools. Members of the profession retain some control because they choose their successors by admitting some and not others to the professional schools.

SUMMARY

This discussion has outlined some important trends within the labor market. Changes in product, technology, and organization affect the demand for workers. Important changes in the supply of workers include the increased participation of women workers and the rising educational level of labor force. The next section examines these trends in relation to the significance of occupation and alternative variables.

THE DECLINING SIGNIFICANCE OF OCCUPATION

Reviewing the preceding developments in the labor force, one is hard pressed to argue for the continued prominence of occupation in contemporary analyses of work. The historical association of occupation with social stratification was based on both the antecedents of occupation and the consequences of occupation, and yet contemporary trends seem to be weakening both associations.

One important antecedent of occupation is education. Specific occupational preparation, or what sociologists might call *anticipatory socialization*, has become less common because occupations are changing so rapidly. As workers compete for entry-level jobs and access to training, the link between education and occupation has been attenuated. The typical direction of this attenuation has been rising levels of education.

The consequences of occupation include income, life-style, and subculture. Organizational innovations have reduced the link between income and occupation, so that the intraoccupational variations in income have become quite large. The link of occupation with life-style and subculture assumes a more orderly stratification system in which occupation (1) is a relatively stable component of identity and (2) is recognized as such by relevant others. Neither condition holds true when workers change jobs rapidly and each job change is *de facto* a change in occupation as well. Nor does the relationship hold if neighbors and others do not understand what occupational incumbents do. For example, there is evidence that the relative ranking of new computer occupations was uncertain, and some reversals in prestige scores occurred (Sullivan & Cornfield, 1979), despite arguments that the new occupations would be easily fit within the existing stratification schemes (Treiman, 1977). In fact, from the earliest research into occupational prestige, it has been noted that the public cannot rate new or unfamiliar occupations (Matras, 1975).

The relationship of occupation to subculture assumes a certain amount of interaction, either in the workplace or elsewhere. A number of organizational innovations, if they become widespread, would militate against subcultural maintenance. Among these are the competition of organizational careers; isolation within the workplace; different reward structures for workers in the same occupation but different organizations; and deliberate creation of different work rewards for workers in the same occupation and same organization. Again, the professions and perhaps the skilled trades may remain exceptions, but the bureaucratized workplace has powerful tools for weakening occupational subcultures.

What is striking about this instrumental use of occupation, which is so widespread in the social sciences, is that it begs the issue of changing job content. Calling an occupation by the same name for 200 years does not mean it is the same job. The differences may be unimportant *if the pace of change in other occupations were similar.* But if change moves unevenly between occupations, or even within the same occupation at different work sites, then occupational titles may conceal more variation than they reveal. Creating new occupational titles, although certainly necessary for many purposes, eliminates the communal basis of occupational identity that is the basis for much of the social significance of occupation.

Arguments for the significance of occupation based on comparative and historical similarities must assume that the pace of change is not so rapid nor so pervasive as I expect. These arguments rest on the predicate that occupations in the United States at the end of the twentieth century are substantially the same as occupations with similar titles in other countries and at other times. The current arguments for stability (Parcel & Benefo, 1987; Treiman, 1977) are based upon measurement tools that *assume* identical or highly correlated job content. They cannot be used to test that assumption.

What would be a better procedure? Arguments that we need to analyze firm and industry are abundant within the literature (Baron & Bielby, 1980). The reluctance to use them is not a hard-hearted resistance by tradition-bound sociologists. Rather, it reflects the relative scarcity of such information, relative to occupation, and the lack of useful measurement tools to use the information when it is available.

Consistent industry codes are far less common than occupational codes in the existing large social science databases. Even when the codes are available, how to use them is a problem. Industry is at best a discrete variable; it can be collapsed into a dichotomy, as has been done in terms of *centrality* to the economy (Beck, Horan, & Tolbert, 1987; Tolbert, Horan, & Beck, 1980). There is no concept analogous to *occupational prestige* and no hierarchical ranking of industry that is readily available to the sociologist.

Thus the methodological argument has been where to draw lines in developing polytomies and not how to assess ordinality. Analysts thus cannot apply to industry the sophisticated techniques used with measures of occupation.

Despite the importance of firm, it is even less available as a variable, nor is it always possible to know how to reclassify it usefully. Hodson (1984) reclassified firms in terms of industry sources that emphasized corporate size, certainly one useful dimension of firm. Firm is most likely to be available for intensive study in relatively small case studies, but there are problems in fully exploiting such data (Cornfield & Sullivan, 1983), even setting aside the issue of generalizing from case studies. Even if national surveys contained questions about firms, it is unclear how respondents would analyze the often complicated corporate structures that offer them employment. Would they report the name of the subsidiary, the parent company, or the holding company? This ambiguity also affects industry data reported by establishments, for the various corporate pieces of a large firm may crosscut industries.

The underlying analytic difficulty in broadening our knowledge of the world of work is that we collect data from individual workers. We use information on occupation because the individual workers who are our respondents can give an answer to that question. But the trends within the labor market suggest that the locus of decision making, with products, technology, and organization, lies with corporate actors of various sorts, not with individuals. We find corporate actors hard to conceptualize, hard to analyze, and certainly hard to access. Like the drunk who looks for his lost money under the street lamp because that is where the light is, we continue to rely on occupation even though its meaning may be changing in significant ways.

CONCLUSION

Underlying my argument is a rather pessimistic view of how workers and occupations will be matched. I view that process as one that is becoming less voluntaristic, less affected by the wishes of the individuals, and far more affected by large-scale forces beyond the control of most workers. By implication, I expect occupational power, as we have generally known it, to wane while organizational power waxes. The remaining correlation between occupation and life-style is likely to be a spurious one, with income the true explanatory variable. This does not mean that "proletarianization" will occur (Wright & Singelmann, 1982); indeed, I would make no prediction about what the distribution of occupations might be.

Current measures of occupation will continue to be used, but if changes are proceeding as rapidly as I project, the meaning of those measures may be in more doubt. It is noteworthy, perhaps, that the 1980 U.S. Census uses occupational codes that are much closer to our understanding of industry (i.e., product or service produced) than to our former understanding of occupation. Thus, "farming, fisheries, and forestry" is an occupational group; "precision production" is a separate occupational group. We may find more efforts to regroup and redraw occupational boundaries so that the resulting studies are more informative.

The logic of my argument implies that the argument itself cannot be adequately tested using the current tools. Short of developing new tools, what could we predict would happen in the labor market within the next, say, 15 years? If I am correct, I believe that we will see the following results:

1. Intraoccupational heterogeneity will increase on a variety of variables—not just education, where it has already increased, but also earnings, hours and weeks of work, and so on. This heterogeneity will be explainable by industry distribution and firm effects.
2. A replication of the occupational prestige studies will find many Americans unable to rate many new specialties, and it will reveal some reversals among the rankings of the lower white-collar workers. Test questions that compare prestige "in a big company" with a work site in "a small firm" will show the larger company to carry more prestige.
3. If asked to rate industries on the basis of prestige, many Americans will be able to offer ratings, and these ratings would tend to "load" on industries that deal with information, communication, and "high" technology.
4. If a new *DOT* were commissioned, job analysts would find greater differences in job descriptions if the work sites were varied in size and if the same occupation were studied in different industries.
5. Americans and not just Japanese will begin to consider lifelong commitment, if it exists at all, as something that is associated with a firm, and not with an occupation.
6. Intergenerational mobility will come to be a concept more associated with relative income levels, industry, and firm than with occupation.

A revolution in work is an exciting time in which to live but a difficult time in which to conduct research. It is said of the military that they are always prepared for the last war. It may also be true of sociologists that we have developed more and more sophisticated ways to study a phenomenon that is of less and less relative importance.

ACKNOWLEDGMENTS

I would like to acknowledge the helpful comments of the conference participants, especially Duane E. Alwin and Randy Hodson, and the comments of my colleagues Harley L. Browning, Joe R. Feagin, Lawrence E. Raffalovich, and Bryan Roberts.

REFERENCES

Baron, J. N., & Bielby, W. T. (1980). Bringing the firms back in: Stratification, segmentation, and the organization of work. *American Sociological Review, 45*, 737–765.

Beck, E. M., Horan, P. M., & Tolbert II, C. M. (1978). Stratification in a dual economy: A sectoral model of earnings determination. *American Sociological Review, 43*, 704–720.

Bell, D. (1973). *The coming of postindustrial society*. New York: Basic Books.

Bielby, W. T., & Baron, J. N. (1984). A woman's place is with other women: Sex segregation within organizations. In B. Reskin (Ed.), *Sex segregation in the workplace* (pp. 27–55). Washington, DC: National Academy Press.

Blau, P. M., & Duncan, O. D. (1967). *The American occupational structure*. New York: Wiley.

Cain, P. S., & Treiman, D. J. (1981). The Dictionary of Occupational Titles as a source of occupational data. *American Sociological Review, 46*, 253–278.

Clogg, C. C., & Shockey, J. W. (1984). Mismatch between occupation and schooling: A prevalence measure, recent trends, and demographic analysis. *Demography, 21*, 235–257.

Clogg, C. C., & Sullivan, T. A. (1983). Demographic composition and underemployment trends, 1969–1980. *Social Indicators Research, 12*, 117–152.

Clogg, C. C., Sullivan, T. A., & Mutchler, J. E. (1986). Measuring underemployment and inequality in the work force. *Social Indicators Research, 18*, 375–393.

Cornfield, D. B., & Sullivan, T. A. (1983). Fieldwork in the oligopoly: Protecting the corporate subject. *Human Organization, 42*, 258–263.

Davies, M. W. (1982). *A woman's place is at the typewriter*. Philadelphia: Temple University Press.

Duncan, O. D. (1961). A socioeconomic index for all occupations. In A. J. Reiss (Ed.), *Occupations and social status* (pp. 109–138). New York: Free Press.

Edwards, A. M. (1943). *U.S. Census of Population, 1940: Comparative Occupational Statistics, 1870–1940*. Washington, DC: U.S. Government Printing Office.

Hauser, P. M. (1949). The labor force and gainful workers—concept, measurement, and comparability. *American Journal of Sociology, 54*, 338–55.

Hauser, R. M., & Featherman, D. L. (1977). *The process of stratification*. New York: Academic Press.

Hodge, R. W., Siegel, P. M., & Rossi, P. H. (1964). Occupational prestige in the United States. *American Journal of Sociology, 70*, 286–302.

Hodson, R. (1984). Companies, industries, and the measurement of economic segmentation. *American Sociological Review, 49*, 335–348.

Hodson, R., & Sullivan, T. A. (1985). Totem or tyrant? Monopoly, regional, and local sector effects on worker commitment. *Social Forces, 63*, 716–731.

Hodson, R., & Sullivan, T. A. (1990). *The social organization of work*. Belmont, CA: Wadsworth Publishing Co.

Matras, J. (1975). *Social inequality, stratification, and mobility*. Englewood Cliffs, NJ: Prentice-Hall.

Mills, C. W. (1959). *The sociological imagination*. New York: Oxford.

Murphree, M. C. (1981). Rationalization and satisfaction in clerical work: A case study of Wall Street legal secretaries. (unpublished doctoral dissertation, Department of Sociology, Columbia University).

North, C. C., & Hatt, P. K. (1947). Jobs and occupations: A popular evaluation. *Public Opinion News, 9*.

Oppenheimer, V. K. (1970). *The female labor force in the United States*. Berkeley: University of California Press.

Parcel, T. L., & Benefo, K. (1987). Temporal change in occupational differentiation. *Work and Occupations, 14,* 514–532.

Reflett, R. (1988). Market's crash continues to take psychological toll. *The Wall Street Journal, 31,* March, p. 25.

Reskin, B. (Ed.). (1984). *Sex segregation in the workplace.* Washington, DC: National Academy Press.

Reskin, B., & Hartmann, H. I. (Eds.). (1986). *Women's work, men's work.* Washington, DC: National Academy Press.

Robinson, J. (1936). Disguised unemployment. *Economic Journal, 46,* 225–237.

Sullivan, T. A. (1978). *Marginal workers, marginal jobs.* Austin: University of Texas Press.

Sullivan, T. A., & Cornfield, D. B. (1979). Downgrading computer workers; evidence from occupational and industrial redistribution. *Sociology of Work and Occupations, 6,* 184–203.

Tolbert, C. N. II, Horan, P. M., & Beck, E. M. (1980). The structure of economic segmentation: A dual economy approach. *American Journal of Sociology, 85,* 1095–1116.

Treiman, D. T. (1977). *Occupational prestige in comparative perspective.* New York: Academic Press.

Wright, E. O., & Singelmann, J. (1982). Proletarianization in the American class structure. In M. Burawoy & T. Skocpol (Eds.), *Marxist inquiries.* Supplement to the *American Journal of Sociology, 88,* 5176–5209.

CHAPTER TWO

Women, Work, and Family
Changing Gender Roles and Psychological Well-Being

CATHERINE E. ROSS AND JOHN MIROWSKY

INTRODUCTION

How do macrolevel social changes affect individual well-being and distress? Specifically, how do lags—situations in which one change lags behind another—affect individuals? Women's labor force participation is changing much faster than the household division of labor. This means that many women are employed, yet solely responsible for the housework. The labor force participation of mothers of young children is changing much faster than the availability of child care. This means many employed mothers have difficulty arranging child care. These lags, and others, may be experienced by individuals as stressful.

Macrolevel social changes, especially increases in women's labor force participation, shape families and in turn the psychological well-being of men and women. American marriages are shifting from the complementary type, in which the husband is employed and the wife does the domestic work, to the parallel type, in which both spouses are employed and both are responsible for child care and housework. This transition, however, is far from complete. So great a change in so central and personal an institution may not occur smoothly for individual couples. Temporary disjunctions and strains in the institution of marriage, its related roles, and its links with other institutions may be experienced by individuals as emotionally distressing.

CATHERINE E. ROSS AND JOHN MIROWSKY • Department of Sociology, University of Illinois at Urbana–Champaign, Urbana, Illinois 61801.

33

Increases in women's labor force participation have set in motion other changes that, on the individual level, shape people's adjustment to women's employment: beliefs and values concerning women and their place, the division of labor at home, the cost of having children on one hand and the employment of mothers of young children on the other, and child care arrangements inside and outside the home. Each of these things (values, division of labor at home, number of children, and child care within the couple and outside the home) are changing in response to the employment of women. But they are changing more slowly. The transition in which one thing—like women's employment—has changed, but others—like responsibility for the children—have not, can produce a gap which is experienced by individuals as stressful.

These transitions are illustrated in Table 1.

The effect of a woman's employment on her psychological well-being and her husband's may depend on values and preferences, the husband's participation in housework, the presence of children, the husband's participation in child care, and the difficulty of arranging child care while parents are at work.

EMPLOYMENT AND MARRIAGE

Community mental health surveys consistently find that married women have higher levels of depression than married men. Perhaps women are more distressed than men because of differences in their social roles. Before the 1970s, the majority of married women were exclusively housewives and men were the breadwinners and job holders. Gove, one of the first sociologists to research gender differences in psychological well-being and distress, reasoned that if women are more distressed than men because of something different in their lives, then women who are employed will be less distressed than women who are exclusively housewives. This is what he found, and many studies replicated the finding (Gove & Geerken, 1977; Gove & Tudor, 1973; Kessler & McRae, 1982; Richman, 1979; Rosenfield, 1980; Ross, Mirowsky, & Ulbrich, 1983). It was an important discovery. Freud argued that women are born to be housewives and mothers and cannot be happy in the competitive world outside the home. Parsons argued that society and the people in it function most smoothly when women specialize in the loving, nurturing family realm and men specialize in the competitive, acquisitive, job-holding realm. Although it may seem obvious now, the discovery that women with jobs are less distressed than women without them overturned a century of armchair theorizing.

Gove's research shook preconceptions about women but did not explain everything. Although employed women are less distressed than

TABLE 1. Changes in Women's Labor Force Participation, Approval of Women's Employment, and the Household Division of Labor

Year	Women's labor force participation — Percentage of married women employed	Values — Percentage who approve of married women working	Household division of labor — Percentage of husbands who share housework equally with employed wife
1900	20%		
1940	30%	20%	
1970	50%	60%	
1978	56%	70%	20%

housewives, employed women are *more* distressed than employed men. Having a job is not the whole story. What explains the difference in distress between men and women with jobs outside the home? Kessler and his colleagues found that employment is associated with less distress among women whose husbands help with housework and child care, but there is little advantage to employment among women whose husbands do not help (Kessler & McRae, 1982). They also found that the extra housework and child care done by husbands of employed women does not increase the husband's distress. Researchers had been comparing different types of women; it was time to compare different types of couples.

Surveys show that American marriages are changing from ones in which the husband has a job and the wife stays home caring for the children and doing housework to ones in which the husband and wife both have jobs and share the housework and child care (Oppenheimer, 1982). Although many today may believe this a positive change, not many would have in 1900. The change did not happen because of preferences and values. Change in values followed changes in women's labor force participation (Smith, 1980). It happened because the logic of social arrangements in 1900 undermined itself as the economy grew and changed from manufacturing to services.

At the beginning of the century, women only took jobs in the period between getting out of school and getting married. A married women worked outside the home only if her husband could not support the family. Women could be paid much less than men with equivalent education and skills because the women's jobs were temporary or supplemental. Many jobs quickly became "women's work," particularly services such as waiting on tables, operating telephone switchboards, elementary-school teaching, nursing, and secretarial work.

The economic incentive for employers to hire women, combined with economic growth and the shift from manufacturing to services, increased the demand for female employees. Eventually there were not enough unmarried or childless women to fill the demand, and employers began reducing the barriers to employment for married women and encouraging those whose children were grown to return to work. Still the demand for labor in female occupations continued to grow faster than the supply of women in accepted social categories, and by the 1950s growth in female employment reached the sanctum sanctorum—married women with young children (Oppenheimer, 1973).

Throughout the century, individual women were drawn into the labor force by contingencies: economic need, the availability of work, and the freedom to work (Waite, 1976). Despite the low pay and limited opportunities, many women came to prefer working and earning money, and many husbands began to realize the benefits of two paychecks instead of one. But who was taking care of the home? This brings us back to the question of why employed women are more distressed than employed men.

We examined this issue with a national probability sample of 680 married couples (Ross, Mirowsky, & Huber, 1983). Respondents, chosen by random digit dialing, were interviewed by telephone in 1978. If the respondent was married, his or her spouse was also interviewed. Thus it is one of the few surveys of a large, representative sample of married persons throughout the United States in which both the husband and wife in each couple were interviewed. We compared the husband's and wife's depression in four types of marriages.

Depression was measured by a modified form of the Center for Epidemiological Studies' Depression scale (Radloff, 1975). Respondents were asked how often during the past week they felt run down, that everything was an effort, felt sad, felt they could not shake the blues, had trouble keeping their mind on what they were doing, felt they could not get going, had trouble falling asleep or staying asleep, did not feel like eating, felt lonely, bothered by things that do not usually bother them, and thought their life had been a failure.

A survey such as this, conducted at one point in time can be thought of as a slice of history. If the slice is taken in the midst of an historical change, then it will contain examples, of old, transitional, and new types. We examined four types of marriages, ordered according to historical change (see Figure 1).

In the first type of marriage the wife does not have a job, she and her husband believe her place is in the home, and she does all the housework and child care.[1] This is the traditional marriage. In 1978 it included roughly 44% of the couples. This type of marriage is internally consistent—preferences match behavior. For this reason it may be psychologically beneficial

---

[1]Housework and child care include the five most time-consuming tasks: who does the cooking, shopping, dishes, cleaning, and child care. Responses were coded from the wife always, to the wife usually, to the husband and wife share equally. Only two husbands usually did the housework and none always did.

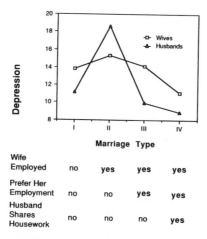

FIGURE 1. The effect of wife's employment, preferences for her employment, and the household division of labor on depression levels of wives and husbands. *Note:* From "Dividing work, sharing work, and in-between: Marriage patterns and depression," by Catherine E. Ross, John Mirowsky, and Joan Huber, 1983, *American Sociological Review, 48.* Copyright 1983 by the American Sociological Association. Reprinted by permission.

but more so for the husband. He is head of the household and has the power and prestige associated with economic resources. The wife, on the other hand, is typically dependent and subordinate. We found that the wife in this type of marriage has a higher level of depression than her husband.

In the second type of marriage, the wife has a job, but neither she nor her husband want her to, and she does all the housework and child care. This is roughly 19% of the couples. It is the first transitional marriage. Both husband and wife believe that he should provide for the family while she cares for the home and children, but she has taken a job because they need the money. Psychologically, this is the worst type of marriage for both of them, and their distress is greater than in any other. The wife may feel that it is not right that she has to work, that her choice of husband was a poor one, that she cannot do all the things a "good" mother should, and she carries a double burden of paid and unpaid work. To the extent that the husband has internalized the role of breadwinner, his wife's employment reflects unfavorably on him, indicating that he is not able to support his family. He may feel guilty and ashamed that she has a job, worry about his loss of authority, and suffer self-doubt and low self-esteem. This is the only type of marriage in which the husband is more distressed than his wife.

Although adjustment may come slowly, people do not long bear a tension between the way they live and the way they think they should live. As economic, demographic, and historical changes nudge lives into new patterns, husbands and wives come to view her employment more positively. This is particularly true as more of their friends and neighbors become two paycheck families. With macrolevel changes, two things are changing: individuals and the context in which they live.

Thus in the third type of marriage the wife has a job, and she and her husband favor her employment, but she remains responsible for the home. About 27% of the couples are in this second transitional category. The husband is better off than ever before. He has adjusted psychologically, his standard of living is higher, and the flow of family income is more secure. He has even lower distress than men in the first type of marriage. Things are not quite as good for his wife. She is better off than in the second type of marriage but still carries a double burden.

In a system in which the wife stays home and the husband goes out to work it makes sense for her to do the most time-consuming household chores. When she also goes out to work, and particularly when she stops thinking of her job as temporary, it becomes clear to her that the traditional division of the chores is no longer sensible or fair. Typically she assigns tasks to the older children, mechanizes tasks like dishwashing, uses frozen foods and eats out more often, cuts down on optional events like dinner parties, and does not clean as often. Even so, the demands on her time are likely to be much greater than those on her husband's (Robinson, 1980). The wife's level of distress in this type of marriage is about the same as in the first type, and the gap between her distress and her husband's is greater than in any other type of marriage.

Once the wife accepts the permanence of her new role as employed worker she may begin pressing for greater equality in the division of household labor. Although the husband may initially resist, once he has grown accustomed to the economic benefits of two paychecks he is likely to be open to negotiation. If his wife presses the issue, he often makes concessions rather than lose her earnings.

In the fourth type of marriage, the wife has a job, she and her husband approve of her employment, and they share housework and child care *equally*. This is about 11% of the couples. Both the husband and the wife are less distressed in this type of marriage than in any other, and the gap between them becomes insignificant. In adapting to the wife's employment, the central problem for husbands seems to be one of self-esteem — of getting over any embarrassment, guilt, or apprehension associated with the wife's employment. For wives the central problem is getting the husband to share the housework.

We began with the fact women are more distressed than men, and housewives are more distressed than women with jobs. In the end we found that couples who share both the economic responsibilities and the household responsibilities also share much the same level of psychological well-being and are less distressed than other couples. The difference in distress between men and women does not appear to be innate. The difference is there because men and women lead different lives, and as their lives converge the difference disappears.

There is a postscript to this research. About 20% of the employed wives are in marriages in which the husband shares the housework and child care. An analysis of the factors that increase the husband's housework shows that husbands with higher levels of education do more. Husbands also do more the higher the wife's earnings, and they do *less* the more their own earnings exceed the wife's (Ross, 1987). Thus equality in the division of labor at home, which provides psychological benefits to the husband and wife, depends on their economic equality in the workplace.

EMPLOYMENT AND CHILDREN

People have strong values about children. Many believe that children bring joy and happiness. Without children, women, especially, are said to feel empty, lonely, and unfulfilled. What about the research evidence on the effect of children on parents' psychological well-being and distress? Does it support our myths? The evidence here is not conclusive, but the picture is beginning to emerge, and some tentative conclusions can be drawn. They do not support the myths.

One finding is clear. Children do not improve the psychological well-being of parents (Brown & Harris, 1978; Cleary & Mechanic, 1983; Bore & Mangione, 1983; Gove & Geerkin, 1977; Kessler & McRae, 1982; Lovell-Troy, 1983; Pearlin, 1975; Radloff, 1975; Ross, Mirowsky, & Huber, 1983). When the presence of children in the home is correlated with psychological well-being of mothers and fathers, in no case do parents have higher well-being than nonparents. Furthermore, there are many instances in which parents—especially mothers—are more psychologically distressed than nonparents (Gove & Geerkin, 1977; Pearlin, 1975). The very group for whom children are believed to be most positive show the most negative effects.

According to Gove and his colleagues, young children put constant demands on mothers who are home all day with the children. They separate them from other adults and make them feel they are "stuck" in the house, at the same time decreasing their privacy and time alone (Gove & Geerkin, 1977). Housewives who are not employed are much more likely to feel that others are making demands on them than are employed mothers or fathers (Gove & Geerken, 1977). The traditional female role of housewife and mother who is not employed outside the home is stressful (Gove & Tudor, 1973). This argument implies that children are most stressful for women in the traditional role of housewife and mother—those who are home all day with the children (Brown & Harris, 1978; Gove & Geerken, 1977).

The opposite argument is also plausible. According to this argument, children are bad for the psychological well-being of employed mothers—because of role overload and conflict. As discussed, marriages are shifting from an arrangement in which the husband is employed and the wife does the domestic work to one in which both spouses are employed and both are responsible for child care and housework. But the transition is far from complete. Many wives are employed yet solely or largely responsible for child care. The result is role strain—overload from the sheer amount of effort it takes to perform in both arenas and conflict from meeting the expectations of people who do not take each other into account (i.e., one's boss and one's children).

Many women face incompatibilities between their role of mother and of employee because the institutional and family support necessary to fulfill both roles often does not exist. Possibly the major lack of support is in the area of child care. Readily available, affordable child care may ease the strain on employed mothers.

To examine some of these issues, we used the data on 680 husbands and wives throughout the United States, described earlier (Ross & Mirowsky, 1988). We examined depression levels of husbands and wives depending on whether or not there are young children (under the age of 12) at home, whether or not the wife is employed, whether the husband shares child care responsibilities with his wife or whether the wife has the major responsibility for child care, and whether child care arrangements for working parents are readily available and easy to arrange or whether arranging child care while the parents are at work is difficult.[2]

Figure 2 shows the deviations from the overall mean depression level for wives. We focus on wives because regression analyses indicated that neither children nor their care affected husbands' well-being one way or the other. The figure shows mean differences, which the regression analyses indicated are not merely spurious consequences of differences in age, education, income, or number of children. Nonemployed wives with young children have significantly higher depression than those without children.

For employed wives, it is not children *per se*, but the difficulty in arranging child care that affects psychological well-being. Employed wives without children and employed wives with young children for whom child care presents no difficulties have significantly lower depression than average. Employed women with young children who have difficulty arranging child care have much more depression than average. There is no significant difference in depression between employed women with no children and those with children for whom child care arrangements present no problem.

In terms of wives' mental health, the best arrangement appears to be

[2]Mothers were asked, "How difficult is it for you to arrange child care while you are at work?" Responses were coded from not at all difficult to very difficult.

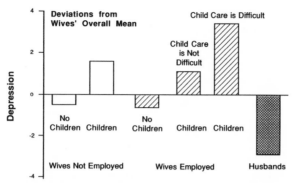

FIGURE 2. Deviations from wives' overall mean depression level, depending on her employment status, the presence of children, and the difficulty of arranging child care. Husbands are shown for comparison. *Note:* From "Child care and emotional adjustment to wives employment," by Catherine E. Ross and John Mirowsky, 1988, *Journal of Health and Social Behavior, 29.* Copyright 1988 by the American Sociological Association. Reprinted by permission.

employment and no children or employment coupled with easy and available child care for the young children. Staying at home with children appears to be more stressful. However, the most stressful situation for wives is one in which they are employed, have young children, and have difficulty in arranging child care. Can the husband's participation in child care help offset the strain on these employed mothers?

Figure 3 adds another factor for employed women: whether or not her husband takes some of the responsibility for child care. It shows the deviations from the mean for employed wives, depending on the presence of young children, difficulty of arranging child care while at work, and the husband's participation in child care. The husband's participation can offset the strain of arranging child care. The situation that is most detrimental to wives' mental health is one in which she is employed, has young children, has difficulty arranging child care, and her husband does not share the child care responsibilities with her.

If employed women with children have no difficulty arranging child care while they are working and their husbands share the child care with them, depression levels are very low. Under these conditions, the mental health of wives is as good as that of husbands. The average depression level is 11.1, which is not significantly different than the average husband's level of 10.9. In contrast, the employed wives who have difficulty arranging child care for young children and have sole responsibility for child care are twice as depressed ($\bar{X} = 22.6$ vs. $\bar{X} = 11.1$).

Child care is the overwhelming concern for employed mothers. We began with the finding that children are bad for mothers' psychological well-being. We end with the finding that it is not children *per se* that create stress for employed mothers but the absence of supportive arrangements.

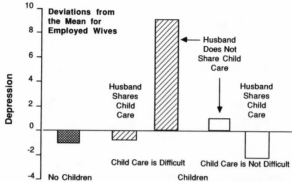

FIGURE 3. Deviations from the mean depression level for employed wives, depending on the presence of children, difficulty of arranging child care, and the husband's participation in child care. *Note:* From "Child care and emotional adjustment to wives' employment," by Catherine E. Ross and John Mirowsky, 1988, *Journal of Health and Social Behavior, 29.* Copyright 1988 by the American Sociological Association. Reprinted by permission.

We find that employed mothers whose husbands share the child care responsibilities and who have no difficulty in arranging child care have depression levels that are as low as employed women with no children and as low as husbands.

Children are much less stressful for employed mothers than for housewives who are not employed, as long as the employed mothers have easily available child care and their husbands share the responsibility of child care with them. Nothing offsets the stress of young children for housewives who are not employed. The women who are home all day with the children may feel, as Gove and his colleagues described, that the children are making constant demands on them, that they have no privacy, that they are isolated from other adults, and that they are "stuck" in the house.

When husbands' and wives' social roles are similar, their depression levels are similar. The gender gap in psychological well-being closes due to lower depression among wives and not due to greater depression among husbands. Some have argued that employment among wives puts a strain on husbands because of added responsibility for child care. We find no evidence that this is the case. *If* the wife's employment increases her husband's depression *at all* when he helps with child care, the increase in his depression is very small compared to the decrease in hers.

What we now think of as a "traditional" family pattern, in which the husband is employed and the wife stays home and cares for the household and children, is actually a consequence of the Industrial Revolution (Tilly, 1983). Parsons (1949) claimed it is functionally imperative that the husband is the provider and his wife is the homemaker and child rearer. Becker (1976) claimed that, from the perspective of maximizing household utilities, it was economically rational for the wife to stay home caring for children because her market wages were typically lower than her husband's. Parsons's and Becker's theories of marital roles seem time bound. The massive labor force entry of married women with children has reduced the credibility of both theories. A pattern that appeared with industrial society may disappear in a postindustrial period.

It is understandable, however, that scholars writing in a transitional period should see a shift away from the complementary marriage pattern in which the husband is employed and the wife stays home as stressful, disturbing, and threatening to the marriage. What is stressful is the transition in which one aspect of family roles has changed (such as employment of mothers of young children), but other family roles (such as the husband's participation in the child care) or the family's links to other institutions (such as the availability of child care) have not caught up.

The plea to return to the "traditional" family of the 1950s is a plea to return wives and mothers to a psychologically disadvantaged position, in which husbands have much better mental health than wives. A shared family pattern in which both spouses are employed and both are responsible for child care and in which there are supportive institutions for child care outside the nuclear family is one in which both husbands and wives have low levels of depression. The well-being of husbands is not taxed by these changes.

Since 1970, the greatest labor force increases have occurred among young married women with young children, and there is no reason to think the trend will be reversed. It is unrealistic to think that Americans can care for their children by going back to a time when mothers were not engaged in productive labor, and child care and homemaking were full-time jobs (a short period of time historically, anyway). As the number of working couples increases, the need for child care policy increases.

There are three things society can do about the high depression levels caused by the stress on employed mothers of not having available, affordable child care. The first is nothing. This is unacceptable because it ignores individual suffering and demoralization. It also ignores the fact that depression may interfere with the ability to work and to care for the children. The second is treat the depression and leave the social problem unsolved. This is the usual response. The third is provide child care for everyone who needs it. Compare the second and third alternatives. If an employed mother receives treatment from a psychiatrist for her depression, the psychiatrist might prescribe medication, monitor her for side effects, listen to her talk, interpret her dreams, hypnotize her, and so on. The one thing a psychiatrist cannot do is solve her child care problem. How much money would we have to spend on psychiatrists, drugs, and therapies to get this woman's depressive symptoms down to a tolerable and humane level? If we spent the money, do we have evidence that it would be effective in reducing symptoms? Let us estimate that it costs about $4,000 a year for child care for one child (Kamerman & Kahn, 1979). And let us estimate that psychiatric care for a woman with high levels of depression who sees a psychiatrist once a week costs $4,800 a year (48 × $100), plus the costs of prescription drugs. The costs of treating this woman's depression are about the same as providing care for her child. The child care can prevent the depression in the first place, instead of exposing her to the stress, frustration, and demoralization that lead her to seek help.

For employed mothers, institutional arrangements *and* family arrangements are important modifiers of the stress of having young children. Readily available, affordable child care is an important way to reduce the strain on employed mothers and improve their psychological well-being. Changing husbands' perceptions of the role of child rearer is also important. Both husbands and wives must be responsible for child care.

This century has been characterized by three trends: increases in educational levels, increases in women's labor force participation and decreases in fertility. The three are closely related because more educated women are more likely to be in the labor force and are less likely to have many children. There is no indication that these trends will be reversed. The association between employment and fewer children is in part due to the fact that the institutional and family arrangements necessary to be employed and be a mother often do not exist. Providing this support reduces the strain on employed mothers and is associated with very high levels of psychological well-being on their part, higher than that of mothers who are not employed. There is nothing necessarily "antifamily" or "antinatalist" about the employment of women. It is the lack of readily available child care and the lack of shared responsibility for children within the couple that puts the stress on the mothers and their families.

WOMEN'S WORK

Not only have changes in values, the division of labor at home, and the availability of child care lagged behind increases in women's employment, characteristics of women's jobs have also changed slowly. Compared to men's jobs, women's are characterized by less autonomy, a smaller likelihood of promotion or of being in a supervisory position, and lower earnings. Thus men's and women's work experiences are different. These characteristics of work may also modify the effect of employment on women's well-being and distress. This is an important direction for future research on changing gender roles and psychological well-being.

CONCLUSION

Over the course of the twentieth century, we have seen a long, slow cultural adaptation to forceful and dramatic trends in female employment.

Ultimately, these trends are themselves the consequences of increasing female education and decreasing family size in a cultural context that viewed women's employment as temporary and supplemental. Greater education made women's labor increasingly valuable; smaller families made it increasingly available. Women constituted a pool of high-quality, low-cost labor. For the most part, this pool has been tapped.

The lags in adaptation to increasing female employment exist for much the same reason as the trend in employment itself. The demand for female labor flows from its relatively low cost per unit of education and experience. On the supplier's side, the low price women get for their labor encourages them or their husbands to view it as temporary or supplemental. Increasingly, it is neither. Nevertheless, the fact of lower earnings combines with the myth of temporary or supplemental employment to slow the rate of adaptation in the division of household chores and childcare responsibility.

What is to come? It is easier to know the past or the present than to know the future. One thing seems clear, though. Trends in the ratio of women's to men's earnings will be the critical factor. A rosy forecast is that the vanishing pool of untapped, inexpensive female labor will lead employers to pay higher wages to women already in the labor force. This would put women in a better position to bargain with husbands, employers, and politicians about child care. Also, to the extent that family income increases with women's wages, the family is better able to pay for child care.

Of course, there is no guarantee this rosy forecast will come true. One would like to think that husbands will accept greater responsibility for care of their own children before it is absolutely forced upon them in tough negotiation. Unfortunately, the trends to date make one question whether husbands will. As for employers, they are likely to be less enthusiastic about paying more to women currently in the labor force than they were about bringing more women in at low pay. There may be an historical, economic inevitability to the eventual demise of differences between men and women in wages and in responsibility for housework and childcare. Even so, the rate at which the lag in adaptation disappears is within the realm of individual and collective action. That adaptation is critical for bringing women's emotional well-being up to the level of men's.

ACKNOWLEDGMENTS

Data collection was supported by the National Science Foundation grant SOC 78-18015 to Joan Huber. Sampling, pretesting, and interviewing were conducted by the Survey Research Laboratory of the University of Illinois. Figure 1 is from "Dividing Work, Sharing Work, and In-Between: Marriage Patterns and Depression," by Catherine E. Ross, John Mirowsky, and Joan Huber, *American Sociological Review*, 1983, *48*, 809–823. Figures 2 and 3 are from "Child Care and Emotional Adjustment to Wives' Employment," by Catherine E. Ross and John Mirowsky, *Journal of Health and Social Behavior*, 1988, *29*, 127–138. Parts of this chapter also appeared in those articles. Figures and text are reprinted with permission. We thank Joan Huber for all her contributions, and particularly for encouraging us to think about the connections between macrolevel social change and individual well-being.

REFERENCES

Becker, G. (1976). *The economic approach to human behavior*. Chicago: University of Chicago Press.

Brown, G. W., & Harris, T. (1978). *Social origins of depression*. New York: Free Press.

Cleary, P. D., & Mechanic, D. (1983). Sex differences in psychological distress among married people. *Journal of Health and Social Behavior, 24*, 111–121.

Gore, S., & Mangione, T. W. (1983). Social roles, sex roles, and psychological distress. *Journal of Health and Social Behavior, 24*, 300–312.

Gove, W. R., & Geerken, M. R. (1977). The effect of children and employment on the mental health of married men and women. *Social Forces, 56*, 66–76.

Gove, W. R., & Tudor, J. F. (1973). Adult sex roles and mental illness. *American Journal of Sociology, 78*, 812–835.

Kamerman, S. B., & Kahn, A. J. (1979). The day care debate: A wider view. *The Public Interest, 54*, 76–93.

Kessler, R. C., & McRae, J. A. (1982). The effect of wives' employment on the mental health of married men and women. *American Sociological Review, 47*, 216–227.

Lovell-Troy, L. (1983). Anomia among employed wives and housewives. *Journal of Marriage and the Family*, May, 301–310.

Oppenheimer, V. K. (1973). Demographic influence on female employment and the status of women. In J. Huber (Ed.), *Changing women in a changing society* (pp. 184–191). Chicago: University of Chicago Press.

Oppenheimer, V. K. (1982). *Work and family: A study in social demography*. New York: Academic Press.

Parsons, T. (1949). The social structure of the family. In R. Anshen, *The family: Its function and destiny* (pp. 173–201). New York: Harper.

Pearlin, L. I. (1975). Sex roles and Depression. In N. Datan & L. H. Ginsberg (Eds.), *Life span developmental psychology: Normative life crisis* (pp. 191–208). New York: Academic Press.

Radloff, L. (1975). Sex differences in depression: The effects of occupation and marital status. *Sex Roles, 1*, 249–265.

Radloff, L. (1977). The CES-D scale: A self-report depression scale for research in the general population. *Applied Psychological Measurement, 1*, 385–401.

Richman, J. (1979). *Women's changing work roles and psychological-psychophysiological distress*. Paper presented at the American Sociological Association annual meeting, Boston.

Robinson, J. P. (1980). Housework technology and household work. In S. F. Berk (Ed.), *Women and household labor* (pp. 53–67). Beverly Hills: Sage.

Rosenfield, S. (1980). Sex differences in depression: Do women always have higher rates? *Journal of Health and Social Behavior, 21*, 33–42.

Ross, C. E., Mirowsky, J., & Huber, J. (1983). Dividing work, sharing work, and in-between: Marriage patterns and depression. *American Sociological Review, 48*, 809–823.

Ross, C. E., Mirowsky, J., & Ulbrich, P. (1983). Distress and the traditional female role: A comparison of Mexicans and Anglos. *American Journal of Sociology, 89*, 670–682.

Ross, C. E. (1987). The division of labor at home. *Social Forces, 65,* 816–833.

Ross, C. E., & Mirowsky, J. (1988). Child care and emotional adjustment to wives' employment. *Journal of Health and Social Behavior, 29,* 127–138.

Smith, T. W. (1980). *A compendium of trends on general social survey questions.* National Opinion Research Center Report No. 129. Chicago: NORC.

Tilly, L. (1983). *The world turned upside down: Age and gender in Europe, 1750–1950.* Paper presented at the annual meeting of the American Sociological Association, Detroit.

Waite, L. J. (1976). Working wives: 1940–1960. *American Sociological Review, 41,* 65–80.

CHAPTER THREE

Gender and the Structural Transformation of the Legal Profession in the United States and Canada

JOHN HAGAN

INTRODUCTION

Two notable features of contemporary legal practice in the United States and Canada are the increasing numbers of women lawyers and the expansion of large firms. Both developments are part of a growth in the profession that has occurred over much of this century, especially during the past two decades, when this expansion has seemed to some to be out of control (see Abel, 1986). Those who see this growth as a problem are divided in their concerns about its effects on the well-being of lawyers and their clients. The former concern is about earnings of lawyers and about competition for work (see, e.g., Stager, 1982). The latter concern is about a propensity for legal conflict that many believe is producing a "litigation explosion" (but see Galanter, 1983a). Of course, competition for work and litigiousness could be related, and this also is a concern.

Although our interest is primarily in the legal profession itself, it is impossible to study this profession without considering its impact on society. The relationship is symbiotic. First, however, we consider dimensions of the growth of this profession and causes and consequences of its structural transformation in the United States and Canada. These two nations provide interesting possibilities for comparison.

JOHN HAGAN • Faculty of Law, University of Toronto, Toronto M5S 2C5, Ontario, Canada.

THE DEMOGRAPHICS OF PROFESSIONAL GROWTH
IN THE UNITED STATES AND CANADA

We begin with census data on the legal profession in the United States and Canada, with further breakdowns for Ontario and Quebec, and by gender. These comparisons are facilitated by data on the U.S. legal profession assembled by Halliday (1986). There is a large literature on cultural and structural differences between the United States and Canada that owes its biggest debts to S. M. Lipset (e.g., 1968, 1986) and S. D. Clark (1942, 1976). Although the two countries are economically entwined and although they share an English legal heritage, the core of Lipset's and Clark's arguments is that there are important value differences between the United States and Canada that derive from their respective revolutionary and counterrevolutionary beginnings. It is argued that these value differences make Canadians more consensual and less conflictual in their social and political behaviors. It also is widely believed that structural differences (Hiller, 1976), for example in procedural and substantive law, have joined with cultural differences in producing substantial differences in crime and lawyering in the two countries.

However, it also is argued that a growing domination of the Canadian economy by the United States is leading to cultural convergence (e.g., Davis, 1971; Horowitz, 1973). There is little evidence of this convergence in terms of the nations' respective crime statistics (see Hagan & Leon, 1978; Hagan, 1984). However, here we compare developments in the legal professions of these nations. Further data is provided on Quebec and Ontario, sometimes called the "two solitudes" of Canadian society.

Table 1 presents census data on the growth of the legal profession and of the populations of Canada and the United States, and in Ontario and Quebec. In contrast with the convergence hypothesis, throughout the time series the ratio of lawyers to population is higher in the United States than in English or French Canada. This national difference persists in the face of dramatic absolute changes in the number of lawyers and the general populations of each jurisdiction. The first half-century represented in this table reveals an approximate doubling of lawyers and the general population in both countries. Until 1961, the ratio of lawyers to population remained at about .7 per thousand persons in Canada and at about 1.25 per thousand in the United States. With only one minor deviation (see 1921), in every decade from 1911 to 1961, the number of lawyers per 1,000 population is more than one and a half times again larger in the United States than in Canada.

Since 1961 the number of lawyers in both countries has increased dramatically. In absolute terms, lawyers in each jurisdiction again more than doubled, this time in the space of the two decades. In relative terms, in the single decade between 1971 and 1981 in Canada, the number of lawyers per thousand population nearly doubled, from .757 to 1.405. Within Canada,

TABLE 1. Growth of the Legal Profession and Populations of Canada, Ontario, Quebec, and the United States, 1911–1981

Year	Canada[a]			United States[c]			Ontario			Quebec		
	Lawyers[b]	Population	Per 1000	Lawyers	Population	Per 1000	Lawyers	Population	Per 1000	Lawyers	Population	Per 1000
1911	5,204	7,206,643	.722	114,704	91,063,200	1.25	1,678	2,527,000	.664	1,716	2,006,000	.855
1921	7,209	8,789,949	.820	122,519	103,819,828	1.16	2,231	2,934,000	.760	2,004	2,351,000	.849
1931	8,058	10,376,786	.777	160,605	122,599,227	1.31	2,792	3,432,000	.814	2,351	2,875,000	.818
1941	8,621	11,506,655	.749	177,643	131,587,407	1.35	2,817	3,788,000	.744	2,587	3,332,000	.776
1951	9,038	14,009,429	.645	180,461	150,384,167	1.20	3,388	4,598,000	.737	2,669	4,056,000	.658
1961	12,088	18,238,247	.663	217,523	179,771,074	1.21	4,902	6,236,000	.786	3,322	5,259,000	.632
1971	16,320	21,568,311	.757	285,466	203,904,286	1.40	6,845	7,703,000	.889	4,400	6,028,000	.730
1981	34,205	24,343,181	1.405	521,874	225,801,739	2.30	13,445	8,625,000	1.559	8,665	6,438,000	1.346

[a]Newfoundland added in 1951 and Yukon and Northwest Territories in 1961.
[b]From Category 2343, Lawyers and Notaries, Standard Occupational Classification, 1980, Statistics Canada.
[c]The U.S. data are taken from Halliday, 1986, Appendix.

the increase in Ontario was from .889 to 1.559, and in Quebec from .730 to 1.346. The increase in the United States was from 1.40 to 2.30. So as of 1981, there were still more than one and a half times more lawyers per thousand population in the United States than in Canada.

Table 2 further elaborates changes in these countries by gender. This table confirms that although law historically has been a male-dominated profession, small but steady gains have occurred for women in both countries through most of this century, with pronounced gains in the past two decades, especially since 1971. In 1911 there were only 7 women lawyers in Canada, whereas there were 785 in 1971 and 5,175 in 1981. A similar pattern of growth occurred in the United States, from 558 women lawyers in 1911, to 13,964 in 1971, to 72,312 in 1981. The ratios of men to women lawyers in Canada in 1911, 1971, and 1981 were about 742:1, 20:1, and 6:1, respectively; and the ratios are comparable in the United States. Over the past two decades women have increased from about 10% of graduating law school classes, to in some cases over 40%. Women will by conservative estimates constitute more than a third of the legal profession in both countries by the year 2000 (Morello, 1986). Women already form a large segment of the younger and larger cohorts of the profession.

Mention should be made of an interesting gender difference between English and French Canada. Table 2 indicates that whereas in 1971 the ratio of men to women lawyers in Ontario and Quebec was nearly identical (about 19:1), in 1981 the ratios were quite different: 6.89:1 in Ontario and 4.45:1 in Quebec. Both ratios declined sharply, but the decline in Quebec was noticeably larger. This difference was clearer still for city-specific comparisons of Toronto and Montreal but was not apparent for comparisons of other professions or occupations in the two cities. This difference may follow from a movement of francophone males into business in the 1970s in Quebec, and there are indications from further afield that this difference between French and English Canada is mirrored in comparisons of France and England (Menkel-Meadow, 1989). This difference in the composition of the legal profession across places is an example of interesting possibilities for research on the causes and consequences of variation in the gender composition of occupational experiences.

Overall, our data indicate differences as well as similarities in the U.S. and Canadian experiences. The most significant differences is that relative to population, there continue to be substantially fewer lawyers in Canada than in the United States. This aside, however, the overall growth of the profession and the increased representation of women are remarkably similar in the two countries. Apparently structural and cultural differences between the United States and Canada have established parameters within which similar processes of social change are operating.

This leaves the question of what has caused these changes. Economists (Pashigian, 1978) point to cyclical changes in the demand for legal

TABLE 2. Growth of the Legal Profession by Gender:
Canada, Ontario, Quebec, and the United States, 1911–1981

Year	Canada			Ontario			Quebec			United States[a]		
	Women	Men	Ratio	Women	Men	Ratio	Women	Men	Ratio	Women	Men	Ratio
1911	7	5,197	742.43	4	1,604	401.00	1	1,715	1715.00	558	114,146	204.56
1921	64	7,145	111.64	23	2,208	96.00	9	1,995	221.67	1,738	120,781	69.49
1931	54	8,004	148.22	32	2,760	86.25	4	2,347	586.75	3,385	157,220	46.45
1941	129	8,492	65.83	73	2,744	37.59	5	2,582	516.40	4,187	173,456	41.27
1951	197	8,841	44.88	107	3,281	30.66	30	2,639	87.97	6,256	174,205	27.85
1961	311	11,777	37.87	162	4,740	29.26	59	3,263	55.05	7,434	210,089	28.26
1971	785	15,585	19.85	345	6,500	18.84	225	4,175	18.56	13,964	273,044	19.55
1981	5,175	29,030	5.61	1,705	11,740	6.89	1,590	7,075	4.45	72,312	452,494	6.26

[a]The U.S. data are taken from Halliday, 1986, Table 2, p. 62.

services that produce wavelike patterns of growth, whereas others (Abel, 1979; Auerbach, 1976; Larson, 1977) have emphasized attempts of bar associations to monopolistically control the supply of new lawyers. However, these approaches better explain the slower growth of the profession during the earlier part of this century than the dramatic expansion in recent years (Halliday, 1983).

These accounts do not consider the aspirations of those who entered the profession in the 1970s and early 1980s. These cohorts are the products of the postwar baby boomers, many of whose parents experienced the Great Depression as children and World War II as adults. Many of the women and mothers who might otherwise have joined the labor force during the Great Depression and World War II stayed out of the labor force during the late 1940s and 1950s, helping to create what has been called "the normative 1950s family." However, many of these same women and mothers returned to work during the postwar boom that extended into the 1960s and that created new demands for female labor (Cherlin, 1983). The children of the baby boom grew up in a period of prolonged economic growth and attendant rising expectations of social and economic well-being—for woman as well as for men. For many, legal education seemed an attractive, multifaceted vehicle for the realization of their aspirations. For some, perhaps more often women than men, the law represented a promising instrument for change, including changes sought by the women's movement (Chester, 1985). For many others of both genders, the law represented a promising means of access to higher social positions of status and power. This brings us to issues of stratification and mobility in the practice of law.

THE SEGMENTATION AND STRATIFICATION OF LEGAL PRACTICE

Census figures can only begin to reveal a segmentation and stratification of the profession that is structured around divisions in work organization and gender. Work organization and gender crosscut one another in the hierarchical stratification of lawyers. Because we already have presented evidence of the growing representation of women in the profession, we now introduce the element of work organization and then return to the ways in which women are located in the organization of legal activity.

The salient factor in the organization of lawyers' work is the growing domination of the large firms, or what Galanter (1983b) has called *megalawyering*. There were only 38 U.S. law firms with 50 or more lawyers in the late 1950s (Smigel, 1964), but by the mid-1980s there were 508 firms of this size (Curran *et al.*, 1985). Meanwhile, a Canadian survey (Arthurs, Willms, & Taman, 1971) reported that while 41% of Toronto lawyers were engaged in solo practice in the 1950s, only 12% were so engaged in the early 1970s. The era of rapid growth in the legal profession that we observed with census data for the United States and Canada was also a period in which there was a shift from solo practice to large firms.

This shift from small to large firms is widely observed (see, e.g., Larson, 1977), and it is the focal point in Heinz and Laumann's (1982) landmark study of Chicago lawyers. Although there are important exceptions (e.g., Goulden, 1971), major corporations usually are represented by large firms, whereas small businesses and individuals of moderate or low income usually are represented by small firms or by lawyers practicing alone (Carlin, 1962; Ladinsky, 1963). Heinz and Laumann (1982, p. 319) emphasize the connections between these firms and corporate clients.

> Much of the differentiation within the legal profession is secondary to one fundamental distinction—the distinction between lawyers who represent large organizations...and those who represent individuals. The two kinds of practice are the two hemispheres of the profession. Most lawyers reside exclusively in one hemisphere or the other and seldom, if ever, cross the equator.

This last observation, that lawyers in Heinz and Laumann's analogy rarely cross the hemispheres of legal practice, leads logically to a broader consideration given in the stratification literature to the segmentation of capital and labor markets.

Sociologists as well as economists now commonly draw distinctions between sectors of the private economy (e.g., internal/external, center/periphery) that are relevant to the practice of law. Hodson and Kaufman (1982) note that these sectors differ in terms of market power, financial size, scale of employment, conglomerate organization, long-term planning capabilities, and relationship to the government. The internal sector is advantaged on each dimension, whereas the external sector is disadvantaged. Emphasis is placed on the extent to which employment is more stable and secure in the internal sector and on the barriers to mobility that may exist between sectors (Doeringer & Piore, 1971; O'Conner, 1973). Internal labor markets shelter employees in large, core firms from competition with workers in external labor markets. Points of entry to the internal markets are limited, and barriers to mobility between labor markets rise as a result of differences in on-the-job training, access to job information, job security, and other institutionalized factors (Bluestone, 1970). Work histories in the external sector therefore may limit entry and advancement into the internal sector (Gordon, 1972), whereas within the internal market, "job ladders" encourage upward mobility (Halaby, 1979; Kanter, 1977; Rosenbaum, 1979) and further intensify the segmentation of markets (Baron & Bielby, 1984; Sorensen & Kalleberg, 1981).

These factors may also divide large law firms from other parts of the profession. Heinz and Laumann's suggestion that there is little movement between the hemispheres of the profession and the emphasis they place on connections between large firms and corporate clients both imply a segmentation of sectors. This view is consistent with studies that show that single occupations, as well as national labor markets, effectively can be understood in terms of internal/external segmentation (Finlay, 1983; Smith, 1983).

Gender crosscuts forms of work organization in the segmentation of the legal profession. The larger stratification literature confirms that gender influences entry and outcomes across occupations (e.g., Featherman & Hauser, 1976; Trieman & Terrell, 1975), operating in different ways within structurally differentiated occupational settings (Boyd, 1982; Kanter, 1977). In general, women may be located disadvantageously both between and within labor markets. So that women may not only be located disproportionately in external labor markets (but see also Bridges, 1980; Kaufman & Daymont, 1981), they may also experience sex segregation within internal as well as external markets (Blau, 1977; Gross, 1986; Halaby, 1979; Kanter, 1977). Finally, although Kalleberg and Hudis (1979) show that firm-internal labor markets offer attainment advantages over other types of job situations for men, Felmlee (1982) demonstrates that for women the overall advantages of being in a firm-internal labor market are modest.

What might these findings mean for men and women in law? One might argue that the legal profession would, especially with the emphasis placed by law in democratic societies on equal treatment, provide protection against gender-based disparities. Such arguments add interest to questions that follow from the preceding discussion of the entry and advancement of women compared to men in internal compared to external sector settings. For example: Do large law firm settings serve as mobility routes? If so, how do women compared to men fare in their use of such firms as mobility routes? Do such routes, as some commentators have suggested (Hodson & Kaufman, 1982), produce vulnerabilities as well as provide resources in the mobility process? Prior research cannot answer these questions because it has not adequately conceptualized or operationalized positions that lawyers occupy in the social structure of legal practice. However, as we see next, prior research on lawyers does give further reason to ask these questions.

PARTNERSHIP, PROFIT, AND PLEASURE IN PRACTICE

Prior research on lawyers has addressed three issues—partnership, earnings, and job satisfaction—and in each area gender has emerged as a significant factor. Research on partnership confronted the issue of gender in the aftermath of *Hishon v. King & Spaulding*, the unsuccessful U.S. Supreme Court case of a female associate denied partnership in an Atlanta firm. This research consists mainly of surveys of firms that were asked to report the numbers of male and female associates and partners. Results are reported in a mixture of unpublished and summary forms that make meaningful interpretation problematic. For example, Fenning (1987) reviews three studies from Los Angeles, Maryland, and Michigan that collectively indicate that women make up about 4 to 8% of the partners and 25 to 33% of the associates in firms. However, these results apparently are derived from tables percentaged in the noncausal direction and without controls for experience.

Findings with regard to earnings are revealing but also inconclusive. White (1967) sampled male and female graduates from the classes of 1956 through 1965 of 134 American law schools and found that "the males make a lot more money than do the females" (p. 1057). Another early study of Harvard law graduates (Glancy, 1970) found fewer than 12% of the women as compared to 57% of the men were making more than $20,000 a year. A 5-year follow-up study (Adam & Baer, 1984) of the 1974 graduating class of Ontario (Canada) law schools reports that women graduates earn about $3,000 a year less on average than men. Finally, a study (Vogt, 1987) conducted in 1985 in seven northeastern U.S. law schools reports that among graduates 11 years out in the same size firms, men earn an average of $75,000 and women $46,500. These studies provide few insights into sources of gender differences in lawyers' incomes, but they demonstrate that substantial differences exist (see also Hagan, 1989).

Finally, there is a much-cited survey by the American Bar Association (1985) of the job satisfaction of lawyers. Women are more dissatisfied than men in every job category except the public sector, and the gender difference in dissatisfaction is greater among younger than older lawyers. Controlling for partnership did not eliminate this difference: Women partners still are more dissatisfied than their male colleagues. When asked about causes, more women than men cited lack of time for their private lives (see also Spangler, 1986). Furthermore, a higher percentage of women cited an impersonal or unfriendly job atmosphere. An exception to these findings is a study by Chambers (1987) of University of Michigan law graduates. He reports that although women have unique problems in practice, they are no more dissatisfied overall than men. Chambers notes that this variance from the ABA survey findings may result from the elite status of the Michigan graduates.

So overall there is evidence that women are less often partners, earn less, and are more dissatisfied. However, we know little about how these differences vary across sectors, about their relationship to stages in lawyers' careers, or about their connection to differences in positions of power. These issues probably are interconnected, but to establish such interconnections it will be necessary to further conceptualize and operationalize the power structure of legal practice.

POWER IN PRACTICE

Few studies analyze power relationships among lawyers. Several factors may account for this. To begin, partners often are uncertain whether to
answer on labor force surveys that they are self-employed. It sometimes is
estimated that from 50 to 60% of all lawyers practice alone (e.g., Sikes,
Carson, & Gorai, 1972). Such estimates may be inflated by the misleading
or misinterpreted answers of partners in firms. In any case, the legal distinction between associates and partners is insufficient for our purposes.
There are partners and there are partners; for example, there are senior
partners, managing partners, tax partners, and junior partners.

If this terminology were consistently applied, there would still be
problems for research purposes. Large law firms prize their privacy, and
issues of power and partnership are more likely to be understood than
discussed, especially with sociologists. Stewart (1983, p. 16) writes that
lawyers in powerful firms are tradition bound and that "of these traditions,
one of the most deeply rooted is secrecy." This tendency toward secrecy
makes penetration of the power structure of large elite firms difficult.

Nonetheless, it is necessary to penetrate these power structures to
effectively reveal the stratification of lawyers and to use this knowledge in
explaining differences in income and job satisfaction. In our work on
Toronto lawyers, we incorporate survey measures developed by Erik
Wright (e.g., Wright et al., 1982). Studying the stratification of a profession
rather than a national labor force requires modification of Wright's measures, although keeping in mind that the legal profession necessarily intersects and overlaps with the larger stratification system. Erlanger (1980, p.
882) makes this point in relation to status attainment when he notes that
although lawyers commonly are portrayed as located at a single point on a
status continuum, they actually are dispersed along a status distribution
that overlaps distributions of other occupations. So, for example, although
physicians collectively may have higher status than lawyers, corporate
lawyers may often have higher status than family physicians. The same
point can be made in relation to the tendency of class theorists, for example, to treat the "professional–managerial class" (Ehrenreich & Ehrenreich,
1978) as an unanalyzed aggregate. The point is that the stratification of the
legal profession involves more than is often assumed in either class or
status traditions. To take an example we discuss further later, it can be
argued that the composition of the legal profession includes not only members of a capitalist class, but in a limited sense, workers as well.

As noted, our own attempt to map the class structure of lawyers in
Toronto (see Tables 3, 4, and 5) has involved an elaboration of a model used
in the recent work of Wright. Grabb (1984, p. 144) notes that for Wright,
"class and power are really inseparable ideas." The power bases of Wright's
occupationalization of class involve indicators of relations of appropriation

TABLE 3. Ranges for the Estimate of the Class Distribution of Toronto Lawyers
(in Percent), 1984 ($N = 995$)

Class location	Best estimate	Minimum	Maximum
Capitalist class	4.5	2.7	12.0
Managerial bourgeoisie	12.4	11.4	13.8
Supervisory bourgeoisie	11.9	11.8	21.9
Small employers	15.7	5.9	19.0
Petty bourgeoisie	9.1	5.0	N.A.
All managers/supervisors	12.1	11.0	36.4
Managers	7.6	7.0	19.9
Advisory managers	3.6	3.4	15.4
Supervisors	.9	.6	1.1
Semiautonomous employees	25.6	9.1	31.8
Working class	8.7	2.9	26.2

Note. Ranges were based on the following criteria:

Capitalists:
  Minimum = employer + more than 30 employees + elite firm + task and sanctioning authority + participates directly in policy making + no level above respondent + two or more levels below respondent.
  Maximum = employer + more than 30 employees + task or sanctioning authority + two or more levels below respondent decision-maker.

Managerial bourgeoisie:
  Minimum = employer + 10 or more employees + task and sanctioning authority + two or more levels below respondent + participates directly in policy making.
  Maximum = employer + 10 or more employees + task or sanctioning authority + two or more levels below respondent.

Supervisory bourgeoisie:
  Minimum = employer + 10 or more employees + two or more lawyers (including self) + one or more levels below respondent.
  Maximum = employer + two or more employees.

Small employers:
  Minimum = employer + two or more employees.
  Maximum = employer + one or more employees.

Petty bourgeoisie:
  Minimum = sole practitioner + no employees.
  Maximum = N.A.

Manager:
  Minimum = employee + decision-maker + task and sanctioning authority + two or more levels of authority.
  Maximum = employee + decision-maker.

Advisory managers:
  Minimum = employee + advisor on decision-making + task and sanctioning authority + two or more levels of authority.
  Maximum = employee + advisor on decision-making.

Supervisors:
  Minimum = employee + nondecision-maker + task and sanctioning authority + two or more levels of authority.
  Maximum = employee + nondecision-maker + two or more levels of authority.

Semiautonomous employees:
  Minimum = employee + high autonomy + minimum criteria for managers.
  Maximum = employee + limited autonomy + minimum criteria for managers.

Workers:
  Minimum = employee + no autonomy + minimum criteria for managers and semiautonomous employees.
  Maximum = employee + some autonomy + minimum criteria for managers and semiautonomous employees.

TABLE 4. Operational Typology of the Class Structure of the Legal Profession[a]

Class name	Legal description	Link to dominant corporation	Ownership relation	Number of employees	Authority	Decision-making	Autonomy	Hierarchical position
Capitalist class	Managing partner in large elite firm	Through firm	Employer	≥30	1-2	1-3	X	1-2
Managerial bourgeoisie	Managing partner in medium to large firm	X[a]	Employer	≥10	1-2	1-3	X	1-2
Supervisory bourgeoisie	Nonmanaging partner in medium to large firm	X	Employer	≥10	3-4[b]	4	X	X
Small employer	Partner in small firm	X	Employer	2-9	X	X	X	X
Petty bourgeoisie	Solo practitioner	X	Employer	0-1	X	X	X	X
Manager	Associate, corporate, or government managing or supervisory lawyer	X	Employee	X	1-2	1-3	X	1-2
Advisory manager	Same as for manager	X	Employee	X	1-2	4	X	1-2
Supervisor	Same as for manager	X	Employee	X	3[c]	5	X	1-3
Semiautonomous employee	Semiautomomous associate, corporate, or government lawyer	X	Employee	X	4[d]	X	1-2	4
Working class	Nonautonomous associate, corporate, or government lawyer	X	Employee	X	4	X	3-4	4

[a]X-criterion not applicable.
[b]Respondents without task and sanctioning authority or without decision-making responsibility are classified as nonmanaging partners.
[c]Respondents with task or sanctioning authority but without any decision-making involvement are classified as supervisors.
[d]"Nonmanagerial decision-makers"—people who make decisions but have no subordinates and are classified as "nonmanagement" in terms of levels of supervision were merged with semiautonomous employees (if they are autonomous) or workers (if they are nonautonomous) throughout.

TABLE 5. Distributions of Criteria Used in Typology ($N = 995$)

	Percent
A. Ownership relation	
Partner	41.7
Solo practitioner	11.8
Employee	46.5
B. Number of employees (for 553 employers only)	
0–1	16.9
2–9	29.2
10–29	15.2
30 +	38.7
C. Decision-making	
1. Directly participates in all or most policy decisions	44.6
2. Directly participates in some policy decisions	15.0
3. Directly participates in at least one area of decision-making	11.0
4. Does not directly participate, but provides advice	17.3
5. Does not directly or indirectly participate in decision-making	12.1
D. Authority	
1. Sanctioning supervisor	33.7
2. Task supervisor	2.7
3. Nominal supervisor	.2
4. Nonsupervisor	62.9
E. Hierarchical position	
1. No level above respondent/two or more levels below	24.9
2. Two or more levels below respondent	10.0
3. One level below respondent	59.3
4. No level below respondent	5.8
F. Autonomy	
1. Designs all or most important aspects of work	58.7
2. Designs some important aspects of work	29.0
3. Designs a few important aspects of work	7.7
4. Not required to design aspects of work	4.7
G. Type of firm	
Elite	15.7
Nonelite	84.3

and domination, including measures of ownership relations, numbers of employees, authority in the workplace, involvement in decision making, work autonomy, and hierarchical position within the organization of work relations. These measures can be applied in the study of lawyers without threatening confidentiality and secrecy. Individually, the items do not seem to pry into the power structure of a firm, but individually and collectively they can reveal much about power relations in everyday legal work. Furthermore, these measures allow a relatively straightforward accumulation of knowledge about power relations across intra- as well as interoccupational settings, in various times and places. However, the gains of applying such measures and models must be weighed against possible problems and misunderstandings.

These problems involve the transferability of class concepts between occupational and professional settings and implications of permanence that some of these concepts carry. For example, the designation of a working class of lawyers raises the question of whether "workers" in the legal profession share the same positions as "workers" in other occupational hierarchies. There are obvious differences as well as some possible similarities. One salient difference involves the income and mobility prospects that characterize work in professional settings. Wright (1985, p. 185) himself observes that "proletarianised white-collar jobs that are really premanagerial jobs should...not be considered in the same location within class relations as proletarianised jobs which are not part of such career trajectories." Yet note that Wright also points to a condition of "proletarianization" that presumably characterizes white- as well as blue-collar work experiences. The challenge is to identify what is similar and different about these respective experiences. Obviously, a first step in doing so is to establish where "proletarianized" experiences occur in professional settings.

Meanwhile, to suggest that there are lawyers who are in any sense workers is to raise the issue of the "proletarianization of the professions." Although "the proletarianization thesis" is widely discussed (Arnowitz, 1973; Larson, 1977; Oppenheimer, 1970), it is largely untested (but see Wright & Singelmann, 1982). As Derber (1982, p. 29) notes, "Bell [1973] and others have argued that it is scarcely meaningful to speak of proletarianization among salaried professional employees unless it can be shown that their labor is effectively subordinate and subject to management authority—an argument with which most Marxist theorists of professional proletarianization would agree." This brings us, then, to the search for similarities. In our survey of the Toronto legal profession (see Hagan, Huxter, & Parker, 1988), we have identified a working class of lawyers as including those respondents who are neither partners nor solo practitioners, who have neither managerial nor supervisory responsibilities beyond the work they pass on to secretaries, and who design few or no important aspects of their work. These lawyers are so "subordinate and subject to management authority" that they have almost no autonomy in their work. Our best estimate is that 8.7% of Toronto lawyers fall into this "proletarianized professional working class." Some of the largest concentrations of these lawyers are in the early years of corporate practice in large elite firms.

Some idea of what work at subordinate levels of large firms is like is provided in the following description by a senior partner of work in the securities area:

> I guess the lower you are the more your priorities are determined by other people, and I guess, and I don't know why it works out this way, because you're called on to be involved in the following three deals and one of them doesn't go,

nothing happens for a while, so you get called on for another one and then the fourth one that you had picks up again and you're buried in that, you go to meetings all day but somebody's got to do the paper at night—it's you. It's probably that, certainly in my practice anyway, there's a meeting function, there's an answering the telephone function and there's a paperwork function. And sort of dealing with the clients tends to go more to the senior people, in terms of structuring or more sophisticated things; the dealing with them at a level of collecting information and things falls to more junior people; the meeting function gets split up in the way I described, but the actual generation of paper tends to go to junior people, and even with word processors and routine and everything, it's a major time consuming task and so if you come around here at night that is mostly what the junior people do. So, at the end of meetings apart from other things I do, I could in theory go home, they come back and do the work and my involvement would be a review of that. It might take me 1/2 hour to review something it takes them 10 hours to produce. And I guess that's the difference.

But how far beyond the circumstances of subordination described do similarities between the positions of professional and other kinds of workers extend? A key part of this issue involves comparative rates and probabilities of movements out of working-class positions over time; in this instance, this requires knowledge of the career trajectories of persons located in legal working-class positions. There are at least two problems in obtaining this knowledge. One problem is that a logical precondition for the exploration of such class trajectories is the development of the kind of positional analysis just described. Class trajectories cannot be analyzed unless there is agreement about the class positions between which these trajectories are established, in the legal profession and elsewhere, so that comparative judgments can be reached. Agreement about a class model such as we have derived from Wright would allow us to do this. Meanwhile, the importance of doing this is reflected in the large number of women found in the bottom ranks of lawyers: in Toronto, 17% of women lawyers, compared to about 6% of men, occupy positions in the working class of the profession. This disparity is reduced but not eliminated by controls for years of experience and other variables. So part of the structural transformation of legal practice that we have described in this chapter involves large numbers of women joining a working class of lawyers that partly populates the internal (large firm) sector of the profession. Are these women gaining in power through advances in the legal profession? Or, are they becoming a part of a new and enlarged source of legal secretarial labor that has a working class (albeit well paid, at least when hours at work are not considered) form?

Attempts to answer this question will encounter a second problem involving the changing social organization of the legal profession and its unestablished capacity to accommodate large numbers of new lawyers within its hierarchical structure (Nelson, 1983; cf. also Spangler, 1986). Because the legal profession has expanded so dramatically over the past decade and a half, it is not possible to determine fully whether the working class of lawyers we have described is a transitory feature of the current period or an incipient structure that is becoming institutionalized. Cross-sectional analyses can only partially address this issue by considering whether ascribed characteristics such as gender are associated with class positions, and whether these associations are eliminated by controlling for class trajectories in the form of years of practice in the profession. We have already noted that in the case of our Toronto data, the answers to these questions are "yes" and "no," respectively. However, retrospective and prospective longitudinal data and dynamic models such as those applied in event history analysis will be required to more definitively answer questions about the effects of the changing structure of the legal profession on the class trajectories of individuals.

So the legal profession has a complicated but measurable power structure, and the emergence of this power structure may in part be a consequence of a structural transformation of the legal profession that we have described in a very general way in this paper. By implication Marxian and postindustrial theories make predictions about the transformation of this profession. For example, Marxian theory (e.g., Wright & Singelmann, 1982) predicts that the structural transformation of the larger economy will result, presumably in law as elsewhere, in a declining ratio of capital to labor; that is, that the capital of the profession will become increasingly concentrated and centralized among partners in very large firms who themselves form a shrinking proportion of the profession, in contrast to a proportionally increasing pool of largely nonautonomous lawyer employees working for these partnerships in large firms.

The predictions of postindustrial theory are somewhat less certain. Wright and Singelmann (1982) suggest that this theory predicts as well a concentration and centralization of the ownership sector, whereas Steinmetz and Wright (1989) suggest a possible exception to this in the form of growth in the number of small firms, and by implication in the partnerships of small firms. Of greater interest, however, is the unambiguous prediction made by postindustrial theory of growth in the middle levels of the economy, and by implication in the middle ranks of the legal profession as well. The argument is that the information and technology demands that drive the formation of a "new class" in postindustrial theory, perhaps especially lawyers (Glazer, 1979), require employees that have new and more rewarding levels of autonomy. Marxian theory also predicts growth in the private and government managerial sectors but with persons in these positions largely assuming responsibility for the management of a growing nonautonomous class. The result is that where Marxian theory predicts an expanding professional class lacking in autonomy, a kind of burgeoning professional proletariat, postindustrial theory predicts the expansion of a more autonomous class occupying a contradictory position between managers and nonautonomous employees, with the latter class expected to decline.

These predictions become particularly interesting in the context of the legal profession because this occupational group deals rather exclusively in cultural symbols, with the assets of individuals and firms in the profession therefore taking the form of cultural capital rather than physical assets. Although the concentration and centralization of physical capital is much studied, we know little about parallel processes affecting cultural capital. It will, of course, be of further interest to explore how gender crosscuts the predicted expansions and contractions of class categories we have described in the transformation of the legal profession. But again, this exploration can only be undertaken with a typology of the kind we have proposed.

LAWYERS' LIVES AND THE STRUCTURAL TRANSFORMATION OF LEGAL PRACTICE

We began by noting that two striking changes in the legal profession in recent decades involve the increased representation of women in law and the growth of large firms. The importance of the intersection of these trends, of course, extends beyond the legal profession: The increased labor force participation of women and the growth of firms are pervasive trends. We also noted the impact that the profession may be having on the larger society in terms of increased litigation. A focal point in this litigation involves the acquisitions and mergers that are central to the transformation of the larger economy.

We certainly are not the first to note interconnections between law and the larger society, although this point often is neglected outside of the sociology of law. Sorokin warned that we (sociologists) ignore the law at our peril. Marx and Weber, despite their differences, both saw the specialization and expertise that are fundamental to the professions, especially the legal professions, as critical to class relations (see, for example, Marx & Engels, 1970, pp. 64–68). C. Wright Mills (1966) went on to explicitly articulate the role of the legal profession in forming class relations. In doing so, Mills portrayed lawyers as both proactive and reactive participants in the economy, observing (122) that "the skills of a profession shift, externally, as the function of the profession changes with the nature of its clients' interests, and internally, as the rewards of the profession are given to new kinds of success." Externally, this means that lawyers are recognized for the proactive roles they often play in shaping "the legal framework of the new economy" (see Fligstein, 1989). Internally, this means that lawyers increasingly are found in highly stratified work environments that reactively mirror the economic arrangements they help to form for client corporations, because "in fulfilling his function the successful lawyer has created his office in the image of the corporations he has come to serve and defend"

(Mills, 1966, p. 122). Note that the choice of male pronouns in Mills state-
ment is an assumed reflection of male dominance among lawyers.

The legal profession offers an important setting to study the intersection of the increasing labor force participation of women and the expanding
internal economic sector precisely because lawyers play such a unique
"interstitial" role between contending forces and actors in the surrounding
economy and society. Parsons (1954) observed this unique role of lawyers
at the microlevel, and as we have noted, Mills and others have observed
this role at the macrolevel. There may be no more interesting and significant setting than law in which to assess the advancement of women. The
challenge is to conceptualize and operationalize this task.

The conceptualization and operationalization of class positions considered in this chapter provides a framework within which these kinds of
issues can be studied. This will be done most effectively with retrospec-
tively and prospectively collected data on lawyers' careers, including, for
example, information on career changes in individual and sectoral position, income, and job satisfaction. Such data will allow consideration of
transitional movements within and between sectors and of the trajectories
these transitions establish. For example, such data would allow us to determine if there are causal processes that move temporally from gender differences in income and promotion within and between sectors to, for
example, gender differences in job satisfaction and absences and exits from
the profession. These individual transitions form the collective base for the
transformation of the profession, and they provide an opportunity to see
consequences of this transformation as it unfolds over time. There may be
no profession more likely than law to signal the advances and/or reverses
that women are experiencing in Western societies.

ACKNOWLEDGMENTS

Research reported in this chapter was supported by a grant from the
Social Sciences and Humanities Research Council of Canada and a fellow-
ship from the Canadian Institute for Advanced Research and Statistics
Canada.

REFERENCES

Abel, R. (1979). The rise of professionalism. *British Journal of Law and Society, 6,* 82–98.
Abel, R. (1986). The transformation of the American legal profession. *Law and Society Review,*
    20, 7–17.
Adam, B., & Baer, D. (1984). The social mobility of women and men in the Ontario legal
    profession. *Canadian Review of Sociology and Anthropology,* 21(i), 21–46.
Arnowitz, S. (1973). *False promises: The shaping of American working class consciousness.* New
    York: McGraw-Hill.
Arthurs, H. W., Willms, J., & Taman, L. (1971). The Toronto legal profession: An exploratory
    study. *University of Toronto Law Journal, 21,* 498–528.

Auerback, J. (1976). *Unequal justice: Lawyers and social change in modern America*. New York: Oxford University Press.

Baron, J., & Bielby, W. (1984). The organization of work in a segmented society. *American Sociological Review, 49*, 454–473.

Bell, D. (1973). *The coming of post-industrial society*. New York: Basic Books.

Blau, F. (1977). *Equal pay in the office*. Lexington, MA: Lexington.

Bluestone, B. (1970). The tripartite economy: Labor markets and the working poor. *Poverty and Human Resources, 5*, 15–25.

Boyd, M. (1982). Sex differences in the Canadian occupational attainment process. *Canadian Review of Sociology and Anthropology, 19*, 1–28.

Bridges, W. (1980). Industrial marginality and female employment: A new appraisal. *American Sociological Review, 45*, 58–75.

Carlin, J. E. (1962). *Lawyers on their own: A study of individual practitioners in Chicago*. New Brunswick: Rutgers University Press.

Chambers, D. (1987). *Tough enough: The work and family experience of recent women graduates of the University of Michigan Law School*. Paper presented to Conference on Women in the Legal Profession. Madison, Wisconsin.

Cherlin, A. (1983). Changing family and household: Contemporary lessons from historical research. *Annual Review of Sociology, 9*, 51–66.

Chester, R. (1985). *Unequal access: Women lawyers in a changing America*. South Hadley, MA: Bergin & Garvey.

Clark, S. D. (1942). *The social development of Canada*. Toronto: University of Toronto Press.

Clark, S. D. (1976). *Canadian society in historical perspective*. Toronto: McGraw-Hill Ryerson, Ltd.

Curran, B., Rosich, K., Carson, C., & Puccetti, M. (1985). *The Lawyer Statistical Report: A statistical profile of the U.S. legal profession in the 1980s*. Chicago: American Bar Foundation.

Davis, A. K. (1971). Canadian society as hinterland versus metropolis. In R. J. Ossenberg (Ed.), *Canadian society: Pluralism, change and conflict* (pp. 6–32). Scarborough, Ontario: Prentice-Hall.

Derber, C. (1982). *Professionals as workers: Mental labor in advanced capitalism*. Boston: G. K. Hall and Company.

Doeringer, P., & Piore, M. (1971). *International labor markets and manpower analysis*. Lexington, MA: Lexington.

Ehrenrich, B., & Ehrenrich, J. (1978). The professional-managerial class. In P. Walker (Ed.), *Between labor and capital* (pp. 5–45). Montreal: Black Press.

Erlander, H. (1980). The allocation of status within occupations: The case of the legal profession. *Social Forces, 58*, 882–903.

Featherman, D., & Hauser, R. (1976). Sexual inequalities and socioeconomic achievement in the U.S., 1962–1973. *American Sociological Review, 41*, 462–483.

Felmlee, D. (1982). Women's job mobility processes within and between employers. *American Sociological Review, 47*, 142–151.

Fenning, L. (1987). *Report from the front: Progress in the battle against gender bias in the legal progress*. Paper presented to the Conference on Women in the Legal Profession, August, 1987, Madison, Wisconsin.

Finlay, W. (1983). One occupation, two labor markets: The case of longshore crane operators. *American Sociological Review, 48*, 306–316.

Fligstein, N. (1990). *State and markets: The transformation of the large corporation, 1880–1985*. Cambridge, MA: Harvard University Press.

Galanter, M. (1983a). Reading the landscape of disputes: What we know and don't know (and think we know) about our allegedly contentious and litigious society. *UCLA Law Review*, 31–108.

Galanter, M. (1983b). Mega-law and mega-lawyering in the contemporary U.S. In R. Dingwell & P. Lewis (Eds.), *The Sociology of the professions* (pp. 152–176). London: Macmillian.

68   JOHN HAGAN

Glancy, D. (1970). Women in law: The dependable ones. *Harvard Law Bulletin, 5.*
Glazer, N. (1979). Lawyers and the new class. In B. B. Briggs (Ed.), *The new class?* (pp. 89–100), New Brunswick, NJ: Transaction Books.
Gordon, D. M. (1972). *Theories of poverty and under-employment.* Lexington, MA: Heath.
Goulden, J. (1971). *The superlawyers.* New York: McKay.
Grabb, E. (1984). *Social inequality: Classical and contemporary theorists.* Toronto: Holt, Rinehart & Winston.
Gross, E. (1986). The sexual structure of occupations over time. *Social Problems, 16,* 198–208.
Hagan, J. (1984). *The disreputable pleasures: Crime and deviance in Canada.* Toronto: McGraw-Hill Ryerson.
Hagan, J. (1989). The gender stratification of income inequality among lawyers. *Social Forces, 68*(3).
Hagan, J., & Leon, J. (1978). The philosophy and sociology of crime control: Canadian-American comparisons. *Sociological Inquiry, 47,* 181–208.
Hagan, J., Huxter, M., & Parker, P. (1988). Class structure and legal practice: Inequality and mobility among Toronto lawyers. *Law and Society Review, 22,* 9–56.
Halaby, C. (1979). Sample selection bias as a specification error. *Econometrica, 45,* 153–61.
Halliday, T. (1983). Professions, class and capitalism. *European Journal of Sociology, 24,* 321–346.
Halliday, T. (1986). Six score years and ten: Demographic transitions in the American legal profession, 1850–1980. *Law and Society Review, 20,* 53–78.
Heinz, J., & Laumann, E. (1982). *Chicago lawyers: The social structure of the bar.* Chicago: Russell Sage Foundation and American Bar Foundation.
Hiller, H. (1976). *Canadian society: A sociological analysis.* Scarborough, Ontario: Prentice-Hall.
Hodson, R., & Kaufman, R. (1982). Economic dualism: A critical review. *American Sociological Review, 47,* 727–739.
Horowitz, I. L. (1973). The hemispheric connection: A critique and corrective to the entrepreneurial thesis of development with special emphasis on the Canadian Case. *Queen's Quarterly, 80,* 327–359.
Kalleberg, A., & Hudis, P. (1979). Wage change in the late career: A model for the outcomes of job sequence. *Social Science Research, 8,* 16–40.
Kanter, R. (1977). *Men and women of the corporation.* New York: Basic Books.
Kaufman, R., & Daymont, T. (1981). Racial discrimination and the social organization of industries. *Social Science Research, 10,* 225–255.
Ladinsky, J. (1963). Careers of lawyers, law practice and legal institution. *American Sociological Review, 28*(1), 47–54.
Larson, M. S. (1977). *The rise of professionalism: A sociological analysis.* Berkeley: University of California Press.
Lipset, S. M. (1968). *Revolution and counterrevolution: Change and persistence in social structures.* New York: Basic Books.
Lipset, S. M. (1986). Historical traditions and national characteristics: A comparative analysis of Canada and the U.S. *Canadian Journal of Sociology, 11,* 113–155.
Marx, K., & Engels, F. (1970). *The German ideology.* New York: International Publishers.
Menkel-Meadow, C. (1989). The comparative sociology of women lawyers: The "feminization" of the legal profession. In R. Abel & P. Lewis (Eds.), *Lawyers in society* (pp. 196–255). Berkeley: University of California Press.
Mills, C. W. (1966). *White collar: The American middle class.* New York: Oxford University Press.
Morello, K. B. (1986). *The invisible bar: The woman lawyer in America, 1683 to the present.* New York: Random House.
Nelson, R. L. (1983). The changing structure of opportunity: Recruitment and careers in large law firms. *American Bar Foundation Research Journal,* 109–42.
O'Conner, J. (1973). *The fiscal crisis of the state.* New York: St. Martin's Press.
Oppenheimer, M. (1970). White collar revisited: The making of a new working class. *Social Policy, 1,* 27–32.

Parsons, T. (1954). The professions and social structure. In *Essays in sociological theory* (pp. 34–49). Toronto: University of Toronto Press.

Pashigian, P. (1978). The number and earnings of lawyers: Some recent findings. *American Bar Foundation Research Journal*, 51–82.

Sikes, B., Carson, C., & Gorai, P. (1972). *The 1971 lawyer statistical report*. Chicago: American Bar Foundation.

Smigel, E. O. (1964). *The Wall Street lawyer: Professional organization man?* Bloomington: Indiana University Press.

Smith, D. R. (1983). Mobility in professional occupational—internal labor markets: Stratification, segmentation and vacancy chains. *American Sociological Review, 48*, 289–305.

Sorenson, A., & Kalleberg, A. (1981). An outline of a theory of the matching of persons to jobs. In I. Berg (Ed.), *Sociological perspectives in labor markets* (pp. 49–74). New York: Academic Press.

Spangler, E. (1986). *Lawyers for hire: Salaried professionals at work*. New Haven: Yale University Press.

Stager, D. (1982). The market for lawyers in Ontario: 1931 to 1981 and beyond. *Canadian–U.S. Law Journal, 6*, 113–124.

Steinmetz, G., & Wright, E. O. (1989). The fall and rise of the petty bourgeoisie: Changing patterns of self-employment in the post war U.S. *American Journal of Sociology, 94*, 973–1018.

Stewart, J. B. (1983). *The Partners: Inside America's most powerful law firms*. New York: Simon & Schuster.

Treiman, D., & Terrell, K. (1975). Sex and the process of status attainment: A comparison of working women and men. *American Sociological Review, 40*, 174–200.

Vogt, L. (1987). *From law school to career: A highlight report of the career paths study of seven northeastern area law schools*. Mimeo.

White, J. J. (1967). Women in law. *Michigan Law Review, 65*, 1051–1116.

Wright, E. O. (1982). *Classes*. London: Versa.

Wright, E. O., & Singelmann, J. (1982). Proletarianization in the changing American class structure. *American Journal of Sociology, 88* (Supplement), 1765–2095.

CHAPTER FOUR

The Changing Composition of Schools

Implications for School Organization

CORA BAGLEY MARRETT

CHANGES IN THE MAKEUP OF SCHOOLS

Classrooms across the United States looked quite different in the 1980s from what had prevailed earlier, for they contained more black, Hispanic, Native American, and Asian-American students than ever before. We can anticipate still further change, for children of minority group background already comprise a significant fraction of the school-age population, and the growth rates for minority groups exceed those for the general population. In 1960 nonwhite students represented around 13% of the population aged 5 to 17 years. That number had risen to above 20% by the mid-1980s (see Table 1). These numbers understate the changes, for they exclude Hispanics—the fastest growing minority population. Birth rates among Puerto Ricans and Mexican-Americans surpasses those of the wider population. Consequently, more Puerto Ricans and Mexican-Americans are under 14 years of age than is the case for the total population of the nation.[1]

The changes have not taken place evenly across the nation. In California, black, Hispanic, and Asian students constitute most of the school enrollees; these students comprise 46% of the pupils found in Texas

---

[1] The Hispanic population consists of persons of Cuban origin, in addition to those of Mexican and Puerto Rican heritage. But children represent a smaller fraction of the Cuban population than of the population for these other groups. See Bean and Tienda (1987) for comparative data on the Hispanic categories.

CORA BAGLEY MARRETT • Department of Sociology, University of Wisconsin–Madison, Madison, Wisconsin 53706.

TABLE 1. Estimates of School-Age[a] Resident Population,
by Race (in Thousands)

Year	Total	White[b]	Black	Other
1960	44,176	86.8	12.1	1.0
1970	52,593	85.1	13.5	1.3
1980	47,236	82.6	14.8	2.6
1986	45,143	80.9	15.4	4.0

[a]School-age population identified as persons 5 to 17 years of age.
[b]Includes persons of Hispanic origin.
Source: *Current Population Reports*, Series P-25, Nos. 519, 917, and 1000.

schools. Minority youngsters are found especially in urban school districts; they dominate the classrooms located within the 25 largest city school systems. The higher birth rates for certain groups, coupled with continued immigration from Asia, Mexico, Central and South America, and the Caribbean, indicate that other states will undergo the changes Texas and California already have encountered. Immigration will continue to bring into school districts persons whose native tongue is not English. But not all of this population will experience difficulty with the English language. Of greatest concern to educators are students whose proficiency in English is limited. Spanish-speaking students and Vietnamese students are more likely to be designated as of limited English proficiency than are students from several other language groups.

More and more students of minority group background are of low-income status as well. Large numbers of black youth live in households headed by a single parent; generally the income in these households falls below that in two-parent households. Exceptions to the generalization exist: The rates of poverty in Hispanic households rose in the 1980s, primarily because of the inadequate wages earned in two-parent and not one-parent households. These low-income minority youth attended schools with declining numbers of nonminority students. The number of black students enrolled in predominantly minority schools dropped between 1968 and 1976 but rose thereafter. By 1984 nearly 64% of black students were in schools that had primarily minority students bodies. In that same year, Hispanic representation in predominantly minority schools stood at 71%.

The presence of large numbers of minority group students—especially Hispanic, black, and Native American students—poses challenges for schools, for these are students who commonly have not performed well on standard measures of achievement. The National Assessment of Educational Progress reports data for blacks, whites, and Hispanics that consistently show gaps in reading, mathematics, science, and other subjects favoring whites over the other groups (see Table 2). The scores compiled for the Scholastic Aptitude Test (SAT) reflect a similar pattern: Whites score

TABLE 2. Percentage of 17-Year-Olds at Selected Proficiency Levels
in Reading and Writing, by Race/Ethnicity

Test area and level	Group		
	White	Black	Hispanic
Reading: Basic level[a]			
1980	99.3	88.8	96.5
1984	99.2	96.5	96.8
Writing: Minimal level[b]			
1979	89.4	72.8	78.1
1984	91.3	79.5	86.1

[a]The assessment defined as *basic* the ability to understand combined ideas and make references based on short, uncomplicated passages about specific or sequentially related information.
[b]The assessment covered three writing areas: informative writing, persuasive writing, and imaginative writing. The results given here are informative writing. For each area, five levels of proficiency were measured. The level here—"minimal"—covered responses that recognized the elements needed to complete the task but were not managed well enough to ensure that the intended purpose of the writing was achieved.
Source: *Digest of Education Statistics*, 1988. Washington, DC: National Center for Education Statistics. Based on National Assessment of Educational Progress data.

higher on both the verbal and mathematical portions of the test than do blacks and Hispanics. Congruent with the results on other measures, Asian-Americans obtain the highest scores, scores that eclipse those of white students.[2]

Black, Hispanic, and Native American students tend more often to drop out of school than do white or Asian-American students. For the nation as a whole, approximately 40% of Hispanic students leave school without a high-school diploma. For some urban areas, the dropout rate for blacks and Hispanics approaches 50%. Those minority students who complete high school are not as likely as nonminority students to continue on to college.

When the National Commission on Excellence in Education (1983) called the United States a nation at risk, it recognized the growing population of minority youth as the component at greatest risk. One effort to reform education, the effective schools movement, implies that these students need not be doomed to the unhappy fate of underachievement and its consequences. The reversal of that trend, according to this movement, requires changes in the management of schools. The progress of minority

[2]It is easy to overlook the problems of Asian-Americans because of the patterns found on tests of quantitative skills. The category is in fact a diverse one, made up of both native born and immigrant students from Hong Kong, Taiwan, Vietnam, Korea, and several other nations. Scores are variable within the category. When the scores are favorable, they seem to result both from the effort the students put forth and the assumptions of teachers and counselors that Asian students can and will do well on tests of quantitative skills (Tsang, 1983). Significantly, the results on these tests are not always matched by those on verbal skills.

students—at least those enrolled in schools with heavy minority represen-tation—depends on the extent to which the central figures of authority exert influence.

This chapter explores the argument for greater involvement by school administrators in the activities of urban or innercity schools. Although one line of work suggests that greater control at the top of the school can improve the performance of these students, an alternative position pre-sents the advantages of looser control. The chapter examines these two lines of work, reviewing the bases for the argument that central manage-ment matters and then analyzing the support for the concept of loose coupling. I reach the following conclusions. First, many of the schools of interest here stand outside of the category for which the term *loosely coupled* was developed. The call for tighter control in these schools may be an attempt to have them resemble more closely the professional, craft-based model than they now do. Second, central involvement—by which I mean involvement at the school-building level by the principal—does not invaria-bly mean supervision. Ends can be achieved as well through the use of persuasion and the building of consensus. We can usefully draw three distinctions of the school as a system: It is a system of roles, a cultural system, and a system of interpersonal relationships. I propose that the loose coupling of relationships poses even greater problems for inner-city schools than does the looseness of connections among roles. The call for greater sharing by principals that appears in the effective schools literature need not imperil the autonomy of the classroom teacher in pedagogical issues. It can be interpreted as an effort to tighten the interpersonal con-nections that prevail.

I am particularly concerned with the issue of relationships, primarily because of the evidence, drawn from diverse arenas, that social networks affect individual functioning and social institutions. If networks matter for educational performance and networks are sparse or flimsy in inner-city schools, then the tightening of roles may do little to produce high achieve-ment. The linkages among persons could be more pivotal.

EFFECTIVE SCHOOLS RESEARCH

More black, Hispanic, and Native American students enroll in public and private schools than ever before. The rise in enrollment rates has not been accompanied by dramatic improvements in the performance rates of these students. For a period, analysts noted that these students came disproportionately from low-income households and argued that schools rarely overcome the deficits students bring with them from their homes and neighborhoods. But not everyone was convinced. The Coleman study (Coleman *et al.*, 1966), used so often to buttress the argument that homes have greater effects than schools, had in fact found schools to make more of a difference for minority than nonminority students. Some observers, aware of schools in which low-income students performed better than usually occurred, began a systematic search for such schools and for their distinctive characteristics.

A study of reading in four urban schools (Weber, 1971) helped launch the search, for it described these schools as successful in raising the test scores of their pupils. Studies followed of successful schools in New York (New York State Department of Education, 1974a, b), Detroit (Brookover & Lezotte, 1979; Lezotte, Edmonds, & Ratner, 1974) as well as other locations. Certain features appeared time and again: strong leadership, clear goals, an orderly school climate, high expectations, and frequent monitoring and assessment of student progress. Analysts found the educational components in these schools to be tightly coordinated, with the curriculum, instruction, and tests carefully aligned and the work directed toward specific goals. A literature now exists that accepts the traits as the ones common to effective schools.

The research on effective schools is not without its limitations, as a set of reviews documents. The reviews caution readers against an uncritical acceptance of the tenets from the effective schools movement. The conclusions often derive from small and unrepresentative samples of schools; emerge from comparisons drawn between "successful" schools and unsuccessful ones rather than between the former and average schools; and build from test scores that in middle-class schools would denote poor performance (Purkey & Smith, 1983; Rowan, Bossert, & Dwyer, 1983). The initial analyses of effective schools measured performance on basic skills, usually in elementary and not secondary schools. From these analyses came the argument that the principal should serve primarily as an instructional leader, but direct involvement with instruction takes place more often in elementary than in secondary schools (Farrar, Neufeld, & Miles, 1984). It appears from subsequent work at the secondary level that the conclusions about the context for the development of basic skills apply across the grades (Lightfoot, 1983; Lipsitz, 1984; and Corcoran & Wilson, 1986, for a review of the research). The general findings are consistent and commonsensical enough to convince most observers that schools serving minority and low-income students are not identical. One way in which they differ: Principals are more active in molding events in some settings than in others.

The case for greater commitment at the top has not come solely from those whose interests center on schools. Students of business practices have increasingly maintained that performance depends on leadership from the top. Spurred by the argument that Japanese businesses succeeded remarkably in the post-World War II era because they attended to organization and management, these students looked for businesses in the United States whose orientations compared favorably with those in Japan. The search yielded a set of conditions, thought to distinguish top-performing businesses from others (see especially Kanter, 1983; Ouchi, 1981; Peters & Waterman, 1982). The conditions usually had to do with leadership: Organizations with active direction and participation by management emerged time and again as distinctive. Thus the view that top management matters is not limited to observations of inner-city schools.

THE ORGANIZATION OF AMERICAN SCHOOLS

Schools have been characterized as loosely coupled systems, in which control—especially over pedagogy—rests at the level of the classroom teacher. Imposing greater structure on such systems might be self-defeating. We face, then, a dilemma. If tighter control enhances performance of minority students but schools are inappropriate settings for such control, then minority students face a future that is bleak. Given the implications for minority education of the loose coupling perspective, that perspective deserves close scrutiny.

ON LOOSELY COUPLED SYSTEMS

Discussions of formal organizations long have acknowledged that these institutions vary in the ways they are structured. Some conform far more closely to the Weberian model of bureaucracy than do others. Yet the bureaucratic model, of hierarchical authority, strict rules, and equitable rewards, often has been the standard against which operating organizations have been judged. Convinced that such a focus blinded analysts to features of and processes within many organizations, Karl Weick in 1976 called for research on "loosely coupled systems."

In loosely coupled systems, events are related, but the events remain identifiable, although they are linked physically or logically. The components of such a system carry out tasks or subtasks that are relatively independent. Tightly coupled systems are woven together in either of two ways: through interdependent tasks or through a formal authority structure. The former approximates what Durkheim termed *organic solidarity* and the latter, *mechanical solidarity*.[3] Schools, Weick concluded, are loosely coupled on both measures. Teachers and counselors carry out their activities rather autonomously, and those in formal positions do not use their positions to direct participants.

[3]Burns and Stalker (1961) used this distinction to draw a contrast between formal organizations. A mechanistic organization essentially operates hierarchically. The organic forms rely on commitment and lateral rather than vertical communication. Others have used such categories as bureaucratic and craft administration to offer a similar contrast.

Weick hoped that others would adopt and refine the notion of schools as loosely coupled systems. The idea has in fact spread widely (see Herriott & Firestone, 1984; Meyer & Rowan, 1978; Wilson & Corbett, 1983). The work points out the features that hinder the tight coupling of tasks and the use of hierarchical authority in schools. First, schools are technological systems, in that they seek to bring about transformations. Yet, the diversity among the students to be transformed and the lack of agreement about how they should be transformed — and toward what ends — work against centralization of activities and authority. Second, schools are staffed by professionals who derive their knowledge and sense of identity from sources external to the given setting. Third, because the number of teachers exceeds the number of administrators and administrators have other tasks to carry out, close supervision of day-to-day events in classrooms proves almost impossible.

One should not regard loose coupling as the result of the difficulty administrators have in imposing structure, Weick suggested. Instead, it is a model that has distinctive advantages over tight coupling. Loosely coupled systems promote a sense of efficacy because they provide greater opportunity for self-determination than do bureaucratic systems. In addition, loosely coupled systems are cheaper to administer because they require less oversight and entail fewer conflicts and discrepancies across activities.

RETHINKING THE MODEL

The model of schools as loosely coupled systems has been widely adopted. Analysts agree that schools are dissimilar, that some are more tightly coupled than are others. What has garnered less attention is the possibility that some schools lie outside of the loosely coupled model that Weick developed. This point is significant, for it suggests that Weick did not intend the term to apply to any nonhierarchical setting. Let me elaborate, for it is my thesis that many inner-city schools, as they are currently structured, do not fit the model of "loosely coupled" that Weick outlined.

The systems Weick described are linked, not through a formal hierarchy or clearly meshed tasks but through ends that are shared extensively. Participants in such systems recognize that the ends can be reached through more than one means and hence do not seek to impose uniformity. Sources often describe loosely coupled systems as *anarchic* systems. But if one restricts the concept of anarchy to situations where confusion and disorder reign, loosely coupled systems are not anarchic. They are not centrally coordinated, but neither are they without any glue to hold them together.

Where the participants have no clear sense of the ends their organization should seek—or think of those ends in only the vaguest sense—the setting could be better described as uncoupled than as loosely coupled. Advocates for effective schools undoubtedly zeroed in on shared goals because they knew that accord on ends rarely marked inner-city schools. I do not mean that dissensus rules. Rather, I mean that the participants do not always develop collective ideas about ends and strategies appropriate for the kinds of students they serve. Obviously, shared goals do not cause high performance, but neither is the presence of goals matched to local circumstances likely to impede such performance.

Many inner-city schools depart from the ideal of the loosely coupled system in another respect: Their staffs are not as highly professional as befits the ideal. Where participants possess the knowledge and skills for producing the intended outcomes, central control over roles produces both resentment and inefficiency. The high turnover rates in inner-city schools leave these settings with inexperienced teachers who cannot readily call on past encounters to determine what engages students and what frustrates them. The shortage of teachers with credentials in particular subject areas—a shortage that afflicts inner-city schools more seriously than others—acts as well as a damper for the professional model that underlies the idea of the school as a loosely coupled system. Currently, half of the newly employed mathematics, science, and English teachers do not have the credentials to teach the subjects to which they are assigned. The heavy use of substitute teachers, teachers working outside of their fields, and teachers with emergency teaching certificates makes the inner-city school less of the professional setting than is the usual portrait of schools.

Studies on the attributes of teachers find no strong connections between the background of teachers and their performance (Eisenberg, 1977; Lawrenz, 1975). It is easy to exaggerate the finding and conclude—erroneously—that background and preparation do not matter. Often teacher qualifications have been measured on the basis of the courses taken and not on the understanding of the content of those courses. In addition, it would be foolhardy to think that even the best qualified teacher could overcome the disorganization and apathy found in many schools. Finally, the studies as a rule are based on those teachers who meet the standards established for the areas in which they work. The studies tell us little about those teachers who instruct outside of the subjects or grade levels for which they were prepared. To suggest that those who are exposed to certain topics perform no better than individuals without such exposure is to offer a grave indictment of education.

The rates of absenteeism among teachers in inner-city schools exceed those of teachers elsewhere. Qualifications count for little if those who possess them are not in their classrooms. High rates of absenteeism and turnover reduce the continuity of instruction in inner-city schools. To designate some of these schools as *loosely coupled* is to portray them as more connected than they are.

Schools that serve minority youth sometimes have roles that are so unconnected that to call for tighter management is to suggest that they are not to the point at which loose coupling can have advantages. In sum, we gain little by treating all schools in an undifferentiated way, as if—by virtue of their designation as schools—they require invariable patterns of involvement centrally.

Beyond the Coupling of Roles

Schools are not only system of roles, however. They are cultural systems as well, settings in which norms, values, and symbols operate. Shared cultural ideals can weld an organization together and affect its overall productivity, but there are signs that cultural norms do not operate this way in inner-city schools. First, in some instances, one has difficulty identifying any norms that pervade the entire organization. Students, teachers, and administrators may have codes, but the codes do not necessarily overlap. Second, where widely held norms exist, they sometimes do little to encourage academic performance. Not uncommonly, students and teachers agree that each group should impose as little strain on the other as possible. The literature on effective schools reports that a noticeable attribute of these schools is the presence of high expectations for achievement as well as practices and behaviors that demonstrate a commitment to excellence. The literature, in other words, reports a strong link between achievement—on basic skills—and the existence of common expectations for high achievement. The cross-sectional design that typifies this research does not allow us to conclude that these expectations produce the achievement. But the possible effects of high expectations should not be dismissed, if in fact they are less common where student performance lags. The recent literature not only accepts the view that the school is a cultural system; it tries as well to specify the way in which school administrators can foster that system. At both the elementary- and secondary-school levels, the principal can shape the culture, sometimes by managing the resources. No administrator can guarantee that classroom teachers will use the resources given to them in specific ways. But if there is some harmony on what should be attained, then the probability increases that the resources will in fact be used, corresponding with management concerns and system goals (Gamoran, 1988).

There is nothing novel in the assertion that nurturance from the center in the shaping of the school culture can and does make a difference. What analysts have given less attention to is the importance of interpersonal relationships for educational consequences. I have chosen to develop this perspective, for several reasons. First, in many respects, the social relationships in urban schools appear to be even more fragmented than are the roles and tasks. Second, a wide-ranging body of work tells us that social relationships often are pivotal for both individual and societal outcomes. Third, some of the actions designed to improve discipline in schools work against the building of schools as communities and hence may do little to produce both the academic achievement and maturity that no one would want to deny to minority youth. Cultivation of the school on a day-to-day basis need not imply control over the ways in which teaching will be carried out. It can operate instead to connect people to one another.

ON THE SIGNIFICANCE OF SOCIAL TIES

Recurring in the social and behavioral science literature is this theme: Interaction has significant consequences for individuals as well as for the society writ large. The theme appears in the classic work on group relations from Simmel, the analysis Durkheim carried out on suicide, and the reflections on alienation from Marx. We find that mortality rates vary, depending on the kinds of social support one receives (House, Robbins, & Metzner, 1982; Litwak & Messeri, 1989); that social support affects mental well-being (Gove, 1984); and that where social interaction is prominent, formal systems of surveillance seem less essential. If social contact makes a difference across so many contexts, it undoubtedly counts in the school setting as well. What should matter most is not just the presence of contacts but rather the existence of social networks.

Two different systems of social networks can be identified: those found within the school and those linking the school to its wider social setting. The school network consists of the web of linkages among students, teachers, and staff within the school. I mean by *community network* the relationships obtaining between students, teachers, and others within the school and parents and other actors in the larger context. Webs can differ, of course, in their density and in the character of the linkages they encompass. Networks in which the linkages are formal—they are created and maintained in highly regulated ways—and segmented produce effects contrasting with those that result when linkages are informal and crosscutting. The effectiveness of interpersonal ties depends on the extent to which they form a network of relationships.

There are several mechanisms through which social networks modify individual and social conditions. First, networks of interaction are means through which individuals can develop trust. Interestingly, studies of organizations, and especially of economic organizations, show an ever greater interest in the effect of trust, not just on the interpersonal relations that take place but also on the kinds of structures that arise (see Dore, 1983; Granovetter, 1985; Ouchi, 1980). Second, networks often are means through which information is exchanged. The broader the social network, the greater the variety of information it is likely to incorporate. Third, networks can serve as mechanisms for social control. They are most likely to sway individual and collective actions if they are inclusive.

ON NETWORKS AND LEARNING

IN-SCHOOL NETWORKS

Educational reforms often take a very individualistic route to learning, seeking to foster those aptitudes thought to lie within the person. Yet, learning may depend heavily on the social context and especially on the kinds of relationships in that context. Students influence one another; peer influence carries considerable weight among minority students. Apparently, black children lean more and more on their counterparts as they grow older and move away from the values the school favors (Castenell, 1983; Cummings, 1977). But even among minority students, the emphases of peer group vary; some groups in fact promote high achievement (Epstein, 1983). The direction depends on the connectedness of the group to adults, especially teachers and parents. The stronger the ties to teachers, the greater the likelihood that the group will use academically based criteria. Where such ties are tenuous, norms rejecting those of adults often prevail.

But the linkages among teachers are not always strong enough to support and sustain norms of achievement. Often, the ties among teachers are as fragile as those between teachers and students. Teachers in inner-city schools describe themselves as relatively isolated from others. There are few incentives for frequent and sustained interaction; poor achievement, weak discipline, deteriorating facilities serve neither as sources of pride nor as rallying points for contact. For neither students nor teachers are the contacts far-reaching or dense.

SCHOOL–COMMUNITY NETWORKS

Educational outcomes, especially performance as often measured in schools, depend more heavily on conditions within the school than those outside of it. Yet, the world outside does intrude, more often to promote the achievement of middle-income and nonminority youth than low-income black, Hispanic, and Native American students. For these groups, experiences in schools match imperfectly those in the neighborhood or on the streets. Erickson (1985) makes this point, as he attempts to explain why students who compute flawlessly in a store fail when given the same computational problem in school.

It is not surprising that a child can display arithmetic competence while dealing with change at the grocery store and yet seem to lack that performance when doing what seems to be the "same" arithmetic problem on a worksheet or at the blackboard in the classroom, even if the problem is presented by using pictures of coins with which the child is familiar rather than using numerals with which the child might be less familiar. Still, a picture of a coin is not a coin, and relations with the teacher and fellow students are not the same as relations with a store clerk (when one has money) and one's little brother or friend (before whom one's display of appropriate performance carries no negative social and emotional consequences). (p. 7)

Erickson is not alone in the observation that students often assess the relationships they have in school as different from those outside of that context. In an autobiographical account, the psychiatrist James Comer (1988) reports that because he excelled in school, people expected him to outperform others in a Sunday School class he attended as well. That was not to be. His bible-class peers, who rarely spoke up in school, outshone him. He muses:

In retrospect, I believe they scored well in Sunday School convention class because it was a place where they were accepted and relaxed. They were intimidated in the public school. (p. 113)

Often, then, the lives that inner-city students lead in school are so loosely linked with events on the outside that the experiences do not reinforce one another in any positive way. Stated another way, inner-city schools are not enmeshed in networks that operate toward the same goals and ends.

ON EFFECTIVE SOCIAL NETWORKS

Some networks are more effective than are others for building trust, exchanging information, and monitoring behavior. The networks most likely to shape outcomes are those where extensive and crosscutting linkages bring the participants together. The greater the closure—or the degree to which the web incorporates most of the ties of the participants—the more likely it is that the network will be reinforcing and hence will affect behaviors. A study of four communities offers some insight on the consequences of personal relationships. The study examined the density of acquaintanceship: the extent to which people shared mutual acquaintances. Regularly, rates of crime and deviance varied inversely with density. The teenagers in the closely knit communities complained that they were continually under surveillance, that everyone watched them. Such monitoring seemingly served to keep behavior in line (Freudenburg, 1986).

The interpersonal linkages that predominate in inner-city schools tend to be segmented. This is true in three respects. First, they operate within but not across categories. The contacts students have most frequently are with their peers: Most of the adults they see in school are teachers, not the personnel who provide other services.[4] The linkages students have with one another frequently center on negative rather than positive matters. Students band together to oppose the demands of teachers and the rules of schools. The two groups—teachers and students—are not connected in ways that would identify mutual or shared interests. Second, the contacts are highly specific in nature. Parents who interact with teachers usually do so in connection with the problems of a given student, not with students or educational matters more broadly in mind. Third, the contacts relate only marginally to those that the actors have elsewhere. Teachers, students, parents, and administrators from inner-city schools rarely encounter one another outside of the school context. Those students whom the teacher finds as unmotivated may perform quite differently beyond the eyes of the teacher, as both Erickson and Comer discovered.

The contacts that bring actors together in schools lack symmetry: The participants do not interact as equals. Students respond to teachers, their superiors; parents who come to the school move from their own turf to that of teachers and administrators. Teacher-to-teacher relations theoretically are more balanced than those between teachers and students, but recall their infrequency: Teachers do not find themselves engaged primarily with their peers.

Contacts among persons of similar status nourish trust more readily than do connections across dissimilar statuses (Allport, 1954). Relationships of unequals do little to remove the mysteries and mystifications that block mutual understanding. Now because teachers and students hold different ranks, equal status contact between them might appear to be impossible. As long as the contacts remain confined to the classroom, they clearly are likely to be between unequals. Outside of that context—in the community, at athletic events, in neighborhood markets—school roles can count for less. It is the sparseness of nonclassroom contacts, not the impossibility of equal status interaction, that makes the relationships between students and teachers so asymmetrical.

Distrustful relationships are not inevitable in urban schools. Metz (1986) marveled at the bonds students and teachers had formed in one of the middle schools she studied in a large city. Any number of policies and practices demonstrated respect. For example:

> Nearly every lunchtime student would knock at the door of the teachers' lounge in search of materials or information. The teachers welcomed them into the lounge and courteously gave what was asked. Teachers also gave students keys to get material from unsupervised locked areas. (p. 67)

---

[4]Newmann (1981) discusses the consequences of limited student–adult contacts for student motivation. He concludes that alienation often characterizes schools, because the connections among participants are too tenuous. His discussion is of schools in general, not of inner-city schools. If the problems plague all schools, they are exacerbated in inner-city schools.

Wehlage and his associates (1989) corroborate the view from Metz that positive relationships can and do occur in some urban schools. The researchers studied 14 high schools that served students at risk of dropping out. They describe the effective schools as "communities," settings that promoted a sense of membership and opportunities for sharing.[5] The comments from the Wehlage *et al.* and Metz studies sustain those from the research on effective schools. But neither these studies nor the analyses of effective schools examine the density of the ties within the school and between the school and the communities from which the students, teachers, and staff come. Whether the bonds cover most or only a handful of students and teachers should have significant implications for overall outcomes in the school.

NETWORKS AND SCHOOL ACHIEVEMENT

The evidence, especially that on peers and performance, shows rather clearly that the networks found within the schools matter for performance. It demonstrates, too, that teachers respond positively to schools where colleagues support one another (Newmann, 1981; Stevenson, 1987). The signs that community–school linkages encourage achievement are more indirect. We do know that students whose parents take part in school affairs generally overshadow those students whose parents remain on the margins. Social class, of course, contributes to this effect: Middle-class parents are more likely to have the time and skills to help their children and to intervene with the schools than are lower-income parents. But differences in the resources of the family cannot explain fully the better outcomes we find for some students. The expectations of teachers count as well. Teachers respond more positively to the students of interventionist parents, whatever the social class. The teachers interpret involved parents as supportive ones whose children deserve attention.

NETWORKS AND SOCIAL CAPITAL

Coleman makes the case for an examination of contextual forces in his comparison of private and public schools. To Coleman, the tendency for students in Catholic schools to outperform many who attend public schools results quite probably from differences in social contexts (Coleman, 1988; Coleman & Hoffer, 1987). Catholic schools operate within com-

[5]These observations about the study appear in Gary Wehlage, "Membership, Engagement and Success with At-Risk Students," *Newsletter* of the National Center on Effective Secondary Schools, 4 (Spring, 1989), 2–5. For the full report, see Gary Wehlage, Robert Rutter, Gregory Smith, Nancy Lesko, and Ricardo Fernandez, *Reducing the Risk: Schools as Communities of Support* (Madison, WI: Falmer Press, 1989).

munities, where complementary contacts exist.[6] This is the case as well for certain private schools without any specific religious identification and for some public schools. The development of private academies in several cities represents the efforts of parents and educators to offer minority and disadvantaged children a supportive environment, an environment in which parents back the staff and the staff concurs on the best path to education.

Disciplinary problems often embroil inner-city schools. To enhance performance and manage these problems, some administrators have instituted more rigid rules and expelled the troublemakers. These strategies might reduce overt conflict, but they do not make achievers of the expelled or foster the development of trust. Maintaining control proves difficult in the troubled schools, for it must be accomplished by a few rather than by most. The wider the support in the system, the less the demand on those charged with keeping it in line. The quality of relationships, consequently, should make a difference for the climate and behaviors found in a school.

The experiences of a team from the Child Study Center at Yale University illustrate the effects that changed relationships can have on school discipline. In one of the schools, fights among students were common occurrences. The intervention program worked to include parents in school activities, to have teachers plan together, and to incorporate support staff more fully into the educational process. The director felt that his team had made inroads in reducing the distrust and improving the relationships, but one vent in particular persuaded him that the changes had been even more dramatic than he had envisioned.

> At the beginning of the fourth year, someone stepped on the foot of a transfer student and his dukes went up. Another youngster said, "Hey man, we don't do that in this school." He looked at the expressions on the faces around him and read, "We don't fight." (Comer, 1988, p. 219)

If networks can indeed exert control, they are worth fostering in inner-city schools, confronted as these schools often are with conflict.

Coleman reminds us that achievement in this society depends on one's social capital, on the resources one can mobilize. Ties to others represent social capital, for they give one potential sources of information and support. Persons who possess few material resources are not always linkage-poor. But in the case of inner-city students, the linkages are so peripheral to the school that they do not enhance the students' social capital in that setting.

[6]Private schools ostensibly can rely less on hierarchical authority to coordinate people and activities, for they rest in far more consensual communities than do many public schools. See Salganik and Karweit (1982) for an elaboration of this argument. As I mentioned earlier, consensus does not inevitably mean strong and reinforcing ties, however.

NETWORKS AND CULTURE

Because a concern with the culture of schools already appears, one might ask if a focus on relationships makes any specific contribution. The study of culture does not substitute for an analysis of networks. First, the effective schools movement, the school improvement efforts, and the policies of ever greater numbers of school districts make the school the unit of analysis. Changes across the school and not in the classroom of any given teacher became the focus of concern. The school is measured as a whole, even though some participants might have contributed to the outcome more than others. In these cases, cases of joint output, actors face the possibility of free riding: Some who have contributed little to a favorable outcome will share any benefits that ensue. The more isolated the actors from one another, the less their ability to monitor behaviors and exert pressures on free riders. A study exclusively of culture will yield little information on how participants in a school interact with one another to respond to the pressures for success at the overall school level. Second, shared norms can operate in highly atomized situations. Coleman and Hoffer (1987) make the case in this way:

> The independent private schools constitute with few exceptions the extreme of individualism in education. The family acts individually, enrolling the child in a school that is not an outgrowth of a functional community, but one that collects children from a set of parents who have similar values and sufficient resources to implement these values. (p. 216)

Participants may share common assumptions that stress individual rather than joint or mutual action.

Third, cultural approaches all too often treat the culture in a rather static way, as a set of forces that, once set in motion, remain relatively fixed. Obviously, culture is not static; norms and values change from one time to the next. The idea that relationships are somewhat fluid—continually being built and rebuilt—appears more often than does the notion that culture changes. Thus it is to highlight the construction of relationships that I have chosen to treat social relationships separately from culture.

Fourth, individuals need not conform to the norms that exist. Knowing, then, the nature of the norms is not synonymous with knowing how a given system will operate. Finally, cultural norms, values, and symbols do not spring up in a vacuum, nor do they persist without reinforcement. The kind of culture one will find at any specific time within a school will depend on who happens to be linked to the school. An understanding of the culture, consequently, may require an understanding of the relationships that give rise to and sustain it.

The Tasks Ahead

The changes in the school population make it urgent that we examine the settings in which the "newcomers" find themselves. That examination might profitably include a reconsideration of our conceptions about schools. We think of them increasingly as more than technical systems, in which technical experts—teachers—carry out the fundamental processes of change. We know that they are cultural systems as well. I ask that we recognize their interpersonal dynamics, particularly because the interpersonal ties seem so ephemeral and problematic in inner city schools. Will stronger networks enhance achievement? Not directly; but they can provide a context of support that goes beyond the given classroom. What remains to be examined are the kinds of linkages that do exist, the conditions that undergird them, the networks that inner-city schools can build, and the consequences for education of strong interpersonal ties.

We look for panaceas that can cure the ills of inner-city schools; organizational changes all too often are set forth as such panaceas. It would be tempting, indeed, to argue that strong networks reduce administrative costs, that when ties are effective, monitoring proves less essential. Let us not overstate the savings, however. The worth of a practice cannot always be assessed by its economic outcomes. In addition, given the difficulty one would have in measuring economic returns, we have little to gain from confining the analysis of networks to their economic results. Finally, let us recall that no form or practice is without any costs. The presence of strong networks may indeed give the schools the support they need to bolster themes. But this will occur, only if those in the networks endorse those notions the educators share. Similarly, teachers may find themselves in a trade-off: For greater support from the wider community, they give up their autonomy; they become more prone to intervention and questions from persons in their multiple networks.

In sum, one need not regard the call for tighter influence at the top as a call for the diminished diligence of teachers. In some instances, it reflects the presence of an uncoupled educational system, with the classroom teachers isolated from one another. In another—and perhaps most—instances, it grows out of the problems attending the tenuousness of interpersonal ties.

Strong networks of relationships are unlikely to spring up spontaneously in inner-city schools. They can be fostered, however. Seemingly, principals in effective schools promote teacher-to-teacher interaction by scheduling meetings, organizing work teams, establishing communication nodes. The principals exercise the skills of socioemotional or expressive leadership.

Schools are changing demographically. What the new cohort needs is not that difference from what any group of students needs. But what these students lack is an embeddedness in networks connected to schools and the educational process. Stronger parent–school linkages clearly warrant development. The performance of minority youth depends on support from more than their own parents, however. A growing segment of such students consists of the "children of children": the offspring of teenage mothers and fathers. Many of the parents themselves left school before graduating or found their experiences so alienating that the endorsement they give for schooling rings hollow. For these students, the building of their social capital requires the creation of stronger linkages to community figures and forces beyond the confines of the family.

The community must transcend neighborhood boundaries, for many inner-city neighborhoods are too problem-ridden to provide solid grounding for education. High rates of crime and drug use are not restricted to central cities, but they occur more frequently in such areas than in other locales. Tightening the coupling of schools to their contexts may require significant time and skill, for it requires that administrators reach well beyond the boundaries of their schools.

Throughout this discussion I have taken achievement as the outcome of greatest import in the case of minority education. There are other outcomes of course—improved discipline, attendance, and morale—and social relationships perhaps shape these outcomes even more than they do achievement. Improved attendance, without a concomitant rise in performance, will not make minority students better able to compete in the society. The other outcomes merit consideration, partly because they capture the quality of life within schools and primarily because they can contribute to achievement.

Much of this is speculative, for we have little data on the quality of relationships in schools and how—if at all—those relationships shape student outcomes. Nonetheless, the arguments in the literature about social networks are so corroborative that only an extreme skeptic would deem them unworthy of further development and analysis. Demographic changes have brought to the schools of America a population vulnerable, at risk for failure. The demographic changes seemingly demand structural changes as well, changes intended to weave the varied elements within and without schools into tapestries of support.

REFERENCES

Allport, G. W. (1954). *The nature of prejudice*. New York: Addison-Wesley.
Bean, F. D., & Tienda, M. (1987). *The Hispanic population of the United States*. New York: Russell Sage.
Brookover, W. B., & Lezotte, L. W. (1979). *Changes in school characteristics coincident with changes in student achievement*. East Lansing, MI: Institute for Research on Teaching, Michigan State University.

Burns, T., & Stalker, G. M. (1961). *The management of innovation*. London: Tavistock.

Castenell, L. (1983). Achievement motivation: An investigation of adolescent achievement patterns. *American Educational Research Journal, 20*, 503–510.

Coleman, J. S. (1988). Social capital in the creation of human capital. *American Journal of Sociology, 94* (1988 Supplement), S95–S120.

Coleman, J. S., Campbell, E. Q., Hobson, C. J., McPartland, J., Mood, A. M., Weinfeld, F. D., & York, R. L. (1966). *Equality of educational opportunity*. Washington, DC: U.S. Government Printing Office.

Coleman, J. S., & Hoffer, T. (1987). *Public and private high schools: The impact of communities*. New York: Basic Books.

Comer, J. (1988). *Maggie's American dream*. New York: New American Library.

Corcoran, T., & Wilson, B. (1986). *The search for successful secondary schools: The first three years of the secondary school recognition program*. Philadelphia: Research for Better Schools.

Cummings, S. (1977). Family socialization and fatalism among black adolescents. *Journal of Negro Education, 46*, 62–75.

Dore, R. (1983). Goodwill and the spirit of market capitalism. *British Journal of Sociology, 34* (December), 459–482.

Duran, R. P. (1986). Hispanics' precollege and undergraduate education: Implications for science and engineering studies. In *Minorities: Their underrepresentation and career differentials in science and engineering* (pp. 73–128). Washington, DC: National Academy of Sciences Press.

Eisenberg, T. A. (1977). Begle revisited: Teacher knowledge and student achievement in algebra. *Journal for Research in Mathematics Education* (May), 216–222.

Epstein, J. L. (1983). The influence of friends on achievement and affective outcomes. In Joyce Epstein & Nancy Karweit (Eds.), *Friends in school: Patterns of selection and influence in secondary schools*. New York: Academic Press.

Erickson, F. (1985). *Conditions for higher order thinking in teaching and learning: An anthropologist's perspective on mathematics, science and technology education*. Paper prepared for the Committee on Mathematics, Science, and Technology Education, National Research Council.

Farrar, E., Neufeld, B., & Miles, M. (1984). Effective schools programs in high schools: Social promotion or movement by merit? *Phi Delta Kappan, 65* (June), 701–706.

Firestone, W. A., & Wilson, B. L. (1985). Using bureaucratic and cultural linkages to improve instruction: The principal's contribution. *Educational Administration Quarterly, 21* (Spring), 7–30.

Freudenburg, W. (1986). The density of acquaintanceship: An overlooked variable in community research? *American Journal of Sociology, 92* (July), 47–63.

Gamoran, A. (1988). Resource allocation and the effects of schooling: A sociological perspective. In David Monk & Julie Underwood (Eds.), *Microlevel school finance: Issues and implications for policy*. 30–62 Ninth Annual Yearbook of the American Educational Finance Association. Cambridge, MA: Ballinger.

Gove, W. (1984). Gender differences in mental and physical illness: The effects of fixed roles and nuturant roles. *Social Science and Medicine, 19*, 77–91.

Granovetter, M. (1985). Economic action and social structure: The problem of embeddedness. *American Journal of Sociology, 91* (November), 481–510.

Herriott, R., & Firestone, W. A. (1984). Two images of schools as organizations; A refinement and elaboration. *Educational Administration Quarterly, 20* (Fall), 41–57.

House, J. S., Robbins, C., & Metzner, H. (1982). The association of social relationships and activities with morality: Prospective evidence from the Tecumseh community health study. *American Journal of Epidemiology, 116*, 123–140.

Kanter, R. M. (1983). *The change masters*. New York: Simon and Schuster.

Lawrenz, F. (1975). The relationship between science teacher characteristics and student achievement and attitudes. *Journal of Research in Science Teaching, 12*(4), 433–437.

Lezotte, L. W., Edmonds, R., & Ratner, G. (1974). *A final report: Remedy for school failure to equitably deliver basic school skills*. East Lansing, MI: Department of Urban and Metropolitan Studies, Michigan State University.

Lightfoot, S. L. (1983) *The good high school: Portraits of character and culture*. New York: Basic Books.

Lipsitz, J. (1984). *Successful schools for young adolescents*. New Brunswick, NJ: Transaction Books.

Litwak, E., & Messeri, P. (1989). Organizational theory, social supports, and mortality rates. *American Sociological Review, 54* (February), 49–66.

Marrett, C. B. (1986). Black and Native American students in precollege mathematics and science. In *Minorities: Their underrepresentation and career differentials in science and engineering* (pp. 7–32). Washington, DC: National Academy of Sciences Press.

Metz, M. H. (1986). *Different by design: The context and character of three magnet schools*. New York: Routledge and Kegan Paul.

Meyer, J. W., & Rowan, B. (1978). The structure of educational organizations. In Marshall Meyer & Associates (Eds.), *Environments and organizations: Theoretical and empirical perspectives*, (pp. 78–109). San Francisco: Jossey Bass.

National Commission on Excellence in Education. (1983). *A nation at risk: The imperative for educational reform*. Washington, DC: U.S. Government Printing Office.

New York State Department of Education. (1974a). *Reading achievement related to educational and environmental conditions in 12 New York City elementary schools*. Albany, NY: Division of Education Evaluation.

New York State Department of Education. (1974b). *School factors influencing reading achievement: A case study of two inner city schools*. Albany, NY: Office of Education Performance Review.

Newmann, F. M. (1981). Reducing student alienation in high schools: Implications of theory. *Harvard Educational Review, 51*, (November), 546–564.

Ouchi, W. (1980). Markets, bureaucracies and clans. *Administrative Science Quarterly, 25*, 129–142.

Ouchi, W. (1981). *Theory Z: How American business can meet the Japanese challenge*. Reading, MA: Addison-Wesley.

Peters, T., & Waterman, R. (1982). *In search of excellence*. New York: Harper & Row.

Purkey, S., & Smith, M. (1983). Effective schools: A review. *The Elementary School Journal, 83* (March), 427–452.

Rowan, B., Bossert, S., & Dwyer, D. C. (1983). Research on effective schools: A cautionary note. *Educational Research, 12*(4), 22–31.

Stevenson, R. B. (1987). Autonomy and support: The dual needs of urban high schools. *Urban Education, 22*, 366–386.

Tsang, Sau-Lim. (1983). *Mathematics learning styles of Chinese immigrant students*. Unpublished manuscript.

Weber, G. (1971). *Inner-city children can be taught to read: Four successful schools*. Washington, DC: Council for Basic Education.

Weick, K. (1976). Educational organizations a loosely coupled system. *Administrative Science Quarterly, 21*, 1–19.

Wilson, B. L., Corbett, H. D. (1983). Organization and change: The effects of school linkages on the quantity of implementation. *Educational Administration Quarterly, 19* (Fall), 85–104.

CHAPTER FIVE

Single Parents and the Schools

Effects of Marital Status on Parent and Teacher Interactions

JOYCE L. EPSTEIN

INTRODUCTION

The one-parent home is one of the major family arrangements of school-children today. Over 15 million children live in one-parent homes, most in mother-only homes and most as a result of separation or divorce. From a total of about 62 million children overall, the number in one-parent homes is an important and growing subgroup of children in the country. Each year over 1 million children under the age of 18 have parents who divorce. In the United States in 1986, 25% of the households with children under 18—about 1 in 4—were single-parent homes (U.S. House of Representatives, 1986). Membership in one-parent homes is even greater for black children, with about half of all black children under 18 years old in one-parent homes (U.S. Bureau of the Census, 1982). It is estimated that over 50% of all children born after 1980 will live with one parent for at least 3 school years before reaching the age of 18. Most will live in poor, female-headed households (Furstenburg, Nord, Peterson, & Zill, 1983; Garbarino, 1982; Glick, 1979; Masnick & Bane, 1980).

In earlier times, single-parent homes were atypical; now they are common. The historic contrast raises many questions about the effects of single-parent homes on the members of the family. Much has been written about single parents, their children, their numbers, and their problems, but little research has focused on how single parents and their children fit

JOYCE L. EPSTEIN ● Center for Research on Elementary and Middle Schools, The Johns Hopkins University, Baltimore, Maryland 21218.

into other social institutions that were designed to serve "traditional" families. When children are in school, the family and school are inexorably linked. Because of this linkage, changes that occur in families must be accommodated by responsive changes in schools.

THEORETICAL PERSPECTIVES

Schools and families are overlapping spheres of influence on student learning and development (Epstein, 1987). The model of overlapping spheres of influence recognizes that there are some practices that schools and families conduct separately but that there are other practices that can best be conducted as partners. This view is in contrast to a long-standing alternative perspective that emphasizes the separateness of these institutions.

An emphasis on separateness. One perspective on institutions and their relationships emphasizes the importance of their *separate* contributions to society. This view assumes, for example, that school bureaucracies and family organizations are most efficient and effective when their leaders maintain independent goals, standards, and activities (Parsons, 1959; Waller, 1932; Weber, 1947). Institutions that are separate and nonoverlapping give little consideration to the ideas or histories of the other groups or to their common or interlocking aims or goals until there are problems or trouble. This is, in effect, a "conflict resolution" model, requiring interventions and interactions only when necessary to solve serious problems.

An emphasis on overlapping spheres of influence. A social-organizational perspective is offered as the basis for research on schools and families (Epstein, 1987) and other interinstitutional connections that influence the education of children (Epstein, 1989). In this model, the key, proximate environments that educate and socialize children are shown as spheres of influence that can, by design, overlap more or less in their goals, practices, messages, and resources for students. Major "forces" are considered in the model, including (1) time—to account for changes in the ages and grade levels of students and the influence of the historic period, and (2) the philosophies, policies, and practices of each institution. These forces affect the nature and extent of "overlap" of families and schools. The model integrates and extends the ecological approach developed by Bronfenbrenner (1979); the educational insights of Leichter (1974); the sociological studies of schools and communities of Litwak and Meyer (1974); the theory of institutions and individuals of Coleman (1974); and a long tradition of sociological research on school and family environments (Coleman et al., 1966; Epstein & McPartland, 1979; McDill & Rigsby, 1973; and others).

The model of overlapping spheres of influence recognizes the interlocking histories of institutions that educate and socialize children and the changing and accumulating skills of the individuals in them as the basis for studying connections that can benefit children's learning and development. This, in effect, is a "conflict prevention" model in which institutions invest resources in shared goals (such as student success) in order to prevent or reduce tensions and problems that could require later, more costly treatment.

These two theoretical perspectives are reflected in the practices of two types of teachers and may influence their interactions with single and married parents. Some teachers believe that families and schools have different responsibilities that can best be accomplished separately and independently. These teachers may make greater distinctions in their opinions about the effectiveness of single and married parents if they view single parents as lacking the resources needed to carry out family responsibilities. Other teachers believe families and schools overlap in their interests and share responsibilities for the education and socialization of their children. They may make fewer distinctions between single and married parents if they view all parents as important contributors to their children's education.

Opinions differ about whether schools and teachers should be informed about parents' marital status or changes in family structure. Some argue that teachers are biased against children from one-parent homes. They suggest that teachers negatively label children of divorced or separated parents, explain children's school problems in terms of the family living arrangement rather than in terms of their own teaching practices or the children's individual needs, or assume parental inadequacies before the facts about parents' skills are known (Hetherington, Camara, & Featherman, 1981; Laosa, 1983; Lightfoot, 1978; Ogbu, 1974; Santrock & Tracy, 1978; Zill, 1983). This view sets schools and families apart as separate spheres of influence, with families expected to cope on their own with changes and problems.

Others argue that schools should be informed about parental separation or divorce because teachers provide stability and support to children during the initial period of family disruption, can be more sensitive to children's situations when discussing families, and can organize special services such as afterschool care for children that may be needed by single parents and working mothers (Bernard, 1984). This view brings schools and families together, as overlapping spheres of influence with both institutions working together to help children cope and succeed even during times of family changes and stress.

The discrepant opinions of how much families should inform schools about family circumstances are each supported by parents' accounts of experiences with teacher bias or with teacher understanding and assistance (Carew & Lightfoot, 1979; Clay, 1981; Keniston, 1977; National Public Radio, 1980; Snow, 1982). There are few facts from research, however, about whether and how teachers respond to students in differently structured families or about how single parents perceive, react to, and become involved with their children's schools and teachers.

Many early studies of single parents and some recent ones are based on a "deficit theory" of family functioning. One major underlying assumption of this work is that the number of parents at home is the key variable for understanding effective parenting and children's success. That is, two parents are always better than one. For example, research based on the "confluence" model argues that crucial intellectual resources are lacking when the father is absent from the home (Zajonc, 1976). This theory asserts that the father is the family member with the highest intelligence and is the educational leader of the family. This is a mechanical theory that has not been well supported in research. It establishes an unequivocal bias against one-parent homes, putting mothers in a fixed and forced subordinate position, discounting the roles most mothers play in encouraging their children's education, and ignoring the roles of schools in guiding family activities that concern school skills.

Other research on single parents based on their deficiencies assumes that one-parent homes are unstable, uncaring, lacking in emotional and academic support or strong role models for students' school success. The number of parents at home is the measure used as a proxy for numerous alleged weaknesses of the one-parent home. Studies that include the number of parents as the only explanatory variable establish a theoretical bias against one-parent homes, without allowing for alternative explanations.

An alternative view focuses more on the strengths and potentials of families, with attention to the activities and practices of families of any size or structure. The underlying assumption of these studies is that the quality of family practices and processes explain more about parental effectiveness than marital status or the number of parents at home (Barton, 1981; Blanchard & Biller, 1979; Dokecki & Maroney, 1983; Hetherington & Camara, 1984; Marotz-Bader, Adams, Beuche, Munro, & Munro, 1979; Shinn, 1978).

The change from a "deficit model" to a "strengths model" has led to more thoughtful studies of children and parents in one *and* two parent homes. Models improved in small steps, from the simple, mechanistic theories of the impact of the number of parents in the home on student achievement or behavior, to only slightly more complex theories that added family socioeconomic status (SES) as another explanatory variable. Researchers recognized that because low eduction and low income often accompany single-parent status, it is necessary to measure these family conditions as well as marital status so that negative effects due to SES or education were not attributed falsely to single-parent status (Barton, 1981; Kelly, North, & Zingle, 1965; Milne, Myers, Rosenthal, & Ginsburg, 1986; Svanum, Bringle, & McLaughlin, 1982). For example, children from well-educated, middle-class, one-parent homes often perform as well as similar children from two-parent homes.

The improvements in knowledge gained from added measures of social class were not enough, however, to clarify the inconsistent results across studies of the effects of marital status on parent behavior and student achievement. Two relatively stable status variables—marital status and socioeconomic status—do not adequately represent the dynamics of family life that contribute to student achievement or success in school (Hanson & Ginsburg, 1986). Even recent studies of family contacts with the schools (Baker & Stevenson, 1986; Garfinkle & McLanahan, 1986; Kurdek & Blisk, 1983; Milne *et al.*, 1986; Zill, 1983) have ignored the roles of teachers in increasing or reducing differences in parent and student behavior in differently structured families. A comprehensive review by Newberger, Melnicoe, and Newberger (1986) calls for studies of the many factors that may ameliorate and explain the negative conditions of one-parent homes.

The present study looks at some potentially important variables that allow schools to change to meet the changing needs and conditions of families. We use data from teachers and parents to examine family and school connections in one- and two-parent homes. We focus on the children's living arrangements that affect the day-to-day communications and interactions between schools and families. We compare single and married *parents' reports* of the frequency of teacher requests for parent involvement. We look next at *teachers' reports* of the quality of involvement of the single and married parents of their students, and the *teachers' reports* of the quality of the homework completed by children from one- and two-parent homes. And we examine other similarities and differences among single and married parents concerning their children's education.

We ask the following questions: Do single and married parents differ in their perceptions of teacher practices of parent involvement? Are teachers' perceptions of parents and children influenced by family living arrangements? How does marital status relate to other family and school connections? And, how do teachers' practices reflect the two theoretical perspectives that emphasize separateness or overlap of families and schools? To address these questions, we introduce, first, a simple model that improves upon earlier research on single parents by accounting for marital status, parent education, and teacher leadership to study parent–teacher exchanges and evaluations. We then test a more complete model that places marital status, parent education, and teachers' practices of parent involvement in a fuller social context with other characteristics of the school and family.

This exploration includes many measures of *family* structure and processes, *student* characteristics, and *school and classroom* structures and processes. The independent variables, introduced as they are needed in different analyses, include *family* size, race, and parent education; *student* grade level, classroom ability, and behavior in class; *teacher* leadership in parent involvement, teaching experience, and overall teaching quality; and specific *teacher–parent* interactions about the child as a student.

Unlike earlier research that often used "special problem" samples to study single-parent families (Shinn, 1978), this is a purposely stratified sample of a normal population of teachers in grades 1, 3, and 5 in public schools in the state of Maryland and the parents and students in their classes (Becker & Epstein, 1982a). Importantly, the data from teachers, parents, and students are linked so that particular teachers' practices can be connected with the parents and students in those teachers' classrooms (Epstein, 1986, 1990a). Few previous studies measured the behavior and attitudes of single parents about the schools their children attend (Clay, 1981), and none link the teachers' and parents' practices and evaluations of each other.

SAMPLE, VARIABLES, AND APPROACHES

Surveys of teachers, principals, parents, and students in 16 Maryland school districts were conducted in 1980 and 1981. About 3,700 first-, third-, and fifth-grade teachers and their principals in 600 schools were surveyed (Becker & Epstein, 1982a; Epstein & Becker, 1982). From the original sample, 82 teachers were selected who varied in their use of parent involvement in learning activities at home. They were matched by school district, grade level, years of teaching experience, and characteristics of their student populations. Among the teachers, 17 were confirmed by their principals as strong *leaders* in the use of parent involvement activities. In all, the 82 teachers ranged along a useful continuum from high to low use of parent involvement, with the "confirmed leaders" making the most concerted use of parent involvement in learning activities at home.

Data were obtained on the achievements and behaviors of the students in the 82 classrooms. The parents of the children in the 82 teachers' classrooms were surveyed about their attitudes toward and experiences with parent involvement. In all, 1,269 parents responded to a questionnaire by mail—a response rate of 59%. Of these, 24% were single parents—close to the national average of 22% (U.S. Bureau of Census, 1982).

We requested that the parent complete the survey who is most familiar with the child's school and teacher. Over 90% of the respondents were female, and virtually all of the single-parent respondents were female. Thus the research provided a sizable, useful sample of single and married mothers whose children were in the classrooms of teachers who differed in their use of practices to involve parents in their children's education.

The categories *one-parent home* and *single parent* come from the parents' reports that only one parent lives at home with the child. We prefer the terms *single-parent home, one-parent home,* or *mother-only/father-only home* to describe the living arrangements of schoolchildren, rather than the pejorative terms *broken home, broken family,* or even *single-parent family.* A single-parent home or a two-parent home may or may not be "broken" by marital, economic, or emotional conditions (Engan-Barker, 1986; Kamerman & Hayes, 1982). To determine if a family is "broken" requires clear and sensitive measures in addition to the structure of living arrangements. A child in a single-parent home may have contact with two parents, although only one parent lives at home when the child leaves for and returns from school. The data do not include information on the cause, choice, or duration of single-parent status, nor can we identify calm or troubled relations in two-parent homes. Our sample does not permit us to study one-parent homes where the father is the custodial parent or the parent most knowledgeable about the child's schooling. These are important characteristics of families that should be included in new studies of family and school effects (Bane, 1976; Eiduson, 1982; Furstenburg & Seltzer, 1983; Shinn, 1978; Zill, 1983).

Parent involvement refers to 12 techniques that teachers used to organize parental assistance at home, including reading, discussions, informal learning games, formal contracts, drill and practice of basic skills, and other monitoring or tutoring activities. For example, the most popular teachers' practices included: ask parents to read to their child or listen to the child read; use books or workbooks borrowed from the school to help children learn or to practice needed skills; discuss school work at home; and use materials found at home to teach needed skills. Eight other activities were also used by teachers to establish parents at home as partners with the teacher to help students do better in school. The activities, patterns of teacher use, effects on parents, and effects on student achievements are discussed fully in other publications (Becker & Epstein, 1982a, b; Epstein & Becker, 1982; Epstein, 1986; Epstein, 1990a). Parent involvement in learning activities at home is a complex, difficult type of teacher–parent partnership (Leler, 1983), but these practices include more parents and have greater positive impact than other forms of parent involvement that occur at the school building (Epstein, 1986). Involvement in learning activities at home is the type of involvement that most parents would like the schools to increase and improve across the grades (Dauber & Epstein, 1989; Epstein, 1990b).

CHARACTERISTICS OF PARENTS

Table 1 shows the characteristics of the single and married parents in the sample. There are several important differences. Significantly more single parents are black, reside in the city, have fewer years of formal schooling, work full-time, or have one child. The single and married parents are about equally represented by children in the three elementary-school grades (1, 3, and 5) in the study and in the classroom of teachers who were confirmed by their principals as *leaders* in the use of parent involvement. These characteristics of the Maryland sample are similar to those expected from a national sample of single parents.

We use mothers' education rather than both parents' education, or either parent's occupation, in order to minimize missing or incomparable data for one- and two-parent homes. Mothers' education has traditionally been used as an indicator of family SES (Sewell & Hauser, 1975). As others

TABLE 1. Characteristics of Single and Married Parents

	Single parents $(N = 273)$ Percentage respondents	Married parents $(N = 862)$ Percentage respondents
Race[a]		
White	35.9	73.2
Black	64.1	26.8
Residence[a]		
City	57.1	27.7
County/suburb	42.9	72.3
Parent education[a]		
Some high school (or less)	27.1	15.2
High-school diploma	32.2	38.4
Some college	28.1	22.6
Bachelor's degree	4.8	10.5
Some graduate school (or more)	7.8	13.3
Employment[a]		
No work outside home	33.1	40.4
Part-time work	11.3	21.4
Full-time work	55.6	38.2
Family size[a]		
0 siblings	24.9	11.7
1–2 siblings	58.3	71.9
3–4 siblings	15.0	14.2
Over 4 siblings	1.8	2.2
Extended family (other adults)	23.8	10.2
Grade level of child		
Grade 1	41.8	38.3
Grade 3	27.8	26.9
Grade 5	30.4	34.8
Teacher leadership in parent involvement		
Confirmed leader	27.5	20.4
Not confirmed leader	72.5	79.6

[a]Chi-square tests yield significant differences in proportions for single and married parents beyond the .001 level.

have noted, mother's education may be more pertinent than other measures for studying family influences on children's school behaviors, or as an indicator of a parent's familiarity with school organizations and procedures (Baker & Stevenson, 1986; Milne *et al.*, 1986). In one-parent homes especially, mother's education may be a more important and accurate indicator of schoollike activities at home than other occupational or economic indicators.

RESULTS: PARENTS' REPORTS OF
TEACHERS' PRACTICES OF PARENT INVOLVEMENT

Parents were asked to report how often their child's teacher requested their involvement on the 12 home-learning activities described earlier. Parents' reports of teachers' requests ranged from 0 to 12 frequently used activities, with a mean score of 4.1 and a standard deviation of 3.4. Table 2 shows how single and married parents' reports differed by the educational level of the parents and by the teachers' leadership in parent involvement. The mean scores and tests of comparisons in the first column of the table show that, compared to married parents, single parents reported significantly more requests from teachers to assist with learning activities at home (4.80 vs. 3.76). The figures in the second column indicate that among single parents, high- and low-educated single parents reported about equally frequent requests from teachers for parent involvement. Among married parents, however, less-educated married parents reported more frequent requests from teachers for parent involvement than did more-educated married parents (4.16 vs. 3.30).

In the third column, the measure of teacher leadership adds important information about the experiences of parents. Single and married parents with children in the classrooms of teachers who were confirmed by their principals as *leaders* in parent involvement reported more requests than parents who children's teachers were *not leaders* in parent involvement. The differences were especially great between married parents in teacher-leader and nonleader classrooms.

Other comparisons noted in Column 4 of Table 2 reveal differences in single and married parents' reports about teachers who were *not leaders* in parent involvement. Highly educated single parents in these teachers' classrooms reported significantly more requests than highly educated married parents (4.47 vs. 3.04). Less-educated single parents reported significantly more requests than less-educated married parents (4.73 vs. 3.97).

If we looked only at the differences in involvement by marital status and educational levels in Columns 1 and 2 of Table 2, we would miss the

TABLE 2. Parents' Reports of Frequency of Teachers' Use of Parent Involvement (12 Techniques) (Means, Standard Deviations, and Test Statistics from Multiple Comparisons of Mean Scores of Single vs. Married, Low vs. High-Educated Parents and Parents of Children in Classrooms of Confirmed Leader vs. Nonleader Teacher in Parent Involvement)

	Family structure		Parent education[a]		Teacher leadership in parent involvement		Other significant comparisons of means
Parents' reports of teachers' use of 12 parent involvement techniques	Single parent	$\bar{X}$ 4.80* s.d. 3.53 N (246)	Low	$\bar{X}$ 4.87 s.d. 3.42 N (144)	Confirmed leader	$\bar{X}$ 5.22 s.d. 3.50 N (41)	Single vs. married, low education in nonleader classroom ($\bar{X}$ = 4.73* vs. 3.97)
					Nonleader	$\bar{X}$ 4.73 s.d. 3.39 N (103)	
			High	$\bar{X}$ 4.70 s.d. 3.70 N (102)	Confirmed leader	$\bar{X}$ 5.28 s.d. 3.52 N (29)	Single vs. married, high education in nonleader classroom ($\bar{X}$ = 4.47* vs. 3.04)
					Nonleader	$\bar{X}$ 4.47 s.d. 3.77 N (73)	
	Married parent	$\bar{X}$ 3.76 s.d. 3.23 N (801)	Low	$\bar{X}$ 4.16* s.d. 3.30 N (433)	Confirmed leader	$\bar{X}$ 4.76* s.d. 3.24 N (103)	Low vs. high education, married parents, in nonleader classroom ($\bar{X}$ = 3.97* vs. 3.04)
					Nonleader	$\bar{X}$ 3.97 s.d. 3.30 N (330)	
			High	$\bar{X}$ 3.30 s.d. 3.08 N (368)	Confirmed leader	$\bar{X}$ 4.63* s.d. 3.04 N (60)	
					Nonleader	$\bar{X}$ 3.04 s.d. 3.03 N (308)	

[a] Parent education is high if the respondent attended or graduated from postsecondary school; low if parent attended or graduated from high school only.
*T-test significant at or beyond the .05 level.

important link between families and schools due to teachers' practices, reported in Column 3. There are two important patterns of results in Table 2:

- Single parents, regardless of their educational level, report more requests from teachers than do married parents to be involved in learning activities at home.
- According to parents, teachers who are confirmed *leaders* in parent involvement make more equal requests of all parents, regardless of education and marital status, whereas other, *nonleader* teachers ask more of single and low-educated parents.

It is not enough, then, to measure only marital status or parent education to explain parents' behavior concerning their children. Research on single parents and the schools must also take into account teachers' practices concerning parents.

Table 3 extends the inquiry by introducing other variables that may explain the simple patterns in Table 2. The first line of Table 3 reports the independent effects of the three variables—marital status, mothers' education, and teachers' practices of parent involvement—that were introduced earlier. With the other two variables statistically controlled, single parents, less-educated parents, and parents whose children are in the classrooms of teachers who were *leaders* report receiving more requests from teachers for their involvement with their children in learning activities at home.

The second line of the table introduces other characteristics of the family, student, and teacher that previous research suggests may also affect parents', teachers', and students' interactions and evaluations of each other. *Race* clearly helps to explain the effect of single-parent status on parents' reports of teachers practices. More black parents head one-parent homes in this sample (as in the nation), and black parents report receiving more requests for parent involvement than do white parents, regardless of marital status. These results reflect the practices of the urban district in which most of the black parents in this sample reside. Teachers in the urban district reported that they used more parent involvement practices (Becker & Epstein, 1982b), and the parents' responses verify the teachers' reports. Teachers tend to reach out to parents when children need extra help. The results also may indicate a continuing trend for black parents to let teachers know that they want to be involved in their children's education (Lightfoot, 1978).

The regression coefficients in line 2 of Table 3 show that six variables in addition to race have significant independent effects on parents' reports of their experiences with teachers' practice of parent involvement. Parents report significantly more frequent requests for involvement from teachers if they have less education (PARED), have younger children (GRADE), have children whose teachers are *leaders* in parent involvement (TCHLDR), or whose teachers use specific strategies to build close family–school relation-

TABLE 3. Effects of Measures of Family, Student, and Teacher Characteristics
on Parents' Reports of Teacher Practices of Parent Involvement

	FAMSTR[a,b]	PARED	TCHLDR	PARWORK	RACE	SEX	ACH	DISC	GRADE	YEARST	TQUAL	PARCOMF	TKNOCH	TALKHLP	R^2
Initial model	-.116*[b]	-.108*	.126*												.048
Full model	-.006	-.102*	.071*	.046	-.238*	-.029	-.055	.003	-.114*	.053	.072*	.071*	.238*	.211*	.286
	(-.138)[c]	(-.133)	(.141)	(.047)	(-.306)	(-.039)	(-.134)	(.020)	(-.195)	(-.029)	(.130)	(.114)	(.328)	(.296)	

[a]Variables are FAMSTR = one- or two-parent homes; PARED = schooling from less than high school (0) to graduate school (5); TCHLDR = teacher's leadership or lack of parent involvement confirmed by principal (0–4); PARWORK = no work (0) or work (1) outside home by parent; RACE = black (0) or white (1); SEX = male (0) or female (1); ACH = reading and math skills ranked by teacher (0–6); DISC = low (–1) or high (+1) discipline problems; GRADE = students' grade in school management (0–4); PARCOMF = parent feeling comfortable and welcome at school (1–4); TKNOCH = parent report that teacher knows child's individual learning needs (1-4); TALKHLP = teacher talked to parent about how to help child at home (0/1). The outcome "parents' reports" refers to the number and frequency of teacher requests for up to 12 techniques to involve parents in learning activities at home.

[b]Standardized regression coefficients are reported. $N = 1135$.

[c]Zero-order correlations are in parentheses.

*Indicates coefficient is significant at or beyond the .01 level.

ships. These interpersonal practices are: parent feels comfortable and welcomed at school (PARCOMF); parent reports that teacher knows child's individual learning needs (TKNOCH); and teacher talks to parent about how to help the child at home (TALKHLP). Separate analyses show that these variables are about equally important for black and white parents.

The percentage of variance explained in parents' reports of teachers' requests for their involvement improved markedly—from 5% to 30%—when we added detailed information on the actual practices that bring schools and families together. It is important, too, that even with teacher–parent interpersonal practices accounted for, *teacher leadership* in the use of specific practices continues to significantly affect parents' reports of their experiences with learning activities at home.

In previous research, the limited focus on marital status has veiled the importance of other variables that influence parents' interactions with their children and their children's schools. Single and married parents' reports about their experiences with parent involvement are influenced by many family and school factors, not simply by the categorical label of marital status.

Single and married parents' reports about what teachers ask them to do at home is one indicator of their treatment by the schools. The next two sections explore teachers' evaluations of single and married parents' abilities to conduct the requested activities and the quality of the home work that their children do.

TEACHERS' REPORTS OF SINGLE AND MARRIED PARENTS' HELPFULNESS AND FOLLOWTHROUGH

Parents' marital status is believed to influence teachers' opinions of parents and their children. Teachers were asked to rate the helpfulness and followthrough on home-learning activities of the parents of each student and the quality of homework completed by each student. In contrast to the laboratory study of Santrock and Tracy (1978) that asked teachers to rate hypothetical children from one- and two-parent homes, our questions were designed *not* to call teachers' attention to the students' living arrangements when the teachers rated parents and students. We were interested in whether, in a natural environment, teachers' evaluations were affected by parent marital status (identified by the parent) or other family characteristics and practices. It is likely that elementary-school teachers are aware of family living arrangements from information provided by parents on emergency cards each year, from informal exchanges with parents or children about their families, or from discussions with other teachers. However, our method for collecting information did not ask teachers to base their evaluations on the explicit criteria of the children's living arrangements.

Table 4 presents teachers' evaluations of the quality of involvement of single and married parents. The ratings of parent helpfulness and followthrough on learning activities at home ranged from $+1$ to -1, with a mean of .18 and a standard deviation of .70, indicating that, on average, parents were perceived as neither particularly helpful nor inept but more were helpful (35%) than not (17%). The comparisons in the first column of Table 4 show that teachers rated married parents significantly higher than single parents on helpfulness and followthrough on home-learning activities. The second column shows that better educated single and married parents received higher ratings from teachers on helpfulness. The difference in ratings was significant between low- versus high-educated married parents (.267 vs. .437) and single versus married high-educated parents (.302 vs. .437).

The third column offers important information about how teachers' practices affected their evaluations of parents' helpfulness. Teachers who were *leaders* in the use of parent involvement practices rated single, less-educated parents significantly higher in helpfulness and followthrough at home than did teachers who were *not leaders* in parent involvement (.366 vs. .102). The same pattern appeared for teachers' ratings of single, high-educated parents (.483 vs. .234). Less-educated married parents were considered less responsible assistants than more-educated married parents, regardless of the teachers' leadership in the use of parent involvement.

If we had not included teachers' practices in our comparisons, we would conclude that, regardless of education, teachers rate single parents as less cooperative and less reliable than married parents in assisting their children at home. What we see instead is that teachers' own practices of parent involvement influence their ratings of the quality of parental assistance. Teachers' frequent use of parent involvement practices reduces or eliminates the teachers' differential evaluations of single and married parents.

Table 5 presents the results of the initial and the better specified models. The regression analyses summarized in Table 5 show, as did the previous tables of simple mean scores, that there are significant independent effects of marital status, parents' education, and teacher leadership in parent involvement on teachers' ratings of their students' parents on helpfulness and followthrough at home. Although each variable has significant, independent effects, the three-variable model explains only 4% of the variance in teachers' reports of parent helpfulness.

On the second line of the table, other measures of family, student, and teacher characteristics that have been found important in other research on family–school connections are added to the basic model. These variables increase the explained variance to 23%. Most dramatically, student achievement levels and behavior *in school* affects how teachers evaluate the students' parents. Teachers rate parents more positively if their children

TABLE 4. Teachers' Estimates of the Quality of Parents' Responses to Requests for Involvement (Means, Standard Deviations, and Test Statistics from Multiple Comparisons of Mean Scores of Single vs. Married, Low vs. High-Educated Parents and Parents of Children in Classrooms of Confirmed Leader vs. Nonleader Teacher in Parent Involvement)

	Family structure		Parent education[a]		Teacher leadership in parent involvement		Other significant comparisons of means
Teachers' estimates of parents' helpfulness	Single parent	$\bar{X}$ .227 s.d. .712 N (255)	Low	$\bar{X}$ .174 s.d. .733 N (149)	Confirmed leader	$\bar{X}$ .366* s.d. .733 N (41)	Single vs. married, low education ($\bar{X}$ = .302 vs. .437*)
					Nonleader	$\bar{X}$ .102 s.d. .723 N (108)	Single vs. married, low education, in nonleader classroom ($\bar{X}$ = .102 vs. .260*)
			High	$\bar{X}$ .302 s.d. .679 N (106)	Confirmed leader	$\bar{X}$ .483* s.d. .738 N (29)	Single vs. married, high education in nonleader classroom ($\bar{X}$ = .234 vs. .436*)
					Nonleader	$\bar{X}$ .234 s.d. .647 N (77)	Low vs. high education, married, in nonleader classroom ($\bar{X}$ = .260 vs. .436*)
	Married parent	$\bar{X}$ .346* s.d. .660 N (813)	Low	$\bar{X}$ .267* s.d. .693 N (438)	Confirmed leader	$\bar{X}$ .291 s.d. .736 N (103)	
					Nonleader	$\bar{X}$ .260 s.d. .680 N (335)	
			High	$\bar{X}$ .437* s.d. .608 N (375)	Confirmed leader	$\bar{X}$ .444 s.d. .690 N (63)	
					Nonleader	$\bar{X}$ .436 s.d. .591 N (312)	

[a]Parent education is high if the respondent attended or graduated from postsecondary school; low if parent attended or graduated from high school only.
*T-test significant at or beyond the .05 level.

TABLE 5. Effects of Family, Student, and Teacher Characteristics
on Teacher Reports of Parent Helpfulness and Followthrough on Learning Activities at Home

	FAMSTR[a]	PARED	TCHLDR	PARWORK	RACE	SEX	ACH	DISC	GRADE	YEARST	TQUAL	PARCOMF	TKNOCH	TALKHLP	R^2
Initial model	.072*[b]	.131*	.135*												.039
Full model	.042	.049	.136*	.014	−.034	−.044	.343*	−.205*	−.099*	.104*	−.009	.041	.029	.056	.226
	(.081)[c]	(.131)	(.121)	(.027)	(.039)	(.025)	(.365)	(−.256)	(−.079)	(.079)	(.051)	(.092)	(.069)	(.050)	

[a]Variables are described in the footnote to Table 3. The outcome "teacher reports" in this table refers to the ratings by teachers of the parent of each student on the quality of parent help at home (scored −1/0/+1).
[b]Standardized regression coefficients are reported. $N = 1135$.
[c]Zero-order correlations are in parentheses.
*Indicates coefficient is significant at or beyond the .01 level.

are high achievers or well behaved in school. Children may be successful in school because their parents help them at home, or parents may give more help to children who are good students and easy to assist, or good students may be assumed by teachers to have good parents as part of a school/home "halo" effect.

Teachers of younger children and more experienced teachers tend to rate parents higher in helpfulness and followthrough than other teachers. Teachers of the lower elementary grades tend to use more parent involvement techniques, and more experienced teachers may be more aware and appreciative of how the efforts of parents supplement the efforts of teachers (Becker & Epstein, 1982a, b). Although race was not an important variable overall for explaining teachers' ratings of parent helpfulness, separate analyses of black and white parents revealed that marital status remained a modest but significant influence on the teachers' ratings of white parents but not of black parents. White, single parents were rated lower in helpfulness and followthrough than white, married parents, with all other variables in the model statistically controlled. White, single parents may be the most distinct group in terms of their marital status because proportionately more white than black parents are married.

These analyses show that it is mainly the characteristics and needs of students—not the simple category of parental marital status—that best explain teachers' evaluations of parents. But, teachers' leadership remained an important influence on their ratings of parents, even after all other variables were statistically taken into account. Teachers who frequently use parent involvement techniques in their regular teaching practice acknowledge the help they receive and view single and married parents in a more positive light than do other teachers. When teachers involve parents in their children's schoolwork on a regular basis, creating more family and school "overlap," they tend to report that the amount and quality of help from single parents is comparable to that of married parents. When teachers use frequent activities as part of their teaching practice, they help parents build better skills to assist their children at home. At the same time, these activities may help teachers develop more positive expectations and appreciation of parents. Teachers who keep schools and families more separate and do not make parents part of their regular teaching practice tend to promote the stereotype of single parents. They rate single parents' assistance and followthrough on learning activities at home lower in quality and quantity than that provided by married parents.

TEACHERS' REPORTS OF THE QUALITY OF HOMEWORK BY CHILDREN FROM ONE- AND TWO-PARENT HOMES

Teachers were asked to rate the quality of homework completed by each of their students. Researchers identified the children from one- and two-parent homes from data provided by parents. Teachers identified the students who were homework "stars" and homework "problems." Scores on the quality of homework ranged from +1 to −1, with a mean of −.01 and a standard deviation of .64, indicating that, on average, students were neither particularly outstanding nor inferior, with about equal numbers of homework stars (20%) and homework problems (21%). Teachers' ratings of children's homework are shown in Table 6 according to children's living arrangements in one- or two-parent homes, parents' education, and their teachers' leadership in the use of parent involvement.

The first column of Table 6 shows that students from two-parent homes were more often rated as "homework stars" and were less often viewed as "homework problems" than were students from one-parent homes. The measures in the second column show that these ratings were linked to parent education. Children whose mothers had little formal education were rated lower in the quality of their homework than other children in one-parent homes (.057 vs. −.101 for more- vs. less-educated mothers) and in two-parent homes (.157 vs. .050). Family socioeconomic status in Column 2 of Table 6 helps to explain teachers' evaluations of children in one- and two-parent homes, as has been reported before (Barton, 1981; Laosa & Siegel, 1982; Scott-Jones, 1983).

Teachers' practices of parent involvement are taken into account in Column 3 of the table. Teachers who were *not leaders* in parent involvement held significantly lower opinions of the quality of homework of children from single-parent homes than from married-parent homes, at both levels of parent education. The results suggest that children from less-educated, single-parent families face disadvantages in school that may be exacerbated by teachers' lack of leadership in organizing parent involvement in learning activities at home.

If estimates of homework quality reflect student achievement in general, children from one- and two-parent homes in teacher *leader* classrooms should have more similar grades and achievement test scores, after other important characteristics are taken into account. In classrooms of teachers who are *not leaders* in parent involvement, children from one-parent homes may do less well than children from two-parent homes in their report card grades and other school achievements.

The regression analyses in Table 7 show how teachers' ratings of the quality of students' homework are influenced by other parent, teacher, and student characteristics. On the first line of the table, the familiar three-variable model shows that marital status and parent education have significant independent effects on teacher ratings of student homework. Students from one-parent homes or whose parents have less education are given lower ratings on homework quality. Teacher leadership in parent involvement is not a significant independent influence on teachers' ratings of students, after the other variables are accounted for. The basic model,

TABLE 6. Teachers' Estimates of the Quality of Children's Homework Completion (Means, Standard Deviations, and Test Statistics from Multiple Comparisons of Mean Scores by Family Structure, Family Education, and Teacher Leadership in Parent Involvement)

Teachers' estimates of students' homework completion

Family structure		Parent education[a]		Teacher leadership in parent involvement		Other significant comparisons of means
Single parent	$\overline{X}$ −.035 s.d. .604 N (255)	Low	$\overline{X}$ −.101 s.d. .601 N (149)	Confirmed leader	$\overline{X}$ .073* s.d. .648 N (41)	Single vs. married, low education ($\overline{X}$ = −.101 vs. .050*)
				Nonleader	$\overline{X}$ −.167 s.d. .572 N (108)	Single vs. married, low education, in nonleader classroom ($\overline{X}$ = −.167 vs. .045*)
		High	$\overline{X}$ .057* s.d. .599 N (106)	Confirmed leader	$\overline{X}$ .207* s.d. .620 N (29)	
				Nonleader	$\overline{X}$ .001 s.d. .585 N (77)	
Married parent	$\overline{X}$ .100* s.d. .619 N (813)	Low	$\overline{X}$ .050* s.d. .640 N (438)	Confirmed leader	$\overline{X}$ .068 s.d. .630 N (103)	
				Nonleader	$\overline{X}$ .045 s.d. .644 N (335)	
		High	$\overline{X}$ .157* s.d. .589 N (375)	Confirmed leader	$\overline{X}$ .254 s.d. .595 N (63)	
				Nonleader	$\overline{X}$ .138 s.d. .587 N (312)	

[a]Parent education is high if the respondent attended or graduated from postsecondary school; low if parent attended or graduated from high school only.
*T-test significant at or beyond the .05 level.

TABLE 7. Effects of Family, Student, and Teacher Characteristics
on Teachers' Ratings of Children on Their Homework Completion

	FAMSTR[a]	PARED	TCHLDR	PARWORK	RACE	SEX	ACH	DISC	GRADE	YEARST	TQUAL	PARCOMF	TKNOCH	TALKHLP	R^2
Initial model	.085*[b]	.106*	.039												.021
Full model	.068*	.022	.042	−.024	−.107*	.058	.392*	−.183*	−.007	.050	−.038	−.024	.058	.055	.236
	(.097)[c]	(.114)	(.026)	(−.005)	(−.007)	(.132)	(.412)	(−.259)	(.001)	(.035)	(.021)	(−.005)	(.105)	(.018)	

[a]Variables are described in the footnote to Table 3. The outcome "teacher ratings" in this table refers to the evaluations by teachers of each student's homework (scored −1/0/ +1).
[b]Standardized regression coefficients are reported. $N = 1135$.
[c]Zero-order correlations are in parentheses.
*Indicates coefficient is significant at or beyond the .01 level.

however, explains only 2% of the variance in teacher ratings of student homework.

The second line of Table 7 shows that 24% of the variance in teacher ratings of student homework is explained by other measures. The most important variables are the work students do in class and their classroom behavior. Brighter students—whatever their behavior or other characteristics—were rated higher on the quality of their homework, and well-behaved students—whatever their ability or other characteristics—were given higher ratings on homework quality. Black students were rated significantly higher in homework quality, after achievement level and behavior were taken into account. Even with these highly influential variables taken into account, the quality of homework of students from two-parent homes was still rated slightly higher by some teachers than that of students from one-parent homes.

Several researchers have questioned whether teachers base children's grades and other ratings on criteria other than performance and whether their ratings reflect bias against children from single parent homes (Barton, 1981; Boyd & Parrish, 1985; Hammond, 1979; Lightfoot, 1978). Our data show that teachers base their judgments about the quality of children's homework mainly on the performance of the children, rather than on other unrelated criteria. There is little bias evident against children in one-parent homes. When they do occur, biased reports are more likely by teachers who have less contact with parents. If teachers do not ask for and guide parent involvement, single parents and their children are assumed to be less qualified than married parents and their children.

The simple lines of inquiry in Tables 2, 4, and 6 suggest that there may be important statistical interactions of marital status, parent education, and teachers' leadership in parent involvement in their effects of school and family communications. For example, when we graph the mean scores in Tables 2, 4, and 6 (not shown here), we see that *teacher leadership* matters more in determining teachers' ratings of single parents' helpfulness and followthrough on learning activities with their children at home, and on their ratings of the homework quality of children in one-parent homes. *Parent education* matters more for married parents on how teachers rate parents' helpfulness and children's homework. New research is needed on the consequences for student learning of these potentially important interactions.

The full models in Tables 3, 5, and 7 reveal other important patterns. *Parents' reports* of teachers' practices of parent involvement are influenced by several characteristics of students, teachers, parents, and family–school communications. *Teachers' reports* of parents are influenced especially by the teachers' interactions with the child in school. It often is said that children are reflections of their parents, but it also seems to work the other way. Parents are evaluated, in part, on the basis of their children's success and behavior in school. *Teachers' reports* of children are mainly determined by the children's school work. However, even after achievement level is taken into account, some teachers report that children from one-parent homes have more trouble completing homework than do children from two-parent homes. The analyses show clearly that the ratings that parents and teachers give each other are significantly affected by teachers' philosophies and practices of parent involvement.

On a related theme, in the full model we also found that whether or not mothers worked outside the home had no important effect on parents' reports about teachers, teachers' reports about parents, or teachers' reports about the quality of children's homework.

PARENTS' AWARENESS, KNOWLEDGE, AND EVALUATIONS OF TEACHERS

Are single and married parents equally aware of their children's instructional program? Is marital status an important variable for explaining parental receptivity to teachers' requests to help their children? Epstein (1986) showed that teachers' practices influenced parental reactions to their children's teachers and schools. For this chapter, we examined whether single and married parents react differently to teachers' efforts to involve and inform parents. The exploration of previous analyses showed that marital status had no significant effect on whether parents think the child's teacher works hard to get parents "interested and excited about helping at home." Rather, frequent experience with teachers' requests to become involved in learning activities at home had a strong effect on parent awareness of the teacher's efforts. Other variables—less education of parents, parents' belief that teachers know the individual needs of their children, and teachers' direct conversations with parents about helping their own child at home—also had significant, independent effects on parents' awareness of teachers' efforts to involve parents.

Similarly, teachers' frequent requests for parent involvement in learning activities at home—not marital status—had strong effects on single and married parents' reports that they get *many ideas* from teachers about how to help at home; that the teacher thinks parents *should help* at home; that they *know more* about the child's instructional program than they did in previous years; and that the teacher has positive *interpersonal skills* and high *teaching quality*.

OTHER REPORTS ABOUT SCHOOL FROM SINGLE AND MARRIED PARENTS

Other data collected from parents also help explain some of the results reported in the previous tables.

Single parents reported significantly more often than married parents that they spent more time assisting their children with homework but still did not have the "time and energy" to do what they believed the teacher expected. Single parents felt more pressure from teachers to become involved in their children's learning activities. It may be that their children required or demanded more attention or needed more help to stay on grade level. Or it may be that parents who were separated, divorced, or never married felt keenly their responsibility for their children and the demands on their time. Single parents divide their time among many responsibilities for family, work, and leisure that are shared in many two-parent homes (Glasser & Navarre, 1965; Shinn, 1978).

Requests from teachers for parents to help on home-learning activities may make more of an impression and may be more stressful for single parents (McAdoo, 1981). Our data show, however, that single parents respond successfully to teachers who involve all parents as part of their regular teaching practice. Like other parents, single parents who were frequently involved by the teacher felt that they increased their knowledge about the child's instructional program. Indeed, teachers who organize and guide home-learning activities may especially help single parents make efficient and effective use of often limited time. When teachers convey uniform expectations and guidance for involvement by all parents, single parents receive an important message about their continuing responsibility in their children's education.

Married parents spent significantly more days in the school as volunteers, as classroom helpers, and at PTA meetings than did single parents. Teachers may be more positive toward parents whom they meet and work with in the school building and classroom. These positive feelings may influence some teachers' ratings of the quality of parental assistance at home. An important fact is, however, that the teacher leaders—whose philosophy and practices emphasized parent involvement at home—*did not* give significantly lower ratings to single parents or less-educated parents on their helpfulness or followthrough on home-learning activities, despite those parents' lower involvement at the school building. Because many single parents work full- or part-time during the schoolday or have other demands on their time that keep them away from school, it is important for teachers to emphasize practices that involve all parents with their children's education at home. If all involvement occurs during school hours, single parents and working parents are excluded from school activities.

There were several measures on which there were no significant differences in the reports of single and married parents. Some common beliefs about single and married parents were not supported statistically. For example, single and married parents gave similar evaluations of the overall quality of their children's teachers, the extent to which the teacher shares the parent's goals for their child, their child's eagerness to talk about school, their child's level of tenseness about homework activities, the appropriateness of the amount and kinds of homework that their children's teachers assigned, and the frequency of most communications (e.g., notes, phone calls, and memos) from the school to the home. These findings support Snow's 1982 conclusion that single and married parents had similar contacts with teachers, similar evaluations of teachers, and that socioeconomic status was more predictive than marital status of parents' contacts with teachers. We show, however, the SES is not the most important variable. Rather, school and family communications of several types reduce or eliminate the importance of marital status and SES.

Marital status is not significantly related to the severity of discipline problems in class. The belief that children from one-parent homes tend to be disruptive in school may be one of the "myths" that has perpetuated from earlier studies based on "special problem" populations and from studies that did not include measures of student, family, and teacher characteristics and practices—all of which are more important influences than marital status on children's classroom behavior. In our study, children's disciplinary problems in the classroom are significantly correlated negatively with gender ($r = -.262$), academic achievement ($r = -.147$), and whether the child likes to talk about school at home ($r = -.124$), as might be expected. Male students, low-achieving students, and those who do not like to talk about school or homework with their parents are more likely than other students to be disciplinary problems in class. But parents' marital status is not significantly associated with behavior problems in class ($r = -.056$).

Marital status is not correlated with parents' willingness to help at home, feeling welcome at the school, or with reports that someone at home reads regularly with the child. Indeed, single *and* married parents are remarkably positive about the general quality of their children's elementary schools and teachers (Epstein, 1986). As in earlier reports by Eiduson (1982), Keniston (1977), and Sanick and Maudlin (1986), our survey shows that, like married parents, single parents are concerned about their children's education, work with their children, and are generally positive about their children's elementary schools and teachers.

SUMMARY AND DISCUSSION

Researchers have contributed three types of information on single parents. First, *descriptive reports* offer statistics about single parents and their children. Many reports have focused on the dramatic increase over the years in the prevalence of single parents, the number of children in single-parent homes, racial differences in marital patterns, and the economic disparities of single versus two-parent homes, especially single-mother homes versus other family arrangements (Bane, 1976; Cherlin, 1981; Newberger & Associates, 1986; Weitzman, 1985). It is important to continue to document and monitor the trends in separation, divorce, the numbers of children affected, and the emergence and increase of special cases such as teenage single parents (Mott Foundation, 1981) and never-married parents (U.S. Bureau of the Census, 1982).

Second, *analytic studies* of the effects of family structure on children or parents go beyond descriptive statistics to consider *family conditions and processes* that affect family members. Research of this type has measured a range of family-life variables—such as socioeconomic status, family history, family practices, and attitudes such as parental commitment to their children (Adams, 1982; Bane, 1976; Epstein, 1983; Furstenburg, Nord, Peterson, & Zill, 1983; Marjoribanks, 1979; Svanum, Bringle, & McLaughlin, 1982; Zill, 1983). These studies increase our understanding of the dynamics of family life under different social and economic conditions.

Third, *integrative, ecological studies* of the effects of family structure on children and parents go beyond the boundaries of family conditions to include *other institutions* that affect family members (Bronfenbrenner, 1979; Epstein, 1987; Leichter, 1974; Litwak & Meyer, 1974; Santrock & Tracy, 1978). These studies show that effects of family structure are, in large part, explained by other variables, including teachers' practices of parent involvement and other measures of family and school interaction.

The present study contributes new knowledge based on data from parents and teachers about single parents and their children's schools:

1. *Single parents are not a single group.* Single parents are highly diverse in their education, family size, family resources, occupational status, confidence in their ability to help their children, and other family practices that concern their children. The diversity in single-parent homes means that we cannot fully understand families by measuring only the simple category of marital status.

2. *There is diversity in teachers' practices that concern families.* Some teachers' philosophies and practices lead them toward more positive attitudes about single parents and about how all parents can assist the teacher as knowledgeable partners in their children's education. Some teachers' practices exemplify the theory that families and schools are overlapping spheres of influence for children, and other teachers' practices exemplify the belief that families and schools are better off when teachers and parents conduct separate and different activities.

Some teachers involve all or most parents successfully. Other teachers demand more but expect less of single parents and their children. Single parents' abilities to help their children may be affected by the teachers' abilities to inform and direct the parent about productive activities for parent involvement at home.

Santrock and Tracy (1978) found that teachers rated hypothetical children from two-parent homes higher on positive traits and lower on negative traits than children from one-parent homes. Levine (1982) reported
that teachers had lower expectations for children from one-parent homes.
In actual school settings, we found that teachers differed in their evaluations of children from one- and two-parent homes. Teachers tend to rate
children from one-parent homes lower on the quality of their homework,
and teachers who were *not leaders* made even greater distinctions between
children from one- and two-parent homes.

3. *Teacher leadership, not parent marital status, influenced parents' knowledge about the school program and the teachers' efforts.* Single and married
parents whose children were in the classrooms of teachers who were
leaders in parent involvement were more aware of teachers' efforts in parent
involvement, improved their understanding of their children's school programs, and rated teachers' interpersonal and teaching skills higher than
did parents of children in other teachers' classrooms.

Evidence has been accumulating in many studies that daily practices
are more important than static measures of family structure for understanding children's experiences. This has often been interpreted to refer to
practices that parents might conduct on their own. But parent involvement
in school is not the parents' responsibility alone. Contexts influence practice. Kriesberg (1967) found a neighborhood effect on parents' practices.
He noted that disadvantaged single mothers in middle-class neighborhoods gave more educational support to their children than similar
mothers in poor neighborhoods. Our study reports a school effect on parents' practices. Teachers' practices that support and guide parents boost the
involvement of all parents, including single parents — the same parents that
other teachers believe cannot or will not help their children.

4. *Research on single parents and their children must include measures of
family and school structure and processes that affect the interactions of parents,
teachers, and students.* Marital status will look more important than it is
unless studies include measures of the teachers' practices. In this study,
teachers' approaches to parent involvement, other teacher, parent, and
student characteristics, and specific family–school communications were
more important and more manipulable variables than marital status or
mother's education for explaining parents' and teachers' evaluations of
each other. Studies of school and family connections must go beyond simple structural labels such as marital status and education and include measures of the practices and attitudes of parents, teachers, and students.
During the school years, it is necessary to measure the characteristics of all
overlapping institutions that influence student behavior and particularly
the family and the school. This is especially true for particular outcomes
such as student learning and development or parental understanding and
practices concerning their children as students.

5. *Schools' interactions with families need to change because families are changing.* Teachers must consider how they perceive and interact with single parents in order to minimize bias and maximize the support that all parents give their children.

Family members may recover relatively rapidly from the disruption caused by divorce or separation (Bane, 1976; Hetherington, Cox, & Cox, 1978; Zill, 1983). But teachers who favor traditional families may have difficulty dealing with families who differ from their "ideal." Some administrators and teachers still consider the primary, two-parent family as the model by which other families should be judged (Bernard, 1984). The primary family—two natural parents and their children—may be an ideal type but it is no longer the "typical" family for all school-aged children. In 1980, 63% of white children and 27% of black children lived in primary families; 14% of all white children and 43% of all black children lived in one-parent homes with their mothers. Most of the others lived in "blended" families in which at least one parent had remarried (Hernandez & Meyers, 1986). Demographic trends indicate that the one-parent home will be "the new norm" as over half of all children will live in a one-parent home for some of their school years. During that time, teachers' practices to assist and involve all parents can help reduce single parents' stress about their children's well-being and help children's learning and attitudes about school and homework.

Schools need to change their understanding of single parents in order to better meet the parents' concerns and children's needs. Most suggestions about how the school should assist single parents and their children focus on providing psychological services, family therapy, discussion groups, or individual counseling for children who experience divorce in their families (Brown, 1980). Although discussion or therapy sessions may help children adjust to family disruptions, this study suggests that a more important general direction is to assist all parents in how to help their children at home in ways that will improve their children's success in school. This includes helping parents make productive use of small amounts of time at home on school-related skills, activities, and decisions.

School policies and practices can minimize or exaggerate the importance of family structure. Although school practices cannot solve the serious social and economic problems that single parents often face, our data show that teachers play a pivotal role in the lives of children from one-parent homes and in their parents' lives as well.

ACKNOWLEDGMENTS

This research was supported by grant NIE-G-83-0002, from the National Institute of Education (now the Office of Educational Research and Improvement) of the U.S. Department of Education. The opinions expressed by the author do not necessarily reflect the position or policy of the OERI, and no official endorsement by the agency should be inferred. An earlier version of the paper was presented at the annual meeting of the American Sociological Association, 1984. The author is grateful to Henry Jay Becker, John Hollifield, Linda Gottfredson, and Gary Natriello for their helpful comments on earlier drafts.

REFERENCES

Adams, B. (1982). *Conceptual and policy issues in the study of family socialization in the United States.* Paper presented at the annual meeting of the American Educational Research Association.

Baker, D. P., & Stevenson, D. L. (1986). Mothers' strategies for children's school achievement: Managing the transition to high school. *Sociology of Education, 59*, 156–166.

Bane, M. J. (1976). *Here to stay: American families in the twentieth century.* New York: Basic Books.

Barton, W. A. (1981). *The effects of one-parentness on student achievement.* Unpublished doctoral dissertation, Pennsylvania State University.

Becker, H. J., & Epstein, J. L. (1982a). Parent involvement: A study of teacher practices. *The Elementary School Journal, 83*, 85–102.

Becker, H. J., & Epstein, J. L. (1982b). *Influences on teachers' use of parent involvement.* Report 324. Baltimore: The Johns Hopkins University Center for Social Organization of Schools.

Bernard, J. M. (1984). Divorced families and the schools. In J. H. Cansen (Ed.), *Family therapy with school related problems* (pp. 91–101). Rockville, MD: Aspen Systems Corporation.

Blanchard, R. W., & Biller, H. B. (1971). Father availability and academic performance among third-grade boys. *Developmental Psychology, 4*, 301–305.

Boyd, D. A., & Parish, T. S. (1985). *An examination of academic achievement in light of familial configuration.* Paper presented at the annual meeting of the AERA.

Bronfenbrenner, U. (1979). *The ecology of human development.* Cambridge, MA: Harvard University Press.

Brown, B. F. (1980). A study of the school needs of children from one-parent families. *Phi Delta Kappan, 61*, 537–540.

Carew, J., & Lightfoot, S. L. (1979). *Beyond bias: Perspectives on classrooms.* Cambridge, MA: Harvard University Press.

Cherlin, A. J. (1981). *Marriage, divorce, remarriage.* Cambridge, MA: Harvard University Press.

Clay, P. L. (1981). *Single parents and the public schools: How does the partnership work?* National Committee for Citizens in Education, Columbia, Maryland.

Coleman, J. S. (1974). *Power and structure in society.* New York: W. W. Norton.

Coleman, J. S., Campbell, E. Q., Hobson, C. J., McPartland, J. M., Mood, A., Weinfield, F. D., & York, R. L. (1966). *Equal educational opportunity.* Washington DC: U.S. Government Printing Office.

Dauber, S. L., & Epstein, J. L. (1989). *Parents' attitudes and practices of involvement in inner-city elementary and middle schools.* CREMS Report 33. Baltimore: The Johns Hopkins University Center for Research on Elementary and Middle Schools.

Dokecki, P. R., & Maroney, R. M. (1983). To strengthen all families: A human development and community value framework. In R. Haskins & D. Adams (Eds.), *Parent education and public policy* (pp. 40–64). Norwood, NJ: Ablex.

Eiduson, B. T. (1982). Contemporary single mothers. In L. G. Katz (Ed.), *Current topics in early childhood education* (pp. 65–76). Norwood, NJ: Ablex.

Engan-Barker, D. (1986). *Family and education: The concepts of family failure and the role it plays in national educational and family policy — A review of the literature.* Masters of arts dissertation, University of Minnesota.

Epstein, J. L. (1983). Longitudinal effects of person-family-school interactions on student outcomes. In A. Kerckhoff (Ed.), *Research in sociology of education and socialization* (Vol. 4, pp. 101–128). Greenwich: JAI Press.

Epstein, J. L. (1986). Reactions of parents to teacher practices of parent involvement. *The Elementary School Journal, 87* (January), 277–294.

Epstein, J. L. (1987). Toward a theory of family-school connections: Teacher practices and parent involvement across the school years. In K. Hurrelmann, F. Kaufmann, & F. Losel (Eds.), *Social intervention: Potential and constraints* (pp. 121–136). New York: DeGruyter.

Epstein, J. L. (1989). *Schools in the center: School, family, peer, and community connections for more effective middle grade schools and students.* Paper prepared for the Carnegie Task Force for the Education of Young Adolescents. Baltimore MD: Johns Hopkins University Center for Research on Elementary and Middle Schools.

Epstein, J. L. (1990a). Effects of teacher practices of parent involvement on student achievement in reading and math. In S. Silvern (Ed.), *Literacy through family, community, and school interaction.* Greenwich CT: JAI Press.

Epstein, J. L. (1990b). School and family connections: Theory, research and implications for integrating sociologies of education and family. *Marriage and Family Review* (Summer, 1990).

Epstein, J. L., & Becker, H. J. (1982). Teacher reported practices of parent involvement: Problems and possibilities. *The Elementary School Journal, 83* 103–113 (November).

Epstein, J. L., & McPartland, J. M. (1979). Authority structures. In H. Walberg (Ed.), *Educational environments and effects* (pp. 293–312). Berkeley CA: McCutcheon.

Furstenburg, F. F., Jr., & Seltzer, J. A. (1983). *Encountering divorce: Children's responses to family dissolution and reconstitution.* Paper presented at the annual meeting of the American Sociological Association.

Furstenburg, F. F., Nord, C. W., Peterson, J. L., & Zill, N. (1983). The life course of children of divorce: Marital disruption and parental contact. *American Sociological Review, 48,* 656–668.

Garfinkle, I., & McLanahan, S. S. (1986). Single mothers and their children: A new American dilemma. Washington, DC: Urban Institute Press.

Garbarino, J. (1982). *Children and families in the social environment.* New York: Aldine.

Glasser, P., & Navarre, E. (1965). Structural problems of the one parent family. *Journal of Social Issues, 21,* 98–109.

Guidubaldi, J., & Perry, J. D. (1984). Divorce, socioeconomic status, and children's cognitive social competence at school entry. *American Journal of Orthopsychiatry, 54,* 459.

Glick, P. C. (1979). Children of divorced parents in demographic perspectives. *Journal of Social Issues, 35,* 170–182.

Hanson, S. L., & Ginsburg, A. (1986). *Gaining ground: Values and high school success.* Washington, DC. Decision Resources Corporation.

Hammond, J. M. (1979). A comparison of elementary children from divorced and intact families. *Phi Delta Kappan,* November, p. 219.

Hetherington, E. M., & Camara, K. A. (1984). Families in transition: The process of dissolution and reconstitution. In R. D. Parke (Ed.), *Review of child development research: Volume 7* (pp. 398–440). Chicago: University of Chicago Press.

Hetherington, E. M., Camara, K. A., & Featherman, D. L. (1981). *Cognitive performance, school learning, and achievement of children for one parent households.* Washington, DC: National Institute of Education.

Hetherington, E. M., Cox, M., & Cox, R. (1978). The aftermath of divorce. In J. H. Stevens, Jr. & M. Matthews (Eds.), *Mother-child, father-child relations* (pp. 149–176). Washington, DC: National Association for the Education of Young Children.

Hernandez, D. J., & Myers, D. E. (1986). *Children and their extended families since World War II.* Paper presented at the annual meeting of the Population Association of America. San Francisco.

Kamerman, S. B., & Hayes, C. D. (1982). *Families that work: Children in a changing world.* Washington, DC: National Academy Press.

Kelly, F. J., North, J., & Zingle, H. (1965). The relation of the broken home to subsequent school behaviors. *Alberta Journal of Educational Research, 11,* 215–219.

Keniston, K., & the Carnegie Council on Children. (1977). *All our children: The American family under pressure.* New York: Harcourt Brace Jovanovich.

Kriesberg, L. (1967). Rearing children for educational achievement in fatherless families. *Journal of Marriage and the Family, 29,* 288–301.

Kurdek, L. A., & Blisk, D. (1983). Dimensions and correlates of mothers' divorce experiences. *Journal of Divorce, 6,* 1–24.

Laosa, L. M. (1983). Parent education, cultural pluralism, and public policy. In R. Haskins & D. Adams (Eds.), *Parent education and public policy* (pp. 331–345). Norwood, NJ: Ablex.

Laosa, L. M., & Sigel, I. E. (1982). *Families as learning environments for children.* New York: Plenum Press.

Leichter, Hope Jensen (Ed.). (1974). *The family as educator.* New York: Teachers College Press.

Leler, H. (1983). Parent education and involvement in relation to the schools and to parents of school-aged children. In R. Haskins & D. Adams (Eds.), *Parent education and public policy* (pp. 114–180). Norwood, NJ: Ablex.

Levine, E. R. (1982). *What teachers expect of children from single parent families.* Paper presented at the annual meeting of the American Educational Research Association, April, New York.

Lightfoot, S. L. (1978). *Worlds apart: Relationships between families and schools.* New York: Basic Books.

Litwak, E., & Meyer, H. J. (1974). *School, family, and neighborhood: The theory and practice of school-community relations.* New York: Columbia University Press.

Marjoribanks, K. (1979). *Families and their learning environments: An empirical analysis.* London: Routledge & Kegan Paul.

Marotz-Bader, R., Adams, G. R., Bueche, N., Munro, B., & Munro, G. (1979). Family form or family process? Reconsidering the deficit family model approach. *The Family Coordinator, 28,* 5–14.

Masnick, G., & Bane, M. J. (1980). *The nation's families: 1960–1990.* Cambridge MA: Joint Center for Urban Studies of MIT and Harvard University.

McAdoo, H. (1981). Levels of stress in single black employed mothers of school-aged children. Washington, DC: Howard University (mimeo).

McDill, E. L., & Rigsby, L. (1973). *Structure and process in secondary schools: The academic impact of educational climates.* Baltimore: Johns Hopkins University Press.

Milne, A., Myers, D., Rosenthal, A., & Ginsburg, A. (1986). Working mothers and the educational achievement of school children. *Sociology of Education, 59,* 125–139.

Mott Foundation. (1981). *Teenage pregnancy: A critical family issue.* Flint, MI: The Charles Stewart Mott Foundation.

National Public Radio (NPR). (1980). *Single parent families,* Parts 1–4, programs 272–275 (November). Washington, DC: National Public Radio.

Newberger, C. M., Melnicoe, L. H., & Newberger, E. H. (1986). The American family in crisis: Implications for children. *Current Problems in Pediatrics, XVI,* Number 12. Chicago: Yearbook Medical Publishers.

Ogbu, John V. (1974). *The next generation: An ethnology of education in an urban neighborhood.* New York: Academic Press.

Parsons, T. (1959). The school class as a social system: Some of its functions in American society. *Harvard Educational Review, 29,* 297–318.

Sanick, M. M., & Maudlin, T. (1986). Single vs. 2-parent families: A comparison of mothers' time. *Family Relations, 35,* 53.

Santrock, J. W., & Tracy, R. L. (1978). Effects of children's family structure on the development of stereotypes by teachers. *Journal of Educational Psychology, 20,* 754–757.

Scott-Jones, D. (1983). *One-parent families and their children's achievement.* University of Pittsburgh (mimeo).

Sewell, W. H., & Hauser, R. M. (1975). *Occupation and earnings: Achievement in the early career.* New York: Academic Press.

Shinn, M. (1978). Father absence and children's cognitive development. *Psychological Bulletin, 85,* 295–324.

Snow, M. B. (1982). Characteristics of families with special needs in relation to school (AEL Report Series). Charleston, WV: Appalachian Educational Laboratory.

Svanum, S., Bringle, R. G., & McLaughlin, J. E. (1982). Father absence and cognitive performance on a large sample of six-to-eleven-year old children. *Child Development, 53,* 136–143.

U.S. Bureau of the Census. (1982). *Marital status and living arrangements: March 1982.* Current Population Report Series. Washington, DC: U.S. Government Printing Office.

U.S. House of Representatives. (1986). *Divorce: A fact sheet.* June 17, 1986. Washington, DC: Select Committee on Children, Youth, and Families.

Waller, W. (1932). *The sociology of teaching.* New York: Russell and Russell.

Weber, M. (1947). *The theory of social and economic organization.* New York: Oxford University Press.

Weitzman, L. (1985). *The divorce revolution: The unexpected social and economic consequences for women and children in America.* New York: Free Press.

Zajonc, R. (1976). Family configuration and intelligence. *Science, 192,* 227–236.

Zill, N. (1983). *Perspectives: Mental health of school children from single-parent families.* Paper presented at the National Conference of Single Parents and the Schools (March), Washington, DC.

CHAPTER SIX

The Changing Contours of the Teaching Profession

BARBARA HEYNS

Teaching, as a profession, has changed considerably in the last several decades. Moreover, by policy design, the profession is likely to undergo even more extensive changes during the next decade. Educational reform has become centered on the teaching force, rather than the schools; accountability, examinations for certification and recertification, and salary incentives are among the most frequently mentioned proposals to enhance the quality and quantity of teachers. Moreover, dramatic increases in educational policy activity by the states have created an altered environment for teachers. States have mandated changes in the standards and legal requirements for graduation and instituted minimum competency tests, causing modifications in both the curriculum and teacher recruitment and staffing patterns. States require exams for certification and recertification, while grappling with career ladders and increased salaries for teaching. Finally, the emphasis on increasing professionalism and enhancing the status of teachers is likely to create change in the profession.

These policy changes are inspired by two central concerns: teacher shortages and perceptions of declining teacher quality, both of which are argued to be the result of teacher attrition. This chapter will analyze patterns of teacher attrition during the last decade and address these issues with a new and fascinating longitudinal data set. First, I will examine changes in the level of attrition as a factor shaping the profession. Second, I

This paper was written while the author was a Fellow at the Center for Advanced Study in the Behavioral Sciences, Stanford. It was funded by the National Science Foundation (SES-8512580).

BARBARA HEYNS • Department of Sociology, New York University, New York, New York 10003.

will examine patterns of talent erosion in education, asking in particular whether or not we should be concerned with declines in teacher quality. Finally, I will discuss recent proposals for reform that include enhancing professional status and rewards. I will argue that the schools losing the most teachers are not the poorest or most disadvantaged schools but are among the best. Teacher attrition has a paradoxical relationship to both school quality and teacher quality. Professionalization, at least in the short run, may improve working conditions for teachers but have no impact on rates of retention.

An era of declining enrollments and budget cuts appears to be ending, and a teacher shortage has been rediscovered; one untapped source of manpower is the "reserve pool" of former teachers. Estimates of the number of former teachers and the likelihood of their returning to the classroom are the basis of calculations of the size of the reserve pool. Former teachers are alleged to have been the best and the brightest members of the teaching corps; their exodus is assumed to be an ominous indictment of public education. For those intent on reforming schools, high rates of attrition imply a general deterioration of education. The former teacher in these accounts is a burnt-out survivor or perhaps a self-serving veteran pursuing a lucrative salary in the private sector. Without doubt, policies that promote retention and enhance the professional stature of teachers are long overdue. Yet most of the discussion of attrition is premised on *ad hoc* myths about former teachers, designed to fit the policy prescriptions at hand, rather than one serious investigation.

One perspective on the teaching shortage views it as largely ephemeral because there is a large, untapped reserve pool of former teachers (Wells, 1987). If we imagine that former teachers are waiting in the wings, eager to return to the classroom, the prospect that the teaching shortage will approach crisis proportions dims. Accepting the "warm body" theory of manpower planning, we need only count former teachers to estimate the reserve pool. The mythical former teacher resembles a young housewife, baking brownies and waiting patiently for the right moment or proper inducements to return. Alternatively, high rates of attrition among qualified teachers are viewed as symptomatic of a general decline in the quality of education. Good teachers are seen as leaving a sinking ship in droves. The former teacher is described as an idealist, disillusioned by bureaucracy and administrative interference. Although such examples are obviously caricatures, they evoke the range of mythical figures surfacing in public policy discussion. Although each of these prototypes can be found among former teachers, the reality is more diverse than such simple stereotypes suggest.

The limitations of available data have contributed to the myths unfolding about former teachers. Data to dispel such myths, at least partially, are not available. In the spring of 1986, the fifth wave of the National Longitudinal Study (NLS-72) of the high-school seniors in 1972 was fielded; along with an extensive follow-up survey of all respondents, a special supplement was sent to all the respondents who identified themselves as either present or former teachers or as having been trained to be teachers.[1]

The NLS-72 provides a unique opportunity to study the career dynamics of teaching. It is the first national survey of teachers encompassing a full 14 years of school and work experience. The sample is representative of high-school seniors in 1972; it was not selected to represent teachers or students in education. NLS-72 allows an examination of the development of teaching careers from an early stage and to follow the students who eventually became teachers, as well as those who did not. It allows us to compare students who aspired to be teachers while still in college with those who chose teaching somewhat later in their lives; to contrast the students who entered teaching directly, and for whom teaching was their first or only job, with those who became teachers by a more circuitous route. In particular, it allows us to compare those teachers who were still teaching in 1986 with those who had left the field.

TRENDS IN ATTRITION[2]

Given the amount of attention devoted to teacher retention in the popular press, one might assume that high rates of attrition were a new phenomenon and that teachers were currently leaving the schools at record rates. It is ironic that teacher attrition has become a national policy issue at a time when retention has improved (Grissmer & Kirby, 1987; National Education Association, 1982, 1986; Talbert, 1986; Weaver, 1983). The predominant trend has been changes in the numbers entering the profession, not the number leaving. For most of the last decade, jobs were scarce in education. Each year, the number and proportion of students aspiring to

[1]The initial interviews for the NLS-72 were conducted in the spring of 1972. Over 20,000 high-school students participated, providing data on their backgrounds and expectations for the future. These students were reinterviewed in the fall of 1973, 1974, 1976, and 1979, and, most recently, in the spring of 1986. The entire sample, irrespective of background or occupational choice, completed extensive work histories and gave detailed information on their educational, marital, and personal experiences at each interview. All those who had majored in education, expected to become a teacher, were certified to teach, or taught before 1980 were included in the NLS-72 fifth wave. Respondents who were identified as present or former teachers or who had been trained to be teachers were sent a supplementary teaching questionnaire. The response rate for the entire cohort was 88.6%; for the teaching pool, the response rate was 91.8%. The response rate to the second stage was 86.0% of those eligible, or 1,147 individuals. All tables and percentages cited in the text are weighted to compensate for sampling probabilities and nonresponse on both surveys. Information on the design of the original cohort sample and the first four waves can be found in Riccobono, Henderson, Burkheimer, Place, & Levinson (1981). For details of the sampling design for the fifth wave, see Tourangeau et al. (1987); for details on the teaching supplement, see Sebring et al. (1987).
[2]Portions of the research to be reported were published in a 1989 paper entitled "Educational Defectors: A First Look at Teacher Attrition in the NLS," Educational Researcher, 17 (3), 24–32.

teach or enrolling in teacher training programs declined. Since 1975, the profession has aged. In 1976, *less* than three-fourths (72.8%) of all teachers had taught for 5 or more years; in 1986, 9 out of 10 public school teachers (90.8%) had 5 or more years experience (National Education Association, 1987).

Attrition rates in education have long been relatively high, particularly in the first 3 or 4 years of teaching (Heyns, 1972; Lortie, 1975). However, there is little evidence that they are increasing. Although there are no national data truly comparable to the National Longitudinal Study, there are good reasons to believe that attrition has declined since the early 1960s. Using census data from 1970, Talbert (1986) estimated that 63% of those teaching in 1965 were still teaching in 1970. Among young teachers, those who were 25 years of age or less, about half taught in both 1965 and 1970, defined as the stable teaching force. The estimated rate of attrition among men under 25 years of age was .48; for young women of the same age, it was .50.

Comparable figures for the NLS-72 cohort suggest substantially less attrition. For teachers employed between 1977 and 1980, Table 1 presents the proportion teaching 5 years later, by year, separately for men and for women. In no year were the rates of attrition for either men or women as high as those calculated by Talbert for the earlier period. These comparisons suggest that retention rates have improved over the last 12 to 15 years and improved more dramatically for women than for men, at least among young teachers.

There are numerous reasons why declines in attrition among teachers should not be surprising, particularly among young cohorts. The scarcity of teaching positions in the 1970s may have convinced many teachers to

TABLE 1. Proportions of National Longitudinal Study Sample Teaching between 1976–1980, by Year, and 5 Years Later, by Sex

NLS-72 teachers[a]	Male teachers	Female teachers	Total
Proportion of those teaching in 1976–1977 who also taught in 1981–1982	53.7	65.6	62.9
Proportion of those teaching in 1977–1978 who also taught in 1982–1983	59.5	61.1	60.7
Proportion of those teaching in 1978–1979 who also taught in 1983–1984	61.7	62.8	62.6
Proportion of those teaching in 1979–1980 who also taught in 1984–1985	72.9	68.9	69.9
Census[a]			
Proportion of those <25 still teaching 5 years later 1965–1970	.50	.48	.49

[a]Ninety-five percent of the NLS cohort had turned 25 by the end of 1979.
Source: Talbert (1986).

hold onto jobs for longer than they would otherwise have done. Women's labor force participation has increased for all age groups, regardless of marital status or family responsibilities. Couples have deferred both marriage and parenthood longer than was true in the past; high divorce rates may also boost labor force participation among women, despite the demands of child rearing. It has been claimed that as new and more rewarding careers open up for women, the teaching profession will necessarily be depleted of talent. Increasing rates of retention, however, imply that women are persisting in or returning to the careers that they have chosen in large numbers as well.

ATTRITION RATES IN THE NATIONAL LONGITUDINAL STUDY

Panel data for teachers allows one to estimate both entry and attrition rates more precisely than can be done with employment data alone. It is estimated that between one-fourth to one-third of all education majors do not enter the profession after they are trained. Calculations of the number of teachers in the reserve pool at any point in time clearly depend on assumptions about what happens to students who are not hired in their first or second year after graduation. Table 2 presents the entry rates for this cohort during the 1976–1986 decade. The pool of teachers available for hire in 1976 consisted of the entire sample of trained NLS-72 teachers, representing 211,000 students. In 1986, 54,100 students, or 26%, had never accepted or were never offered a teaching job. In each intervening year, the numbers of first entrants depletes the original pool as teachers are hired. By far the largest entry rate is the first year of this cohort's teaching career, 1976–1977; however, as Table 2 makes clear, entry rates stabilize after 3 or 4

TABLE 2. Pattern of First Entry by Date: National Longitudinal Survey, 1972

Date	Total pool of trained teachers with no entry at beginning of period	Number teaching for the first time during period	Entry rate[a]
1976–1977	211,587	66,262	.3132
1977–1978	145,327	30,426	.2094
1978–1979	114,901	15,835	.1378
1979–1980	99,066	21,587	.2179
1980–1981	77,479	4,889	.0631
1981–1982	72,590	3,006	.0414
1982–1983	69,584	2,912	.0419
1983–1984	66,672	3,432	.0515
1984–1985	63,240	3,323	.0526
1985–1986	59,917	5,819	.0971

[a]The entry rate is calculated as the ratio of first entrants during a given year to the pool at the beginning of the period.

TABLE 3. Pattern of First Exit by Date, NLS-72

Date	Total teaching force at specific dates	Number of teachers leaving for the first time at year's end	Proportion leaving
1976–1977	66,262	5,924	.0894
1977–1978	90,764	7,853	.0865
1978–1979	98,745	22,381	.2267
1979–1980	98,617	10,617	.1077
1980–1981	96,982	9,887	.0981
1981–1982	94,430	8,647	.0916
1982–1983	92,683	8,930	.0963
1983–1984	89,114	3,964	.0445
1984–1985	92,092	6,998	.0760
1985–1986	91,970	—	—

years at between 4% to 5% of those remaining. Although the numbers of first-entry teachers dwindle as the pool is depleted, new teachers were drawn from those initially trained throughout the decade.

Table 3 presents a parallel "career table" for teachers leaving the profession for the first time during the decade, by year of exit. The annual attrition rates tend to decline as the cohort ages, but they remain substantial throughout the decade.[3] After the initial 2 or 3 years, attrition, like entry, stabilizes at between 4% and 10% for this cohort. Survival rates, based on years of experience and sex are presented in Table 4. The rates are calculated only for those who could have taught the prescribed number of years; hence, the probabilities reflect attrition after a fixed number of years but not at a specific date. For the total sample of teachers, the probability of teaching 2 consecutive years was .87. Nearly half, 46%, had left teaching at least once by the end of their fifth year. Rates of first attrition are quite similar for men and for women. Women are, however, much more likely than men to reenter at a later date and therefore more likely to be teaching in 1986.

Teacher attrition and reentry during the decade can be viewed as a series of events, in which experienced teachers are employed during specific time periods with specific probabilities. Each time a teacher enters,

[3]The reasons for the inexplicably high attrition in 1979 are probably threefold. First, this was the year in which NLS-72 college graduates in the class of 1976 would have ended their first 3-year teaching contract. Second, 1979–1980 was a year of particularly high reductions in force in particular states. Grissmer and Kirby (1987) estimated rates of attrition nearly three times larger than usual for 1980, based on files constructed from state data. Third, NLS-72 work history data for the early years were not based on the 1986 interviews, which only included jobs held since 1979. The earlier NLS panels asked questions that were not strictly comparable. Combining the two different data sets may have artificially inflated attrition rates in 1979–1980. It is possible that some of the teachers "leaving" education in 1979 actually left somewhat earlier and that the attrition rates in the initial years are underestimated.

TABLE 4. Survival Rates for NLS-72 Cohort,
Consecutive Years of Experience, by Sex

Proportion still teaching after specific year of experience	Male	Female	Total	[N]a
First	.87	.83	.87	[761]
Second	.79	.73	.77	[748]
Third	.66	.61	.64	[730]
Fourth	.61	.54	.59	[717]
Fifth	.56	.49	.54	[706]
Sixth	.49	.48	.49	[683]
Seventh	.41	.41	.41	[595]
Eighth	.38	.39	.38	[517]
Ninth	.38	.37	.38	[351]

aThe number of cases depends on date of first entry; these rates exclude reentry. The probability of surviving the fifth year, for example, is calculated only for those having entered more than 6 years before.

leaves, or reenters teaching, an event is observed with a specific probability; the time period, or the spell, has a specific observed duration (Allison, 1984; Murnane, Singer, & Willett, 1988). Spells of employment are assumed to be at least 1 year; the duration of a teaching spell and the likelihood of the spell ending are summarized in Table 5. Over half of the NLS-72 teaching sample (55%) left teaching during the decade; less than

TABLE 5. Teacher Attrition and Reentry as Employment Spells, NLS-72

	All experienced teachers					
	All trained teachers	Ever entered	Ever left	Ever reentered	Left two or more times	Entered two or more times
Number of teachers	211,588	156,754	85,200	27,629	8,887	2,810
Number still in given situation (censored)	54,834	71,554	57,571	18,743	6,076	1,473
Probability of event, given prior event	—	.741	.545	.324	.322	.316
Mean years duration of spell, given spell ended	1.76	3.67	2.02	3.2	1.9	1.4
Years duration of event, given spell ended						
1 year or less	42.1	21.7	44.7	56.2	70.7	73.0
3 years or less	71.5	58.1	88.2	80.2	95.6	90.2
5 years or less	79.3	74.8	94.4	95.5	100.0	100.0
Sample size	[1038]	[786]	[440]	[144]	[46]	[14]

5% of the teachers left two or more times during the 1976–1986 decade; however, one-third (32%) of those who ever left reentered at a later date. More than half of those reentering (56%) did so after only 1 year; four out of five who reentered did so within 3 years. These data suggest that for a large number of teachers, leaves or breaks from teaching of 1 or 2 years are customary and accepted practice.

Teachers reentering the profession tend to be similar to those who never left on most characteristics. The characteristics that best distinguish teachers who return from those who do not is subsequent work experience and level of education taught. Primary-school teachers and those who have not taken another job since leaving are the most likely to return, and the most likely to expect to return in the future. Table 6 compares former teachers with work experience to those without on a number of salient characteristics. The teachers who reentered are more likely to be female, to teach the primary grades or in junior high school, to hold regular certification, and to have master's degrees. The teachers who first taught in 1976–1977 are slightly more likely to have reentered than those who first entered later, because they had more time to both leave and reenter; the differences, however, are not large.

WHO LEFT TEACHING AND WHO WANTS TO RETURN?

Former teachers in the NLS-72 resemble current teachers on most demographic characteristics. In the aggregate, men are slightly more likely to have left teaching than females and to have left earlier in their careers; the differences between men and women teachers are, however, largely a function of the type of teaching entered. For both sexes, the highest rates of attrition are among high-school teachers; numerically men dominate the schools at that level. Controlling for the level of schooling taught, a larger proportion of women teachers left teaching at both the primary and secondary levels. As we have observed, the largest sex differences among the NLS-72 teachers is the likelihood of returning.

Former teachers are commonly assumed to have been disappointed with public schools and discontented with their jobs. Yet in the aggregate, former teachers do not appear to be overwhelmingly disaffected. Former teachers are more dissatisfied than current teachers but not as much as one might suspect. Over two-thirds of the current teachers report either that they are satisfied all (9.9%) or most of the time (68.4%); in contrast, 7% of the former teachers report that they were satisfied with their teaching job all of the time, and over half (51.5%) were satisfied most of the time. Twenty-nine percent of the current teachers said they would certainly become teachers again if they could start over; 18% of the former teachers said they would. Most significantly, almost half of the former teachers (43.9%)

TABLE 6. Comparisons between Former Teachers
with Work Experience since Leaving Teaching and Those without

| | Former teachers[a] | |
	With subsequent work experience (75.1%)	Without work experience since leaving teaching (18.1%)
Years of teaching experience		
2 or less	39.5	22.9
3–4	29.0	24.8
5–6	12.2	32.4
7+	19.3	19.9
Year left		
1978 or prior	22.3	10.9
1979–1982	45.0	44.4
1983+	32.7	44.7
Grade level taught		
Prekindergarten/kindergarten	5.6	6.9
Elementary	29.7	48.8
Middle school/junior high	18.9	14.6
Secondary	44.6	31.0
Supplemented income when last taught		
Yes	51.3	24.3
No	48.7	75.7
Gender		
Male	33.5	9.1
Female	66.5	90.9
Desire to teach in future		
Yes	42.2	72.5
No	57.8	27.5

[a]Excludes 3.3% of the former teachers who had left in the last year, and 3.5% who were currently looking for a teaching position. These cases uniformly wished to return to teaching.

want to return to teaching but are not sure when. This percentage is considerably higher than that reported by the only other national survey of former teachers conducted in recent years.[4]

[4]The Metropolitan Life Survey of Former Teachers in America (1985) collected data on teachers who had left to take another job within the previous 5 years. The survey reported that 26% of the women in the sample thought it very likely or fairly likely that they would return within the next 5 years; 12% of the males thought so. The sample was neither random nor representative of former teachers; it consisted of respondents identified by a colleague or by a principal in a parallel study. The Metropolitan Life sampling design eliminated former teachers who were either in school or who were not working full-time. Two-thirds were male, nearly three-fourths had taught in secondary schools, and all had full-time jobs at the time of the survey. Restricting the NLS-72 cohort to comparable ex-teachers produces substantially more agreement between the findings. Among NLS-72 males who formerly taught secondary school and who worked full-time at a job not in education, 17% want to return.

The single largest determinant of wanting to return to teaching is experience in the labor market. Among NLS-72 former teachers, over half took a full- or part-time job the first year after they left, one-fifth went back to school (22%), and nearly one-third (31%) were keeping house. By 1986, 72% of the former teachers were working full-time; the proportion going to school had fallen by an equivalent amount, whereas the proportion keeping house had not changed. Although 79% of the housewives want to return to the classroom, less than one-third of those working full-time do. Experienced teachers, with 4 or more years in the classroom behind them or those who have reentered previously are the most likely to want to return. In short, the more teaching experience a respondent has had, or the less opportunity to explore other jobs, the more likely he or she is to express a desire to return (Heyns, Mottina, & Dodd, 1988).

TEACHER ATTRITION AND TEACHER QUALIFICATIONS

Studies of attrition have typically found that teachers leaving the field were more talented academically and more qualified than those who remained. The standard measures of talent are college grades, achievement test scores, or the scores on the National Teaching Examination (Schlechty & Vance, 1981, 1983; Vance & Schlechty, 1982; Weaver, 1983). The decline in the number of college entrants who aspire to be teachers has been particularly severe among the most talented students (Peng, 1982; Roberson, Keith, & Page, 1983). These patterns, combined with the fact that education majors are often not at the top of their class, have suggested to numerous analysts that the major problem in education is teacher quality (Weaver, 1981, 1983). High attrition, particularly among talented potential teachers is worrisome. Weaver (1983), among others, has argued that talented teachers can and do find more lucrative employment outside the academy. Increasing opportunities for women and minorities and the declining attractiveness of schools as workplaces are seen to exacerbate these trends (Darling-Hammond, 1984).

Analysts have worried that changing patterns of recruitment presage general declines in academic quality over time. Schools of education have rarely been as selective in admissions as other liberal arts graduate programs. The undergraduate population as a whole has dipped academically; potential teachers may have fallen below an acceptable level. Within schools of education, teacher training programs are generally thought to be less intellectually exciting or rigorous than the doctoral programs. Sykes (1983b) has argued that prestigious universities have colluded in the process of lowering standards, by abandoning teacher education, or by favoring equity issues over excellence as criteria for admissions. If the best students avoid entering teaching or the most qualified teachers leave after a few years, talent in education declines. Extrapolating such processes over time implies a steady erosion of teacher quality over time.

The NLS-72 data do not altogether disprove the talent loss theory, but they surely temper massive foreboding. On the whole, the sample of teachers came from lower socioeconomic backgrounds and scored less well on standardized tests, compared to all college graduates in the cohort. They were more likely to attend public universities or colleges, rather than private ones, and they were less likely to graduate in 4 years. Moreover, those who became teachers scored less well on standardized tests than those who were trained but never entered. On average, the former teachers in 1986 have a slight edge on current teachers, in terms of both socioeconomic background and tested ability. Current teachers had, however, received higher grades in both high school and college, and they were significantly more likely to have graduate training and advanced degrees.

Former teachers in the aggregate scored slightly better than current teachers on SAT tests and on high-school achievement tests in math and slightly worse on tests of verbal skills. These differences, however, are quite small and not significant. Current teachers are more likely than former teachers to have earned a master's degree. Thirty-nine percent of the current teachers held a master's degree in 1986, compared to 23% of the former teachers.

These aggregate patterns do not, however, imply a steady erosion of talent in the teaching profession. If we compare the career patterns of current and former teachers and look at patterns of entry and reentry, the results are distinctly more mixed. Teachers entering the profession late after other work experience are more talented (again assuming that high-school tests and SAT scores measure academic talent) than teachers entering directly after college. Moreover, teachers taking breaks from teaching, but reentering later, tend to score higher than those who have never left. Finally, former teachers who want to return to the classroom tend to score more highly than those who do not want to return, although these differences are not significant.

Table 7 presents the mean SAT scores for the NLS-72 cohort teaching in a given year and the level of schooling they taught. No clear trends are evident over the decade of teaching experience represented. These results suggest it is premature to assume that attrition necessarily depletes the profession of the most talented teachers. Although the most talented teachers are more likely to leave, they are also more likely to reenter. Those who enter late, or who return after a break, or who want to return in the future, tend to raise the averages for current teachers.

TABLE 7. Mean SAT Scores for Experienced Teachers
by Level Taught and Year Teaching: National Longitudinal Study, 1986

	Elementary-school teachers		Secondary-school teachers		Proportion of sample teaching in specific years	
Year	SAT Verbal	SAT Math	SAT Verbal	SAT Math	Elementary	Secondary
1976–1977	439	460	438	499	.45	.37
1977–1978	440	460	450	497	.61	.53
1978–1979	435	457	447	495	.64	.62
1979–1980	432	464	455	513	.63	.62
1980–1981	433	460	442	502	.62	.62
1981–1982	426	453	438	487	.61	.58
1982–1983	433	456	446	502	.59	.57
1983–1984	436	459	449	495	.59	.51
1984–1985	438	459	448	487	.61	.53
1985–1986	437	458	445	493	.65	.47
[N]	[182]	[180]	[73]	[73]	[519]	[250]

The contrast between early and late entrants is somewhat surprising.[5] Late entrants are more likely to have delayed college graduation, perhaps due to financial or academic difficulty in college. Among the late-entry teachers, about half took more than 4 years to graduate; however, a larger number entered with graduate training and advanced degrees as well. Late-entry teachers, like those who reentered, were more likely to have children than current teachers. For many teachers, entering the profession late appears to be equivalent to taking an early break from teaching, to pursue educational credentials, to start families, or both.

The composition of the pool of late-entry and reentry teachers suggests a second explanation of these patterns. Teachers entering after 1980 were more likely to come from relatively advantaged families; moreover, late-entry teachers tended to have higher than average family incomes in both 1985 and 1986. This is also true of the teachers who had taken breaks between 1977 and 1986. It seems likely that the same measure of economic security is a prerequisite for leaving education, whether or not one returns.[6] Such correlates help to explain, at least in part, the higher test scores. As a profession, teaching is unique in that it allows individuals

[5]Although these results are surprising, they are not unique in the literature. Pavalko (1970), for example, studied a cohort of 1957 high-school graduates from Wisconsin, who were followed up in 1964. He reports that late-entry teachers tended to have the highest ability of all those entering teaching.

[6]One could also argue that as the decade progressed, getting a teaching job became harder; hence those who entered at successively later dates were more select. The evidence is rather sparse on this point; there were no trends in the test scores of teachers by year of entry after 1981.

with the motivation and the wherewithal to take extended leaves. Teachers who chose to exercise this option were disproportionately drawn from the more privileged socioeconomic sectors and more likely to score well on ability tests.

These results can perhaps mitigate fears that attrition among high-quality teachers means the inevitable decline of teaching quality, at least in the aggregate. However, teachers were not the most talented graduates in their class. Moreover, it is still the case that those leaving teaching tend to have higher scholastic aptitude than those who remain. Teaching can be an exhausting and stressful business; it is not surprising that teachers who can afford to do so choose to take leaves or breaks from teaching. The teachers who report the most satisfaction with teaching as a profession are those who have either entered late or taken breaks during their tenure. Retaining highly qualified teachers may involve providing sources of re-vitalization and renewal outside the classroom, such as paid sabbaticals. Ironically, the teachers who have the most access to leaves, or at least choose to use them the most often, teach or have taught in the least stressful or discouraging educational environments. To this paradox we now turn.

Schools and Patterns of Attrition among Teachers

Teacher shortages tend to be found in the same sorts of schools that report high levels of teacher dissatisfaction. Innercity schools or integrated schools with large minority enrollments are, on average, schools that are chronically underfunded and understaffed. Levels of dissatisfaction are understandably high. Generally, public-school teachers tend to be more dissatisfied than teachers in private schools, whether religious or not. School level makes a difference, however; elementary-school teachers are typically more satisfied than high-school teachers, in both public and private schools, irrespective of gender, school location, or composition of the student body. The teachers who would certainly or probably become teachers if they were choosing a career again are more likely to report that their students are high or above average in ability and relatively advantaged socioeconomically. And, as we have seen, former teachers are less likely to report they were usually satisfied or that they would become teachers again than are current teachers. These patterns are hardly revelations.

Such findings invite the conclusion that former teachers are refugees from the most depressed and most depressing educational environments, from the schools in which no one wants to teach. Teaching shortages in ghetto schools or in the innercity, by this logic, reflect the high rates of

attrition in these schools. The distribution of unfilled vacancies in education reinforces such inferences.[7]

Surprisingly, however, teacher attrition tends to be inversely related to
the characteristics of schools alleged to enhance teacher satisfaction. Private schools, whether religious or not, have higher rates of attrition than do
public schools. Suburban schools lose more teachers every year than do
urban schools; rural schools lose the least of all. Large schools tend to have
lower rates of attrition than small- or medium-sized schools. Secondary-
school teachers are far more likely to leave the profession than elementary-
school teachers, although elementary schools have fewer resources or are
less professionally rewarding places to teach. Former teachers report that
their students were of high or average ability and from upper- or upper-
middle-class families, more often than current teachers do. Although the
differences by race are not significant, it is clear that current teachers are
more likely to teach minority pupils in minority schools than former
teachers were.

Attrition rates by type of school are presented in Table 8. All of the
comparisons, except that for racial composition, as noted, are significant.
The measure of retention used is the ratio of teachers in the category who
identify themselves as former to the total number who entered teaching
and taught in the schools in question. This rate reflects the proportion of
teachers who left without returning, or at least had not returned by 1986.
The measure of attrition used reflects teachers leaving the profession,
rather than leaving a particular school; it measures attrition from the profession, not merely turnover rates in particular types of schools. Rates of
turnover typically confound attrition with transfers between schools. The
differences between schools in attrition presented in Table 8 are conservative estimates, because most of the former teachers left their first teaching
position, whereas the majority of current teachers have held more than one
post. For both past and present teachers, the schools described were their
most recent or present positions. Experienced teachers can usually command more desirable positions than new graduates can; a second teaching
job is typically in better, more sought-after schools than the first position.

Professional status and working conditions are widely viewed as the

[7]The factors that are assumed to explain the distribution of teacher shortages are changes in
the demographic and intellectual composition of students and changes in the general "quality" of schools. Shortages in specific fields, such as math, science, and computer training are
long-standing, although they have been exacerbated by recently mandated increases in
requirements for graduation. Shortages in special education, bilingual programs, and pre-
schooling reflect increases in the demand for education for certain kinds of children. Unfilled
positions in the West or in the Sunbelt generally reflect population shifts. But one can only
explain shortages in areas that are losing population, such as ghetto schools or the inner city,
as based on the quality of the school. See National Center for Education Statistics (1985) and
the National Education Association (1982, 1986).

TABLE 8. Teacher Satisfaction and Rate of Attrition
by School Characteristics: National Longitudinal Study, 1986

School characteristics[a]	Proportion who would certainly or probably be teachers if they could do it again (current teachers)	Rate of (former teachers/all experienced teachers)
Secondary schools (including junior high and middle schools)	48.3	.508
Elementary schools	60.5	.409
Control of school		
Public	54.2	.401
Parochial	65.9	.621
Private	79.9	.624
School location		
Rural	59.0	.404
Urban	52.9	.435
Suburban	56.5	.579
Racial composition		
All white (less than 10% minority)	59.0	.475
Integrated (10%–60% minority)	57.0	.439
Minority (over 60% minority)	56.3	.415
Economic status of students		
Upper or upper middle class	54.2	.503
Lower and lower middle class	55.6	.455
Mixed	63.5	.377
Ability levels of students		
High or average ability	58.7	.491
Low ability	54.3	.441
Mixed	56.6	.382

[a]School characteristics are based on teacher reports for the last or most recent school in which they taught. All the differences in attrition, except those for racial composition, are significant ($p \leqslant .05$). Only the differences by level and control of the school are significant for current teachers.

most important reasons for high rates of teacher attrition. Moreover, one would like to believe that improving schools and increasing teacher's professional status will increase retention. Unfortunately, however much school reform designed to increase professionalism may be needed in education, it is not clear that greater autonomy, improved working conditions, or enhanced professional status will stem attrition among teachers. Attrition seems more related to the market position and to alternative possibilities for work than to school conditions.

Teaching is, in the last analysis, very hard work. At the highest levels of education, in elite universities, with high professional status, instructors seem eager to avoid it. We do not, however, expect teachers in elementary or secondary schools to escape teaching responsibilities because of increased administrative burdens. In a variety of contexts, school reform comes hand-in-hand with prolonged and often acrimonious meetings, discussions of goal setting, reports, evaluations, and a torrent of paperwork. Although such activities may improve education, it is much less clear that they improve the lot of teachers. At the very least, they take valuable time away from class preparation and student contact. Increasing professional autonomy and responsibility for policy decisions may improve the relative professional status of teaching; however, such reforms will not improve the work load of teachers. The need to reduce teaching loads by a commensurate amount to permit time for such responsibilities should not be overlooked. In both 1981 and 1986, teachers mentioned heavy work loads and extra responsibilities as the major hindrances to teaching more often than any other impediment (National Education Association, 1987).

The goal of reducing attrition should be clearly separated from the intent of improving schools. The teachers most likely to leave the profession are not those found teaching in the most troubled and troubling schools; they have taught in some of the most desireable settings. Linking school reform with proposals to enhance the prestige of teaching and increase retention has considerable appeal; however, poor work conditions do not necessarily mean higher attrition. Working conditions could, of course, be improved; and it is possible that deteriorating conditions have produced a general decline in morale. However, in the aggregate, working conditions do not seem to have changed noticeably in the last decade (National Education Association, 1987). It is possible that reductions in class size improved the working conditions of teachers more than most reforms.

In a series of reports published by Rand, teacher attrition is argued to be strongly related to the tendency for schools to undermine teacher efficacy. Further, highly qualified teachers are judged to be more dissatisfied than less qualified teachers (Darling-Hammond, 1984; Darling-Hammond & Wise, 1983; Wise & Darling-Hammond, 1984/1985; Wise, 1986). The NLS-72 data raise questions about these interpretations, however. Secondary-school teachers, who tend to have more control over both curriculum and teaching schedules and who are more likely to have graduate degrees as well are much less satisfied with their jobs than elementary-school teachers. The most dissatisfied teachers are not those with the best qualifications, if higher degrees are an adequate measure of qualifications. Within either elementary or secondary schools, teachers with advanced degrees are more satisfied with their jobs than teachers with fewer credentials; not coincidentally, they tend to make more money as well.

CONCLUSIONS

The present study presents results from possibly the best longitudinal data on teachers ever assembled and makes three fairly controversial claims. The first and the least disputable assertion is that teacher attrition has declined over time. Nonetheless, there are substantial amounts of career mobility among American teachers and frequent breaks in service. Teacher turnover may be higher than the levels of attrition; however, turnover in general has probably declined. The majority of current teachers from the high-school class of 1972 either entered or reentered the profession since 1980.

The second claim is that former teachers are quite similar to current teachers, except that they have typically been employed in work settings that seem better than average. Differences in background are small; differences in ability are insignificant. Former teachers are disproportionately drawn from the best rather than the worst schools. Although the majority do not want to return to the classroom, former teachers do not constitute a cadre of disaffected outcasts. Moreover, the patterns of entry and reentry suggest that some of the "best" teachers, in terms of their academic qualifications, have had careers that are somewhat erratic. To be sure, the teachers in the NLS-72 are still quite young; perhaps the patterns discerned during their first decade of teaching will change with time. At present, however, high rates of mobility and attrition do not seem incompatible with either academic excellence or job satisfaction.

Finally, these results have implications for educational policy designed to enhance teacher professionalism and the retention of teachers. Although improving the lot of teachers by raising professional standards and providing better remuneration and working conditions are entirely worthwhile goals, it is not clear that such reforms will reduce attrition. It is comforting to endorse the complete package: professionalism, school improvement, and reduced attrition. These goals are not necessarily incompatible; however, they are not equivalent. Some of the most progressive and favored schools have quite high rates of attrition. Although such patterns may seem paradoxical, it is important to remember that for many teachers, ease of transfer and reentry, geographic mobility, and the capacity to take extended leaves are benefits unique to the field of education. If professionalism substitutes career ladders, peer evaluations, mentors (or an opportunity to mentor), and remuneration that is tied to work experience in a specific school or district for teacher autonomy, it may well be less appealing than current career benefits.

REFERENCES

Allison, P. D. (1984). *Event history analysis: Regression for longitudinal event data*, Sage University Paper Series, Quantitative Applications in the Social Sciences, Number 46. Beverly Hills, CA: Sage Publications.

Carnegie Forum on Education and the Economy: Task Force on Teaching as a Profession. (1986). *A nation prepared: Teachers for the 21st century*. New York: The Carnegie Corporation.

Carnegie Foundation for the Advancement of Teaching. (1986, September/October). Future teachers: Will there be enough good ones? *Change*, 27–30.

Chapman, D., & Hutcheson, S. M. (1982). Attrition from teaching careers: A discriminant analysis. *American Educational Research Journal, 19*, 93–105.

Darling-Hammond, L. (1984). *Beyond the commission reports: The coming crisis in teaching*. Santa Monica: The Rand Corporation.

Darling-Hammond, L., & Wise, A. E. (1983, October). Teaching standards or standardized teaching? *Educational Leadership*, 66–69.

Darling-Hammond, L., Wise, A. E., & Pease, S. R. (1983, Fall). Teacher evaluation in the organizational context: A review of the literature. *Review of Educational Research, 53*(3), 285–328.

Grissmer, D. W., & Kirby, S. N. (1987). *Teacher attrition: The uphill climb to staff the nation's schools*. Santa Monica, CA: The Rand Corporation.

Harris, Louis, & Associates, Inc. (1985, April–June). *The Metropolitan Life Survey of former teachers in America*. Conducted for Metropolitan Life Insurance Company, New York.

Heyns, B. (1972). Down the up staircase: Sex roles, professionalization, and the status of teachers. In S. Anderson (Ed.), *Sex differences and discrimination in education* (pp. 54–60). New York: Charles Jones.

Heyns, B. (1988). Educational defectors: A first look at teacher attrition in the NLS-72. *Educational Researcher, 17*(3), 24–32.

Heyns, B., Mottina, F., & Dodd, J. (1988). *Is there a reserve army of teachers?* Washington, DC: National Education Association.

Lortie, D. C. (1975). *Schoolteacher: A sociological study*. Chicago: University of Chicago Press.

Murnane, R. J., Singer, J., & Willett, J. B. (1988). The career paths of teachers: Implications for teacher supply and methodological lessons for research. *Educational Researcher, 17*(6), 22–30.

National Commission for Excellence in Teacher Education. (1985). *A call for change in teacher education*. Washington, DC: American Association of Colleges for Teacher Education.

National Education Association (1982). *Teacher supply and demand in the public schools, 1980–1981*. Washington, DC: NEA.

National Education Association (1986). *Teacher supply and demand*. Washington, DC: NEA.

National Education Association (1987). *Status of the American public school teacher, 1985–1986*. Washington, DC: National Education Association.

Pavalko, R. M. (1970). Recruitment to teaching: Patterns of selection and retention. *Sociology of Education, 43*, 340–355.

Peng, S. S. (1982, December). Education attracts fewer academically high achieving young women. *National Center for Education Statistics Bulletin*, 82–249b.

Riccobono, J., Henderson, L. B., Burkheimer, C. J., Place, C., & Levinson, J. R. (1981). *National longitudinal study: Base year (1972) through fourth follow-up (1979) data file user's manual*, Vols. 1, 2, and 3. Washington, DC: Center for Education Statistics, U. S. Department of Education.

Roberson, S. D., Keith, T. Z., & Page, E. B. (1983 June/July). Now who aspires to teach? *Educational Researcher*, 13–21.

Schlechty, P. C., & Vance, V. S. (1981, October). Do academically able teachers leave education? The North Carolina case. *Phi Delta Kappan, 63*(2), 106–112.

Schlechty, P. C., & Vance, V. S. (1983, March). Recruitment, selection, and retention: The shape of the teaching force. *The Elementary School Journal, 83*(1), 469–487.

Sebring, P., Richardson, K., Campbell, B., Glusberg, M., Tourangeau, R., & Singleton, M. (1987). The National Longitudinal Study of the Class of 1972, fifth follow-up. Teaching Supplement, Data File User's Manual. Chicago: National Opinion Research Center.

Sykes, G. (1983a). Public policy and the problem of teacher quality: The need for screens and magnets. In L. S. Shulman & G. Sykes (Eds.), *Handbook of teaching and policy*, (pp. 97–125). New York: Longman.

Sykes, G. (1983b, October). Contradictions, ironies and promises unfulfilled: A contemporary account of the status of teaching. *Phi Delta Kappan, 65,* 87–93.

Talbert, J. E. (1986, August). The staging of teachers' careers: An institutional perspective. *Work and Occupations, 13*(3), 421–443.

Tourangeau, R., Sebring, P., Campbell, B., Glusberg, M., Spencer, B., & Singleton, M. (1987, June). *The national longitudinal study of the class of 1972.* Chicago: National Opinion Research Center.

Vance, V. S., & Schlechty, P. C. (1982). The distribution of academic ability in the teaching force: Policy implications. *Phi Delta Kappan, 64,* 22–27.

Weaver, W. T. (1981). Demography, quality, and decline: The challenge for education in the eighties. In *Policy for the education of educators: Issues and implications.* Washington, DC: American Association of Colleges for Teacher Education.

Weaver, W. T. (1983). *America's teacher quality problem: Alternatives for reform.* New York: Praeger.

Wells, A. S. (1987, April 12). "Wanted: A million schoolteachers," *The New York Times,* Education Life (Section 12), pp. 29–30.

Wise, A. E. (1986, May). Three scenarios for the future of teaching. *Phi Delta Kappan, 67*(9), 649–652.

Wise, A. E., & Darling-Hammond, L. (1984, December/1985, January). Teacher evaluation and teacher professionalism. *Educational Leadership, 42*(4), 28–33.

Chapter Seven

Contradiction and Change in Organized Religion

Roman Catholicism in the United States and Spain

Lawrence A. Young and Richard A. Schoenherr

At midcentury, to be American was to be confidently Protestant, Catholic, or Jew (Herberg, 1955). True elites were WASP by birthright, but Catholics and Jews were accepted as part of the mainstream and nonaffiliation was simply un-American. Institutional religion in the United States was not only the heart of the "American Way of Life," but its moral conscience, political legitimator, and economic backbone as well. Church religion was not isomorphic with civil religion, to be sure, but they were comfortable bed partners (Bellah, 1968).

Although secularization appeared to be ravaging religion in other parts of the world, churches thrived in the United States. Luckmann (1967) argued that church-oriented religion had been relegated to the periphery of modern society especially in Europe and probably in America as well. Some social scientists, however, had their doubts, and many thought the secularization argument limped badly when applied to the United States (Bellah, 1970; Greeley, 1972a, b; Parsons, 1963; Swanson, 1968).

The 1960s, though, brought undeniable religious "decline." Several social trends added confirming evidence of the secularization hypothesis.

LAWRENCE A. YOUNG ● Department of Sociology, Brigham Young University, Provo, Utah 84601.   RICHARD A. SCHOENHERR ● Department of Sociology, University of Wisconsin–Madison, Madison, Wisconsin 53706.

For example, in the aftermath of the Second Vatican Council, church attendance plummeted among Catholics (Hout & Greeley, 1987). Liberal Protestant denominations faced decline in membership for the first time in
history (Kelley, 1972). Marty (1979) assessed the "seismic shift" in the religious terrain with his usual perspicacity. And Robinson (1963) boldly proclaimed the "death of God."

As the twentieth century and the second Christian millennium enter
their last decade, the face of religion is changing again dramatically —
nationally and worldwide. Sociologists ponder the beginnings of "yet another great awakening" (Barker, 1985). Some boldly proclaim the death of
the "myth of secularization" (Greeley, 1972a; Hadden & Shupe, 1985; Stark
& Bainbridge, 1985). All marvel at the return of the sacred — in old and new
guise (Barker, 1985; Bell, 1977). In truth, however, the decline of religion in
the 1960s and its reawakening in the 1980s were symptoms of more fundamental transformations underway within institutional religion.

Luckmann and others who argued that religion had become a peripheral institution in modern society clearly misspecified the situation. Glob-
ally, the resurgence of Islamic fundamentalism in the past decade
represents one of the most significant ideological shifts of the century.
Likewise, institutional forms of Christianity have been at the center of
notable political–economic conflicts during the 1980s. For example, Roman
Catholicism is an agent for change in Eastern Europe (Poland), Asia
(Philippines), and Latin America (Nicaragua and several other countries).
Other political hot spots, including Northern Ireland, South Africa, and
the Middle East, continue to be influenced by institutional forms of
religion.

The persistent influence of religion does not mean it has remained
unchanged. With growing consensus, social theorists argue that the core
element transforming institutional religion, at least in North America, is
increased privatization and voluntarism associated with religious belief
and practice (Bellah et al., 1985; Roof & McKinney, 1987; Wuthnow, 1988).
Although this change is characterized by growing numbers and higher
status of those claiming no religious affiliation, it is more fully demonstrated by greater independence of those involved in formal religion. For
example, Catholics in the United States have moved from general compli-
ance with church teaching to a whole gamut of individualistic behaviors,
from choosing whether to eat meat on Fridays to open disregard for papal
teaching on birth control.

The privatization and new voluntarism that characterize contemporary religion have facilitated both "growth" and "decline." Consequently,
although relational shifts both within religion and between religion and
other institutions have occurred, the changes do not represent monotonic
growth or decline. Roof and McKinney (1987) document several key modifications in the contemporary religious landscape. Liberal Protestantism,

which once acted as the moral conscience of the American Way of Life, has experienced sustained decline in membership since the 1960s. At the same time, Roman Catholics and black and conservative Protestants have witnessed growth in their membership and societal influence.

The decline of liberal Protestantism left a vacuum with respect to religion's traditional function of producing societal cohesion and consensus. That is to say, whereas the WASP elite was once considered the embodiment of the moral order that made national community possible — perhaps as recently as the 1950s — today the center no longer holds. Public morality has become a contested terrain. Undoubtedly, religion's ability to act as a hegemonic agent of societal consensus has been significantly reduced. At the same time, however, religious groups that were traditionally relegated to the margins, such as conservative Protestants and Catholics, are now vying for influence over the center. The emergence of a new middle consisting of Protestant moderates and Catholics — with some participation from liberal and black Protestants — is a distinct possibility. As evidence of growing Catholic influence on public affairs, for example, observers point to the unique role of Catholic bishops as the voice of Christian morality in the United States.

In the meantime, the privatization and new voluntarism of recent years has led to a basic change in the relationship between religion and society. Wuthnow (1988) argues that one of the primary components of the restructuring of American religion is the emergence of a liberal–conservative split within and across denominations. Since Niebuhr (1929), sociologists have argued that denominational divisions were primarily based on social differences arising from class, ethnicity, region, and race. Roof and McKinney demonstrate that traditional social sources of denominationalism, in particular class and ethnicity, have declined in importance and are being replaced by religious switching and affiliation based on theological and moral preferences.

The theological and moral shift not only leads to increased liberal–conservative polarization within religion but also undermines organized religion's ability to speak with one dominant voice. Nowadays, several denominations claim to represent the centrist position on moral order. Because denominations are increasingly differentiated along theological and moral dimensions rather than traditional social dimensions of class and ethnicity, religion is turning away from its historic function of producing consensus and cohesion and, instead, is beginning to define and sharpen societal conflict. Thus with respect to a broad range of issues including abortion, the role of women, gay and lesbian rights, the place of nuclear weapons in national defense policy, foreign policy in Central America and South Africa, and the national political process (including the new Christian right, Pat Robertson, Jesse Jackson, etc.), religion has played an important but divisive role in the 1980s.

Along with shifting beliefs and values, Roof and McKinney (1987) also highlight demographic forces in understanding changes within religion. Modifications in the underlying demography of churches have a significant impact on the political economy of religion and, in turn, on the way religion relates to other institutions in society. Fertility and migration patterns have produced significant growth among conservative and black Protestants as well as Catholics, groups that historically had marginal influence on society. The same demographic forces produced significant decline among liberal and moderate Protestants and Jews, groups that traditionally exerted significant societal influence. This difference is also accentuated by patterns of religious switching that tend to produce younger, and hence, more fertile converts for groups that are growing. Furthermore, the pattern of switching intensifies the liberal–conservative split between denominations as liberals who switch tend to join liberal denominations and conservatives who move tend to join conservative ones.

Wuthnow (1976) also notes the importance of demographic forces in understanding religious change. He reapplies Mannheim's concept of generational unit to analyze the impact on religion of the baby-boom generation and the "legacy of the sixties" and concludes that religious change is marked more by "discontinuities" than unilinear change, be it growth or decline. He also suggests that similar generational unit dynamics affect religious change worldwide. In his most recent reflections on restructuring American religion, Wuthnow (1988) describes how demography has affected the dramatic expansion of higher education, which leads to further privatization and voluntarism associated with American religion. Higher levels of education, in turn, intensify the liberal–conservative split within religion.

ORGANIZATIONAL DEMOGRAPHY AND THE CATHOLIC CHURCH

Sociologists of religion are paying systematic attention to social demography as more and more studies show that the demographics surrounding religious organizations are a driving force for social change. Nowhere are demographic trends creating a more dramatic transformation of organized religion than within Roman Catholicism. Although the birth rate and age structure of Catholics are having strong positive effects on membership size and growth, other components of demographic change within diocesan organizations are having powerful negative effects on the size and growth of the priesthood. Countervailing demographic forces for change are operating in basic contradiction in the Catholic church. One set of social trends seems to be impelling the Catholic church into a position of expanded influence and prominence—in the United States, at least—whereas another may be undermining the very foundation of its organizational strength.

Roof and McKinney (1987, pp. 230–231) discuss the steady growth of the Catholic population in the United States throughout this century. Between 1926 and 1980, the absolute number of American Catholics has grown from fewer than 20 million to more than 50 million. Catholicism's share of the total population has also increased from less than 20% to more than 25%. Demographic forces such as high fertility and the influx of Hispanic and Asian immigrants suggest that the Catholic population will continue its historic pattern of growth.

Human resources are the key element in a service organization's internal political economy (Zald, 1970). The vitality of organized religion, however, is not just a function of the size and growth of church membership. Hoge, Carroll, and Sheets (1988) note that providing religion, as in other service organizations, is affected by supply and demand. Thus the ratio of laity to clergy is also an important indicator of well-being within religious organizations. Hoge and colleagues studied parish leadership in Catholicism and three comparable Protestant denominations and found significant Catholic–Protestant differences in the availability of clergy to serve church members. The differences they document epitomize one of the fundamental demographic contradictions within American religion today. Catholicism, on the one hand, is experiencing growth in membership but a shrinking priesthood. Churches within mainline Protestantism, on the other hand, are characterized by declining church membership but a surplus of clergy.

Weber's (1963, 1978) prolonged attention to professional functionaries, in his study of the organization of both religion and law, leads us to pay close attention to changes in the population of priests in the Catholic church. Because of the strategic position of professional clergy in the hierarchy, structural change in the priestly ministry has pervasive organizational consequences (Schoenherr, 1987). We focus on the transformation of the Catholic priesthood not only because of the structural importance of this key cadre of human resources but also because the demographic forces of decline stand in such stark contrast with the growing power, influence, and membership size of Catholicism in general (Roof & McKinney, 1987).

In this chapter, we address the question of how extensive priest decline is in a large metropolitan Roman Catholic diocese in the United States and one in Spain. An obvious limitation of our study is its focus on just two cases. The aim of the analysis, however, is a preliminary step toward assessing differences in the speed and extent of clergy decline, as well as possible effects of the decline in the dioceses' organizational structure and internal political economy. In spite of its limits, a reconnaissance of the situation enables us to demonstrate the techniques involved in mapping out such demographic change and explore some of the dynamics behind the change. Furthermore, research based on national data reports sustained decline in priest populations in both the United States (Schoenherr & Sorensen, 1982) and Spain (Payne, 1984), indicating that these two dioceses may well be local examples of widespread demographic processes.

The application of demographic concepts and techniques to organizational analysis has been an important development during the past decade. Matras (1975) distinguishes between the demographic analysis of populations of organizations and the analysis of the individual organization as a population. Clearly, the area of greatest research interest has been the demographic analysis of organizational survival in populations of organizations (Brittain & Freeman, 1980; Carroll & Delacroix, 1982; Carroll, 1983; Freeman, 1982; Freeman & Hannan, 1983; Freeman *et al.*, 1983; Hannan & Freeman, 1977; Singh *et al.*, 1986).

Our focus, however, is on the individual organization as a population of its professional members. This type of organizational demography is most frequently represented by studies of the effects of changing cohort size (Gusfield, 1957; Pfeffer, 1985; Reed, 1978; Ryder, 1965; Stewman & Konda, 1983) or the impact of an organization's demography on career mobility and turnover (McCain *et al.*, 1983; Wagner *et al.*, 1984). We take a somewhat different approach by focusing on the phenomenon of population change itself, as it relates to a particular cadre of organizational members. The study of population change provides a foundation for other types of demographic analyses in that a sustained change affects cohort size, career mobility, and turnover.

POPULATION CHANGE AND THE DEMOGRAPHIC TRANSITION

Population change refers to differences in population size and composition at different times (Shryock, Siegel, & Associates, 1976). Unidirectional population change—either growth or decline—is inherently a transitory state with a beginning and an end (Barclay, 1958). When either growth or decline is sustained over a long period, however, the population undergoes a transformation (Barclay, 1958; Matras, 1975; see also Hernes, 1976). Population transformations have important consequences to the extent they produce major changes in population size and composition. The most widely studied sequence of population transformations began in the seventeenth century in Western Europe; it is commonly known as the demographic transition and has had global repercussions, resulting in population growth and eventual stability in some regions of the world but continuous growth in others. Matras (1975, pp. 304–305) summarizes this population transformation as a sequence of changes marked by:

1. High mortality and high fertility ("high balance" in a relatively small population).
2. Declining mortality and high fertility.

3. Declining mortality and declining fertility.
4. Low mortality and declining fertility.
5. Low mortality and low fertility ("low balance" in a relatively large population).

Thus the theory of the societal demographic transition focuses on the transition as *explanandum* and deciphers the structure of the demographic process (see Hernes, 1976) whereby a relatively small and stable population with high mortality and fertility is transformed into a relatively large and stable population with low mortality and fertility. Our interest is in adapting the theory of the societal demographic transition to organizations as a first step toward explaining the causes and consequences of particular historical events, namely the social forces that are creating structural transformation in religious organizations. We assume the demographic transition of the clergy, which is underway during the second half of the twentieth century, is the driving force for pervasive structural change in the Roman Catholic church.

Our assumption about the causal consequences of the clergy population transformation is based on insights from Weber, Hirschman, and Zald. Weber (1963, p. 1) observes that "religious...behavior or thinking must not be set apart from the range of everyday purposive conduct, particularly since even the ends of the religious...actions are predominantly economic." Hirschman (1970) points out that exiting an organization that is already in a state of decline creates economic pressure for reform. Zald (1970) argues from his data on the YMCA that drastic changes in the internal economy are always accompanied by correspondingly pervasive changes in an organization's polity and ideology.

As a first step toward formulating a theory of the demographic transition of Roman Catholic clergy in an organizational setting, we examine a series of historical and projected changes in priest populations during the period 1966–2045. Because the populations are experiencing mostly decline, however, our model of the demographic transition includes a sequence of population transformations different from that which characterizes the societal demographic transition.

The theoretical stages of population transformation in our model may be illustrated by the typical male–female pyramids displayed in Figure 1. The series represents overall decline geometrically, in that the area covered by each successive pyramid is smaller than that of the previous one. The changing pattern of how the age bars are pyramided on top of one another depicts the changing age structure of the population. The triangular shape delineating the first stage of low attrition and high recruitment reflects a large, young population that is either growing slowly or is in a state of stationary stability. At this stage, recruitment must be higher than or at least as high as attrition. Whether the youngest or the second youngest age bar is the longest one in the pyramid will depend on the average age at recruitment.

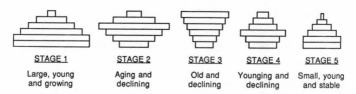

FIGURE 1. Impact of demographic transition on population pyramids.

The smaller pyramid for Stage 2 assumes increasing attrition and declining recruitment. With attrition higher than recruitment, growth stops and decline begins; the pyramid takes on a beehive shape indicating an aging and declining population. Stage 3 of the demographic transition is pictured by an inverted triangle that has shrunk further in size. The third phase of high attrition and declining recruitment produces an old and declining population. Stage 4, which incorporates declining attrition and low recruitment assumptions, reverts to the beehive shape but one that is likewise smaller than the beehive in Stage 2. These changes show that the population is both declining and "younging." If the vital rates stabilize at any time during the younging process and remain constant over an indefinite period, the population will have entered the fifth stage of the transition.

Once the period of balance between relatively low attrition and low recruitment is sustained over time, the population will have become young again. The shape of the pyramid also returns to a normal triangle if the average age at recruitment is relatively young during the period. If, however, the average age at recruitment settles at a relatively older level, the youngest age bar will be shorter than the one above it. At this end stage, the population could remain stable, with regard to age composition, as long as the relationship between the vital rates remained constant. If, however, the constant crude recruitment rate settled at a higher level than the constant crude attrition rate, the population would start to grow and perhaps return to its former size; it would also retain its triangular shape throughout the growth period.

We analyze the component processes of this transformation as it unfolds over eight decades and document its consequences for changing the size and age distribution of the clergy in two contrasting dioceses. Although our exploratory analysis employs a limited data set, in discussing our findings we argue that there is a correspondence between local trends reported here and national trends found in earlier studies. Because local evidence reflects the wider picture, we also speculate on the possible impact of the demographic transition of the clergy for changing other aspects of the organizational structure and internal political economy of Roman Catholic dioceses in general.

Data and Methods

We base the investigation on original data from two organizations. One is a large urban diocese in Spain and the other a moderate size urban diocese in the United States. For each we have constructed a census registry of all diocesan priests. The registries contain full names and complete individual-level data for all entrances into and exits out of the pool of active priests from 1966 to 1984. Entrance events include ordination, incardination (inmigration from another diocese or a religious order) and returns from temporary exit events lasting for at least 1 year, namely resignation, sick leave, and "awaiting assignment"; the latter is a catch-all category for leaves not elsewhere classified. Exit events include resignation, excardination (outmigration to another diocese or a religious order), retirement, death, and temporary exits lasting for at least 1 year, namely sick leave and awaiting assignment.

Demographic data were provided by church officials from a variety of sources including specially prepared lists of entrance and exit events, diocesan directories, priest seniority lists, necrologies (archival lists of deceased priests), the book of ordinations (archival lists of newly ordained priests), and various personnel records. Both dioceses were visited during data collection to assist officials in providing reliable information. Greater detail concerning data collection and other aspects of our methodology is included in Schoenherr et al. (1988).

We use standard and modified demographic techniques to estimate the various entrance and attrition rates and to analyze change in size and composition of the clergy population. Projections beyond the last year of observation are based on average numbers of entrances and age-specific attrition rates experienced during the previous years. Formulas are given in the tables and figures. Techniques used in selecting assumptions for the projections were based on a variety of organizational, historical, mathematical, and statistical considerations that are summarized in Schoenherr et al. (1988, pp. 506–509). The resulting assumptions produce a band of possible future outcomes based on past historical trends.

Analysis

Trends in Growth Rates, 1966–1984

The data displayed in Table 1 present the annual entrance, exit, and net growth rates for the two diocesan clergy populations over the 19-year census period. Although both have suffered severe population decline, the loss has been much greater in the Spanish than in the U.S. diocese. One of the major causes of decline is the sharp reduction in ordination rates in

TABLE 1. Estimates of Growth and Decline Rates in a U.S. Catholic Diocese and in a Spanish Catholic Diocese, 1966–1984a (Number of Entrances and Exits per 100 Active Priests)b

	United States					Spanish				
	Average annual rate				Percentage gross change	Average annual rate				Percentage gross change
Event	1966–1969	1970–1974	1975–1979	1980–1984	1966–1984c	1966–1969	1970–1974	1975–1979	1980–1984	1966–1984c
Entrance										
Ordination	2.86	4.46	3.24	1.42	52.11	2.75	0.79	0.23	0.23	17.10
Incardination	0.00	0.27	0.26	0.27	3.61	0.00	0.05	0.06	0.11	0.93
Other entranced	0.00	0.00	0.07	0.20	1.20	0.00	0.00	0.00	0.00	0.00
Exit										
Resignation	1.54	2.63	1.12	1.35	28.92	0.27	0.99	1.24	0.43	13.14
Excardination	0.08	0.00	0.07	0.20	1.51	0.00	0.00	0.02	0.07	0.34
Retirement	2.32	1.89	1.32	1.08	28.31	0.00	0.02	1.17	0.70	7.83
Death	1.31	0.41	0.46	0.54	11.45	1.77	1.54	1.66	1.31	27.21
Other exite	0.00	0.14	0.00	0.07	0.90	0.00	0.00	0.00	0.00	0.00
Net growth or decline	−2.39	−0.34	0.59	−1.35	−14.16	0.72	−1.71	−3.80	−2.16	−30.50

aCrude rates: $(O/P)k$; $(I/P)k$; $(N/P)k$; $(R/P)k$; $(E/P)k$; $(T/P)k$; $(D/P)k$; $(L/P)k$; $[(O+I+N-R-E-T-D-L)/P]k$. Where O is the number of ordinations, I of incardinations, N of returns from leaves, R of resignations, E of excardinations, T of retirements, D of deaths, and L the number of leaves of absence during the calendar year; P is the total population of active incardinated priests at the beginning of the calendar year; and k is 100.
bRange of $N = 287$–333 for United States; 845–1232 for Spanish.
cUsing 1966 base figures and the cumulative numbers of entrance and exit events for numerators.
dIncludes all other entrance events such as returns from sick leave, awaiting assignment, and resignation.
eIncludes temporary exit events such as sick leave and awaiting assignment.

both dioceses. The ordination rate in the U.S. diocese declined 68% since peaking in the early 1970s. Over the 19 years, the diocese experienced ordinations yielding a 2.7% average annual increase and a 52% overall gross increase. The rate fell even more dramatically in the Spanish diocese. Ordinations dropped 92% since the mid-1960s, yielding only a 0.9% average annual increase and a 17% cumulative gross increase during the two decades. Incardinations and returns from leave played a relatively minor demographic role in both religious organizations.

Both dioceses initially experienced an increase in the crude resignation rate. The exodus of American priests peaked at a high of 2.6% in the early 1970s and then declined. The resignation drain among the Spanish clergy peaked 5 years later at only 1.2% and then began to decline in the 1980s. One of the most striking aspects of the drop in ordination and rise in resignation rates is that, since 1970 in the Spanish diocese, proportionately more young men have decided to leave the active clergy than have chosen to enter. Similarly, in the U.S. diocese since the early 1980s, almost the same proportion are resigning each year as are being recruited to the ordained ministry. Moreover, if trends experienced in the last decade continue, the situation in the U.S. diocese will soon be the same as that in the Spanish one.

Retirement is a relatively new avenue of exit for priests. Most U.S. dioceses did not encourage general retirement for aged priests until after the close of the Second Vatican Council, which occurred in 1965. Thus, during the late 1960s many dioceses—including the one in this study—had a large pool of priests who qualified for retirement. As Table 1 shows, retirements peaked immediately after the new policy went into effect and then declined to the point at which the rate reflects a normal actuarial process. In Spain, social security benefits were not awarded to priests until 1978, so prior to that year retirements were practically nonexistent. Note the huge jump in the Spanish rates for the 1975–1979 period and the notable decline thereafter.

Not surprisingly, both dioceses had relatively high crude death rates among active priests prior to full implementation of the new retirement policies. Once a retirement program was in place, however, death rates among the actives declined and then, particularly in the U.S. diocese, stabilized immediately. In the Spanish diocese, the late institution of a retirement policy is reflected in a notably high annual crude death rate among active priests. As we shall see, the relatively high crude death rate also reflects a higher proportion of older priests in the Spanish than in the U.S. diocese. Thus, although during the census period the U.S. diocese lost 3-1/2 times as many active priests through retirement as did the Spanish one, the latter lost more than 2-1/2 times as many through death as did the former. Note, too, the diocese in Spain experienced a cumulative death rate more than one and a half times higher than its total ordination rate for the

19-year period. The other exit rates—excardination, sick leave, and awaiting assignment—are zero or close to nil and so have had no impact in the Spanish and minimal effects in the U.S. diocese.

The net gain or loss in population size is displayed in the bottom row of the table. The clergy population in the U.S. diocese experienced a sustained net decline for 10 years following the end of the Second Vatican Council. A short growth spurt in the second half of the 1970s was followed by another precipitous drop, which reinforced the prior downward trend. As we have noted, high resignations and retirements accounted for the early period of decline, whereas low ordinations and sustained resignations can be blamed for the more recent period of net loss. During the 19 years under study, the clergy of this diocese suffered a cumulative net loss of more than 14%. In absolute numbers, the population had declined to 285 active priests by the end of 1984 from its original high of 332 in 1966.

Table 1 shows that the Spanish diocese was still climbing to the zenith of a growth period during the late 1960s but then entered a sharp downward plunge that continued unchecked for a decade and a half. During the mid-1960s, this diocese enjoyed high ordination rates that were followed, however, from the mid-1970s onward, by a shattering drop in the number of newly ordained. The decline resulting from extremely low recruitment was then reinforced during the late 1970s as the new retirement program was inaugurated and resignations peaked. Overall, this diocese suffered a loss of more than 30% of its priest population during the 19-year period. The census counts show that the diocese reached its high-water mark in 1969 when the active priest population totaled 1,231. By the end of 1984, it had dropped to 844—a net loss of nearly 400 priests in just 15 years.

A demographic transition of some magnitude is underway in the two dioceses, as the table has demonstrated. To determine the continuing force and direction of change in size and age distribution of the clergy and whether the population transformation is developing according to the hypothesized pattern, we completed a series of long-range projections of these past trends.

ESTIMATES AND PROJECTIONS
OF SIZE AND AGE DISTRIBUTION, 1966–2045

We attempt to analyze the demographic transition of the clergy for a period of almost 80 years, only 19 of which are covered by empirical data. The plausibility of population projections decreases quickly with each passing decade, so results of the analysis are presented with growing caution once the projections go beyond 20 years. It is only for theoretical purposes that we are willing to hazard any projections beyond 2015, realizing that future historical events will probably intervene to make them untenable. The long-range projections are not entirely useless, however, because they shed light on the consequences of the "what-if" models contained in our assumptions. Stable population theory posits the question, "*What* would happen to population size and composition over time *if* entrance events and attrition rates continued into the future at constant levels?" The final segments of our model address this theoretical issue; they will be discussed after describing the less futuristic and more plausible results of the projections.

Change in Population Size, 1966–2015

Table 2 and Figure 2 show the census estimates of population size for the U.S. diocese from 1966–1984 and projections to the year 2045. Corresponding data for the Spanish diocese are contained in Table 2 and Figure 3. We begin the analysis with the first part of the model, which covers the

TABLE 2. Estimates of Number of Active Priests in a U.S. and a Spanish Catholic Diocese, 1966–1984; Projections 1985–2045; and Percentage Decline since 1966[a] (Percentages in Parentheses)

Assumption	Year								
	1966	1975	1985	1995	2005	2015	2025	2035	2045
U.S. diocese:									
Optimistic			279	249	266	263	266	271	272
			(16)	(25)	(20)	(21)	(20)	(18)	(18)
Moderate	332	296	281	232	189	155	133	130	130
		(11)	(15)	(30)	(43)	(53)	(60)	(61)	(61)
Pessimistic			272	176	121	87	74	74	74
			(18)	(47)	(64)	(74)	(78)	(78)	(78)
Spanish diocese:									
Optimistic			794	650	545	337	228	237	241
			(33)	(45)	(54)	(72)	(81)	(80)	(80)
Moderate	1187	1119	794	611	423	194	95	88	88
		(6)	(33)	(49)	(64)	(84)	(92)	(93)	(93)
Pessimistic			787	576	349	119	38	31	31
			(34)	(51)	(71)	(90)	(97)	(97)	(97)

[a]Projection model:
$$X_{ij} = [X_{i-1,j-1} + (A_{j-1}/2)]S_{j-1} + (A_{j-1}/2)$$
Where X_{ij} is the age-specific population at the beginning of the year for age group j in year i; A_{j-1} is the additions to age group $j-1$; and S_{j-1} is the survival probability for age group $j-1$.
And: $$A_{j-1} = N_{j-1} + O_{j-1} + I_{j-1}$$
Where N_{j-1} is number of returns from leaves of absence for age group $j-1$; O_{j-1} is number of ordinations for age group $j-1$; and I_{j-1} is the number of incardinations for age group $j-1$.
And: $$S_{j-1} = (R_{j-1})(E_{j-1})(T_{j-1})(D_{j-1})(L_{j-1}).$$
Where R_{j-1} is the resignation survival probability for age group $j-1$; E_{j-1} is the excardination survival probability for age group $j-1$; T_{j-1} is retirement survival probability for age group $j-1$; D_{j-1} is the death survival probability for age group $j-1$; and L_{j-1} is the leave of absence survival probability for age group $j-1$.

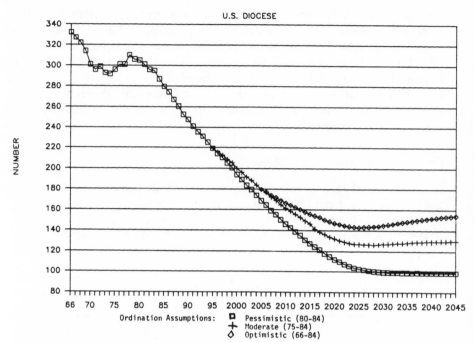

FIGURE 2. Estimates of number of active priests, 1966–1984; projections, 1985–2045. See Table 2, footnote a for projection model.

historical census period from 1966–1984 and the first 30 years of the projections from 1985–2015. We believe the population transformation revealed during that period is reasonably probable. Examining the time span from the beginning of the historical data to the year 2015, the sustained dramatic drop in numbers is the most obvious and important trend of note. By the most optimistic assumptions, the decline in clergy population for the U.S. diocese would reach 21% in the five-decade period between 1966 and 2015. If the pessimistic assumptions hold true, the loss would be in the area of 74% since 1966. For the Spanish diocese, the decrease is even more precipitous, ranging between 72% and 90% since 1966.

Such alarming figures raise questions about how realistic the assumptions are and whether one is more trustworthy than the others. The single most important component of the model in determining future trends is the ordination assumption. That is, relative to the other assumptions built into the model, changes in the ordination assumption have much greater importance in assessing the likelihood of various future outcomes. Because both dioceses have experienced a long period of declining recruitment, we can see little probability that the actual outcomes in these dioceses will be above the curve projected in Figures 2 and 3 by the moder-

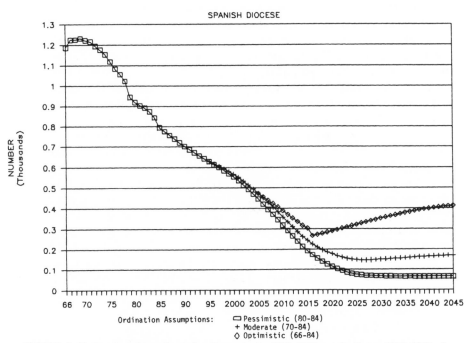

FIGURE 3. Estimates of number of active priests, 1966–1984; projections, 1985–2045. See Table 2, footnote a for projection model.

ate assumptions. Thus if recruitment stabilizes at the 1980–1984 level, the likely population size would approach the trend projected by the moderate assumptions. If, however, recruitment continues to decline in the fashion projected by the regression models used in setting the assumptions—and the models are statistically significant at the .01 level in both dioceses—then the likely outcome would be closer to the losses indicated by the pessimistic assumptions. Hence, the most reasonable future trend would probably fall somewhere between the projection curves produced by the moderate and pessimistic assumptions.

Change in Age Composition, 1966–2015

One of the most important and immediate concomitants of sustained decline in size is transformation of a population's age composition. Table 3, along with Figures 4 and 5, illustrates the changing age distribution of active priests in the two dioceses at 10-year intervals—the first is a 9-year period since our historical data begin in 1966. The bar graphs display absolute numbers in order to show the differences in the overall size of the total population as well as in the numbers at each age.

Both models are based on the moderate assumptions, which incorporate the 1980–1984 or most current entrance and attrition events. Note these assumptions assume that declining ordinations have leveled off at their current rates that will continue indefinitely. The regression analysis has shown, however, that ordinations are most likely to continue to drop in both dioceses. As a consequence, the data for age composition presented in this chapter can be viewed as somewhat optimistic, at least over the next decade or two. Beyond 2015 it is impossible to weigh the plausibility of any assumption. Nevertheless, we continue to maintain the same constant rates to 2045 for theoretical reasons, that is, in order to analyze results of our stable population model.

We again concentrate on that part of the graph that is based on the empirical data and the first 30 years of the projections, namely age composition changes between 1966 and 2015. Figure 4 shows that the U.S. diocese enjoyed a fairly well-balanced age distribution in 1966 with 22% of its population in the youngest age category and 27% in the combined 55 to 64, 65 to 74, and 75 and over age cohorts. By the end of the census period (1984), however, the population had aged notably, with only 11% in the

TABLE 3. Distribution of Active Priests by Age in a U.S.
and a Spanish Catholic Diocese: Estimates, 1966–1984
and Projections Using Moderate Assumptions, 1985–2045[a]

Age group	Year								
	1966	1975	1985	1995	2005	2015	2025	2035	2045
U.S. diocese:									
25–34	73	68	32	19	19	19	19	19	19
	(22)	(23)	(11)	(8)	(10)	(12)	(14)	(15)	(15)
35–44	97	79	73	39	30	30	30	30	30
	(29)	(27)	(26)	(17)	(16)	(20)	(23)	(23)	(23)
45–54	72	71	75	65	39	31	31	31	31
	(22)	(24)	(27)	(28)	(21)	(20)	(23)	(24)	(24)
55+	90	78	102	109	101	75	53	50	50
	(27)	(26)	(36)	(47)	(54)	(48)	(40)	(38)	(38)
Spanish diocese:									
25–34	430	155	15	12	12	12	12	12	12
	(36)	(14)	(2)	(2)	(3)	(6)	(13)	(14)	(14)
35–44	236	428	130	20	18	18	18	18	18
	(20)	(38)	(16)	(3)	(4)	(9)	(19)	(20)	(20)
45–54	92	194	367	116	19	17	17	17	17
	(8)	(17)	(46)	(19)	(5)	(9)	(18)	(19)	(19)
55+	429	342	281	462	374	147	48	41	41
	(36)	(30)	(36)	(76)	(88)	(76)	(56)	(46)	(46)

[a]See Table 2 for projection model.

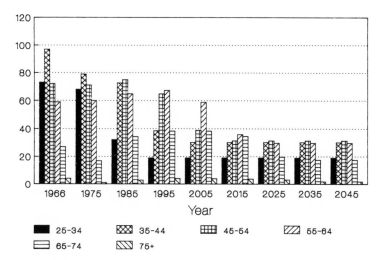

FIGURE 4. Age distribution of active priests in a U.S. diocese, 1966–2045. (Projections for 1985–2045 are based on moderate assumptions.)

youngest and 36% in the senior groups. If the 1980–1984 assumptions — which we believe are realistic if not slightly optimistic—hold true to 2015, the imbalance will have increased considerably; nearly half of the active priests will be 55 or older, whereas only about one-eighth will be under 35.

As Figure 5 demonstrates, the Spanish diocese was very evenly but somewhat artificially balanced in 1966; the number of active priests 25 to 34 years old and the number 55 and older each represented 36% of the total population. The age profile for that year and for 1975, however, is influenced by period effects—probably the events of the Spanish Civil War. In the late 1930s, 4,185 diocesan priests and some 3,000 other ecclesiastics were assassinated (Payne, 1984). The small number of priests in the age bracket 45 to 54 produces a "hollow" in the 1966 pyramid and the same relatively small cohort, after surviving 9 years, has a similar effect on the 1975 pyramid. These men would have been between 18 and 28 years old in 1939, the age of many seminarians and young priests who were killed during the war.

By 1985, the population transformation in the Spanish diocese had already begun in earnest. Whereas the proportion of active priests in the older age groups continued at 36%, the youngest age category had dwindled to an unbelievable 2%, representing a 94% drop in the youngest age category in just 19 years. As Table 1 has shown, this is the combined result of a drastic cut in ordinations and sustained high resignations. Projecting these trends for the next three decades, under the moderate assumptions, would result in an age pyramid in 2015 with an astonishing 76% of the active priests at least 55 years old (after peaking at 88% in 2005)

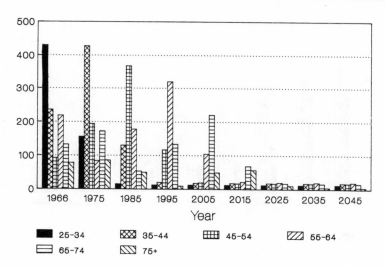

FIGURE 5. Age distribution of active priests in a Spanish diocese, 1966–2045. (Projections for 1985–2045 are based on moderate assumptions.)

and a mere 6% under 35 years of age. Thus, by the end of the census period, both the U.S. and Spanish dioceses have been transformed from relatively balanced and healthy into older, and in the case of the Spanish diocese extremely older, populations. According to our projections, the aging trends will continue unabated well into the twenty-first century.

Stages of the Demographic Transition, 1966–2045

Figures 4 and 5 also permit us to examine our hypotheses and theoretical assumptions about the incidence, stages, speed, and extent of the demographic transition of the clergy. *Mutatis mutandis*, the bar graphs contained in these figures may be interpreted as a series of population pyramids similar to those shown in Figure 1. Because the Roman Catholic priesthood is exclusively male, only the left side of the typical population pyramid can be constructed. And to simplify the graphing techniques, we present the age bars vertically as a bar chart rather than horizontally, which is the traditional manner.

Careful study of the observed and projected age distributions in the series of pyramids reveals that the demographic transition is well underway in both dioceses and is following the process as hypothesized. In addition, the similarities and differences among and between the two groups of pyramids show that whereas the same social forces are at work in the two organizations, the pattern, speed, and extent of the population transformation is different in each. If we ignore the hollow in the first Spanish pyramid in Figure 5, which was probably caused by military losses, the bar chart for 1966 is a striking example of a Stage 1 pyramid. It shows a large, young population with a characteristic triangle-shaped pyramid. The chart for the 1966 U.S. data in Figure 4 is very similar except that the second age bar is the longest one instead of the first. Thus, although the Spanish is somewhat younger overall than the U.S. population, nevertheless, in view of subsequent pyramids, they could both well be in the launching stage of a demographic transition.

Following the changes along at 10-year intervals reveals that the longest bar begins to move across each successive distribution—and thus up the age pyramid—until the bar charts for 1995 in both the U.S. and Spanish diocese take on the beehive shape of the Stage 2 pyramid illustrated in Figure 1. In addition, the size of the pyramids has continued to shrink over the three-decade period since 1966. The length of the longest age bar relative to the two youngest age bars indicates that the population in the Spanish will be much older than that in the U.S. diocese.

The smaller inverted pyramid shape, indicating an old, continuously declining population, appears in both dioceses by 2015. The similarity between these shapes and the Stage 3 pyramid in Figure 1 is not quite exact but is close enough to provide evidence for our hypotheses. In the Spanish diocese, the oldest age bar is slightly smaller than the second oldest age bar, whereas in the U.S. diocese the oldest age bar is extremely small in comparison to all the others. We should probably revise our theoretical expectations accordingly. Only an extremely old population will take on the exact shape of an inverted pyramid—the Spanish approximation is very close, and the population is extraordinarily old. Other aged populations will have the characteristic inverted triangle shape but with a small cap or needle-size oldest age bar on top, as does the U.S. pyramid.

The younging process begins during the next 10 years of the transition and by 2025 beehive-shaped pyramids, which are close replicas of the Stage 4 pyramid in Figure 1, characterize the age distribution in both dioceses. The size of the pyramids is also much smaller in comparison to previous ones. Again, in the case of the Spanish diocese, the reduction in size is severe.

Recall that all age distributions displayed from 1985 onward are the result of a constant set of attrition and recruitment assumptions, which we incorporate to test the implications of stable population theory. The data in the two figures show that stability would be reached by 2035, and the transition process would stop short of reaching a pyramid shape characterizing a young Stage 5 population because the average recruitment age would be relatively high, probably owing to a rising average age at ordination and the influx of incardinations at older ages. The final size and age composition of both populations would thus continue without alteration so long as the attrition and recruitment assumptions remained unchanged.

Discussion

As a preliminary step toward understanding social change in organized religion, we attempted to demonstrate that the theory of the demographic transition and model of the stable population are useful tools. A 19-year census of clergymen in two religious organizations provided data for analyzing trends in recruitment and attrition and served as the basis for projections circumscribing the stages of a dramatic population transformation. Our data described the movement of a large, young, and growing population of diocesan priests through theoretically predictable phases of transformation that included, midway, a stage depicting an old declining population and, eventually, a final stage with a pyramid reflecting a small, young, and stable population. We concluded that the well-known structure of the societal demographic transition characterizes, *mutatis mutandis*, the process of population transformation that takes place in organizations undergoing sustained membership decline.

Comparing organizations in two countries revealed that the demographic transition is not limited to the United States. Also questions about the speed, timing, and duration of the transformation could begin to be addressed. For example, the Spanish diocese has progressed faster and further in the transition than the U.S. diocese. Attritions through resignation and retirement, however, peaked earlier in the United States than in Spain, whereas ordinations dropped much more swiftly in the latter country than in the former. Clearly, comparative studies with a sufficiently large case base are needed to explain these and other important variations in the demographic transition of the clergy. Explicit causal models must be used to examine antecedents of the demographic transition and its consequences for changing the structure of the ministry, not only in local diocesan organizations but also in the Roman Catholic church as a whole.

We contend that countervailing demographic forces within the Roman Catholic church are producing internal organizational contradictions. Mounting evidence shows the U.S. Roman Catholic church growing in power, influence, and membership size (Roof & McKinney, 1987), whereas its clergy is undergoing rapid decline. Contradictions within organizations, however, are not uncommon; in most modern organizations they are the rule rather than the exception. For example, in his critique of Weber's ideal-type bureaucracy, Merton (1952) noted how dysfunctions of the bureaucratic personality give rise to "trained incapacities." Bureaucratic organizations establish rules and decision-making parameters that lead to efficiency but also contradict the need for flexibility in the face of change. Acting according to rules and established decision-making procedures often creates a trained incapacity to react to changing conditions.

Contradictory demands and countervailing social forces can have dire consequences for organizations. In his analysis of organizations in crisis,

Starbuck (1983) describes a case study of the Facit corporation, which lost its unrivaled first place in the calculating machine international market in a relatively short time. By ignoring the electronics revolution, top managers—mesmerized by the success of producing and marketing the best mechanical calculator in the world—allowed the organization to go beyond the point of no return and were never able to recover from the rapid degeneration process.

The fate of the Facit corporation exemplifies Marx's insight that contradictions inherent in social systems are the seeds of change. In the case of the Facit company, the contradiction between technical rational efficiency of tried-and-true procedures, on the one hand, and the need to adapt swiftly to changing technology, on the other, led to organizational demise. In other organizations, change spawned by inherent contradictions can lead to organizational transformation.

Organizational contradictions embodied in the demographic forces within the Roman Catholic church are a powerful driving force for change. Whether the seeds of change will lead to organizational strength or decline in the long run is an empirical question. Bottomore (1975, pp. 161–162) summarizes how demographic processes can produce organizational change:

> One obvious source of variation in the social structure is the continual circulation of membership.... [B]y the elaboration of new ideas and values, younger generations clearly play a part in the destructuring and restructuring of society; they may do so...by interpreting roles differently and...by forming new groups which engage in different types of action.

Several dynamics are at work in late twentieth-century Catholicism creating circulation of new members, new roles, and different types of action, which are transforming the structure of the Catholic church. Clergy decline, primarily, but in interaction with other social preconditions for structural transformation, is modifying the internal political economy of Roman Catholicism (Schoenherr & Sorensen, 1982). A second trend at work is the doctrinal changes legitimated by the Second Vatican Council, which have introduced unprecedented individualism and voluntarism regarding beliefs and values. Critical among the dogmatic redefinitions is a weakened belief in the absolute necessity of celibacy as a way of holiness and a strengthened importance of the charism of marriage as an equal but different means of grace (Schillebeeckx, 1985; Schoenherr & Greeley, 1974). Third, the feminist movement, particularly among nuns and laywomen in church-related careers, is beginning to erode male hegemony over the church's ministry and to establish a growing sense of female equality (Gilmour, 1986). Fourthly, the ordained clergy's political monopoly is being called into question by increased lay participation in ministerial roles (Leege, 1986). Last and inevitably, the sacramental and in particular the eucharistic focus of the Catholic church's "means of justification"

(Troeltsch, 1931) is being dimmed by the growing recognition of the "saving power" of the scriptures as fewer priests are available for mass and more laypeople preside at liturgies of the word.

These political and social conditions have been gaining momentum along with the economic force of the clergy decline. If and when these trends reach a threshold, they could produce an impetus for dramatic social change (Collins, 1980). If in the hearts and minds of believers, for example, the sacrament of marriage would balance the institution of celibacy as a way of Christian holiness and male hegemony would give way to female equality, the Roman Catholic church could allow the ordination of married men and women and thereby stem the clergy decline. At the same time, however, such reforms would dramatically change the structure of the ministry as well as the entire internal political economy of the church. Or, on the other hand, if, in place of the mass, a future Catholic generation became satisfied with worship limited to scripture services and communal prayer led by layministers, this modification in the means of grace would constitute a very different but nonetheless significant structural change in the church's pattern of belief and cultic worship as well as its internal political economy.

We expect continued resistance to such radical changes in the short run. Research findings suggest that conservative resistance in the church is linked to strong period and cohort effects. Schoenherr and Greeley (1974) reported that during the exodus following the Second Vatican Council, liberal priests in the United States were more likely to resign than conservative ones, and Schoenherr and Pérez Vilariño (1979) found the same was true in Spain. In a recent replication of the National Opinion Research Center (NORC) (1972) study of the U.S. clergy, Hoge, Shields, and Verdieck (1988) document that in 1984 young priests were significantly more conservative than their age peers who were surveyed in 1970, scoring lower on liberal items than many of their older confreres. In addition, Verdieck et al. (1988) replicated the NORC commitment model and found strong evidence that the same social processes leading to resignations in 1970, particularly problems with celibacy, were still operative in 1984. The net result, according to the cumulative data, is that active clergy of the 1980s, as a group, are less open to innovation and change than those of the previous decade. Furthermore, as the demographic transition of the clergy progresses, this conservativism will continue to grow.

In addition to the conservative influence of period effects, other research shows that, as complex organizations, dioceses can expect to suffer the social consequences of an aging clergy. Data provided by Lipset (1960), Downs (1967), and Reed (1978), for example, show that various types of organizations with relatively large senior cohorts are more resistant to change than those with predominantly younger members.

Our hunch that, in spite of growing conservatism, the demographic transition of the clergy will be the driving force for structural change in the Roman Catholic church—including, as Wilson (1986) suggests, the ordination of married men and possibly of women—is based on the recognition that substantial population change unleashes powerful economic forces. We contend that although the theology and tradition identified with the church's magisterium are strongly opposed to such change, church leaders will find it increasingly more difficult to resist the enormous economic pressure that is building up as diocese after diocese loses half of its ordained ministers, whereas most of those remaining are aged and overburdened. This situation is exacerbated by slow but steady growth of the Catholic population, especially in the United States (Roozen & Carrol, 1979; Roof & McKinney, 1987). Hence, the most probable options for the church would be to initiate radical restructuring of the ministry along the lines suggested or to modify its traditional emphasis on the mass and sacraments. Whatever direction is taken, however, the Roman Catholic church bears careful scrutiny over the next several decades. Conflict and change will inevitably emerge as demographic forces gain momentum on a collision course.

ACKNOWLEDGMENTS

This research was supported by a grant from Lilly Endowment, Inc., to the United States Catholic Conference and by a grant from the Fulbright Commission, Comite Conjunto Hispano-Norteamericano para la Cooperacion Cultural y Educativa. Supplemental grants were provided by the Family and Demographic Research Institute and College of Family, Home and Social Science, Brigham Young University.

REFERENCES

Barclay, George W. (1958). *Techniques of population analysis.* New York: John Wiley.
Barker, Eileen. (1985). New religious movements: Yet another great awakening? In Phillip E. Hammond (Ed.), *The sacred in a secular age* (pp. 36–57). Berkeley: University of California Press.
Bell, Daniel. (1977). The return of the sacred? The argument of the future of religion. *British Journal of Sociology, 28*(4), 419–449.
Bellah, Robert N. (1968). Civil religion in America. In Donald R. Cutler (Ed.), *The religious situation* (pp. 331–388). Boston: Beacon Press.
Bellah, Robert N. (1970). *Beyond belief.* New York: Harper & Row.
Bellah, Robert, Madsen, Richard, Sullivan, William, Swidler, Ann, & Tipton, Steven. (1985). *Habits of the heart.* Berkeley: University of California Press.
Bottomore, Tom. (1975). Structure and history. In Peter Blau (Ed.), *Approaches to the study of social structure* (pp. 159–171). New York: Free Press.
Brittain, Jack, & Freeman, John. (1980). Organizational proliferation and density dependent selection. In John Kimberly & Robert Miles (Eds.), *Organizational life cycles* (pp. 291–338). San Francisco: Jossey-Bass.

Carroll, Glenn R. (1983). *Concentration and specialization: Dynamics of niche width in populations of organizations.* Unpublished manuscript.

Carroll, Glenn R., & Delacroix, Jacques. (1982). Organizational mortality in the newspaper industries of Argentina and Ireland: An ecological approach. *Administrative Science Quarterly, 27,* 169–198.

Collins, Randall. (1980). Weber's last theory of capitalism: A systematization. *American Sociological Review, 45,* 925–942.

Downs, Anthony. (1967). *Inside bureaucracy.* Boston: Little, Brown.

Freeman, John. (1982). Organizational life cycles and natural selection processes. In Barry M. Staw & Lawrence L. Cummings (Eds.), *Research in organizational behavior, 4* (pp. 1–32). Greenwich, CT: JAI Press.

Freeman, John, & Hannan, Michael T. (1983). Niche width and the dynamics of organizational populations. *American Journal of Sociology, 88,* 116–145.

Freeman, John, Carroll, Glenn R., & Hannan, Michael T. (1983). The liability of newness: Age-dependence in organizational death rates. *American Sociological Review, 48,* 692–710.

Gilmour, Peter. (1986). *The emerging pastor: Non-ordained Catholic pastors.* Kansas City, MO: Sheed & Ward.

Greeley, Andrew M. (1972a). *The denominational society: A sociological approach to religion in America.* Glenview, IL: Scott, Foresman and Company.

Greeley, Andrew M. (1972b). *Unsecular man: The persistence of religion.* New York: Shocken.

Gusfield, Joseph R. (1957). The problem of generations in an organizational structure. *Social Forces, 35,* 322–330.

Hadden, Jeffrey K., & Shupe, Anson. (1985). Introduction. In Jeffrey K. Hadden & Anson Shupe (Eds.), *Prophetic religions and politics: Religion and the political order* (pp. xi–xxix). New York: Paragon House.

Hannan, Michael T., & Freeman, John. (1977). The population ecology of organizations. *American Journal of Sociology, 82,* 929–964.

Herberg, Will. (1955). *Protestant, Catholic, Jew.* New York: Doubleday & Company.

Hernes, Gudman (1976). Structural change in social processes. *American Journal of Sociology, 82,* 513–547.

Hirschman, Albert O. (1970). *Exit, voice and loyalty: Responses to declines in firms.* Cambridge, MA: Harvard University Press.

Hoge, Dean R., Carroll, Jackson W., & Sheets, Francis K. (1988). *Patterns of parish leadership: Cost and effectiveness in four denominations.* Kansas City, MO: Sheed and Ward.

Hoge, Dean R., Shields, Joseph J., & Verdieck, Mary Jeanne. (1988). Changing age distribution and theological attitudes of Catholic priests, 1970–85. *Sociological Analysis, 49,* 264–280.

Hout, Michael, & Greeley, Andrew M. (1987). Church attendance in the United States. *American Sociological Review, 52,* 325–345.

Kelley, Dean. (1972). *Why conservative churches are growing.* New York: Harper & Row.

Leege, David C. (1986). Parish life among the leaders. Report No. 9, *Notre Dame study of Catholic parish life.* Notre Dame, IN: University of Notre Dame.

Lipset, Seymour Martin. (1960). *Political man: The social bases of politics.* Garden City: Doubleday.

Luckmann, Thomas. (1967). *The invisible religion.* New York: Macmillan.

Marty, Martin E. (1979). Foreword. In Dean R. Hoge & David A. Roozen (Eds.), *Understanding church growth and decline, 1950–1978* (p. 10). New York: Pilgrim Press.

Matras, Judah. (1975). Models and indicators of organizational growth, changes and transformations. In Kenneth C. Land & Seymour Spilerman (Eds.), *Social indicator models* (pp. 301–318). New York: Russell Sage Foundation.

McCain, Bruce, O'Reilly, Charles A., & Pfeffer, Jeffrey. (1983). The effects of departmental demography on turnover: The case of a university. *Academy of Management Journal, 26,* 626–641.

Merton, Robert K. (1952). Bureaucratic structure and personality. In Robert K. Merton, Ailsa P. Gray, Barbara Hockey, & Hanan C. Sevlin (Eds.), *Reader in bureaucracy* (pp. 361–371). Glencoe, IL: The Free Press.

National Opinion Research Center (1972). *The Catholic priest in the United States: Sociological investigations.* (Andrew M. Greeley & Richard A. Schoenherr, principal investigators.) Washington DC: United States Catholic Conference Publications.

Niebur, H. Richard. (1929). *The social sources of denominationalism.* New York: Holt.

Parsons, Talcott. (1963). Christianity and modern industrial society. In Edward A. Tiryakian (Ed.), *Sociological theory, values and sociocultural change* (pp. 33–70). Glencoe, IL: Free Press.

Payne, Stanley G. (1984). *Spanish Catholicism: An historical overview.* Madison: University of Wisconsin Press.

Pfeffer, Jeffrey. (1985). Organizational demography: Implications for management. *California Management Review, 28,* 67–81.

Reed, Theodore L. (1978). Organizational change in the American Foreign Service, 1925–1965: The utility of cohort analysis. *American Sociological Review, 30,* 843–861.

Robinson, John A. T. (1963). *Honest to God.* Philadelphia: Westminster Press.

Roof, Wade Clark, & McKinney, William. (1987). *American mainline religion: Its changing shape and future.* New Brunswick, NJ: Rutgers University Press.

Roozen, David A., & Carroll, Jackson W. (1979). Recent trends in church membership participation: An introduction. In Dean Hoge & David Roozen (Eds.), *Understanding church growth and decline* (pp. 21–41). New York: Pilgrim Press.

Ryder, Norman B. (1965). The cohort in the study of social change. *American Sociological Review, 30,* 843–861.

Schillebeeckx, Edward. (1985). *The church with a human face: A new and expanded theology of ministry.* New York: Crossroads.

Schoenherr, Richard A. (1987). Power and authority in organized religion: Disaggregating the phenomenological core. *Sociological Analysis, 47 S,* 52–71.

Schoenherr, Richard A., & Greeley, Andrew M. (1974). Role commitment processes and the American Catholic priesthood. *American Sociological Review, 39,* 407–426.

Schoenherr, Richard A., & Sorensen, Annemette. (1982). Social change in religious organizations: Consequences of clergy decline in the U.S. Catholic church. *Sociological Analysis, 43,* 23–52.

Schoenherr, Richard A., & Pérez Vilariño, José. (1979). Organizational role commitment in the Catholic church in Spain and the USA. In Cornelis Lammers & David Hickson (Eds.), *Organizations alike and unalike: International and interinstitutional studies in the sociology of organizations* (pp. 346–372). London: Routledge & Kegan Paul.

Schoenherr, Richard A., Young, Lawrence A., & Vilariño, José Pérez. (1988). Demographic transitions in religious organizations: A comparative study of priest decline in Roman Catholic dioceses. *Journal for the Scientific Study of Religion, 27,* 499–523.

Shryock, Henry S., Siegel, Jacob S., and Associates (1976). *The methods and materials of demography.* New York: Academic Press.

Singh, Jitendra V., House, Robert J., & Tucker, David J. (1986). Organizational change and organizational mortality. *Administrative Science Quarterly, 31,* 587–611.

Starbuck, William H. (1983). Organizations as action generators. *American Sociological Review, 48,* 91–102.

Stark, Rodney, & Bainbridge, William. (1985). *The future of religion.* Berkeley: University of California Press.

Stewman, Shelby, & Konda, Surresh L. (1983). Careers and organizational labor markets: Demographic models of organizational behavior. *American Journal of Sociology, 88,* 637–685.

Swanson, Guy E. (1968). Modern secularity: Its meaning, sources, and interpretation. In Donald R. Cutler (Ed.), *The religious situation* (pp. 801–834). Boston: Beacon Press.

Troeltsch, Ernst. (1931). *The social teaching of the Christian churches*. New York: The Macmillan Company.

Verdieck, Mary Jeanne, Shields, Joseph T., & Hoge, Dean R. (1988). Role commitment processes revisited: American Catholic priests, 1970 and 1985. *Journal for the Scientific Study of Religion, 26*, 524–535.

Wagner, W. Gary, Pfeffer, Jeffrey, & O'Reilly, Charles A. (1984). Organizational demography and turnover in top-management groups. *Administration Science Quarterly, 29*, 74–92.

Weber, Max. (1963). *The sociology of religion*. Trans. by Ephraim Fischoff. Boston: Beacon Press.

Weber, Max. (1978). *Economy and Society*. 2 vols. Guenther Roth & Claus Wittich (Eds.). Berkeley: University of California Press.

Wilson, George B. (1986). The priest shortage: The situation and some options. *America* (May 31), pp. 450–453.

Wuthnow, Robert. (1976). Recent patterns of secularization: A problem of generations? *American Sociological Review, 41*, 850–867.

Wuthnow, Robert. (1988). *The restructuring of American religion: Society and faith since World War II*. Princeton, NJ: Princeton University Press.

Zald, Mayer N. (1970). *Organizational change: The political economy of the YMCA*. Chicago: University of Chicago Press.

CHAPTER EIGHT

The "Unmaking" of a Movement?

The Crisis of U.S. Trade Unions in Comparative Perspective

LARRY J. GRIFFIN, HOLLY J. MCCAMMON, AND CHRISTOPHER BOTSKO

INTRODUCTION

The sad particulars about the "House of Labor" in the America of the 1980s are well known: Labor quiescence predominates, and the trade union movement, demoralized and disorganized, has rapidly lost momentum. The number of union members began to decline in 1979 and continued to do so for another decade, representing the greatest sustained loss of unionists since the 1920s. Unions have since lost between 4½ and 5½ million members. The rate of decline of "union density" (i.e., union membership as a percentage of the nonfarm labor force), already visible since 1954, began to steepen around 1979: It averaged about 0.4% per year for the period 1954–1978 but between 1% and 1.25% annually since 1979, more than double the previous rate.[1] In the 1950s, unions won about two-thirds of the National Labor Relations Board certification elections held; in the 1960s, almost 60%. Since the late 1970s, however, unions have been win-

[1]The exact figures here and elsewhere depend upon the definition of a "union member." The post-1979 decline of 1% is a conservative estimate, based on union membership of 20.661 million members in 1979; 1.25% is the more liberal estimate based on a 1979 membership of 22.579 (Goldfield, 1987, p. 11). We use the higher 1979 value of union membership in the remainder of the chapter because it and all post-1979 U.S. data are from the same source.

LARRY J. GRIFFIN AND CHRISTOPHER BOTSKO • Department of Sociology, Indiana University, Bloomington, Indiana 47405.   HOLLY J. MCCAMMON • Department of Sociology, Vanderbilt University, Nashville, Tennessee 37235.

ning only about 45% of NLRB certification elections, and during the Reagan years the number of such elections declined by about 50% (Moody, 1987). Finally, labor's strike activity, too, is much lower today than it was even two decades ago, with production time lost to strikes during the mid-1980s reaching an historic low.

One dramatic result of this decline in both organizational strength and workplace insurgency is that the very nature of collective bargaining and labor–management relations have been altered. By the early 1980s, "concession bargaining" among some of the major unions—a process kicked off by the pivotal contract between Chrysler Motor Company and the United Automobile Workers in 1979—had become a widespread phenomenon, replacing traditional forms of wage bargaining institutionalized for 40 and more years (Cappelli & McKersie, 1985; Cullen, 1985). Under this emerging collective bargaining regime, unions traded reductions in wage and fringe demands (and also often relaxed work rules) for nonfinancial benefits, especially employment security, deferred bonus and profit-sharing plans, and representation on company boards of directors (Uchitelle, 1987). Often these "gains" look better on paper than in practice; the job "guarantees," for example, are rather easily circumvented (Massing, 1988; Schlesinger, 1987). By 1982 a number of firms in key industries had engaged extensively in concession bargaining, affecting 36% of the unionized firms in one national survey (Cappelli & McKersie, 1985).

The damaging economic consequences of concession bargaining are clear: In the 1982–1985 period, for example, the average collective bargaining settlement advanced the total compensation received by covered workers by only 4% as compared to 9.8% for the 1974–1982 years (U.S. Bureau of the Census, 1987, p. 407). In real terms, the hourly earnings of production and nonsupervisory workers, including overtime pay, declined almost 5% in the decade from 1975 to 1985. Perhaps most startling, Troy (1986, p. 104) reports that in 1985 compensation gains for unionized labor averaged 2.6% compared to 4.6% for unorganized workers.

Concession bargaining coincided with both the recession of the 1980s and the industrial deregulation wave, which especially hurt union organization in trucking, airlines, and communications (Farber, 1987; Troy, 1986). Economic fluctuations and policies, moreover, are not the only forces combining with concession bargaining to weaken labor's public posture in the last decade. Heartened by President Reagan's firing of more than 10,000 air controller workers, and thereby the breaking of the Professional Air Traffic Controllers Organization in 1981, employers also began adopting new and more sophisticated antiunion strategies. They are increasingly aware of the consequences of "union avoidance" investment decisions, actively relocating in nonunion geographical regions or in countries with unorganized and cheap labor (Goldfield, 1987; Troy, 1986). In the early 1980s, the AFL-CIO (1985) estimated that 75% of all companies were hiring professional "antiunion" consultants, at an estimated cost of more than $100 million a year. Farber (1987) suggests that evidence of increasing employer resistance to unionism comes from the increasing number of unfair labor practice claims filed by unions charging employers with harassment during organizing drives; in 1960, the average of such claims was 1.78 per NLRB election; in 1977, 3.99; in 1982, 7.45.

If unions hope to find relief from government strike breaking and corporate antiunionism in public opinion or just pure political clout, here, too, the tide seemingly has turned. Public "approval" ratings, averaging in the 65 plus percentage range throughout much of the postwar period, and as high as 70% in as recently as 1965, fell to 55% in 1979 and stayed there for the next 6 years; union "disapproval" in the mid-1980s was at an historic high (Lipset, 1986a). Union participation as a powerful actor in the polity, especially so as an essential component of the "Democratic coalition," is now deeply jeopardized. Labor is increasingly unable to get its legislative agenda passed by a Congress fearful of being tagged "prolabor" (Freeman & Medoff, 1984; Lipset, 1986b).

So although organized labor in this country has, at least on some dimensions, been losing ground for several decades, the declines—both to its pocketbook and its public position—have been especially damaging since the late 1970s. Kochan, Katz, and McKersie (1986) suggest that all of this—"concession bargaining," labor passivity, political weakness, and renewed employer harassment and antiunionism—indicates that the New Deal industrial relations system governing collective bargaining from 1935 until 1980 and one of the foundations of the post-World War II "capital–labor accord" (Bowles, 1982; Gordon, Edwards, & Reich, 1982) is giving way to a "new industrial relations system" in which unions are even more distinctively the junior partner. It is thus fair to say that American labor is now at its lowest ebb in more than 50 years, certainly since the pre-Roosevelt Great Depression years.

The "crisis" of labor is such that the very existence of what has been one of the most effective instruments of working-class economic and political advancement ever witnessed in this country—unionization—is now seriously jeopardized. Unions, in our view, represent the single most important market-driven mechanism available to the bulk of workers in their struggles to achieve their material interests (Griffin, O'Connell, & McCammon, 1989; Griffin, Wallace, & Rubin, 1986). They are a key component of labor's "organizational capacity" (Wright, 1978, p. 101) and of its mobilization of the resources needed for collective action (Przeworski, 1985; Tilly, 1978). Organized labor has shaped the contours of political debate, exchanging votes and campaign funds for national and local Democratic party support for its social agenda, an agenda sometimes transcending the narrow economic interests of union members (AFL-CIO, 1985; Greenstone, 1977). The self-organization of labor into trade unions must therefore be understood as an attempt by the working class (or at least that component organized) to present a solid front of opposition to employers in struggles for greater social benefits, higher wages, better fringe benefits, job protection, and the preservation of skill and a degree of worker control and autonomy (Gordon *et al.*, 1982; Montgomery, 1979; Perlman, 1928). In this, American unions were for almost half a century at least relatively successful. "Big" labor, neither revolutionary nor especially militant by comparative standards, delivered the goods to its members in the first three decades after World War II (Freeman & Medoff, 1984; Rubin, 1986), thereby contributing in no small part to the postwar "American economic miracle."

Lest it seem we exaggerate the past political power and economic clout of organized labor and thereby the magnitude and severity of the change, it is worth remembering that in 1950 "the historian Arthur Schlesinger assessed the ten events 'that profoundly shaped and shook history' in the first half of the twentieth century. Second only to the two world wars, Schlesinger placed the 'upsurge of labor'" (Brody, 1980, p. 173). A labor intellectual writing in 1951, J. B. S. Hardman, noted with confidence that "American labor unions have become a social power in the nation and are conscious of their import" (quoted in Brody, p. 174). Popular approval ratings during the period, moreover, were up and still climbing (Lipset, 1986a). Similar assessments from the popular press, the intelligentsia, and academia could easily be multiplied. All point in the same direction: Organized labor clearly came into its own in the early postwar years, and it was casting a long shadow indeed.

That this is no longer the case frames the issue explored in this chapter. Why do we now have a "crisis" of labor? There is no dearth of answers: Explanations of American labor's most recent decline range from the changing demography of the labor force, to shifts in industrial and occupational structures, to overt and covert employer opposition and an indifferent or hostile public policy, and even to worker indifference induced by union complacency and ineptitude (Farber, 1987; Goldfield, 1987; Kochan *et al.*, 1986; Raskin, 1986; Troy, 1986). No doubt all or many of these factors have indeed played their part in reducing the import and presence of organized labor in the United States. But without denying for a moment the special urgency of these questions for U.S. workers and for our polity more generally, the survival or growth of "the labor movement" is not uniquely an American concern: Unions in more than three-fourths of the 18 largest, politically stable capitalist democracies experienced sustained declines or stagnation in the depth or density of their organization from the late-1970s to the mid-1980s. In half of these nations, labor suffered, again as it did in the United States, *absolute* losses in union members. Strike-induced lost production time, too, fell in 11 countries during this same period. Thus we must conclude that many of the challenges confronting American labor in the mid-1980s, and perhaps too some of its few opportunities, characterize not only the United States but also an entire historical epoch and mode of economic and political organization.

Given these concurrent trends, we believe that comparative analysis may yield a more "general" understanding of labor's most recent past and its possible futures—here in this country, as well as elsewhere—than narrowly focused attention to the experiences of any single nation. Our analyses therefore will pertain to the 18 largest capitalist nations with continuous histories of political democracy since the complete reconstruction of the post-World War II capitalist order (roughly the mid-1950s): Australia, Austria, Belgium, Canada, Denmark, Finland, the Federal Republic of Germany, France, Ireland, Italy, Japan, The Netherlands, New Zealand, Norway, Sweden, Switzerland, the United Kingdom, and the United States.[2] Our expectation is that by understanding more thoroughly both similarities and differences among the advanced capitalist democracies in basic social processes—of organization and collective action, of markets and distribution, and of politics and power—in a particular historical period, we will be able to develop a more general accounting for the recent decay of the trade union movement in the United States.

In this chapter, we therefore raise and attempt to answer three specific questions, all directed toward developing a comparative appreciation of the decline of organized labor in the most recent phase of capitalist development: (1) What are the actual patterns of union growth or decay in virtually all of the large, politically stable capitalist democracies during the period of general decline? (2) What are the cross-national causes of these patterns? (3) What implications are there from these comparative analyses for understanding the "crisis" of labor in the United States in the mid- and late-1980s?

UNIONIZATION BEFORE AND DURING THE DECLINE

For the purposes of our analyses and discussion, we define as the *downturn period* those years during which union density either (1) actually declined, or (2) experienced an accelerated rate of decline if it was already in decline, or (3) stopped growing relative to its trend from the mid-1950s (e.g., stagnation). The initial year of the decline or stagnation period is dated separately for each nation from time plots of each country's union density. It terminates with the last year for which we have appropriate data (typically 1985, but for some countries as early as 1981).[3] Our procedure thus preserves the integrity of each nation's unique timing while simul-

[2]Data constraints forced us to exclude two small members of this population—Iceland and Luxembourg.
[3]No nation experiencing a recent period of "decline" (as defined) also saw an "upturn" by the last year for which we have data.

taneously posing cross-national differences in the magnitude of the downturn as the "general" phenomena to be explained, regardless of exactly when they occur within the historical period dating from late 1970s and early 1980s.

A small handful of nations (Belgium, Denmark, and Sweden) experienced no decline or appreciable stagnation in any period temporally proximate to the late 1970s. We analyze the recent unionization patterns of virtually all of the stable capitalist democracies, not simply those actually experiencing a downturn, and those few nations where unions were still growing as of 1985 represent "negative cases" in our explorations (Skocpol & Somers, 1980). To exploit these "negative cases" quantitatively, however, their recent histories must be periodized, just as are those for nations with downturns. We use the modal year of those nations experiencing a downturn, 1979, as the first year of the period to be analyzed for nations not suffering a downturn and the last year for which data are available as the termination year.

Table 1 presents for each country the magnitude of recent shifts in union density and the years included in the downturn period. Union density is defined as the number of union members divided by the "potentially unionizable labor force" (e.g., wage and salary workers plus the unemployed; see Bain & Price, 1980). Between 1979 and 1985 union density in the United States fell, absolutely, by 7.5% (Column 1) or 1.2 percent per year (Column 3). These statistics, reflecting the dimension of the crisis of union labor in the United States, are quite large by any comparative standard, but they are not idiosyncratic. Fifteen countries recorded density declines. Some of these nations, most notably Australia and Japan, actually gained union members during their downturn periods (Column 5) but nonetheless did so at a less rapid pace than the growth of the unionizable labor force.

Where the decline in density is small (e.g., Finland, Ireland, and Norway), we can conclude that organized labor has stagnated; that is, no real organizational gains, relative to the growth of the labor force, were made during the downturn period. Where the declines are large, unions suffered real organizational losses when compared to the growth in the number of potentially unionizable workers. Big losers during this period here are, in addition to the United States, Austria, The Netherlands (with the largest recorded absolute decline), New Zealand, and Britain. New Zealand, with only 2 years in the downturn period (1982–1984), saw the most severe annual decline in density (Column 3), and the United States experienced the largest proportional loss. *From 1979 to 1985 almost a third of American labor's already rapidly declining organizational strength was wiped out* (Column 2).

Union density loss or stagnation during the downturn is all the more striking when compared to union *gains* before this most recent period.

TABLE 1. Union Density Growth or Decline during and before
Nation-Specific Downturn Periods

	Change union density	Percentage change union density	Yearly change union density	Predecline yearly density growth	Change union membership (thousands)	Downturn years
Australia	-1.076	-5.397	-.179	-.136[a]	280	1979–1985
Austria	-4.831	-7.648	-1.610	-.344	-4	1981–1984
Belgium	2.109	2.890	.703	.739	118	1979–1982
Canada	-1.208	-3.636	-.403	-.063	49	1982–1985
Denmark	3.277	4.330	.546	.503	225	1979–1985
Finland	-.885	-1.092	-.22	2.56	103	1980–1984
France	-2.910	-12.902	-.728	.266	-390	1977–1981
Germany	-2.256	-5.630	-.376	.108	-136	1979–1985
Ireland	-.966	-1.750	-.322	.556	35	1979–1982
Italy	-2.379	-5.311	-.793	.690	-71	1978–1981
Japan	-2.567	-8.420	-.513	-.020	184	1979–1984
Netherlands	-9.471	-23.462	-1.579	-.081	-168	1979–1985
New Zealand	-5.291	-12.226	-2.646	-.041	-41	1982–1984
Norway	-.394	-.596	-.099	-.069	86	1981–1985
Sweden	6.659	7.765	1.110	1.04	428	1979–1985
Switzerland	-3.892	-9.729	-.487	-.203	-58	1977–1985
United Kingdom	-9.018	-16.658	-1.503	.524	-2128	1979–1985
United States	-7.489	-31.781	-1.248	-.399	-5583	1979–1985

[a] All predownturn trends are significant at the .05 level (two-tailed test) except Japan, The Netherlands, and New Zealand.

Union density was increasing in nine countries in the "predownturn" years (Column 4). In six of those, however, density growth was slowed or reversed by the early- to mid-1980s: Finland, France, Germany, Ireland, Italy, and the United Kingdom. Among the nine nations with declining densities in the predownturn years, almost all, like the United States, saw density decrease at a much faster rate during the downturn years. Compare, for example, Austria's and Japan's predownturn and downturn rates of decline. Only in Belgium (with truncated data), Denmark and Sweden were gains in labor's organizational strength not severely slowed or reversed. Aside from these exceptions, which figure prominently in subsequent analyses, we see a quite pronounced pattern, both in the generality and in timing of the downturn. Trade unions in three-fourths of the largest, politically stable capitalist democracies experienced generally sustained periods of downturn, defined here either as decline, accelerated decline, or stagnation in union density, during the late 1970s and early 1980s. The downturn started or was exacerbated in 1977 in France and Switzerland, 1978 in Italy, 1979 in most of the larger economies (Germany, Japan, the United Kingdom, and the United States) and also in Australia, Ireland, and The Netherlands, 1980 in Finland, 1981 in Austria and Norway, and 1982 in Canada and New Zealand.

The last decade or so, then, has proved to be a difficult time generally for the union movement throughout the capitalist democracies. Yet organized labor has not suffered equally in these countries: Labor lost dearly in some nations, remained relatively stagnant in other countries, and actually gained in a small number of cases. What accounts for this variability among labor movements even within a population of nations all organized around capitalist economics and democratic politics?

THEORETICAL EXPLANATIONS OF THE DECLINE

Extant theories of and past research on unionization suggest several clusters of cross-nationally variable economic and political factors may be responsible for these recent trends in organized labor's growth or decline.

1. *Unemployment and inflation.* Among the most important macroeconomic determinants of union growth historically within, and cross-sectionally between, countries are unemployment and inflation (Ashenfelter & Pencavel, 1969; Bain & Elsheikh, 1976). Unemployment is likely to empower employers in their use of the "surplus" labor to smash worker solidarity and to foster the belief among workers that the competition for jobs and employment security is of greater importance than organization or collective bargaining. Unemployment also probably reduces the amount of union funds that can be used for organizing and may represent the consequence of "capital flight"; that is, of capital, and hence jobs, actually physically leaving a locale or even a country, possibly as a profitable "union avoidance" strategy (Goldfield, 1987; Kochan et al., 1986). During the downturn periods, unemployment grew in fully 17 of the 18 countries we examine. It increased in the United States by 1.35%, less than the average across the population as a whole (2.5%).

Unlike unemployment, inflation tends to stimulate union growth (or slows union declines) as workers actively organize new unions or continue their membership in extant unions in order to bargain collectively for wage increases designed to reverse real wage declines (Bain & Elsheikh, 1976; Griffin et al., 1989). Labor in nations with high and/or increasing inflation has a heightened interest in recouping or avoiding real wage loss due to the reduced purchasing power of the currency and to the "inflation tax." Though possibly of reduced efficacy recently, unions, through their market power and contractual "cost-of-living" adjustments, are a prime market mechanism for doing precisely that (Mitchell, 1980). Disinflation, or a reduction in inflation rates, predominates generally during the downturn phase, with the steepest inflation decline observed in Canada, New Zealand, Britain, and the United States. Inflation increased appreciably only in Belgium, France, Ireland, and Italy.

2. *Economic "openness" and trade dependence.* The "openness" of the

economy, also often labelled *trade dependence*, is the sum of imports and exports as a percentage of Gross Domestic Product (GDP). Trade dependence may exert contradictory effects on the union movement. On the one hand, Cameron (1978) argues that a high level of foreign trade tends to generate industrial concentration as intense competition in the export sector drives out smaller and weaker capital. Industrial concentration, in turn, tends to promote both industry- or even economywide collective bargaining and probably reflects the growth of production conditions and relations in the export sector favoring labor organization: a mass working class sharing similar work experiences, market positions, material interest, and even employers (Cameron, 1978; Stephens, 1980). By introducing the domestic economy to extensive international trade, however, openness may indirectly retard unionization. To the extent that unions increase per unit labor costs (Freeman & Medoff, 1984) in relatively open economies and thereby reduce the competitiveness of the import or export sectors domestically, private employers and corporatist states (see Lehmbruch, 1984) may perceive the necessity for wage reduction. That, in turn, may require reducing the power of the trade unions (Farber, 1987; Troy, 1986).[4] Openness to the international economy grew for all but two nations (Finland and Ireland); overall, almost 6% more GDP was funneled through the import/export sectors by the time our data terminate than at the beginning of the downturn. United States openness increased marginally during the downturn period but in funneling about 19% of its GDP through its import and export sectors the American economy nonetheless remained the least trade dependent during those years.

3. *Social democratic modes of political governance.* States dominated by social democratic rule are characterized by parliamentary efforts by the organized working class to transform the basis of distribution from that regulated by market principles to that regulated by political principles themselves subject to periodic electoral evaluation and sanction (Cameron, 1984; Hibbs, 1987; Stephens, 1980). Cross-national differences in social democratic representation may affect how unions have fared during the

---

[4]Unfortunately, we lack the data necessary to test directly either interpretation of the possible effect of trade dependence. It is clear, however, that international competitiveness or even dominance is neither a necessary nor a sufficient condition for avoiding union decline. First the necessary condition: Belgium, at least until our data end for that country in 1982, was among the few nations with a growing labor movement. Yet its economy was also the most "open" in the population during the downturn, had an above average increase in foreign trade during the downturn period, and has an acknowledged problem with uncompetitive export markets (Blanpain, 1984). Unions in Ireland, although stagnant, were doing better as of 1982 than would be predicted from its international position; it also has the second most "open" economy and is severely "noncompetitive" (O'Connell, 1989). As for the sufficiency condition, Japan and Germany are much vaulted for the productivity of their export sector (Marshall, 1986), but both also suffered about average density loss during the downturn. Germany even witnessed an absolute loss of union members (Table 1).

downturn years either indirectly, through patterns of aggregate economic performance, and international trade favoring union organizing (Cameron, 1984; Griffin *et al.*, 1989; Hibbs, 1987), or directly, through "leftist corporatism" centered around the "citizen wage," class legislation protecting unions from employer assaults, and incomes policies. Social democratic governments almost universally owe their existence and incumbency to the labor movement (Cameron, 1984; Stephens, 1980); if they strongly displease unionists, by passing antiunion legislation, for example, they would likely be removed from office. Such regimes are in some sense the political arm of the mass working-class movement, suggesting that labor's organizational density and growth should be higher in social democratic regimes than in other nations.

Botsko (1989) and Hobsbawm (1989), however, suggest that the historic link between "labor-in-government" and "labor-on-the-shopfloor" may now be obsolete, a time-conditioned artifact of both the birth of the modern labor movement and, more recently, the "better times" of the 1950s and 1960s. Thus estimates of the impact of social democracy on unionization require a measurement strategy that recognizes possible period-specific effects. We constructed two distinct temporally grounded measures of social democratic governance that combine the electoral strength and success of leftist parties with their representation in cabinet.[5] The first, "long-term" social democratic rule, is a time-series average of the years dating from 1956 until the beginning of the downturn and acknowledges both (1) that left political rule may heighten labor's self-organization only over the "longer term," after social democratic governments have had the time and accumulated institutional power to enact legislation or pursue economic policies favorable to sustained union growth; and (2) that the "historic relationship" may not have lasted in the late 1970s and 1980s. The second measure taps the short-term and more-or-less immediate effects of levels and changes in social democratic incumbency during the downturn period. Going into the downturn, Austria, Denmark, Norway, and Sweden had the most sustained social democratic rule since the mid-1950s. Canada, Japan, and the United States had none, at least at the federal level. About a third of these 18 nations had visible social democratic participation in the management of the state during the downturn period.

4. *Characteristics of the labor movement.* Centralized labor movements should reduce labor's downturn or even stimulate union growth. The concept essentially taps (1) the degree to which rank-and-file unionists are controlled by the central labor confederation, (2) the degree to which the state negotiates with a solitary and identifiable institutional body representing organized labor, and (3) the degree to which capital confronts a

---

[5]"Leftist" parties include Socialist, Social Democratic, Labour, and Communist parties and several less well known "left-of-center" parties. The latter were determined by a content analysis of their platforms. We label for convenience all such parties "social democratic."

unified labor movement.[6] Centralization typically gives unions greater resources with which to organize the unorganized and to defend themselves against union-busting tactics of capital and the state. It can also help reduce the weakening consequence of fragmentation and intraunion competition (Cameron, 1984). Collective bargaining was most centralized in Austria, Denmark, Finland, Norway, and Sweden during late 1970s and early 1980s and least centralized in Canada, Japan, New Zealand, and the United States.

Another attribute of labor movements—strike activity—may also stimulate union growth. Militant labor often presses economic and political demands that are best realized through organization—primarily trade unions (Griffin et al., 1989; Tilly, 1978). A small but not trivial proportion of strikes, moreover, is held precisely over the right to form a union, to bargain collectively, and to organize in the market. Industrial disputes are, or may be converted into, organizing devices for the unions (Rubin, Griffin, & Wallace, 1983). Labor, on the whole, was less militant by the mid-1980s than when it entered the downturn period. In Australia, Canada, France, Ireland, the United Kingdom, and the United States especially, workers were much more quiescent as the downturn deepened. Only in Denmark and Sweden (with comparatively low levels of militancy initially) did workers become considerably more strike oriented.

The level of union density at the beginning of the downturn period is the final labor movement characteristic we examine. A strongly organized working class may have greater institutional and moral resources with which to expand further their organizational base even during periods of recession and antiunion corporate and state action. More weakly organized labor movements, lacking such resources, may be more subject to union losses during economic and political "hard times." This implies that "lagged" union density should stimulate changes in density. But there are also reasons to believe that prior organization will reduce further organizational gains. To the extent that union density represents or taps a "saturation" effect (Ashenfelter & Pencavel, 1969), highly unionized labor movements may find further organization increasingly difficult because each incremental union member takes more and more organizational effort. Going into the downturn, Denmark and Sweden had the highest level of union density; France and the United States, the lowest.

5. Industrial composition. Service industries are alleged to be difficult to organize for a variety of familiar reasons centering on the economic insecurity of the typical employer in this sector, who is most prone to antiunionism, and on the structure of work, the employment relationship, and

[6]Following Cameron (1984), we define union centralization as the numerical power of central labor confederations in the labor movement, confederation power in collective bargaining, scope of collective bargaining (ranging from restricted to economywide), and the presence of "co-determination" in decision making.

the market position and status concerns of "white-collar" workers (Dickens & Leonard, 1985; Farber, 1987; Freeman & Medoff, 1984; Troy, 1986). Troy (1986, pp. 76–77) suggests that the decline in unionization in the five largest capitalist countries (the United States, the United Kingdom, France, Germany, and Japan) "may be common to industrial economies making the transition to service-dominated labor markets" (but observe the Swedish labor movement, in which more than 85% of white-collar workers are organized). He goes on (p. 77) to state that the "service domination" of labor markets in the United States is "one of the keys to understanding the long-run decline of unionization in this country."

In the last 10 years or so, many of the traditionally "unionized industries" (heavy manufacturing, transportation, mining, etc.) have begun to lose workers. In 14 of the 18 countries, the number of employees in these sectors absolutely declined since the late 1970s or early 1980s. In Britain, an astounding 21% of jobs in the unionized sector disappeared. Even more dramatic is the loss of union sector jobs *relative* to growth of the service sector. *Every* single country experienced a decline in the proportion of the nonfarm labor force employed in these traditionally organized or possibly more easily organized industries. Service sector employment, and here we are including all services and trade sectors (but excluding government), grew, on the average, from slightly over 30% of the labor force in the first year of the downturn to 34% at the terminal year. Four nations saw service-sector increases (as measured as a percentage of the labor force) of 5% or more, with Switzerland, Britain, and the United States registering the greatest gains. Overall, service sector employment grew by 15% during this period, whereas "union sector" employment declined about 5%, just about the loss observed for the United States.

In brief, our expectations about the almost universal union decay generally since the late 1970s are that the decline should be greater in countries with high or increasing (1) unemployment and (2) service-sector employment/domination of the labor force, and lower in countries with high or increasing (1) inflation, (2) social democratic governance, (3) union centralization, and (4) strike activity. Trade interdependence and the level of unionization at the onset of the downturn have contradictory implications.[7]

[7] Another hypothesized explanation for union decline is that the state, through publicly financed transfers, is a "compensatory" mechanism, providing the working class adequate current and future living standards so that labor no longer needs to organize in the market to secure minimal subsistence (Neumann & Rissman, 1984). This argument strikes us as wrong on the surface: First, it is in precisely those states having the largest transfers and the highest "social wage" that labor is still growing organizationally (Belgium, Denmark, and Sweden); second, the cross-national correlations between the "*predownturn*" 1975–1980 average "social" wage and union growth and change in union density *during the downturn* are, respectively, .42 and .43, precisely opposite what the "compensatory" hypothesis predicts.

ANALYZING THE DECLINE

Our attempts to explore the utility of these hypothesized explanations are pursued with regression analysis. The design resembles most cross-national research in that the units of analysis are nations and differences among nations on one set of characteristics are used to "explain" differences among nations in some dependent variable (here, of course, changes in union density). The one important difference between our cross-national design and those more typically seen is that the time period used to measure variables in our study varies from country to country.

Using the theoretical arguments outlined, and aided in our choice of specific measures of the presumed determinants (e.g., change scores during the downturn period versus downturn averages) by a correlational analysis not presented here, we developed a series of regression equations specifying the effects of the hypothesized influences on change in union density.[8] Extensive preliminary analyses indicated that only change in inflation, percentage change in strike volume, and the level of prior union organization significantly stimulated change in union density. Increases in unemployment and in the percentage of the labor force employed in "non-unionized" service industries, conversely, were the only variables to depress significantly change in density. Net of the influences of these factors, no other variable we examined, whether operationalized as a change score or a period average—trade dependence, union centralization, or social democratic representation[9]—influenced changes in union density even using generous criteria of statistical significance. They are thus not retained in the final equation estimated with two-stage least squares (Col-

---

[8]Operationalizations and data sources are contained in the Appendix. Change in a variable is defined as the difference between the value of the variable at the beginning of the downturn and its value for the year in which our data terminate.

[9]The dynamic nature of our dependent variable and the specification of the equation, however, must always be in mind. We are analyzing *changes* in unionization, not levels, and we are controlling for the initial level of union density. "Long-term" social democratic rule, specified to assess cumulative socialist or leftist representation in the state for the quarter century preceding the downturn, *does* stimulate both level of union density and changes in density if the lagged density level is not controlled statistically in the equation. Social democracy certainly "matters" to unionists and to the working class more generally; it simply has no efficacy on cross-national change in unionization independent of its effect on level of labor organization during this particular historical period.

umn 1 of Table 2).[10] Unemployment, as noted, weakens labor's ability to attract new members or keep veterans because it allows capitalists to use the jobless against the employed (Gordon et al., 1982; Griffin et al., 1989). Increasing proportional employment in the service sector also harms union organizing or retention efforts, probably for the reasons already discussed. Heightened density (or smaller reductions of it), on the other hand, results from increased inflation, the growth of economic insurgency, and the level of union density at the onset of the downturn. Increasing inflation is a boon to organized labor, providing, we think, incentives (recouping real wages lost to inflation) both to nonorganized workers to join unions and to those already organized to remain in unions. It may also represent other long-term social and economic forces, such as a reduction in status deference and citizenship "push" generally, perhaps stimulating unionization (Goldthorpe, 1978). The stimulative impact of lagged level of union density probably reflects the organizational inertia effect mentioned; highly organized labor movements have the financial and moral resources and the societal legitimation needed to sustain or even deepen organization. That the rate of increase in strike volume spurs density perhaps suggests that strikes arouse the consciousness of workers against their employers and heightens the salience of workers' self-organization into unions (Przeworski, 1985). Strikes, finally, are sometimes about the very right to organize, and those that are victorious necessarily increase unionization (Rubin et al., 1983).

REGRESSION DIAGNOSTICS

We performed a number of diagnostic assessments of the robustness of these findings under alternative estimation techniques, population, and period definitions, operationalizations of the variables, and equation specifications. Our more important findings are summarized next.

---

[10]Inclusion of the "lagged" density variable also controls for both those statistical problems associated with the use of change scores as dependent variables (e.g., "floor" and "ceiling" effects inducing spurious correlations, etc.) and for omitted variables highly correlated with levels of union density (e.g., federalist vs. centralized state systems; population of the country). The inclusion of the lagged level of union density violates the assumptions of classical regression because the error term in the equations is correlated with the lagged dependent variable. Instrumental variables or 2SLS estimation thus is required to purge the equations of this correlation. Similarly, we have specified strike volume to be a determinant of union downturn, but strikes may also depend on the level of labor organization (Tilly, 1978). The possible nonrecursivity between changes in union density and strike activity also violates the classical regression assumptions and necessitates the use of 2SLS estimation procedures.

TABLE 2. Cross-National Determinants of the Change in Union Density:
Capitalist Democracies during Their Downturn Periods

	(1) 2SLS b (t)	(2) OLS b (t)	(3) 2SLS[a] b (t)	(4) 2SLS[b] b (t)	(5) 2SLS[c] b (t)	(6) 2SLS[d] b (t)
Change in unemployment	− .627 (3.01)	− .628 (3.02)	− .661 (2.81)	− .736 (3.11)	− .579 (2.44)	− .741 (3.68)
Change in inflation	.303 (2.50)	.299 (2.47)	.348 (2.39)	.311 (2.30)	.422 (2.36)	.330 (2.04)
Percentage change in strike volume	.015 (2.50)	.014 (2.42)	.032 (1.54)	.016 (2.66)	.019 (2.97)	.018 (3.04)
Change in proportion employed in service sector	− .453 (1.35)	− .482 (1.45)	− .321 (.787)	− .402 (1.14)	− .282 (1.12)	− .549 (1.65)
Level of union density$_{t-1}$	.065 (1.94)	.062 (1.87)	.052 (1.35)	.063 (1.77)	.034 (.943)	.027 (.712)
R^2	.822	.823	.677	.816	.814	.887
Adjusted R^2	.749	.749	.516	.739	.736	.816
S.E.E.	2.05	2.04	2.24	2.08	2.18	2.16
N	18	18	16	18	18	14

[a]Sweden and Denmark excluded.
[b]Change in unemployment and inflation assumed endogenous.
[c]All variables measured from 1979.
[d]Belgium, France, Ireland, and Italy excluded.

(1) Ordinary least squares (OLS) estimates (Column 2) are virtually the same as the 2SLS coefficients presented in Column 1, demonstrating that our results are not solely a function of the specific instruments used to identify the 2SLS equation or of the assumption of nonrecursivity. (2) Sweden and Denmark are statistical outliers in the strike volume series, but estimates of the 2SLS model with both countries omitted from the estimation suggest an even greater strike effect (Column 3) and only modest change in the coefficient indexing the reduction in union density due to the employment shift to the service sector. (3) 2SLS estimates, assuming that changes in inflation and unemployment are endogenous, are quite similar to those presented in Column 1, suggesting that even if changes in unemployment and inflation are both cause and consequence of changes in union density that does not unduly bias our results (Column 4). (4) The general similarity in the patterning of the 2SLS results presented in Column 1 and those obtained from an analysis using the modal year of nations experiencing a union downturn, 1979, to date the initiation of the decline in *all* countries (Column 5), demonstrates that our results are not generally a function of the strategy to date each country's downturn separately and

that we have not "sampled" on the dependent variable.[11] (5) The notion
that truncated data for Belgium, France, Ireland, and Italy (see Table 1) may
have induced distortions in the 2SLS estimates obtained over all 18 countries is explored in Column 6, where these nations are excluded from the
estimation. Again, we see little of importance beyond the reduced statistical significance and magnitude of the lagged union density coefficient.
(6) Further diagnostic checks on the 2SLS model in Column 1 indicate that
the coefficients are not materially affected by the presence or absence of
any single country, by the precise functional forms of the variables analyzed, or by multicollinearity among the predictors (average $r = .23$). (7)
Our results are not limited to changes in union density: We successfully
replicated the same patterning of coefficients using union growth (i.e.,
percentage change in union members) as the dependent variable. (8) We
entered sequentially measures of all of the concepts discussed as possible
determinants of change in union density (e.g., union centralization, social
democratic rule, economic "openness") into the equation estimated in Column 1, finding that none exerted a stable, statistically significant effect not
heavily conditioned by the presence of a single country.[12]

In sum, all of these diagnostics generally confirm or even strengthen
our original inferences. Moreover, the OLS equation has considerable explanatory power, accounting for about 75% of the variation in changes in
union density across the 18 countries after corrections for the loss of degrees of freedom (Column 2; the explained variances obtained with 2SLS
are of dubious utility). Our findings thus suggest that contradictory movements in the domestic macroeconomy, increases in both shop-floor militancy and (though less robustly) in the employment dominance of the
service sector, and the level of union density at the outset of the decline
period are all responsible for a large component of the recent growth or
decline of union density in almost the entire population of stable capitalist
democracies.

"IMPLIED" UNION GROWTH AND DECLINE

The statistical "fit" between the observed patterns of change in union
density (Column 1 of Table 3) and that implied by the regression estimates

[11]We correlated the number of years of the downturn with change in density, finding it to be
essentially 0 and included it, again with no effect, in the regression equation presented in
Column 1 of Table 2. We also converted all change scores to yearly averages (i.e., the annual
change in union density; Column 2 of Table 1) and reestimated the final model. Only
annual change in percentage of the labor force employed in service industries failed to
obtain statistical significance in that analysis, and, even here, the coefficient was about 70%
of its original size.
[12]Specification problems, however, can never be ruled out, and that truism may have even
greater import here because we are unable to test directly some arguments.

TABLE 3. Observed and Implied Changes in Union Density:
18 Capitalist Democracies during the Downturn (Equation 1, Table 2)

	Observed change in union density	Implied change in union density	Residual
Australia	−1.08	−3.85	2.77
Austria	−4.83	−1.78	−3.05
Belgium	2.11	.07	2.04
Canada	−1.21	−3.19	1.99
Denmark	3.28	4.04	−.76
Finland	−.88	.42	−1.31
France	−2.91	−2.94	−.03
Germany	−2.26	−4.15	1.90
Ireland	−.97	−2.51	1.55
Italy	−2.38	.71	−3.09
Japan	−2.57	−3.21	.64
Netherlands	−9.47	−8.17	−1.30
New Zealand	−5.29	−4.35	−.94
Norway	−.39	−1.91	1.51
Sweden	6.66	6.52	.14
Switzerland	−3.89	−3.62	−.28
United Kingdom	−9.02	−7.82	−1.19
United States	−7.49	−6.84	−.65

(Column 2, Table 3) is generally quite good. In all cases except Finland (with a very small decline) and Italy, the estimated equation correctly predicts the *direction* of the change. Sizable errors, at least as a percentage of the observed score, are observed for Australia, Belgium, and Canada (where, in all countries, unions have fared better than we predict) and Austria and Italy (where, in both countries, organized labor lost more than we predict). But the big density "losers," Britain and The Netherlands (leaving aside for the moment the United States), are identified and their losses generally accounted for. And, with the exception of Belgium, already discussed, those few countries in which the labor movement continued through the late 1970s and 1980s to add greater organization strength, Denmark and Sweden, are also extremely well predicted. No separate explanation is needed for these "negative" cases. Our model is thus generally useful for understanding cross-national differences in the magnitude of change in nations experiencing both union growth and decline, accounting even for the extreme values in the population. But does the estimated equation help us understand what happened to American unions between 1979 and 1985? It is to that question that we turn.

"EXPLAINING" THE U.S. DENSITY REDUCTION

Among the causal forces *generally* affecting changes in density (Column 1 of Table 2), two—increases in unemployment and employment shifts favoring the service industries—drive density downward. Consider how the United States fared on these causal variables. The joblessness rate in the United States increased 1.35% during the downturn period, accounting for about .85 of a percentage point (or about 11%) of the total 7.5% drop in density (i.e., the unemployment coefficient from Column 1, Table 2, −.627, multiplied by the increase in unemployment, 1.35). The proportion of the labor force employed in the service sector increased by 5.5 percentage points, leading to a 2.5 point drop (−.45 × 5.5) in density, or about a third of the entire decline.

Consider now the three variables inducing union gains, increases in both inflation and in strike volume, and the lagged level of union density. Inflation decreased in the U.S. by 7.2%; strike volume, by 48%. These declines generated additional declines in density of around 2 (−7.2 × .30, 29%) and about .7 (−48 × .015, 9%) percentage points, respectively. Finally, the lagged level of density accounted for about 20% of the decline (.065 × 23.5 = 1.5 density percentage points). Our model (including the constant) implies a decline of −6.84 (see Table 3); the observed decline is −7.49. The degree of predictive error for the United States, therefore, is trivial, less than 9%. During the downturn, American labor lost considerable organization because, perversely, the United States does "well" on things that generally defeat organization—increased unemployment and proportional employment shifts away from "unionized" blue-collar jobs—and "poorly" on things that generally stimulate organization—increases in inflation and strike volume and high levels of prior working-class organization. The black box of "American exceptionalism"—the values, for example, of the "free market" and "competitive individualism" (Lipset, 1986b)—need not be evoked to explain the recent history of union decline in the United States.

Comparatively, U.S. labor's organizational decline was the third largest in the population, less severe only than The Netherlands and Britain (see Table 3). The analyses reported in Table 2 can help us understand this relative ranking, too. Increased unemployment in the United States was lower than the average, but the increases in the proportion of the labor force with jobs in the service industries was almost twice the 18-country average, clearly behind only Switzerland in the transformation to "postindustrial" labor. Disinflation and decreased strike volume, too, were much greater than the population averages; the United States ranked number three in disinflation, and only Austria and Switzerland, with tiny levels of labor militancy, had larger proportional reductions in strike volume during the downturn. Finally, this country's level of union density at the onset of the most recent decline was less than half the average of the capitalist democracies and was the lowest in the entire population. Labor here thus had comparatively few organizational resources with which to weather the antiunion forces. The United States, therefore, comparatively ranks as a big "labor loser" because it ranks well toward the top in things that stymie labor and toward the bottom in things that aid unions.

CONCLUSION AND IMPLICATIONS

Labor in most of the advanced capitalist democracies suffered an organizational decline beginning in the late 1970s. Even where the union movement was already declining, in Austria, Japan, and the United States, organizational maintenance became more difficult. The severity of the decline varied, however, from country to country. Unions in The Netherlands, the United Kingdom, and the United States lost a large percentage of their organization. Labor organization in other nations, such as Finland and Canada, merely stagnated. In Belgium, Denmark, and Sweden, on the other hand, the labor movement continued to register gains, enrolling new members into their unions even faster than the growth of their "potential" members.

Exceptional union gains in those three countries indicate that there is nothing about contemporary unionization dictating that organized labor *must* necessarily decline as capitalist democracies "mature" into welfare states with institutionalized citizenship rights and historically high levels of working-class consumption, or that advanced industrialization and the transformation to a "service economy" obliterates the realities of "class" and "class organization," as traditionally understood. It is surely a lesson well worth remembering. But is there any implication from these "deviant" cases for the future of unions in the United States?

Before answering, we must first determine what it is "generally" about Belgium, Denmark, and Sweden, or about labor in those countries, that contributed to working-class organizational gains there. To identify what these three nations share in terms of the determinants of changes in union density, we computed a nominal variable, scored 1 for the three "union gainer" nations and 0 otherwise, correlated it with the five determinants of union change already discussed, and found it was highly associated only with percentage change in strike volume (excluding for the moment level of prior organization). The correlation is .76; the other correlations range from .19 (change in inflation) to −.05 (change in unemployment). So, these three countries, considered as a group, resemble each other and, simultaneously, differ from all other nations, again considered as a single group, primarily because of their similarity in recent changes in labor unrest. Strike volume increased dramatically in Denmark (333%) and Sweden (256%) and declined slightly in Belgium. Belgium's data stop in 1982 and this, coupled with its drop off in militancy, suggest that the following discussion be limited to the two Scandinavian countries.

What are the unionization consequences "generally" of change in

TABLE 4. The Contribution of Change in Strike Volume
to Change Union in Density

	Downturn average in change in strike volume	×	b	= Impact on density
Denmark	333	×	.015 =	5.00
Sweden	256	×	.015 =	3.84

The United States	Time "t" volume	−	1985 volume	Percentage change in volume	×	b	=	Impact on density
"t" = 1959	740	−	210	252	×	.015 =		3.78
"t" = 1969	695	−	210	231	×	.015 =		3.47
"t" = 1954–1978 average	511	−	210	143	×	.015 =		2.15

strike volume, and how did it affect labor organization in Denmark and Sweden? The answer is summarized in Table 4. Given the "general" salutary effect of the rate of increase in strike volume of .015 (Column 1, Table 2), Denmark, with its change of 333%, would have increased its absolute level of union density by 5% had not countervailing forces (especially increased service-sector employment) worked to offset partially *potential* gains resulting from Danish labor's militancy. As it turned out, Denmark's net density gain was 3.3%. The absolute density gain attributable to Swedish labor's strike activity was 3.8%, or almost 60% of the entire increase in density (6.7%). Big increases in strike volume coupled with an already densely organized labor movement, then, are the main reasons why the working class in Denmark and Sweden continued to deepen its class organization.

Now to return to the United States. "It has all been said before," Lane Kirkland (1986, p. 393) wrote about the supposed death of the organized labor in America. He went on to argue, perhaps somewhat wistfully, that the recent downturn in union fortunes is less significant than at first appears and that, anyway, workers of "tomorrow... will succeed in overcoming the threat to their economic and social well-being and they will be joined increasingly by those who seem, for the moment, to have surrendered their right to a voice in their own wages and working conditions" (p. 403). U.S. unions will recover, it seems, sometime "tomorrow."

Well, yes and no. Consider again the "general" determinants of increases in union density. The shift out of traditional blue-collar industries will in all likelihood continue, and for the time being, this will work against U.S. unions. Also, the United States is unlikely to soon witness an inflationary upsurge on the order of that recorded in the 1970s, so unions can not expect quick relief there. Joblessness may fall further, so unions may get some help from tighter labor markets. But the unemployment coefficient ($-.627$) implies that unemployment will have to fall 5% for density to increase 3%; considering that we now have a jobless rate of under 6%, it will take an unemployment rate of *less* than 1% to produce even that hypo-thetical union gain. That extraordinarily unlikely low unemployment rate has not been witnessed in this country since the end of World War II, not even during the period of tight labor markets induced by the Korean and Vietnam wars. Assuming even a realistic near-future increase in the *size* of the unemployment coefficient, it is unlikely that reductions in joblessness, so essential in many other ways, will pull labor out of its current doldrums. Finally, U.S. labor will get only minimum help from its current level of union organization because density is already extremely low and still fall-ling. So where does that leave us? With labor militancy, with struggle.

To return to the two Scandinavian countries for a moment, organized labor there benefited from its strike activity. So there may be something to learn from the experience of Danish and Swedish labor after all: The lesson appears to be that radically intensified class struggle at the point of pro-duction *can* stimulate workers' self-organization. Allow us to apply this to the United States. Had labor militancy not declined at all during America's most recent downturn but simply stabilized at its historically low level in 1979 (obviously an historical counterfactual), density would have, accord-ing to our model, been about .7 of a percent higher than it actually was as of 1985. But if labor were as militant "tomorrow" as it was in 1969, unions would increase, absolutely, their organizational depth by about 3.5% (for computational specifics, see Panel B, Table 4). If 1959 militancy levels were observed, density would increase by almost 4%. Levels of industrial con-flict in both 1959 and 1969 were higher than typical in this country. If labor were "only" as militant as it actually was, *on the average*, throughout the entire period from 1954, when union density first began declining, until 1978, the least year before the most recent downturn, density, absolutely, would increase by more than 2%. Thus more than 25% of the union density lost during the downturn would be recouped if strike activity were to increase "tomorrow" to "just" average predecline strike volume.[13]

How realistic is such an increase in the American context? If U.S. labor were to return to the militancy levels of any of the previously mentioned dates or periods, the percentage increase would be less than that of Danish

---

[13]This counterfactual, although based on cross-national patterns, obviously presupposes that the model presented in Column 1 of Table 2 has historical validity for the United States. As a check on this assumption, we estimated a time-series regression model for the United States from 1955 to 1979, specifying the influence on change in density of unemployment and inflation rates (both lagged 1 year), percentage change in strike volume, change in the proportion of the labor force employed in the traditionally "unionized" industries (lagged 1 year), and lagged level of union density. All coefficients were in the direction expected from the cross-national analyses. The strike coefficient, though smaller than estimated before ($b = .007$), was statistically significant ($t = 2.03$). The strike volume data, both in the U.S. time-series and in the analyses reported throughout this chapter, were analyzed as 3-year moving averages to smooth out unusually high (e.g., France in 1968) or low values (e.g., the United States in 1985). Thus, we are not capitalizing in this exercise, or anywhere else in this chapter, on such statistical abnormalities. Smoothing of the strike series is common in this literature (Griffin *et al.*, 1989; Korpi & Shalev, 1980).

labor during the downturn and no more than that of Swedish labor (see Table 4). No more, in fact, than the increase in this country from 1962 until 1969. We are speaking then not of 1930s-style militancy, but rather of 1960s strike levels. But we must still pose the question of just how much "room" there is in the capitalist democracies for a resurgence of labor activism. In analyses not reported, we found that cross-national differences in percentage change in strike volume was influenced by inflation, unemployment, and both levels and changes in the industrial employment patterns. About 78% of the variance was explained by this equation. At least two of the factors affecting militancy, moreover, inflation and unemployment, are at least partly a function of the clout of organized labor (Hibbs, 1987; Stephens, 1980). There is, then, apparently some "open space" for the ideological and political realms of class struggle. Greater insurgency appears possible. The comparative experiences of Sweden and Denmark, with trivial levels of strike activity before the current downturn (Hibbs, 1987), bear witness to this.

Troy (1986) may be correct that new labor laws are necessary before American unions will again grow, but such legislation must also restore workers' full right to engage in strikes. The strike is labor's ultimate weapon; it stops production and, if sustained, can dig into profit levels. Capitalists and courts realize this quite clearly. U.S. labor law has been increasingly interpreted in order to hamper militancy and minimize the impact of the strike (McCammon, forthcoming). But the law is not yet so constructed as to select out entirely recourse to economic insurgency.

Strikes are costly, and there are good reasons, for both individuals and institutions, to avoid them. Workers on strike risk employer and legal retaliation in the form of loss of pay, of employment security, of freedom, and, at least historically, of life. Unions risk loss of respectability and "maturity," even—as the PATCO case makes all too clear—organizational extinction. The AFL-CIO leadership understands this, generally presenting itself as a voice of reason and moderation (AFL-CIO, 1985). Strikes are economic and political weapons (Hibbs, 1987; Korpi & Shalev, 1980; Tilly, 1978), and those who will suffer the consequences of using the strike or not should and will make the decision to call them.

Whatever the risks, and they loom large indeed, workers have since the inception of capitalism struck to improve their material and political positions. There have also been profound moments of silence. American labor is quiet now, but there is no reason to believe that it will always remain so. There is no general "withering" away of the strike (Hibbs, 1987), and if labor loosens its restraints, self-imposed and otherwise, organizational gains may follow. Only collective action, in the final analysis, builds collective organization.

DATA APPENDIX

This appendix contains the operationalizations of the variables used in the analyses and data sources. More detailed information concerning the data is available from the authors upon request. The following abbreviations for sources are used:

BP: Bain & Price, 1980
E: Europa, various years
ILO: International Labor Office, various years
K: Kjellberg, 1983
L: Lybeck, 1986
N: National source
OH: Organization for Economic Cooperation and Development (OECD), 1986, *Historical Statistics*
OL: OECD, various years, *Labor Force Statistics*
ON: OECD, various years, *National Accounts*
UN: United Nations, various years
V: Visser, 1984

Potential unionizable labor force: Total wage and salary earners plus those not currently working for wages (e.g., the unemployed) but subject to wage labor. Sources: Australia, BP, OL; Austria, OL, V; Belgium, OL; Canada, BP, OL; Denmark, BP, V, OL; Finland, OL; France, OL, V; Germany, BP, V, OL; Ireland, OL; Italy, OL, V; Japan, OL; The Netherlands, OL, V; New Zealand, N, OL; Norway, BP, V, OL; Sweden, BP, V, OL; Switzerland, OL, V; United Kingdom, BP, V, OL; United States, BP, OL.

Union membership: Sources: Australia, BP, N; Austria, K, V, E; Belgium, K, L; Canada, BP, N; Denmark, BP, V, N; Finland, N; France, K, V; Germany, BP, V, N; Ireland, N, O'Brien (1981), Rottman and O'Connell (1982); Italy, K, V; Japan, N; The Netherlands, N, V; New Zealand, N; Norway, BP, V, N; Sweden, BP, V, N; Switzerland, N, V; United Kingdom, BP, V, N; United States, BP, N.

Union density: Union membership divided by dependent labor force.

Strike volume: Number of working days lost to strikes per 10,000 "dependent workers." Source for strike days: all countries, ILO; United States, ILO, N.

Unemployment: Number unemployed expressed as a percentage of the civilian labor force. Sources for unemployed: Australia, OL, UN; Austria, OL; Belgium, OL; Canada, OL; Denmark, OL, UN; Finland, UN; France, OL; Germany, UN; Ireland, OL; Italy, OL; Japan, OL; The Netherlands, UN; New Zealand, UN; Norway, UN; Sweden, UN; Switzerland, UN; United Kingdom, UN; United States, OL. Source for civilian labor force: OL.

Inflation: Rate of change in consumer price index. Source: International Monetary Fund, 1984.

Economic "openness" or trade dependence: Imports and exports expressed as a percentage of GDP. Source: ON.

Social democratic representation in government: Number of votes received by left-wing parties participating in cabinet expressed as a percentage of total votes received by all parties with cabinet representation. Source for votes: Mackie and Rose, various years. Source for cabinet composition: E. Source of party platform: McHale, 1983; Day and Dagenhardt, 1980.

Industrial composition: (1) The "unionized sector" consists of mining, manufacturing, construction, public utilities, and transportation; (2) the "nonunionized or service sector" consists of wholesale and retail industries, finance, real estate, and all other services. Source: OL.

ACKNOWLEDGMENTS

An earlier version of this paper was presented as part of the Distinguished Visiting Scholars Series at the University of Notre Dame. We would thank our colleagues both there and at the Indiana University Political Economy Workshop for their valuable comments on an earlier version of this chapter. The research was supported by the National Science Foundation, the Center for West European Studies at Indiana University, and the Division of Research and Graduate Development at Indiana University.

REFERENCES

American Federation of Labor–Congress of Industrial Organization. (1985). *The changing situation of workers and their unions*. AFL-CIO Committee on the Evolution of Work.

Ashenfelter, O., & Pencavel, J. H. (1969). American trade union growth: 1900–1960. *Quarterly Journal of Economics, 83*, 434–448.

Bain, G., & Elsheikh, F. (1976). *Union growth and the business cycle*. Oxford: Basil Blackwell.

Bain, G., & Price, R. (1980). *Profiles of union growth: A comparative statistical portrait of eight countries*. Oxford: Basil Blackwell.

Blanpain, R. (1984). Recent trends in collective bargaining in Belgium. *International Labour Review, 123*, 319–332.

Botsko, C. (1989). *Labor after Keynes: The evolving relationship between trade unions and left-wing parties in the advanced capitalist states* (Master's thesis, Indiana University).

Bowles, S. (1982). The post-Keynesian capital-labor stalemate. *Socialist Review, 65*, 45–72.

Brody, D. (1980). *Workers in industrial America*. New York: Oxford.

Cameron, D. (1978). The expansion of the public economy: A comparative analysis. *American Political Science Review, 72*, 1243–1261.

Cameron, D. (1984). Social democracy, corporatism, labour quiescence, and the representation of economic interest in advanced capitalist society. In J. Goldthorpe, (Ed.), *Order and conflict in contemporary capitalism* (pp. 143–178). Oxford: Clarendon Press.

Cappelli, P., & McKersie, R. (1985). Labor and the crisis in collective bargaining. In T. Kochan (Ed.), *Challenges and choices facing American labor* (pp. 227–245). Cambridge: MIT Press.

Cullen, D. (1985). Recent trends in collective bargaining in the United States. *International Labour Review, 124,* 299–322.

Day, A., & Dagenhardt, H. (1980). *Political parties of the world.* Detroit: Gale Research Company.

Dickens, W., & Leonard, J. (1985). Accounting for the decline in union membership, 1950–1980. *Industrial and Labor Relations Review, 38,* 323–334.

Europa Publications. (Various years). *The Europa yearbook.* London: Europa Publications Ltd.

Farber, H. (1987). The recent decline of unionization in the United States. *Science, 238,* 915–920.

Freeman, R., & Medoff, J. (1984). *What do unions do?* New York: Basic Books.

Goldfield, M. (1987). *The decline of organized labor in the United States.* Chicago: The University of Chicago Press.

Goldthorpe, J. (1978). The current inflation: Towards a sociological account. In F. Hirsch & J. Goldthorpe (Eds.), *The political economy of inflation* (pp. 186–214). Cambridge: Harvard University Press.

Gordon, D., Edwards, R., & Reich, M. (1982). *Segmented work, divided workers.* Cambridge: Cambridge University Press.

Greenstone, J. D. (1977). *Labor in American politics.* Chicago: The University of Chicago Press.

Griffin, L., O'Connell, P., & McCammon, H. (1989). National variation in the context of struggle: Post-war class conflict and market distribution in the capitalist democracies. *Canadian Review of Sociology and Anthropology, 26,* 37–68.

Griffin, L., Wallace, M., & Rubin, B. (1986). Capitalist resistance to the organization of labor before the New Deal: Why? How? Success? *American Sociological Review, 51,* 147–167.

Hibbs, D. (1987). *The political economy of industrial democracies.* Cambridge, MA: Harvard University Press.

Hobsbawm, E. (1989). Farewell to the classic labour movement. *New Left Review, 173,* 69–74.

International Labor Office. (Various years). *Yearbook of labor statistics.* Geneva: ILO.

International Monetary Fund. (Various years). *International financial statistics.* Washington, DC: IMF.

Kirkland, L. (1986). It has all been said before.... In S. M. Lipset (Ed.), *Unions in transition: Entering the second century* (pp. 393–404). San Francisco: Institute for Contemporary Studies.

Kjellberg, A. (1983). *Facklig organisering i tolv lander.* Lund: Arkiv.

Kochan, T., Katz, H., & McKersie, R. (1986). *The transformation of American industrial relations.* New York: Basic Books.

Korpi, W., & Shalev, M. (1980). Strikes, power and politics in the Western nations, 1900–1976. *Political Power and Social Theory, 1,* 301–334.

Lehmbruch, G. (1984). Concertation and the structure of corporatist networks. In J. Goldthorpe (Ed.), *Order and conflict in contemporary capitalism* (pp. 60–80). Oxford: Clarendon Press.

Lipset, S. M. (1986a). Labor unions in the public mind. In S. M. Lipset (Ed.), *Unions in transition: Entering the second century* (pp. 287–322). San Francisco: Institute for Contemporary Studies.

Lipset, S. M. (1986b). North American labor movements: A comparative perspective. In S. M. Lipset (Ed.), *Unions in transition: Entering the second century* (pp. 421–452). San Francisco: Institute for Contemporary Studies.

Lybeck, J. (1986). *The growth of governments in developed economies.* Aldershot, England: Gower.

Mackie, T., & Rose, R. (Various years). *The international almanac of electoral history.* New York: Facts on File, Inc.

Marshall, R. (1986). America and Japan: Industrial relations in a time of change. In S. M. Lipset (Ed.), *Unions in transition: Entering the second century* (pp. 133–149). San Francisco: Institute for Contemporary Studies.

Massing, M. (1988). Detroit's strange bedfellows. *New York Times Magazine,* February 7, pp. 20–27, 52.

McCammon, H. (forthcoming). Legal limits on labor militancy: U.S. labor law and the rights to strike since the New Deal. *Social Problems.*

McHale, V. (1983). *Political parties of Europe.* Volumes 1 and 2. Westport, CT and London: Greenwood Press.

Mitchell, D. (1980). *Unions, wages, and inflation.* Washington, DC: The Brookings Institute.

Montgomery, D. (1979). *Workers' control in America: Studies in the history of work, technology and labor struggles.* Cambridge: Cambridge University Press.

Moody, K. (1987). Reagan, the business agenda and the collapse of labour. *Socialist Register 1987*, 153–176.

Neumann, G., & Rissman, E. (1984). Where have all the union members gone? *Journal of Labor Economics, 2*, 175–193.

O'Brien, J. (1981). *A study of national wage agreements in Ireland.* Pub. Series No. 104. Dublin: Economic and Social Research Institute.

O'Connell, P. (1989). *Transnational economic linkages, class politics, and the fiscal crisis of the state* (Doctoral dissertation, Indiana University).

Organization for Economic Cooperation and Development (OECD). (1986). *Historical statistics, 1960–1984.* Paris: OECD.

OECD. (various years). *Labor force statistics.* Paris: OECD.

OECD. (various years). *National accounts statistics: detailed statistics.* Volume 2. Paris: OECD.

Perlman, S. (1928). *A theory of the labor movement.* New York: Macmillan.

Przeworski, A. (1985). *Capitalism and social democracy.* Cambridge, MA: Cambridge University Press.

Raskin, A. H. (1986). Labor: A movement in search of a mission. In S. M. Lipset (Ed.), *Unions in transition: Entering the second century* (pp. 3–38). San Francisco: Institute for Contemporary Studies.

Ross, A., & Hartman, P. (1960). *Changing patterns of industrial relations.* New York: Wiley.

Rottman, D., & O'Connell, P. (1982). The changing social structure of Ireland. In F. Litton (Ed.), *Unequal achievement* (pp. 63–88). Dublin: Institute of Public Administration.

Rubin, B. (1986). Class struggle, American style: Unions, strikes and wages. *American Sociological Review, 51*, 618–633.

Rubin, B., Griffin, L., & Wallace, M. (1983). "Provided only that their voice was strong": Insurgency and organization of American labor from NRA to Taft-Hartley. *Work and Occupations, 10*, 325–347.

Schlesinger, J. (1987). Job-guarantee contracts are becoming more common. *Wall Street Journal,* June 29.

Skocpol, T., & Somers, M. (1980). The uses of comparative history in macrosocial inquiry. *Comparative Study of Society and History, 22*, 174–197.

Stephens, J. (1980). *The transition from capitalism to socialism.* Atlantic Highlands, NJ: Humanities Press.

Tilly, C. (1978). *From mobilization to revolution.* Reading, MA: Addison-Wesley.

Troy, L. (1986). The rise and fall of American trade unions: The labor movement from FDR to RR. In S. M. Lipset (Ed.), *Unions in transition: Entering the second century* (pp. 75–109). San Francisco: Institute for Contemporary Studies.

Uchitelle, L. (1987). Bonuses replace wage rises and workers are the losers. *New York Times,* June 26.

United Nations. (Various years). *Statistical yearbook.* New York: UN.

U.S. Bureau of the Census. (1987). *Statistical abstract of the United States.* Washington, DC: U.S. Government Printing Office.

Visser, J. (1984). *Dimensions of union growth in postwar Western Europe.* Florence: European University Institute Working Paper No. 89.

Wright, E. (1978). *Class, crisis and the state.* London: New Left Books.

CHAPTER NINE

Medicine, the Medical Profession, and the Welfare State

ROBERT ZUSSMAN

If every doting mother once wanted nothing more for each of her dutiful sons than that he should become a white-coated doctor, it was with good reason. For from the triumph of medicine's "professional project" at the end of the nineteenth century until the mid-1960s, physicians enjoyed a position unrivaled by any other American occupation. Dominating the hospitals in which they worked (and the other health professionals with whom they worked), exercising broad cultural authority over the ways in which sickness would be conceived and treated, and earning generous incomes secured by a monopoly of the market for medical services, physicians represented the very model of a successful profession. Since the mid-1960s, however, a few cracks have begun to show in the success of medical professionalism. If doting mothers (and fathers) may have to find new ambitions for their sons (and daughters), so, too, will sociologists have to rethink their understanding of medicine as well as of the professions more generally.

Professionalism is, of course, both a complex phenomenon and a term of many meanings. Professionalism is sometimes used to refer to any technically skilled occupation. It is also often used, as a number of recent observers have pointed out, in an ideologically charged context: It is a term invoked by occupations (social work, engineering, and accounting, among others) that aspire to the status of medicine. (On professionalism in general, see Abbott, 1988; Freidson, 1986; Sarfatti-Larson, 1977. For discus-

ROBERT ZUSSMAN • Department of Sociology, State University of New York–Stony Brook, Stony Brook, New York 11794, and Center for the Study of Medicine and Society, Columbia University, New York, New York 10032.

sions of medical professionalism, in particular, see Freidson, 1970, 1985; Ritzer & Walczak, 1988; Starr, 1982.) In this chapter, however, I intend to reserve for professionalism a significantly more restrictive meaning: By *professionalism* I mean the distinctively Anglo-American phenomenon by which much of the responsibility for certain key social values is assigned to occupational authorities licensed by, but not formally a part of, the apparatus of the state. Thus, by professionalism, I mean that system in which responsibility for justice is turned over in large parts to lawyers, by which responsibility for the generation of new knowledge is turned over to university professors, and responsibility for health is turned over to physicians. Professionalism in the restricted sense I have reserved for it here, is the creation of societies characterized by weak states, unprepared to assume broad burdens of public administration. It is the contention of this chapter that such professionalism cannot survive in unaltered form the development and maturation of the welfare state.

MEDICINE'S PROFESSIONAL PROJECT

By the middle of the nineteenth century, American medicine was in disarray (Rothstein, 1972; Starr, 1982). Licensing laws, on the books but lightly enforced since Colonial days, had been repealed in every state. Anyone who chose to practice medicine could—and many did. So-called "regular" physicians faced competition from various self-proclaimed healers, ranging from midwives to untrained medical sectarians and lay practitioners armed with little more than one of the many manuals of medical home care, published and bought at a prodigious rate over the course of the century. The United States had embarked on its first (and only) great experiment in providing medical care through the mechanisms of a market.

The experiment did not last long. By the beginning of the twentieth century, medicine had taken on its now familiar form. First, by the beginning of the century, every state in the Union had reinstated licensing laws, limiting the practice of medicine to graduates of accredited medical schools—a restriction that took on all the more importance in light of the sharp decline in the number of such schools, from 162 in 1906 to 95 less than a decade later. The point, as Abraham Flexner (1910, p. 155) argued in his famous 1910 Carnegie Commission report on medical education, was "fewer and better doctors." Second, medicine was granted not only relief from competition but also the right to regulate itself—to determine collectively not only who would practice medicine but also what good medicine would consist of. Third, and perhaps most important, medicine had convinced a sometimes leery American public that its services were essential to good health (Conrad & Schneider, 1980). By incorporating an ever-expanding roster of human problems—ranging from childbirth to public sanitation—into the realm of medical practice, physicians were able to ensure a mounting demand for their services at the very same time that the restriction in the number of physicians ensured that those services would be in short supply. What medicine had won amounted to nothing less than an exemption from the normal controls of the market place.

The remarkable success of medicine's "professional project" depended, in large part, on the collective efforts of physicians themselves. But physicians did not simply seize authority: They were granted it both by public legislatures and by the public at large. The public willingness to grant such authority depended, in part, on a faith in science, a somewhat paradoxical notion but one altogether characteristic of the century's turn. More important, though, it depended on a willingness to accept medicine's insistent claims to public service. "Medicine," as Flexner (1910, p. 17) observed, "curative and preventive, has indeed no analogy with business. Like the army, the police, or the social worker, the medical profession is supported for a benign, not a selfish, for a protective, not an exploiting, purpose." If health, like justice or public safety, is too important a matter to be bought and sold like any other commodity, then medicine—according to Flexner and the other medical reformers—had to be entrusted to a profession that was itself financially disinterested. If the public was prepared to protect physicians from the effects of a free market for their labor, then physicians asserted that they would, in turn, protect the public from the vagaries of a market for their services.

It is, to be sure, easy to be cynical about medicine's claims to self-regulation and public service (Freidson, 1970; Millman, 1976; Sudnow, 1967). Certainly, many physicians have turned their degrees to personal gain, shunning public service for a wealthy (and well-paying) clientele. Equally certain, one of the immediate consequences of the decline in the number of medical schools at the beginning of the century was the virtual exclusion of blacks and women from the field—an exclusion that was not to be rectified, and then only partially, until the past two decades. And neither has medicine done a great deal to regulate itself: Quite the reverse, the profession has demonstrated nothing less than a remarkable reluctance to discipline those practitioners who fail to meet those high standards that, in other circumstances, are proclaimed so loudly (Bosk, 1986; Derbyshire, 1983). Yet, as in the old joke, the surprise should not be that the dog sings so badly but that it sings at all.

In arguing that twentieth-century American medicine has, in fact, been characterized by a commitment (if only partially realized) to public service, I do not mean to imply that physicians are any more altruistic than the rest of us. They are not. Rather, I mean to argue that medicine is characterized by what Robert Merton (1982) has called *institutionalized altruism*—a system of rewards that encourages the deferral of short-term self-interest in the name of long-term self-interest. Medicine, in particular, has rewarded certain types of public service, most notably research and teaching, with high status within the profession. It has insisted on other types of public service, most notably ministering to the poor, as part of its training process (in the form of internships and residencies) and as the first step in a medical career ladder (Duff & Hollingshead, 1968; Rosenberg, 1974). None of this is to say that medicine has ever served the poor as well as it has served the wealthy. It has not. Yet, there is a significant tradition in medicine of both charity care and sliding fees (in which the poor are charged less for the same services as those better able to pay). All this—whatever its limits—takes medicine some distance from the practice of business, which answers to nothing other than the demands of the market.

In stressing the institutionalized altruism of medicine, I am invoking a hoary (and, now, often neglected) tradition in the study of the professions. In this tradition—elements of which can be found among the Fabian Socialists and the American Progressives, in the work of T. H. Marshall (1965, originally published in 1939), Thorstein Veblen (1921), and, finally, Talcott Parsons (1954, originally published 1939, 1968)—the significance of the professions was both deeply political and, in an old-fashioned sense, fundamentally liberal. For, in this tradition, the professions represented an alternative mode of organization not only to the market but also to the state: The professions provided—the phrase is Parsons's (1968, p. 545)—"new leadership...based on cultural criteria of legitimacy rather than criteria of political power or economic success" and promised nothing less than to "become the most important single component in the structure of modern society [displacing both] the 'state'...and...the 'capitalistic' organization of production."

But like many of Parsons's arguments, his analysis of the professions makes far more sense as a set of keen historical observations than as an inevitability of social structure. For, whereas the professional ordering of services represents an alternative to both the market and the state, its relationship to each is different: Historically, the professions, particularly, medicine, represented a defensive response to the vagaries of the market. In contrast, they are not so much a defense against, as an alternative to, the state. The legitimacy of the professions—as Parsons himself observed—depends on their role as a guarantor of key values. But this role devolved on the professions only in the absence of a strong state. Parsons's analysis of the professions, like that of Marshall and Veblen, the Fabian Socialists and the American Progressives, was formulated at a moment before the maturation of the contemporary welfare state. And it is by no means clear that professions, particularly medicine, can continue to claim legitimacy as the guarantor of health in face of the expansion of that state.

MEDICINE AND THE WELFARE STATE

The welfare state came late to America and even later to American medicine. Social security and unemployment compensation were introduced in the United States only in 1935, nearly 25 years after similar programs began in the United Kingdom and nearly 50 years after they began in Germany. And, even then, any system of health care or sickness insurance was among the notable absences in Roosevelt's New Deal. Indeed, there was to be no sustained national presence of any sort in health care until the end of World War II, when the federal government began, first, to underwrite large-scale medical research and, second, to subsidize new hospital construction in medically underserved areas.

Where the financing of medical research and hospital construction involved the federal government in the periphery of American health care, the passage of Medicaid and Medicare in 1965 brought it to the very center. Perhaps the crowning achievement of Lyndon Johnson's Great Society—and the last before his program of domestic reform gave way to the disruptions of the Vietnam War—Medicaid and Medicare were enacted over the long-standing and often bitter opposition of the medical profession. To the American Medical Association, in particular, the programs represented a threat to medical professionalism: By interposing a third party between doctor and patient and by introducing a powerful new actor to the health care scene, virtually any form of national health insurance threatened professional sovereignty in the field of health. To be sure, most physicians' opposition to Medicaid and Medicare disappeared almost as soon as the ink was dry on the new legislation. A threatened boycott never developed. Within a year, well over 90% of physicians had treated at least some Medicare patients (Colombotos, 1969). And physicians everywhere were discovering that, rather than endangering their economic security, both programs were providing new and more secure sources of income. Yet, ironically, Medicaid and Medicare helped set in motion a transformation of medical professionalism of much the sort that physicians had originally feared.

Medicaid and Medicare, as they were eventually passed, represented not two, but three distinct principles of health care insurance. "Part A" of Medicare, a program intended for those over 65 (and later extended to include a number of young people with disabilities of various sorts), is compulsory insurance. Based on the social security system and funded through social security taxes, it consists primarily of insurance for in-hospital costs. In contrast, "Part B" of Medicare, which provides supplementary medical insurance, primarily for physicians' services, is voluntary insurance, with enrollees electing to participate and funding the program (in part) through their own monthly payments. Although both Parts A and B of Medicare are unambiguously "entitlement" programs,

Medicaid is equally unambiguously a welfare program: It is intended for the "medically indigent" and like most welfare programs in the United States is administered by individual states, each of which can set its own eligibility and benefit levels while drawing matching funds from the federal government.

Despite the very different principles underlying them, both Medicaid and Medicare shared one critical characteristic. Both were reimbursement systems. Neither involved the federal government, in any way, as a direct employer of physicians, and neither was intended, in any way, to alter the structure of medical care. Quite the reverse, both programs limited the role of the federal government to that of a guarantor of payment and explicitly excluded any role as a direct provider of services.

The most immediate effect, then, of Medicaid and Medicare was to dramatically increase the access of the old and, even more clearly, the poor to medical services. In 1964, before the passage of Medicaid and Medicare, the poorest segment of the population (those with family incomes under $4,000 a year)—and the segment of the population likeliest to have health problems—were seeing physicians 15% less frequently than the wealthiest segment of the population: By 1975 the poorest segment of the population was actually seeing physicians over 20% more frequently than the wealthiest segment. In 1964, as Davis and Schoen (1978) have observed, "whites averaged 42% more visits to physicians than blacks and others; by 1973 the gap had been narrowed to 13%." To be sure, none of these developments should be overestimated. Corrected for health status, the poor still see physicians less frequently than do the wealthy and—although hard to document—most likely continue to receive health care of a somewhat lower quality. Moreover, a significant (and rising) proportion of the American public falls between the cracks of Medicaid, Medicare, and private health insurance: In 1986, 15% of the population under 65 years of age— and 37% of the poor—were protected by no health insurance of any sort, public or private (*Health*, 1988, p. 169). Yet, even with these caveats, it is clear that Medicaid and Medicare had succeeded in their most immediate intentions. They did not, taken together, amount to a system of comprehensive national health insurance. They were not, in any meaningful sense, socialized medicine. But they did, with all their limitations, make medical care more available than it had ever been before. The surprise was that the implications of Medicaid and Medicare went well beyond this simple effect.

Most important, Medicaid and Medicare transformed the structure of the market for medical services. The inclusion of health care benefits as part of collective bargaining agreements in the two decades immediately following World War II had already increased the share of health care expenditures accounted for by private insurance. Without disrupting that trend, the passage of Medicaid and Medicare dramatically increased the share accounted for by government expenditures (see Table 1). In 1950, nearly two-thirds of health care expenditures consisted of individual direct payments, under one-tenth consisted of private insurance, and under one-quarter of government payments. In 1965, the final year before the introduction of the two programs, individual direct payment accounted for slightly more than half of all health care expenditures and private health insurance, for approximately a quarter, whereas government expenditures remained at slightly under a quarter. By 1986 direct payment and private health insurance each accounted for roughly 30% of health care expenditures whereas government spending accounted for 40%. To put it somewhat differently, in 1965 direct payments for health care accounted for roughly $2.50 for every one dollar spent by the government; by 1986 the government was spending roughly $1.30 for every dollar of direct payments. If we exclude spending on hospital and nursing home care and limit ourselves to spending on physicians' services alone, the transformation is even more dramatic. In 1965 direct payment accounted for $9 for every dollar spent by the government; by 1986 government spending accounted for more of the cost of physicians' services than did direct payment. And equally important, the increase in the share of government spending was accounted for entirely by the federal government: The share of state and local government in health care expenses actually fell between 1965 and 1986 (*Health*, 1988, pp. 158–159). Taken in conjunction with an inflation of health care costs, the expansion of government spending for health care created a public stake in the control of those costs of a sort that had never existed before.

The federal government, along with large industrial concerns, constitutes a market for medical services different from any physicians had served in the past. For until the second half of the twentieth century, that market had consisted almost entirely of individual patients and their families. Such "consumers" could, of course, vote with their feet, preferring to

TABLE 1. Health Care Expenditures, in Percent, by Source of Funds

	1950	1965	1986
All expenditures			
Direct payment	65.5	51.6	28.7
Private insurance	9.1	24.2	30.4
Government	22.4	22.0	39.6
Federal	10.4	10.1	30.2
State and local	12.0	11.9	9.4
Physician's services			
Direct payment		61.6	28.5
Private insurance		31.4	42.1
Government		6.9	29.4

patronize one physician rather than another. But they lacked the political and organizational resources necessary to challenge medical authority at a broader level—to challenge medical conceptions of health and illness or physicians' claims as guarantors of proper health care. In contrast, the federal government possesses precisely those resources necessary to provide an effective counterweight to professional dominance. Its increased role in health care financing, particularly in the context of growing budget deficits, provided it with the impetus to do so.

COSTS AND CONTROLS

The passage of Medicaid and Medicare created a dilemma. Congress had committed the federal government to becoming the primary funder of health care in the United States. But it had also committed the federal government to leaving the structure of health care delivery largely untouched. As Richard Scott (1982, p. 192) has observed, there "is no U.S. Ministry of Health" with the result that "federal controls tend to be fragmented—different departments and bureaus each focusing on the enforcement of some specific program of requirement." Moreover, the federal government, with only a few exceptions, has made little attempt to alter the organization or the division of labor within health care. Physicians continue to dominate both hospitals and the growing number of nurses, technicians, and therapists who work in them.

Yet, it is hard to imagine that a single consumer of nearly one-third of a particular service would not have a significant influence on the producers of that service. For although the federal government has not, for the most part, attempted to determine how health care should be provided, it has stipulated what care to which clients will be reimbursed. This is, in itself, quite a lot. Thus, for example, when Congress in 1972 amended Medicare to include funding for dialysis of patients with end-stage renal disease, the result was, predictably enough, an enormous surge in the number of patients receiving that treatment (Fox & Swazey, 1978). Control over the general direction of medical care, over medical priorities, had passed from the profession of medicine to the federal government.

The conviction that such direction should be exercised has been fueled by an extraordinary expansion of health care costs. Not only did the public share of health care financing increase with the passage of Medicaid and Medicare, but, at the same time, health care costs themselves have been subject to hyperinflation—an inflation above and beyond the inflation that has characterized other parts of the post-World War II economy. In 1950 health care expenditures accounted for 4.4% of the gross national product. In 1965, just before the introduction of Medicaid and Medicare, they accounted for just under 6%. By 1986, they had reached nearly eleven percent (*Health*, 1988, p. 158).

Every administration since Nixon's has mounted a major effort to control health care costs—with the growing intensity of these efforts matching the growing intensity of concerns over the budget deficit. The most recent and most significant of these efforts has been the inclusion in Medicare of a prospective payment system. In its original form, Medicare had reimbursed both hospitals and physicians on the basis of their "usual and customary" fees for particular services. Insofar as these fees were already profitable, it provided an economic incentive to treat more and treat longer. In contrast, the prospective payment system, introduced in 1983, limits reimbursements for hospital charges to a fixed payment based on a patient's diagnosis at the time of admission. Because reimbursement does not increase with additional tests, procedures, or days in the hospital, the system supplies a powerful economic incentive to limit treatment. So far, prospective payment has been limited to reimbursements for hospital costs, although the Reagan administration did propose extending them to physicians' services as well (a proposal the Bush administration is likely to push with added vigor). Moreover, the experiment with prospective payment is still too new to judge how effectively it will control costs, although there is some emerging evidence that it has had at least some success (Iglehart, 1986; Sloan, Morrisey, & Valvona, 1988). Nonetheless, it is clear that prospective payment has altered the climate of medical practice. A number of states, including Massachusetts and New Jersey, have followed the lead of the federal government and extended prospective payment to other hospital reimbursement systems besides Medicare. And most important for the purposes at hand, physicians—faced with explicitly limited resources—are now being asked not simply to advocate on behalf of patients, their traditional role, but also to allocate resources among them. And this change in weather is a wind blowing from the federal government, not the medical profession.

THE RISE OF BIOETHICS

Even beyond introducing the federal government as the major financier of health, the passage of Medicaid and Medicare contributed to the deterioration of professional authority in medicine in another, less direct way. There is, in the United States, no general, legally recognized right to health care. But the passage of Medicaid and Medicare helped to establish the perception of such a right. Before 1965, those unable to pay depended for medical care on the charity of hospitals, of physicians, of philanthropists. After 1965 and the passage of Medicaid, they began to assert claims to health care not as a matter of charity but as a matter of entitlement.

The courts have generally responded without enthusiasm to claims for rights *to* health care. However, they have expressed considerably more sympathy for rights *in* health care. Most important in this respect is the elaboration of the doctrine of informed consent. Intended explicitly to contribute to the "self-determination" of patients in medical treatment, the doctrine, first formulated in a 1957 California court case, has been greatly expanded since the 1960s. Now physicians are routinely required to disclose potential risks to patients not on the basis of usual medical practice (the standard in most malpractice law), but, in the language of one 1972 landmark decision, on the basis of "a standard set by law for physicians" (Katz, 1984).

The recognition of rights in health care is part and parcel of two related developments, which are also helping to transform the relationship between doctor and patient—the growth of a consumer movement in medicine and the emergence of bioethics. Although it is easy to overestimate the extent of the consumer movement in medicine, it is nonetheless clear that at least some patients—primarily younger and better educated—are now more willing to challenge "doctor's orders," to ask for more information about the treatments they are receiving, and to demand more participation in critical decisions than at any other time in the recent past (Haug & Lavin, 1983; Reeder, 1972). Moreover, even if the consumer movement is limited to a small segment of the population and, as Eliot Freidson (1985) has suggested, to the political actions of a few public interest groups, it has nonetheless helped to reshape the expectations of physicians. Rather than assuming that they may unilaterally determine what is in the best interests of their patients, a notion that is an expression of professionalism in full flower, physicians are slowly moving toward a relationship with patients based on the model of contract, in which they provide services in response to the expressed wishes of their clients (Colombotos & Kirchner, 1986; Louis Harris and Associates, 1982).

If the model of contract is implicit in the consumer movement, it is explicit in the bioethics movement. As a social movement—as distinct from simply an intellectually discipline—bioethics was born in response to a number of widely publicized abuses of human rights in medical experimentation, a response to the early stages of federal involvement in medicine. Its first triumph was the establishment of a review process for the consent procedures of federally funded research—a response to the first stages of federal involvement in medicine. Since the 1960s the bioethics movement has moved well beyond its original preoccupation with human experimentation to the ethics of reproduction, the allocation of scarce resources, and the proper character of the doctor–patient relationship more generally. In this, there should be no mistake as to the perspective that bioethics brings to bear on the issue it considers. As Paul Ramsey (1970, p. xi), one of the founders of the bioethics movement, has explained in his classic discussion, *The Patient as Person*, the issues of bioethics "are by no means technical problems on which only the expert (in this case, the physician) can have an opinion. They are rather the problems of human beings in situations in which medical care is needed." Bioethics, like the consumer movement, is an explicit challenge to the prerogatives of physicians.

Given the dominant perspective of the bioethics movement, it is perhaps surprising how quickly the movement has been institutionalized. Two national commissions—one dealing specifically with the protection of human subjects in biomedical research, the other with a broad mandate to examine ethical problems in medicine more generally—have given quasi-official recognition to many of the insights of bioethics. Moreover, bioethics has developed its own organizations, including not only the Hastings Center in New York and the Center for Bioethics at Georgetown University but also "scores of other independent, academic, professional, and public interest associations, institutes, departments, and programs that have a major commitment to reflection, research, teaching, publishing and action in matters pertaining to bioethics" (Fox, 1989, p. 227). Not least, medical ethics has found a place within the core institutions of medicine itself. Articles on medical ethics, virtually unheard of before the mid-1960s, now appear routinely in the prestigious *New England Journal of Medicine* and the *Journal of the American Medical Association* (Barber, Lally, Makarushka, & Sullivan, 1973). Courses on medical ethics, similarly rare before the mid-1960s are now taught at a majority of American medical schools. Such articles and courses are, from the point of view of many physicians who remain committed to the older prerogatives of medical professionalism, the enemy within.[1]

Where federal involvement in financing has tilted responsibility for setting the broad agenda of health care from the medical profession to the government, the consumer movement and the bioethics movement—themselves spawned and nurtured by a federal presence—challenge physicians at the level of clinical decisions. These joint challenges to physicians' authority go hand in hand.

PROFESSIONS AND PROPRIETORS

The increased federal role in health care is not, of course, the only transformative force in contemporary medicine. Rather, it has corresponded with (and contributed to) two other much noted developments—a trend toward the bureaucratic employment of physicians and the growth of proprietary medicine. Both of these developments have been identified frequently as threats to medical professionalism. It is, however, my conten-

---

[1] I am drawing here on my own sometimes painful (and occasionally rewarding) 4-year experience of teaching in a medical school.

tion that neither is as central to the decline of that professionalism as the coming of the welfare state.

There can, to be sure, be no doubt that there has been a significant movement away from sole practice and toward practice in organizational settings. In 1940, just before World War II, 86% of practicing American physicians were in office-based practice; only 14% were primarily hospital based, in administration, teaching, or research, or employed directly in federal service. By 1965, just before the introduction of Medicaid and Medicare, office-based practice had declined to 66%, whereas the proportion practicing in other settings had reached over one-third of all physicians. Since 1965, the trend away from office-based practice has slowed, but the character of that practice has itself changed: Although all but a few percentage of office-based physicians were solo practitioners before World War II, by the 1980s nearly half were part of a group practice. And finally, roughly two-fifths of all American physicians enjoy some sort of contractual relationship with a Health Maintenance Organization, an organizational form developed over the last two decades to provide health care to enrollees on the basis of a single, prepaid fee. If solo, fee-for-service practitioners are not yet extinct, they are surely not the dominant figures in the medical profession that they once were (Derber, 1983; McKinlay & Arches, 1985).

It is, however, one thing to note a trend away from solo practice and quite another to argue that the trend is incompatible with professionalism. First, even when they practice in organizational settings, physicians are often not exactly employees. The relationship between physicians and the organizations in which they work involves an often bewildering assortment of arrangements, from straight salaried employment to partnership and fee splitting. Moreover, hospitals, in particular, are typically as dependent on physicians to provide patients as physicians are on hospitals to provide facilities and salaries. As a result, very few health care organizations even attempt to exercise any significant degree of control over the physicians who work in them.[2] Second, even in health care organizations, decisive administrative positions are usually occupied by physicians. As Eliot Freidson (1985, p. 22) has emphasized, a profession is not simply "composed of individuals doing their daily work...[but] is also corporate in character." Thus the organizational employment of physicians may produce a new form of stratification in the occupation, with sharp divisions between presidents of hospitals and chiefs of departments, on the one hand, and staff physicians, on the other. But the profession, taken as a collectivity, continues to shape the policies and directions of the very organizations that are its nominal employers.

[2]Derber argues that health care organizations are able to exercise effective control over physicians only when they join what he calls "proprietary sponsorship" with "market sponsorship," a situation found only in some prepaid medical plans.

A perhaps more serious threat to medical professionalism is repre-sented by the rise of what Arnold Relman (1980), the editor of the *New England Journal of Medicine*, has called the "medical–industrial complex." For-profit hospitals are not new to the American scene. In fact, the majority of American hospitals in the nineteenth century were doctor-owned, giv-ing way only in the twentieth century (and never completely) to the now dominant mode of control by nonprofit institutions, including churches, municipalities, and universities. What is new is the development of propri-etary multihospital chains. In 1970, as Paul Starr (1983, p. 430) has ob-served, "the largest for-profit chain controlled twenty-three hospitals; by 1981, the same company, Hospital Corporation of America, owned or man-aged three hundred hospitals with 43,000 beds." In all, for-profit chains now own or manage hospitals with approximately one of every seven acute-care beds in the United States.

According to Relman and other critics of the medical–industrial com-plex, the rise of proprietary hospitals represents a profound threat to pub-lic confidence in physicians. And, indeed, the specter of physicians with direct financial interests in proprietary hospitals is fundamentally incom-patible with the notion, at the very core of medical professionalism, of the physician as a trustee of the public interest. Yet, it is also easy to overesti-mate the threat to professionalism represented by the rise of proprietary hospitals. First, after an expansion of between 10% and 20% annually during the 1970s, the growth rate of the proprietary sector has slowed dramatically. With many states continuing to ban multihospital chains, it seems likely that the for-profit hospital is rapidly nearing a point of satura-tion. Second, and more important, the expansion of the proprietary sector is not, as some have suggested, an ironic counterpoint to the expansion of a federal presence in health care but is itself contingent on that presence. For, it is the presence of the federal government as a financier of medical ser-vices that has made health care profitable over the last two decades. Like physicians themselves, the proprietary sector has become dependent upon the public and vulnerable to shifts in health care policy. Moreover, the presence of the federal government as a guarantor of health care has been essential to the political acceptance of the proprietary sector. Only because the federal government, rather than the medical professional, has assumed the role of guarantor is the public prepared to turn to a sector that they might otherwise distrust. In this sense, the rise of the proprietary sector is not so much a cause of declining professionalism as its consequence.

THE LIMITS OF PROFESSIONALISM

Medical professionalism emerged at the end of the nineteenth century as a guarantor of health care services, as an alternative to the treatment of health simply as a commodity like any other and in the absence of a government able and willing to provide (or even regulate) those services directly. In this sense, medical professionalism was the expression of a now old-fashioned-seeming liberalism, one shaped by suspicion of both the market and the state. For the conditions under which medical professionalism emerged are very different from those of the contemporary welfare state: With a government both willing and able to finance and regulate medical care, the broad grant of public authority to an occupation licensed by, but separate from, the state—the core of medical professionalism— begins to seem unwarranted.

The coming of the welfare state to medicine has displaced professional authority in two ways. First, as the financier of medical care, the state has assumed responsibility for setting the broad agenda of health care. And second, as the guarantor of the public interest in health care, the state has undermined the cultural authority of medicine, based on its long-standing claim to public service. None of this is to suggest that medicine will cease to be a profession in other senses: Medicine is likely to remain a high-status and well-paying occupation, even if there is some slight slippage compared to its current position. It is equally likely that physicians will remain, in a favored phrase among them, "captains of the ship," in their relations with nurses, technicians, and therapists. Certainly there is very little evidence to suggest that physicians are undergoing a process of "proletarianization." A medical degree is almost sure to please doting parents for some time to come. Rather, medical professionalism seems likely to diminish only in a limited but critical sense. If, in the phrase cited earlier, physicians once exercised "leadership...based on cultural criteria of legitimacy rather than criteria of political power or economic success," they are unlikely to continue to do so in the future.

The welfare state came to medicine in a Democratic administration, committed to expanding equality in health care. Yet, whatever its origins, the welfare state in medicine has been presided over by an almost unbroken stream of Republican administrations with very different priorities. Where the Democratic administration that introduced Medicaid and Medicare was committed to equality, it was also careful to tread lightly on professional prerogatives. It is, rather, under the succeeding Republican administrations that the incompatibility of the welfare state with medical professionalism has become clear. The great irony in the recent history of American health care is that, at the very moment the state has assumed a role as a guarantor of health care, its most intense efforts have been not to improve access to health care, but to control health care costs. If, in the 1960s, medicine seemed to be waging its last-ditch fight against the welfare state solely in the name of professional privilege, today it may be waging that fight more genuinely in the name of patient care.

REFERENCES

Abbott, A. (1988). *The system of professions*. Chicago: University of Chicago Press.

Barber, B., Lally, J., Makarushka, J., & Sullivan, D. (1973). *Research on human subjects*. New York: Russell Sage Foundation.

Bosk, C. (1986). Professional responsibility and medical error. In L. Aiken & D. Mechanic (Eds.), *Applications of social science to clinical medicine and health policy* (pp. 460–477). New Brunswick, NJ: Rutgers University Press.

Colombotos, J. (1969). Physicians and medicare: A before-after study of the effects of legislation on attitudes. *American Sociological Review, 34*, 318–334.

Colombotos, J., & Kirchner, C. (1986). *Physicians and social change*. New York: Oxford University Press.

Conrad, P., & Schneider, J. (1980). *Deviance and medicalization*. St. Louis: C. V. Mosby.

Davis, K., & Schoen, C. (1978) *Health and the war on poverty*. Washington, DC: The Brookings Institute.

Derber, C. (1983). Sponsorship and the control of physicians. *Theory and Society, 12*, 561–601.

Derbyshire, R. (1983). How effective is medical self-regulation? *Law and Human Behavior, 7*, 193–202.

Duff, R., & Hollingshead, A. (1968) *Sickness and society*. New York: Harper & Row.

Flexner, A. (1910). *Medical education in the United States and Canada*. New York: Carnegie Foundation for the Advancement of Teaching, Bulletin Number 4.

Fox, R., & Swazey, J. (1978) *The courage to fail*. Chicago: University of Chicago Press.

Fox, R. (1989). *The sociology of medicine*. Englewood Cliffs, NJ: Prentice-Hall.

Freidson, E. (1970). *The profession of medicine*. New York: Harper & Row.

Freidson, E. (1985). The reorganization of the medical profession. *Medical Care Review, 42*, 11–35.

Freidson, E. (1986). *Professional powers*. Chicago: University of Chicago Press.

Haug, M. R., & Lavin, B. (1983). *Consumerism in medicine*. Beverly Hills: Sage.

Health, United States, 1987. (1988). GPO: Department of Health and Human Services.

Iglehart, J. (1986). Early experience with prospective payment of hospitals. *New England Journal of Medicine, 314*, 1460–1464.

Katz, J. (1984). *The silent world of doctor and patient*. New York: The Free Press.

Louis Harris and Associates. (1982). View of informed consent and decision-making: Parallel surveys of physicians and the public. In President's Commission for the Study of Ethical Problems in Medicine and Biomedical and Behavioral Research. In *Making health care decisions*, Volume Two: Appendices, Empirical Studies of Informed Consent (pp. 17–314). Washington, DC: Government Printing Office.

Marshall, T. H. (1965). The recent history of professionalism in relation to social structure and social policy. In T. H. Marshall, *Class, citizenship, and social development* (pp. 158–179). Garden City, NY: Anchor.

McKinlay, J., & Arches, J. (1985). Towards the proletarianization of physicians. *International Journal of Health Services, 15*, 161–195.

Merton, R. (1982). Institutionalized altruism. In R. Merton, *Social research and the practicing professionals* (pp. 109–133). Cambridge: Abt Books.

Millman, M. (1976). *The unkindest cut*. New York: Marrow.

Parsons, T. (1954). The professionals and social structure. In T. Parsons, *Essays in sociological theory* (pp. 34–49). Glencoe, IL: Free Press.

Parsons, T. (1968) The professions. In *The international encyclopedia of the social sciences* (Vol. 12, pp. 536–547). New York: Macmillan.

Ramsey, P. (1970). *The patient as person*. New Haven: Yale University Press.

Reeder, L. (1972). The patient as client-consumer: Some observations on the changing professional-client relationship. *Journal of Health and Social Behavior, 13*, 406–12.

Relman, A. (1980). The new medical-industrial complex. *New England Journal of Medicine, 303*, 963–970.

Ritzer, G., & Walczak, D. (1988). Rationalization and the deprofessionalization of physicians. *Social Forces, 67*, 1–22.

Rosenberg, C. (1974). Social class and medical care in nineteenth century America: The rise and fall of the dispensary. *Journal of the History of Medicine, 29*, 32–54.

Rothstein, W. (1972). *American physicians in the nineteenth century: From sects to science*. Baltimore: The Johns Hopkins University Press.

Sarfatti-Larson, M. (1977). *The rise of professionalism*. Berkeley: University of California Press.

Scott, W. R. (1982). Health care organizations in the 1980's: The convergence of public and professional control systems. In A. W. Johnson, O. Grusky, & B. H. Raven (Eds.), *Contemporary health services*. Boston: Auburn House.

Sloan, F., Morrisey, M., & Valvona, J. (1988). Effects of the Medicare prospective payment system on hospital cost containment: An early appraisal. *The Milbank Quarterly, 66*, 191–220.

Starr, P. (1982). *The social transformation of American medicine*. New York: Basic Books.

Sudnow, D. (1967). *The social organization of dying*. Englewood Cliffs, NJ: Prentice-Hall.

Veblen, T. (1921). *The engineers and the price system*. n.p.: Huebsch; reprint, New York: Viking, 1965.

CHAPTER TEN

Mass Media and Public Opinion
Emergence of an Institution

JAMES R. BENIGER AND SUSAN HERBST

Although the concept of institution enjoys wide use in American sociology, it has different implications for different theoretical traditions. Institutions fulfill macrosocietal functions in structural theories, serve ideology and hegemony according to critical theories, and are continuously created, modified, and adapted by individuals under action theories (contrary to the tendency to reify institutions as given or unchanging). In its fullest sense, the concept of institution embraces all three of these levels of social control—those of processor, program, and processing, respectively.

American sociologists have argued for most of this century about whether institutions include formally organized social processors like the family or are restricted to more abstract systems of interacting roles (Parsons, 1960, p. 171), to still more systematized and transcendent processes like language (Bierstedt, 1963; Ginsberg, 1965; MacIver, 1937), or to more explicitly controlling programming like norms (Davis, 1949). "Always in human society there is what may be called a double reality," Kingsley Davis (1949, p. 52) argues. "On the one hand a normative system embodying what *ought* to be, and on the other a factual order embodying what *is*" (emphasis in original).

Bridging the gap between *is* and *ought* is the fact that institutions exist apart from any one individual and in that sense, at least, constrain and control all individuals. At the same time, they also enable or facilitate

JAMES R. BENIGER ● Annenberg School of Communications, University of Southern California, Los Angeles, California 90089-0281.   SUSAN HERBST ● Department of Communication Studies, Northwestern University, Evanston, Illinois 60208.

much individual action, an often-overlooked side of institutional control that Anthony Giddens (1979, 1984) has termed *structuration*. Such control will necessarily involve all levels and components of open processing systems: preprocessing (the Whorf–Sapir view of language [Whorf, 1956]), programs (norms), the process of programming (socialization), and processors themselves (formal social structures). This range is perhaps best covered, in American sociology, by Erving Goffman's view of institutions as extending from what he calls "total institutions" (like prisons and mental hospitals) to the seemingly "natural" and timeless institutions of language, ritualized behavior, and other cultural programming. Although total institutions appear to exert greatest control over the individual, Goffman (1961) maintains that "every institution has encompassing tendencies."

The gap between the social *is* and the cultural *ought*—between process and program—is best understood at the highest level: language. More than merely a means of communication, language constitutes what Berger and Berger (1976, Chapter 4) call "the social institution above all others." Like other institutions, language constrains and controls each individual, translating the collective flood of personal sensation and experience into a classified, ordered, shared reality but also making interpersonal communication—and hence society—possible. Although an individual might construct what Julian Huxley (1966, p. 259) terms *private ritualizations*, communication will be effective only to the extent that each individual approximates the "socially standardized concept" (Carroll, 1964; Smith, 1977, pp. 76–77). Thus language, though it does not function apart from other cultural systems, nevertheless constitutes the primary institution through which collective reality is continuously renegotiated and reproduced, thereby enabling the social organization and mobilization of individual experience.

Public opinion and mass communication, although subordinate to language, play much the same role in institutionalization. Like language, the system of mass communication serves to classify and order the collective experience, thereby enhancing that shared reality—based ultimately in language—that facilitates social interaction and upon which large-scale societies depend. Within this system, the continuous monitoring of public opinion—by increasingly rationalized means—serves both to influence individual thought and behavior and to legitimate institutional decisions. It matters little that family and community opinions remain influential or that subcultural and regional variations in language persist. Within a separate and growing sphere of thought and behavior, public opinion *is* what the monitoring system measures, and reality *is* what the mass media system reports—not by scientific or technical achievement but by institutional intent.

MASS SOCIETY REVISITED

This argument for mass media and public opinion as a relatively new social institution smacks of an earlier, largely alarmist literature on mass society. Mass society, a concept nascent in the writings of many nineteenth-century social theorists and made explicit by founders of the Frankfurt school in the 1920s, currently has little standing in American sociology. The last major American contributions to the mass society model came in the late 1950s (Kornhauser, 1959; Lerner, 1958; MacDonald, 1957; Mills, 1956; Vidich & Bensman, 1958).

The same period brought steadily mounting criticism both of mass society themes in general (Bell, 1960; Bramson, 1961; Greer, 1958; Shils, 1957, 1962), and of their underlying assumptions about mass media influence on public opinion (Bauer & Bauer, 1960; Bramson, 1961, Chapter 5; Freidson, 1953; Katz, 1957, 1960; Parsons & White, 1960; Riley & Riley, 1959). By 1962, discussion of mass society had reached exhaustion—it is difficult to find the term indexed in an American book after that year. The article "Mass Society" in the *International Encyclopedia of the Social Sciences,* published in 1968, contains only 1 reference—out of 28—published after 1962 (Kornhauser, 1968, p. 64).

The problem has been that mass society imagery implies an undifferentiated public, lacking interpersonal ties, politically apathetic, and thus readily manipulated—via mass media—by bureaucracies and ruling elites. The preponderance of sociological research, by contrast, has found modern societies comprised of increasingly differentiated groups, with family and community ties still strong and mass media influence weak or nonexistent. So devastating did such findings prove for mass society imagery that by the mid-1950s leading social researchers had begun to abandon the study of mass communication. In 1958, when Bernard Berelson, director-designate of the Bureau of Applied Social Research at Columbia University, delivered his eulogy for communication research at the annual conference of the American Association for Public Opinion Research (Berelson, 1959), many who had worked in the field—including Harold Lasswell, Carl Hovland, and Paul Lazarsfeld—had already left it.

The combined study of mass media and public opinion, a wedding inspired by Lazarsfeld and Robert Merton (Lazarsfeld 1940, 1942; Lazarsfeld et al., 1944; Lazarsfeld & Merton, 1948; Merton, 1946) and institutionalized at Columbia's BASR (Sills, 1987), virtually ended in 1960 when Joseph Klapper published a revised and expanded version of his 1949 doctoral dissertation as *The Effects of Mass Communication,* a major synthesis of media effects studies. Not only did Klapper's book minimize the effects of mass communication relative to those of interpersonal influence, it also demonstrated that even small changes due to the former will rarely constitute more than a blip in opinions already held or in what audience members already intend to do. In the summer of 1960, a special issue of *Public Opinion Quarterly* devoted to attitudinal change served to commemorate the passing of media effects research (D. Katz, 1960).

The view of modern societies as characterized by strong family and community ties, increasingly differentiated groups, and only indirect mass media influences need not negate the implications of mass society theories, however. Nor does it necessarily undermine the combined study of mass media and public opinion. In only recent years has public opinion, a phenomenon well understood for preindustrial societies by the ancient Greeks, come to be separated from its traditional institutional domains and to be subject to prediction, planning, engineering, and monitoring on a mass scale. Mass media as well as public opinion have been increasingly rationalized since the 1950s; both have been increasingly integrated in a single institutional domain since the late 1960s. A new and growing sphere of thought and behavior has resulted, one in which mass media influences do prevail, simultaneously with—but largely apart from—the spheres dominated by family, community, or work relationships.

All of these changes imply that mass media will play an increasingly important role in modern societies. Unfortunately, the social effects of mass media have become virtually impossible to determine because *public opinion* and *mass communication* have increasingly become merely different terms for the same phenomenon. As a result, so-called media effects will no longer be found as the direct causal consequences of particular mass media content, nor in the predictions of social structural or systems theories, but rather as the intended consequences of carefully engineered social control.

For this reason, we argue, the time has come to reconsider, if not the mass society theories of old, at least the value of mass society imagery as a basis for new social theory. Toward this end, our chapter has three specific aims: First, to document the increasing rationalization of mass media and public opinion and their convergence in a new social institution. Second, to demonstrate that this institution has increasingly assimilated the functions of other ones, including the family, education, religion, and polity, and to describe the growing conflict between the new institution and these others. And finally, to suggest some of the effects of the new institution's growth upon modern society and culture, as well as upon individual thought and behavior. One of these effects, as we shall see, has been the emergence of a new paradigm—beginning in the late 1960s—for the study of mass media and public opinion.

THE EMERGENCE OF A PUBLIC OPINION

Because institutionalization is not absolute but a matter of degree (Parsons & Shils, 1951, p. 20), it is difficult to specify the precise origins of many institutions. To extend the distinction made by William Graham Sumner (1906) for law, institutions may be either crescive or enacted, that is, they may develop unconsciously out of collective action (as did common law) or they may be intentionally created (as is constitutional law). Public opinion, at least before the advent of advanced industrial societies, can best be described as a crescive institution (Herbst, 1988).

Mention of the institution, most often in the context of political decision making, can be found at least as far back as ancient Greece. In the *Antigone* (443–441 B.C.), for example, the role of public opinion seems clear enough to Sophocles, if not to his King Creon:

> HAEMON [to his father, Creon, King of Thebes]: It is my natural office to watch, on thy behalf, all that men say, or do, or find to blame. For the dread of thy frown forbids the citizen to speak such words as would offend thine ear; but I can hear these murmurs in the dark, these moanings of the city.... It were far best, I ween, that men should be all-wise by nature; but otherwise—and oft the scale inclines not so—'tis good also to learn from those who speak aright....
>
> CREON: Is it a merit to honour the unruly?
>
> HAEMON: I could wish no one to show respect for evildoers.
>
> CREON: Then is she [Antigone, Oedipus's daughter, whom Creon has ordered to be buried alive for disobeying his command] not tainted with that malady?
>
> HAEMON: Our Theban folk, with one voice, denies it.
>
> CREON: Shall Thebes prescribe to me how I must rule?
>
> HAEMON: See, there thou hast spoken like a youth indeed.
>
> CREON: Am I to rule this land by other judgment than mine own?
>
> HAEMON: That is no city, which belongs to one man.
>
> CREON: Is not the city held to be the ruler's?
>
> HAEMON: Thou wouldst make a good monarch of a desert....

Historians Charles Tilly (1983) and Robert Darnton (1985) have documented the institutionalization of collective behavior to express public opinion as early as the seventeenth century. By the late seventeenth century, beginning in England, petitions gained acceptance as a formal means to communicate public opinion to government (Emden, 1956). In the eighteenth century, statesmen of France monitored public opinion in the exclusive *salons* of the newly powerful French bourgeoisie (Palmer, 1967), whereas their counterparts in England could do much the same in the coffeehouses and cafes of London (Coser, 1970).

That public opinion might be engineered or controlled via mass media found early demonstration in the development of fashion. Most costume historians agree that fashion did not exist before the beginnings of mercantile capitalism and the growth of cities in medieval Europe in the fourteenth century (Wilson, 1987, p. 16). Trade flows, the first routinized international communication, gave birth to fashion at various geographical centers of trade, perhaps first at the court of Burgundy, center of the trade corridor stretching from Flanders to the Mediterranean (Mukerji, 1983, Chapter 5). By the sixteenth century, costume manuals depicting fashionable variations in dress—among the earlier books printed in Europe—had become commonplace, and with them the first discarding of clothing simply because it had gone out of style (Laver, 1969). John Locke, writing in the late seventeenth century, used the terms *fashion, reputation,* and *opinion* interchangeably, noting that all are transitory, time and place dependent, manipulable, and coercive (Locke, 1690).

Not until the Industrial Revolution and the beginnings of mass production and advertising, however, did fashion begin to fall under the rationalized elite control—via mass media—so dominant today. "One cannot really talk of fashion becoming all powerful before about 1700," writes Fernand Braudel (1981), after which "the word gained a new lease of life and spread everywhere with its new meaning: keeping up with the times." The first modern dress designer, Englishman Charles Frederick Worth, rose to prominence in the 1850s—just the time that the mass production and advertising of fashion had begun to develop (Wilson, 1987, p. 32).

Elections, which date from the ancient Greek democracies like Athens, provided the first highly rationalized means to measure public opinion. Associated with the parliamentary process in England from the thirteenth century, elections became institutionalized through legislation—beginning with the Triennial Act of 1694 and the Septennial Act of 1716—that prescribed their frequency by a succession of nineteenth century reform bills that extended the franchise and by the adoption of the secret ballot in 1872. The so-called Australian ballot, printed, distributed, and collected by the government at a specified polling place, thus assuring an anonymous vote, first appeared in Australia in 1858 and in the United States 30 years later (Fredman, 1967). Corrupt practices legislation, primary elections, poll watching, and—after 1892—the first voting machines all helped to institutionalize the modern election system as an important means of measuring public opinion by the turn of this century.

CONVERGENCE OF MASS MEDIA AND PUBLIC OPINION

Although mass media date from the development of printing in the sixteenth century, mass communication did not begin to converge with public opinion as an identifiable social institution until mid-nineteenth century. Underlying technological and economic causes include the application of steam power to the printing press in the 1820s, the rise of the so-called penny press (led by the *New York Sun* in 1833), telegraphic newspapers and electric-powered printing by the 1840s, double cylinder rotary printing after 1846, and the gradual emergence of a mass press (Beniger, 1986, pp. 264–278).

Although transportation and telecommunications infrastructures have played crucial roles in the control of large territories since the Roman Empire, it is difficult to imagine consolidation of the modern nation-state, over the nineteenth and early twentieth centuries, without the cultural integration made possible by parallel development—in addition to the mass press—of a wide range of mass media: lithographic reproduction (1820s), photography (1830s), high-speed printing (1840s), cheaper wood pulp publications (1850s), transatlantic telegraphic news reporting (1860s), illustrated daily publications and mass mailing (1870s), halftone photoreproduction (1880s), motion pictures and mass circulation magazines (1890s), and finally broadcasting (1900s). Consolidation of the modern nation-state, in turn, has meant further convergence of public opinion and mass communication, both increasingly controlled by the state itself.

Modern mass-circulation dailies, the first powerful U.S. mass media institution, developed rapidly after 1883, when Joseph Pulitzer took control of the *New York World*. The potential mass audience increased during the same period as the U.S. illiteracy rate fell from 22% in 1840 to 17% in 1880 and 7.7% in 1910 (U.S. Bureau of the Census, 1975, pp. 365, 382). With the growth of a mass readership, by the turn of the century, came a proliferation of inexpensive popular magazines, many with suggestive titles like *Public Opinion* and *Everybody's* (Keller, 1977). James Bryce, among the keener political observers of the time, became the first of many to note that periodicals, formerly the biased organs of political parties, had begun to cover and influence public opinion more generally (Bryce, 1888).

Simultaneously with these developments came the first *mass feedback technologies* (Beniger, 1986, pp. 376–389) with which the mass media and their advertisers could assess public opinion: straw polling in the 1820s (Robinson, 1932), formalization of market research after 1910, a postcard-questionnaire survey in 1911, house-to-house market interviewing in 1916, and finally full-blown attitudinal and opinion surveys—a U.S. bibliography listed nearly 3,000 by 1928 (Boorstin, 1973, p. 155). Nowhere can the impact of mass media and the new mass feedback technologies be seen more dramatically than in the changes in the popular symbolic repertoire that occurred after 1850. As historian Charles Tilly summarizes the changes:

> We now live in a world in which the idea of a defined aggregate set of preferences at a national level, a sort of public opinion, makes a certain amount of sense. It makes enough sense that nowadays we can consider the opinion survey a complement to, or even an alternative to, voting, petitioning, or protesting. However, if we push back into the strange terrain of western Europe and North America before the middle of the nineteenth century, we soon discover another world. In that world, most people did not vote, petition, or take positions on

national affairs in anything like the contemporary meanings of those terms. Yet they did act together on their interests, broadcasting their demands, complaints, and aspirations in no uncertain terms. (Tilly, 1983, p. 462)

About mid-nineteenth century, according to Tilly, "the people of most western countries shed the collective-action repertoire they had been using for two centuries or so, and adopted the repertoire they still use today" (Tilly, 1983, p. 464). The repertoire of the seventeenth to nineteenth centuries was, in Tilly's terms, *parochial* (addressed to local actors or to the local representatives of national actors) and relied heavily on *patronage*. The repertoire that appeared after 1850 and still prevails today, by contrast, is *national* in scope (or at least lends itself to coordination among many localities) and relatively *autonomous*. It includes public meetings, demonstrations, strikes, petition marches, invasions of government assemblies, planned insurrections, and even social movements (Tilly, 1983, pp. 464–466).

The shift that Tilly notes might be explained by the roughly simultaneous shift in dominant communication channels from local to mass, with a corresponding shift in audience from local powerholders to a growing national elite. To describe these changes in terms of communication: As the audience for popular collective action shifted from local to national power brokers, the symbolic repertoire was forced to shift to the more autonomous (we would say more *generalized*) messages necessary if one hoped to be understood by the more diverse audience of the national mass media that developed rapidly after 1850 (Beniger, 1983b).

As evident from new technologies like demographic surveys, national censuses, and straw polls, the impetus for better mass feedback did not come from citizens but from business and government. These institutions have showed increasing interest in measuring, predicting, and controlling mass audience behavior in advanced industrial societies (Galbraith, 1967). Therein lies a second explanation for the repertoire change noted by Tilly: It was not only that people shifted the focus of their communication from local audiences to national ones but also that the audiences themselves, especially big business and big government, were increasingly attentive to what people had on their minds and listening—thanks to the new mass feedback technologies—whether people intended to communicate or not.

Certainly business and government had many motives to do so: to influence purchasing decisions and voting behavior, to legitimate their own decisions, to control specific and aggregate demand, and to maintain what has come to be known as good public relations (the industry dates from 1904). Development of mass feedback technologies as means toward these ends awaited only the other half of the mass control loop—the national mass communications infrastructure that emerged between the 1830s and 1920s.

EMERGENCE OF AN INSTITUTION

By the early 1920s, the growing convergence of mass media and public opinion led Walter Lippmann to conclude that newspapers actually *created* public opinion. The public no longer could be considered the powerful collectivity of democratic theory, Lippmann argued, but had to be exposed as a dangerous creation of journalists and editorial writers (Lippmann, 1922, 1925). Over the next decade, U.S. doctoral programs in the social sciences began to introduce journalism into their curricula (Weaver & Mc-Combs, 1980). Emphasis on observing and measuring public opinion became a staple of good journalism as taught in the new journalism schools, especially after the development of scientific survey research in the 1930s.

Not until the late 1930s, however, and especially following World War II, did the convergence of public opinion and mass communication begin to be formally institutionalized. This dramatic transformation has been due largely to two powerful new technologies, scientific survey research and national network television, that emerged in the 1930s and 1940s. Philip Meyer (1973) has coined the term *precision journalism* for the rationalization of his profession through the incorporation of quantification, survey research, and other social science methods in reporting. With such mass feedback technologies to supply reciprocal communication to the mass press, the convergence of public opinion and mass communication — with a resulting potential for mass control — had itself begun to be rationalized.

Modern survey research derives from the technical breakthrough of Morris Hansen, a mathematical statistician at the U.S. Census Bureau, who about 1930 began to extend formal sampling theory to large-scale survey design. Hansen's new theory and methods, by drastically reducing the sizes of samples while maintaining the accuracy of results, made economically feasible the first national public opinion surveys by George Gallup and Elmo Roper in 1935. Another important technology for monitoring mass audiences which depended on large-scale sampling was A. C. Nielsen's adoption of the audimeter to the measurement of radio audiences in 1935 and to television audiences by 1950.

Scientific survey research and electronic monitoring of mass audiences like that of Nielsen, because they yield quantitative data that is hence readily processable, proved a major advance in the rationalized monitoring and potential control of public opinion. Television, which by 1962 could be found in 90% of U.S. households, where it was already on an average of 5½ hours per day (Sterling, 1984, Section 6), provided the first real-time visual mass access to private homes.

Not only have national network television and scientific survey research developed in parallel over the past half-century, but they have also increasingly converged. National public opinion polls, for 30 years conducted independently of the mass media by well-known firms like Gallup, Harris, Roper, and Yankelovich, have been recently and rapidly incorporated directly into the media as integral parts of their news reporting operations. News coverage of the 1988 presidential campaign, for example, was dominated by the almost daily release of polls conducted by *The New York Times*/CBS News, NBC News/*Wall Street Journal*, ABC News/*Washington Post*, *Los Angeles Times*, and *Newsweek*.

A 1980 study finds that one-third of U.S. daily newspapers have in-house polling capabilities, including telephone banks, a trained staff of interviewers, and computers for data analysis; almost all dailies subscribe to at least one polling service (Atkin & Gaudino, 1984). As part of a continuing public relations campaign, the *Times Mirror* media conglomerate has featured the findings of periodic national surveys, commissioned from Gallup, in weekly advertisements run in its own and rival newspapers (*Times Mirror*, 1986). Many of the news media commission polls to bolster scheduled interpretive or feature stories; virtually all cover the releases of at least some new poll data as news stories.

Even in their published and broadcast interviews with government officials and political activists, the media often transmit survey research and public opinion poll data cited by their interviewees. For example, Paletz and Entman (1981) find that the lobbying group Common Cause has enjoyed especially extensive and favorable coverage by the news media precisely because it commands quantitative social science data so effectively. Scientific opinion surveys and other mass feedback data would seem to have privileged access to media channels, regardless of whether such information comes from the media themselves or from external sources — further evidence that mass communication and public opinion, through their parallel rationalization, have increasingly converged in a new institutional sphere.

Emergence of this new institution, in addition to consolidating public opinion and mass communication in a single integrated function of journalism and entertainment, also has the effect—because media-conducted polls are more consistently, prominently, and thoroughly reported than are independent ones—of better feeding mass public opinion back upon itself. Such feedback can play an important role in changing public opinion from what it would otherwise be, an effect described by sociologists and social psychologists under various guises: the outcomes of experiments on conformity (Asch, 1951; Wheeler & Jordan, 1929), social patterns described by Allport (1924) as *pluralistic ignorance*, Schanck's treatment of *public opinion* versus *private attitudes* (1932), the *social self* of Mead (1934, Part 3) that emerges by assuming the attitudes of *significant others*, reference group theory (Hyman, 1942; Newcomb, 1943; Sherif, 1936), bandwagon modeling (Simon, 1954), and the *spiral of silence* of Noelle-Neumann (1974).

Despite the new importance of polls—and related quantitative measures like Nielsen ratings—in feeding mass public opinion back upon it-self, such technologies constitute only some of the means by which mass feedback might facilitate social control. However mass communication is supplemented by a reciprocal flow of information back to the writers and programmers who seek to attract and hold the mass attention, to the adver-tisers who seek to stimulate and control mass consumption behavior, or to the politicians who seek to influence mass public opinion and voting, social control might be effected in at least the weak probabilistic sense. This is the sense in which, for example, economists say that advertising serves to control specific demand, or political scientists say that direct mail helps to control issue voting (Beniger, 1986, pp. 7–8). Audience and market feedback, the flow of information from retailers, consumers, and voters back to those who would influence mass behavior, includes the entire range of data—increasingly collected, stored, processed, and utilized via computer—in what has come to be called *market research.*

NEW MASS MEDIA

Just as control of public opinion has included an expanding repertoire of quantitative, rationalized techniques in recent years, so too has mass communication expanded beyond broadcasting and publishing. With the diffusion of computers, microprocessing, and related hardware and soft-ware has come a rapid blurring of the distinction between mass and inter-personal sources of information. Leading this change have been the progressively more targeted and processable channels into households: digital telephone, multidigit postal codes, and computer-linked cable tele-vision. Examples of the new mass communications include targeted and personalized "hand-written" mass mailings, fully automated and targeted mass telephoning, and interactive household cable services (Beniger, 1987a).

Early in 1986, for example, using laser-print technology, a U.S. senator mailed 40,000 copies on personal stationary of a fund-raising letter that—according to *Time Magazine* (1986)—"looked as if it had been handwritten" (p. 23); by October some 100 House members had tried laser printers, and the Senate pondered installing them as standard office equipment. In that same month, using a network of 400 computers located throughout the country, Republicans telephoned hundreds of thousands of registered party members *each day* with a recorded message from President Reagan urging them to vote in the November elections; hang-up rates ranged from 5% to 17%, unprecedentedly low for a prerecorded solicitation. As a politi-cal consultant explained in *The New York Times*: "We've found that if you use the politician's voice, there's a psychological bonding. You'd be amazed at the number of people who say the next day that 'the President called me on the phone last night'" (Eichenwald, 1986).

A major database marketing industry, including geodemographic targeting of mass mailings using census block statistics, ZIP codes, and postal carrier routes, has sprung up around the modern postal system. The Claritas Company of Alexandria, Virginia, for example, can link national address and telephone lists to neighborhood units with an average size of only 340 households. Based on a growing wealth of consumer information on these units (Claritas routinely links to more than two dozen different databases), mass mailing and telephoning cannot only be personalized by name but by likely housing value, social status and mobility, purchase and credit behavior, and media preferences.

Thus have public opinion, as redefined by survey and market research, and mass communication, as effected by national network television and other increasingly computerized new media, come to converge in a new social institution—one that could not be said to have existed 80 years ago, nor even 30 years ago with anything of the pervasive power that it has today. This new convergence has by now acquired all of the characteristics of a major social institution: It involves highly organized, systematized, and stable macrolevel processes—transcending the life spans of individuals—that have central significance for society.

Nor could the new institution be confused with any of its antecedents: It is not a proper subset of the economy, which serves to produce and distribute goods and services, nor of the polity, which regulates access to—and use of—legitimate power, nor of the stratification system, which determines individual statuses and rewards. Although it intersects and conflicts with all of these and other institutions, as we shall see, the convergence of public opinion and mass communication represents in large part an entirely new institutional domain: engineered and continuously intentional mass control, at least potentially pluralistic, which can influence public opinion independently of economic and political forces.

CONFLICT WITH OTHER INSTITUTIONS

Max Weber (1915) was first to point out that different spheres of rationality might come into conflict with each other. The more rationalized a society, Weber argued, the greater would be the conflict among its various institutions. Because each institution has its own internal logic, which becomes rationalized in ever more explicit principles and procedures, individuals become increasingly conscious of "the inner and lawful autonomy" of each institution, "thereby letting them drift into those tensions which remain hidden to the originally naive relation with the external world" (p. 328).

For this reason, Weber believed that institutional conflict would grow worse in the twentieth century as modern societies differentiated and institutionalized increasing numbers of social spheres, and as these grew increasingly rationalized. Even in 1915, Weber could see the result—the growing independence of institutions so obvious today: Mass media and education, universalized and intellectualized culture, impersonal science, new religions formulated by intellectuals for mass audiences, the planned economy of corporate capitalism, the corporate state of technocrats and bureaucracy. As each sphere became increasingly rationalized, Weber argued, each would grow more independent and come into greater contradiction with the others.

This view of the tensions and conflict inherent in rationalization is borne out by the convergence of public opinion and mass communication. As the new institution has assimilated the functions of others, including the family, education, religion, and polity, it has come into increasing conflict with their divergent values and norms. Mass media challenge the social control of these institutions by presenting a wider range of values, although possibly, as the hegemonic theorists (Gitlin, 1979, 1980; Gramsci, 1929–1935; Hall, 1977; Hall *et al.*, 1978) have argued, within narrow ideological bounds. At the same time, by continually promulgating representations of "public opinion," the media may challenge the view of what others believe (ultimately of what "society" demands) implicit in all institutional norms and values.

CONFLICT WITH THE FAMILY

Much as Weber saw the ancient family (kinship and household) challenged by the New World religions whose charismatic leaders asked followers to renounce family ties, modern family authority and cohesion might similarly be seen to be undermined by conflicting values and norms represented in the mass media and reinforced by media-legitimated sources of public opinion (whether polls, man-on-the-street interviews, expert testimonials, or celebrity endorsements). Just as Jesus, for example, asked true believers to forsake their families to follow him, so too do the mass media ask or at least suggest, daily or even hourly, that their audience take up attitudes and behavior that might conflict with family norms (whether drinking alcohol, practicing "safe" sex, or showing tolerance for minorities).

Because no true social interaction can take place between individual families and the mass media, media socialization can be neither as coercive nor as seductive as that based on interpersonal communication. Efforts to personalize mass communication by disguising the size of intended audiences, targeting messages, and contriving intimacy in content have a long history, however, with the recent diffusion of computers, microprocessing, and related hardware and software blurring even further the distinction between interpersonal and mass communication (Beniger, 1987a). This suggests that it would be a mistake to dismiss the role of the mass media in early socialization and family dynamics, a conclusion bolstered by a growing corpus of media research, much of it recent.

According to a 1982 review of research on television and behavior delivered to the National Institute of Mental Health (NIMH, 1982), most research on television and socialization makes little effort to demonstrate empirically a connection between specific media content and role socialization. That research that does study media effects on socialization, the report found, relies mostly on correlational measures to link television content to ideas about roles expressed by viewers (Greenberg, 1982). Research bearing on mass media and the family conducted since the NIMH report tends to find conflict between the two institutions on values and socialization.

As early as 1955, Raymond Forer found that adolescents who listened to a radio program called "Mind Your Manners" would follow the personal advice given by its teenage panel unless this conflicted with the advice of parents, grandparents, siblings, an aunt or uncle, older friend, or religious leader (Forer, 1955). In 1966, Walter Gerson found black adolescents more likely than whites to say that they use the mass media to learn about or reinforce social norms about "dating" (Gerson, 1966), a result that has held up for lower status groups and norms more generally (Dervin & Greenberg, 1972). James Chesebro (1982) similarly finds that television can influence individual norms. As Herbert Hyman (1974) argues, the mass media might also affect early socialization indirectly by providing parents with information on the proper training of children.

More recent studies have found that mothers actively attempt to turn television content into messages more appropriate for their children (Messaris & Sarett, 1981; Messaris, 1982). In direct reference to family values, a complex series of studies have found that the more television children watch, the more likely they are to adopt that medium's view of even family behavior—a relationship actually *strengthened* by every one of the observed ways that parents attempt to intervene in the process (Buerkel-Rothfuss *et al.*, 1982).

In sum, broadcasting enables centralized sources—for the first time in human history—to speak over the heads of traditional institutional gate-keepers like parents directly to family members in their home. Although parents recognize the potential conflict and actively seek to counter it with intervention that can modify if not lessen the effect (Buerkel-Rothfuss *et al.*, 1982, pp. 200–201), evidence mounts that family control over family norms and values has begun to shift—however slowly—to the newer institution of mass media and public opinion. Although such media socialization can rarely be as effective as that based on interpersonal communication, mass media have become increasingly able to create "pseudo-Gemeinschaft"

(Merton, 1945, 1946, 1975, 1987) or "pseudo-community" (Beniger, 1987). In this they are bolstered by a growing control over "public opinion" that includes even the media-created spokespersons, panels, and celebrities most likely to overcome the lack of true social interaction by eliciting para-social behavior (Horton & Wohl, 1956).

CONFLICT WITH EDUCATION

The new institution's values also undermine those of formal education, much as the values of formal education once undermined those of the family, from which it was differentiated and institutionalized with the growing industrialization of the eighteenth and early nineteenth centuries. Just as the new institution has begun to encroach on family socialization, so too has it begun to usurp more formal educational functions bestowed upon increasingly rationalized public school systems. Nowhere is the conflict generated by the new institution greater than in its competition with schools to educate the young, one arena in which mass media are not disadvantaged for lack of genetic or affective relationships (as they are in the family), of face-to-face social interaction (as with religion), or of legitimated authority and coercion (as in the polity).

On many current topics, students frequently tuned to radio or television know more than their classroom teachers, who are disadvantaged by having to divert time to professional duties. Steven Chaffee *et al.* (1970) find that high-school students rate mass media as their single most important sources of both information and popular opinion on current events—higher even than parents, friends, or teachers. Howard Tolley (1973) finds that relatively heavier users of mass media among elementary-school and junior-high-school students were more informed about the Vietnam war than students who relied more on teachers, clergy, or family.

Mass media programming—even that not intended to cover news or to provide formal knowledge or practical information—may play an equally important role in the education of adults, especially those lacking full access to more traditional educational institutions. In the early 1940s, Herta Herzog found that people listened to daytime radio serials to get "prescriptions" for handling practical problems (Herzog, 1944). Brenda Dervin and Bradley Greenberg (1972) reach the same conclusion for television in general among contemporary adults, especially low-income blacks as compared to middle-class whites.

Even though television seems to have become the educator of first choice, however, the medium remains relatively ineffectual in teaching abstract or complex materials, especially outside of formal classroom settings. Like television newscasts, so-called educational television, because of its mass audience, concentrates on topics that are of general interest,

visually exciting, and tractable using available footage. Public-school textbooks, themselves heavily influenced by television graphics, have difficulty competing with more popular mass media, as do lecturers—even
those supported by audiovisual equipment. Postman (1987) finds that
teachers have difficulty holding the attention of classes, a problem he attributes to students' familiarity with the brief, highly stylized segments of
television. Faced with such competition, teachers increasingly assign students magazine articles or television programs: In 1982, 35% of parents of
school-age children reported that watching television had become part of
homework assignments in their household (Roper, 1983, p. 19). By leaping
over the educational system to communicate directly with students, even
in formal school activities, the mass media have become increasingly associated with formal education itself in the public's mind.

Although little research has yet been conducted on the effect of quan-
tified and legitimated public opinion on student positions and opinion in
classroom discussions, the studies most relevant to this question are
highly suggestive. In the late 1960s, Neil Hollander asked high-school
seniors about 18 possible influences on their opinions about the Vietnam
War and found that the mass media—especially television—ranked first,
beating out family, friends, and teachers (Hollander, 1971). Margaret Conway et al. (1981) also find the mass media more effective in influencing
children's political attitudes than are schools.

Conflict with Religion

Because the mass media serve the economy, much of what Weber
(1915) wrote about rationalized religion's conflict with economic institutions applies equally well to the new institution. Governed by economic
rationality, mass media follow market dynamics, unimpeded by other
forces save some regulation by the state. Market forces, in turn, dictate the
content of mass communication; television exists, in the words of Todd
Gitlin (1983), to "rent the eyeballs" of viewers to advertisers. But such
economic rationalization clashes with ethical tenets of rationalized religions, which stress the worth of individuals, whereas the resulting com-
mercialism of media content undermines religious injunctions to eschew
materialism.

At the same time, however, religions formulated by intellectuals for
mass audiences can be further rationalized by precisely the same mass
communication and advertising techniques exploited by the market. In
short, rationalized religion may be condemned to mass media and materialism by the same structural forces that condemned the medieval monas-
tery, in Weber's view, to wealth, power, and reactionary politics. Thus
rationalized religion has much the same conflict with the new institution as

has the family—a conflict involving divergent values and norms, for social control of the individual (the same conflict Weber found between religion and the family in ancient times). The little empirical evidence available suggests that, just as religion once prevailed against the family, it may now be gradually losing ground to the mass media. Hollander (1971), for example, finds that of 18 possible influences on thoughts and opinions about the Vietnam War, mass media ranked first—clergy ranked near the bottom.

Even active churchgoers would rather watch religious broadcasts than attend local services, according to Gaddy and Pritchard (1985). George Gerbner (1987) argues that a major function of traditional religions, to provide myths with which to interpret the world, has now been usurped by the mass media. Fiske and Hartley (1978, Chapter 6) see this as the "bardic function" of mass media that have become a distinct and identifiable social institution, its major role being to mediate between state and society much as did the bardic orders in medieval Celtic societies—and as did rationalized religion until recent times.

If religion has accommodated itself better to mass media than has the family, it is only because many religious leaders have found the new institution a ready means to reach mass audiences and to control mass attitudes and behavior. Indeed, many of the new mass media already discussed— including computerized telephoning and personalized mass mailing—have been pioneered by religious organizations. If only a few denominations currently have their own television channels or daily newspapers, many others use televised services, weekly programs like inspirational soap operas, and frequent public service announcements. Rationalized public opinion has been exploited by some religious leaders to bolster their teachings (as on capital punishment), even though it may undermine them on some other issues (on contraceptive use, for example, or on abortion).

Religious leaders who do embrace the mass media have, as a result, occasionally become national celebrities and even political leaders. Father Charles E. Coughlin, the "Radio Priest" of the 1920s and 1930s who received as many as 1.2 million letters from listeners following a single program, may have been the first religious figure to discover the power of broadcasting (Beniger, 1986, pp. 370–374). Such figures run the risks of intense scrutiny by national media and the possibly harsh judgment of nationally legitimated public opinion, however, with concomitant risks of running afoul of the political system. Coughlin's support faded after he attempted to build his political organization, the National Union for Social Justice, into an American voice for Adolf Hitler.

CONFLICT WITH THE POLITY

The new institution's relationship with the polity also remains ambiguous. As Weber (1915) points out, the state depends on power—including force and violence—to enforce the social order. Communication is a necessary though not necessarily sufficient component of power, whereas mass communication coupled with highly rationalized feedback is an unusually powerful means of social control. Although the state may ultimately be more powerful, public opinion and mass communication are more effectively powerful from day to day, in military dictatorships no less than in democracies. The new institution can also serve both sides—the polity as a public relations arm and other institutions as a government watchdog and counterbalance to state power. Tensions between these seemingly contradictory roles have been described, for example, by Gladys and Kurt Lang (1983), for the Watergate crisis.

In terms of ideology, the polity has much the same conflict with the new institution as do the family and religion, a conflict involving divergent values and norms for ideological control of the individual manifest through *political socialization*. Herbert Hyman introduced this term in 1959 in his pioneering study of the differential socialization of children and adolescents to political orientation and behavior focused primarily on the role of the family (Hyman, 1959). By the late 1960s, research interest had converged on mass communication as an important determinant of early political cognitions, beliefs, knowledge, attitudes, opinions, and behavior, and eventually even of adult political activities like voting.

Several studies (Hollander, 1971; Tolley, 1973) demonstrate positive correlations between the exposure of children and youth to mass media, on the one hand, and their political knowledge or interest in political affairs, on the other. Charles Atkin (1981) finds that attention to the mass media—especially to news and public affairs programming—increases political interest, affects attitudes toward political leaders, and influences political opinions. As Charles Wright concludes, "It may turn out that persons who are socializing the youth about political behavior—whether in organizations, in the family, in the classroom, or elsewhere—use mass communication in the process" (Wright, 1986, p. 191).

The new institution also exerts independent control over the polity through its depiction of political events to the mass audience. Martin Wattenberg (1984) finds that the media focus on individual candidates and leaders at the expense of parties, platforms, and ideologies, thereby thwarting party attempts to educate, inform, and influence voters. Candidates, in response, increasingly structure their campaigns around visually interesting "photo opportunities," colorfully worded "sound bites," and the schedules of national network newscasts. As a result, party officials rarely campaign with national candidates, whereas media representatives follow them in packs, often on the same plane (Paletz & Entman, 1981). By covering candidates in this way, mass media leap over parties to present politics directly to the electorate.

Just like religious leaders who attempt to ride the media to national fame, however, political candidates and leaders who try to manipulate media coverage to their own ends run considerable risks. Meyrowitz (1985) argues that television especially has restructured government and politics by exposing their often mundane and occasionally unsavory "backstage" behavior. The result he terms *lowering the political hero to our level*, which he describes in terms of information flows and feedback:

> The backstage exposure of our high status performers dramatically changes the relative flow of social information. With respect to our national leaders, for example, we have essentially reversed the nonreciprocal flow of information that traditionally supported their high status.... Through television, "the people" now have more access to the personal expressive behaviors of leaders than leaders have to the personal behaviors of the people. This reversed status is being reinforced by the current demands for "full disclosure" on the part of officials and the complementary demand by the public for protection from government spying and for controls on government access to personal records. With this new reversed nonreciprocal information flow, we are witnessing dramatic changes in our conceptions of Presidents, members of Congress, and the heads of intelligence agencies. (Meyrowitz, 1985, p. 168)

At the same time, the mass media also wield against the polity power drawn from near-monopoly control of legitimated public opinion. Everett Ladd (1980), for example, argues that poll data can be "very useful to the press in its adversary relationship with leaders of the old representative institutions." As he describes polls:

> They offer the means of articulating "what the people really want." They provide a tool for charting popular dissatisfactions with the performance of the political leadership and with that of other institutions like business. They even serve to break down the legitimacy of the claims of political bodies as they hold up the prospect for a purer, more direct and immediate representation of vox populi. (Ladd, 1980, p. 582)

The convergence of mass communication and the legitimated measures of public opinion has given the new institution increasing power once wielded by older political institutions. In ways not imagined as late as the mid-1960s, the new institution may become the new polity of advanced postindustrial or information societies. Consider what the mass media, as currently constituted, can now influence: political agendas both public (Erbring et al., 1980; McCombs & Shaw, 1972; McLeod et al., 1974) and individual (Behr & Iyengar, 1985; Iyengar et al., 1982; Iyengar & Kinder, 1987), the shared symbolic environment in which issues are understood (Beniger, 1983), how wide the political spectrum should be (Gerbner, 1984), even individual opinions themselves (Paletz & Entman, 1981). Mass media can also affect public opinion by feeding it back upon itself, thereby effecting political control through forces as potent as social conformity, pluralistic ignorance, positive and negative bandwagons, and the so-called spiral of silence.

THE NEW INSTITUTIONAL PARADIGM

As further evidence of the convergence of mass media and public opinion in a new social institution, research on the two phenomena has itself begun to converge in a single institutional paradigm, the most far-reaching paradigm shift in this field since the widespread acceptance of the minimal-effects model in the late 1950s. The shift might be summarized as a change in dependent variables from attitudes to cognitions, as a shift in independent variables from persuasion to less-directed but more institutionalized media processes ranging from "framing" through "discourse" to the social construction of reality, or as a refocusing of interest from simple change (like political conversion) to the institutional structuring or restructuring ("structuration") of cognitions and meaning. One result has been that stability—central to the analysis of social institutions—has become no less interesting than change (Beniger, 1987b, pp. 52–55).

Although most often identified with the study of social cognition, the new paradigm transcends both cognitive and social psychology to include political information processing, historical and institutional analysis, and much of the traditional subject matter of the humanities. New interest focuses on *processes*, not only on the processing of information inside each citizen's head (the "black box" of traditional survey research) but also on more public processes involving the new social institution: news coverage and dissemination, public opinion measurement and reporting, interest group advertising and public relations, and public policy debates—all conducted in public, mostly via the mass media, and all affecting public opinion, though often in ways too complex to be tractable by simple structural or causal models or experiments (Beniger, 1987b, pp. 53–54). Social scientists have begun, in short, to rediscover the word *public* in public opinion.

This institutional paradigm began to emerge in the late 1960s in a rapid succession of new approaches to mass media and public opinion by researchers and theorists throughout the social sciences and humanities. No fewer than 10 distinct approaches first appeared in the 12 years between 1969 and 1980, including studies of audience "uses and gratifications" provided by mass media (Blumler & McQuail, 1969; Blumler & Katz, 1974; Katz *et al.*, 1973); the "knowledge gap" exacerbated by media campaigns (Tichenor *et al.*, 1970, 1973); individual "agenda setting" by the mass media (Erbring *et al.*, 1980; McCombs & Shaw, 1972; McLeod *et al.*, 1974); "convergence and co-orientation" of media effects (Chaffee & Choe, 1980; McLeod & Chaffee, 1973); political cognition (Axelrod, 1973, 1976; Becker *et al.*, 1975; Lau *et al.*, 1979; Modigliani & Gamson, 1979; Sears *et al.*, 1980); "audience decoding" of media messages (Bourdieu, 1980; Hall, 1974; Turner, 1977; Worth & Gross, 1974); the "spiral of silence" that suppresses minority views (Noelle-Neumann, 1974, 1980); audience "cultivation" (Gerbner & Gross, 1976; Gerbner *et al.*, 1980); media hegemony (Gitlin, 1979, 1980; Hall, 1977; Hall *et al.*, 1978); and potent "media events" (Katz, 1980).

Although there are many obvious differences within and among these separate approaches, they look surprisingly similar when collectively compared to the older tradition of minimal effects. In sharp contrast to this tradition, all of the new approaches sidestep questions of persuasion and conversion to concentrate on more complex *processes involving information*, whether on the individual level as cognitions or on the institutional level as ideology or culture. Uses and gratifications research, for example, establishes the audience of mass communication as an active processor of information in pursuit of individual needs, so that the media might be seen to supply information—including cognitive structures like "schemata"—to think with. Similarly, work on the knowledge gap shows that people who acquire information are the most likely to acquire still more, presumably because information creates cognitive structures that require "fleshing out," but with the important institutional effect that the knowledge-rich get richer, whereas the knowledge-poor remain at least relatively poor.

SUMMARY

Because most social changes occur so gradually, they are all but imperceptible to contemporary observers. Social changes rarely result from a few discrete events, despite the best efforts of historians to associate the change with such events. Both generalizations apply, as we have seen, to the gradual convergence of mass communication and public opinion and to their emergence as a new social institution. No sign of such an institution can be found in the nineteenth century; there can be little doubt of its appearance in the United States by the late 1960s.

When precisely the new institution emerged, or the specific events that may have precipitated its arrival, may be impossible to say. Certainly it seems to be a post-World War II development, still confined to the more advanced postindustrial societies. We have suggested the rise and convergence of scientific survey research and national network television as major contributing causes. More important than questions of timing or causation, however, is the simple fact that something new has occurred: the emergence of a new institution. With its continuing rationalization, we can predict (following Weber) that it will increasingly conflict—in perhaps ironic realization of much earlier premonitions of the mass society—with other more venerable social institutions.

REFERENCES

Allport, F. H. (1924). *Social psychology*. Boston: Houghton Mifflin.
Asch, S. E. (1951). Effects of group pressure upon the modification and distortion of judgments. In H. S. Guetzkow (Ed.), *Groups, leadership and men: Research in human relations* (pp. 177–190). New York: Russell and Russell, 1963.

Atkin, C. K. (1981). Communication and political socialization. In D. D. Nimmo & K. A. Sanders (Eds.), *Handbook of political communication* (pp. 299–328). Beverly Hills, CA: Sage.

Atkin, C. K., & Gaudino, J. (1984). The impact of polling on the mass media. *Annals of the American Academy of Political and Social Science, 472*, 119–128.

Axelrod, R. M. (1973). Schema theory: An information-processing model of perception and cognition. *American Political Science Review, 67*(4) (December), 1248–1266.

Axelrod, R. M. (1975). *Structure of decision: The cognitive maps of political elites*. Princeton, NJ: Princeton University Press.

Bauer, R. A., & Bauer, A. H. (1960). America, "mass society" and mass media. *Journal of Social Issues, 16*(3), 3–66.

Becker, L. B., McCombs, M. E., & McLeod, J. M. (1975). The development of political cognitions. In S. H. Chaffee (Ed.), *Political communication: Issues and strategies for research* (pp. 21–63). Beverly Hills, CA: Sage.

Behr, R. L., & Iyengar, S. (1985). Television news, real-world cues, and changes in the public agenda. *Public Opinion Quarterly, 49*(1), 38–57.

Bell, D. (1960). America as a mass society: A critique. In *The end of ideology: On the exhaustion of political ideas in the fifties* (21–38). New York: Free Press.

Beniger, J. R. (1983a). Does television enhance the shared symbolic environment? Trends in labeling of editorial cartoons, 1948–1980. *American Sociological Review, 48*(1), 103–111.

Beniger, J. R. (1983b). The popular symbolic repertoire and mass communication. *Public Opinion Quarterly, 47*(4), 479–484.

Beniger, J. R. (1986). *The control revolution: Technological and economic origins of the information society*. Cambridge, MA: Harvard University Press.

Beniger, J. R. (1987a). Personalization of mass media and the growth of pseudo-community. *Communication Research, 14*(3), 352–371.

Beniger, J. R. (1987b). Toward an old new paradigm: The half-century flirtation with mass society. *Public Opinion Quarterly, 51*(4, Pt. 2), 46–66.

Berelson, B. R. (1959). The state of communication research. *Public Opinion Quarterly, 23*, 1–6.

Berger, B., & Berger, P. L. (1976). *Sociology: A biographical approach*. New York: Basic.

Bierstedt, R. S. (1963). *The social order: An introduction to sociology* (2nd ed.). New York: McGraw-Hill.

Blumler, J. G., & Katz, E. (Eds.). (1974). *The uses of mass communications: Current perspectives on gratifications research*. Beverly Hills, CA: Sage.

Blumler, J. G., & McQuail, D. (1969). *Television in politics: Its uses and influence*. Chicago: University of Chicago Press.

Boorstin, D. J. (1973). *The Americans: The democratic experience*. New York: Random House, Vintage.

Bourdieu, P. (1980). The production of belief, trans. L. Richard Nice. *Media, Culture and Society, 2*(3) (July).

Bramson. (1961). *The political context of sociology*. Princeton, NJ: Princeton University Press.

Braudel, F. (1981). *Civilization and capitalism from the fifteenth to the eighteenth century, Volume 1, The structures of everyday life: The limits of the possible*. London: Collins.

Bryce, J. (1988). *The American commonwealth*. 2 vols. New York: MacMillan, 1931–1933.

Buerkel-Rothfuss, N. L., Greenberg, B. S., Atkin, C. K., & Neundorf, K. (1982). Learning about the family from television. *Journal of Communication, 32*(3), 191–201.

Carroll, J. B. (1964). Words, meanings and concepts. *Harvard Educational Review, 34*(2), 178–202.

Chaffee, S. H., & Choe, S. Y. (1980). Time of decision and media use during the Ford-Carter campaign. *Public Opinion Quarterly, 44*(1), 53–69.

Chaffee, S. H., Ward, L. S., & Tipton, L. (1970). Mass communication and political socialization. *Journalism Quarterly, 57*, 647–666.

Chesebro, J. (1982). Communication, values, and popular television series—A four-year assessment. In H. Newcomb (Ed.), *Television: The critical view* (pp. 8–46). New York: Oxford University Press.

Conway, M. M., Wyckoff, M., Feldbaum, E., & Ahern, D. (1981). The news media in children's political socialization. *Public Opinion Quarterly, 45*(2), 164–178.

Coser, L. A. (1970). *Men of ideas.* New York: Free Press.

Darnton, R. C. (1985). *The great cat massacre and other episodes in French cultural history.* New York: Vintage.

Davis, K. (1949). *Human society.* New York: Macmillan.

Dervin, B., & Greenberg, B. (1972). The communication environment of the urban poor. In F. G. Kline & P. J. Tichenor (Eds.), *Current perspectives in mass communication research* (Vol. 1). Beverly Hills, CA: Sage.

Eichenwald, K. (1986). "Hi, Voter, This Is Your President." *New York Times* (November 2), Section 3, p. 19.

Emden, C. S. (1956). *The people and the constitution* (2nd ed.). London: Oxford University Press.

Erbring, L., Goldenberg, E. N., & Miller, A. H. (1980). Front-page news and real-world cues: A new look at agenda-setting by the media. *American Journal of Political Science, 24*(1), 16–49.

Fiske, J., & Hartley, J. (1978). *Reading television.* London: Methuen.

Forer, R. (1955). The impact of a radio program on adolescents. *Public Opinion Quarterly, 19*(2), 184–194.

Fredman, L. E. (1967). The introduction of the Australian ballot in the United States. *Australian Journal of Politics and History, 13*(2).

Freidson, E. (1953). Communications research and the concept of mass. *American Sociological Review, 18*, 313–317.

Gaddy, G. D., & Pritchard, D. (1985). When watching religious TV is like attending church. *Journal of Communication, 35*(1), 123–131.

Galbraith, J. K. (1967). *The new industrial state.* Boston: Houghton Mifflin (3rd rev. ed., 1978).

Gerbner, G. (1984). Political correlates of television viewing. *Public Opinion Quarterly, 48*, 283–300.

Gerbner, G. (1987). Television: Modern mythmaker. *Media and Values, 40–41* (Summer/Fall), 8–9.

Gerbner, G., & Gross, L. (1976). Living with television: The violence profile. *Journal of Communication, 26*, 173–199.

Gerbner, G., Gross, L., Morgan, M., & Signorielli, N. (1980). The "mainstreaming" of America: Violence profile No. 11. *Journal of Communication, 30*(3), 10–29.

Gerson, W. (1966). Mass media socialization behavior: Negro-white differences. *Social Forces, 45*, 44–50.

Giddens, A. (1979). *Central problems in social theory.* London: Macmillan.

Giddens, A. (1984). *The constitution of society: Outline of the theory of structuration.* Cambridge, U.K.: Polity Press.

Ginsberg, M. (1965). *On justice in society.* London: Heinemann.

Gitlin, T. (1979). Prime time ideology: The hegemonic process in television entertainment. *Social Problems, 26*, 251–266.

Gitlin, T. (1980). *The whole world is watching: Mass media in the making and unmaking of the new left.* Berkeley: University of California Press.

Gitlin, T. (1983). *Inside prime-time.* New York: Pantheon.

Goffman, E. (1961). *Asylums: Essays on the social situation of mental patients and other inmates.* Garden City, NY: Doubleday Anchor.

Gramsci, A. (1929–1935). *Selections from the prison notebooks.* Trans. and Ed. by Q. Hoare & G. H. Smith. New York: International, 1971.

Greenberg, B. S. (1982). Television and role socialization: An overview. In D. Pearl, L. Bouthilet, & J. Lazar (Eds.), *Television and behavior: Ten years of scientific progress and implications for the eighties* (Vol. 2, pp. 329–342). National Institute of Mental Health, Rockville, Md. Washington, DC: U.S. Government Printing Office.

Greer, S. (1958). Individual participation in mass society. In R. Young (Ed.), *Approaches to the study of politics* (pp. 329–342). Evanston, IL: Northwestern University Press.

234   JAMES R. BENIGER and SUSAN HERBST

Hall, S. (1974). The television discourse: Encoding and decoding. *Education and Culture, 25,* 8–14.

Hall, S. (1977). Culture, the media, and the "ideological effect." In J. Curran, M. Gurevitch, & J. Woollacott (Eds.), *Mass communication and society* (pp. 315–348). Beverly Hills, CA: Sage.

Hall, S., Critcher, C., Jefferson, T., Clarke, J., & Roberts, B. (1978). *Policing the crisis: Mugging, the state, and law and order.* New York: Holmes and Meier.

Herbst, S. (1988). *Effects of public opinion technologies on political expression: Putting polls in historical context.* Paper presented at the 43rd Annual Conference of the American Association for Public Opinion Research, Toronto, May 19–22.

Herzog, H. (1944). What do we really know about daytime radio serial listeners? In P. F. Lazarsfeld & F. Stanton (Eds.), *Radio research, 1942–1943* (pp. 3–33). New York: Duell, Sloan and Pearce.

Hollander, N. (1971). Adolescents and the war: The sources of socialization. *Journalism Quarterly, 58,* 472–479.

Horton, D., & Wohl, R. R. (1956). Mass communication and parasocial interaction: Observations on intimacy at a distance. *Psychiatry, 19*(3), 215–229.

Huxley, J. (1966). A discussion on ritualization of behaviour in animals and man: Introduction. *Philosophical Transactions of the Royal Society of Britain, 251,* 249–271.

Hyman, H. H. (1942). The psychology of status. *Archives of Psychology, 38,* 5–94.

Hyman, H. H. (1959). *Political socialization: A study in the psychology of political behavior.* Glencoe, IL: Free Press.

Hyman, H. H. (1974). Mass communication and socialization. In W. P. Davison & F. T. C. Yu (Eds.), *Mass communication research* (pp. 5–94). New York: Praeger.

Iyengar, S., & Kinder, D. R. (1987). *News that matters: Television and American opinion.* Chicago: University of Chicago Press.

Iyengar, S., Peters, M. D., & Kinder, D. R. (1982). Experimental demonstration of the "not-so-minimal" consequences of television news programs. *American Political Science Review, 76*(4) (December), 848–858.

Katz, D. (Ed.). (1960). Attitude change—A special issue. *Public Opinion Quarterly, 24,* 163–365.

Katz, E. (1957). The two-step flow of communication: An up-to-date report on an hypothesis. *Public Opinion Quarterly, 21,* 61–78.

Katz, E. (1960). Communication research and the image of society: Convergence of two traditions. *American Journal of Sociology, 65,* 435–440.

Katz, E. (1980). Media events: The sense of occasion. *Studies in Visual Communication, 6,* 84–89.

Katz, E., Gurevitch, M., & Haas, H. (1973). On the use of the mass media for important things. *American Sociological Review, 38,* 164–181.

Keller, M. (1977). *Affairs of state: Public life in late nineteenth-century America.* Cambridge, MA: Harvard University Press.

Klapper, J. T. (1960). *The effects of mass communication.* Glencoe, IL: Free Press.

Kornhauser, W. (1959). *The politics of mass society.* Glencoe, IL: Free Press.

Kornhauser, W. (1968). Mass society. In D. L. Sills (Ed.), *The international encyclopedia of the social sciences* (Vol. 10, pp. 58–64). New York: Macmillan and Free Press.

Ladd, E. C. (1980). Polling and the press: The clash of institutional imperatives. *Public Opinion Quarterly, 44*(4), 574–584.

Lang, G. E., & Lang, K. (1983). *The battle for public opinion: The president, the press, and the polls during Watergate.* New York: Columbia University Press.

Lau, R. R., Sears, D. O., & Centers, R. (1979). The "positive bias" in evaluations of public figures: Evidence against instrument artifacts. *Public Opinion Quarterly, 43,* 347–358.

Laver, J. (1969). *A concise history of costume.* London: Thames and Hudson.

Lazarsfeld, P. F. (1940). *Radio and the printed page.* New York: Duell, Sloan and Pearce.

Lazarsfeld, P. F. (1942). The effects of radio on public opinion. In D. Waples (Ed.), *Print, radio, and film in a democracy* (pp. 95–118). Chicago: University of Chicago Press.

Lazarsfeld, P. F., Berelson, B., & Gaudet, H. (1944). *The people's choice.* New York: Duell, Sloan and Pearce.

Lazarsfeld, P. F., & Merton, R. K. (1948). Mass communication, popular taste and organized social action. In L. Bryson (Ed.), *The communication of ideas: A series of addresses* (pp. 95–118). New York: Institute for Religious and Social Studies, Harper.

Lerner, D. (1958). *The passing of traditional society: Modernizing the middle east.* Glencoe, IL: Free Press.

Lippmann, W. (1922). *Public opinion.* New York: Harcourt, Brace.

Lippmann, W. (1925). *The phantom public.* New York: Harcourt, Brace.

Locke, J. (1690). *An essay concerning human understanding,* ed. P. H. Nidditch. Oxford, U.K.: Oxford University Press, Clarendon, 1975.

MacDonald, D. (1957). A theory of mass culture. In B. Rosenberg & D. M. White (Eds.), *Mass culture: The popular arts in America* (pp. 59–73). Glencoe, IL: Free Press.

MacIver, R. M. (1937). *Society: A textbook of sociology.* New York: Farrar and Rinehart.

McCombs, M. E., & Shaw, D. L. (1972). The agenda-setting function of mass media. *Public Opinion Quarterly, 36,* 176–187.

McLeod, J. M., & Chaffee, S. H. (1973). Interpersonal approaches to communication research. *American Behavioral Scientist, 16,* 469–499.

McLeod, J. M., Becker, L. B., & Byrnes, J. (1974). Another look at the agenda-setting function of the press. *Communication Research, 1,* 131–166.

Mead, G. H. (1934). *Mind, self, and society: From the standpoint of a social behaviorist,* ed. C. W. Morris. Chicago: University of Chicago Press.

Merton, R. K. (1945). The sociology of knowledge. Reprinted as pp. 510–542 in *Social theory and social structure,* enl. ed. New York: Free Press, 1968.

Merton, R. K. (1946). *Mass persuasion: The social psychology of a war bond drive.* New York: Harper.

Merton, R. K. (1975). On the origins of the term: Pseudo-Gemeinschaft. *Western Sociological Review, 6,* 83.

Merton, R. K. (1987). The focussed interview and focus groups: Continuities and discontinuities. *Public Opinion Quarterly, 51*(4), 550–566.

Messaris, P. (1982). Parents, children, and television. In G. G. Gumpert & R. Cathcart (Eds.), *Inter/media: Interpersonal communication in a media world* (2nd ed., pp. 580–598). New York: Oxford University Press.

Messaris, P., & Sarett, C. (1981). On the consequences of television-related parent-child interaction. *Human Communication Research, 7,* 226–244.

Meyer, P. (1973). *Precision journalism: A reporter's introduction to social science methods.* Bloomington: Indiana University Press.

Meyrowtiz, J. (1985). *No sense of place: The impact of electronic media on social behavior.* New York: Oxford University Press.

Mills, C. W. (1956). *The power elite.* New York: Oxford University Press.

Modigliani, A., & Gamson, W. A. (1979). Thinking about politics. *Political Behavior, 1,* 5–30.

Mukerji, C. (1983). *From graven images: Patterns of modern materialism.* New York: Columbia University Press.

National Institute of Mental Health. (1982). *Television and behavior: Ten years of scientific progress and implications for the eighties.* Rockville, MD: National Institute of Mental Health.

Newcomb, T. M. (1943). *Personality and social change: Attitude formation in a student community.* New York: Holt, Rinehart & Winston.

Noelle-Neumann, E. (1974). The spiral of silence: A theory of public opinion. *Journal of Communication, 24,* 43–51.

Noelle-Neumann, E. (1980). *Die Schweigespirale.* Published in English as *The spiral of silence: Public opinion, our social skin.* Chicago: University of Chicago Press, 1984.

Paletz, D., & Entman, R. (1981). *Media power politics.* New York: Free Press.

Palmer, P. A. (1967). The concept of public opinion in political theory. In C. Wittke (Ed.), *Essays in history and political theory in honor of Charles H. McIlwain,* pp. 230–257. New York: Russell and Russell.

Parsons, T. (1960). *Structure and process in modern societies*. Glencoe, IL: Free Press.
Parsons, T., & Shils, E. A. (Eds.). (1951). *Toward a general theory of action*. Cambridge, MA: Harvard University Press.
Parsons, T., & White, W. (1960). The mass media and the structure of American society. *Journal of Social Issues, 16,* 67–77.
Postman, N. (1987). The teachings of the media curriculum. In D. Lazere (Ed.), *American media and mass culture: Left perspectives* (pp. 421–430). Berkeley, CA: University of California Press.
Riley, J. W., Jr., & Riley, M. W. (1959). Mass communication and the social system. In R. K. Merton, L. Broom, & L. S. Cottrell (Eds.), *Sociology today: Problems and prospects* (pp. 537–578). New York: Basic.
Robinson, C. (1932). *Straw votes: A study of political prediction*. New York: St. Martin's.
Roper Organization. (1983). *Trends in attitudes toward television and other media: A twenty-four year review*. New York: Television Information Office.
Schanck, R. L. (1932). A study of a community and its groups and institutions conceived of as behaviors of individuals. *Psychological Monographs, 43,* 2(195), 1–133.
Sears, D. O., Lau, R. R., Tyler, T. R., & Allen, Jr., H. M. (1980). A self-interest vs. symbolic politics in policy attitudes and presidential voting. *American Political Science Review, 74,* 670–684.
Sherif, M. (1936). *The psychology of social norms*. New York: Harper.
Shils, E. A. (1957). Daydreams and nightmares: Reflections on the criticism of mass culture. *Sewanee Review, 65,* 587–608.
Shils, E. A. (1962). The theory of mass society. *Diogenes, 39,* 45–66.
Sills, D. L. (1987). Paul F. Lazarsfeld, February 13, 1901–August 30, 1976. In *Biographical memoirs* (Vol. 56, pp. 251–282). Washington: National Academy Press.
Simon, H. A. (1954). Bandwagon and underdog effects and the possibility of election predictions. *Public Opinion Quarterly, 18,* 245–253.
Smith, W. J. (1977). *The behavior of communicating: An ethological approach*. Cambridge, MA: Harvard University Press.
Sophocles. 443–441 B.C. Antigone. In *The Plays of Sophocles*, trans. Richard C. Jebb. Cambridge, U.K.: Cambridge University Press, 1952.
Sterling, C. H. (1984). *Electronic media: A guide to trends in broadcasting and newer technologies, 1920–1983*. New York: Praeger.
Sumner, W. G. (1906). *Folkways: A study of the sociological importance of usages, manners, customs, mores, and morals*. Boston: Ginn, 1940.
Tichenor, P. J., Donohue, G. A., & Olien, C. N. (1970). Mass media flow and differential growth in knowledge. *Public Opinion Quarterly, 34,* 159–170.
Tichenor, P. J., Rodenkirchen, J. M., Olien, C. N., & Donohue, G. A. (1973). Community issues, conflict, and public affairs knowledge. In P. Clarke (Ed.), *New models for mass communication research* (pp. 45–79). Beverly Hills, CA: Sage.
Tilly, C. (1983). Speaking your mind without elections, surveys, or social movements. *Public Opinion Quarterly, 47*(4) (Winter), 461–478.
Time Magazine. (1986). Politics' unholy writ. *Time* (October 20), p. 43.
Times Mirror. (1986). *The people and the press. A Times Mirror investigation of public attitudes toward the news media conducted by The Gallup Organization*. Los Angeles: Times Mirror.
Tolley, H., Jr. (1973). *Children and war: Political socialization to international conflict*. New York: Teachers College Press.
Turner, V. (1977). Process, system, and symbol: A new anthropological synthesis. *Daedalus, 106,* 61–80.
U.S. Bureau of the Census. (1975). *Historical statistics of the United States, Colonial Times to 1970,* 2 vols. Washington, DC: U.S. Government Printing Office.
Vidich, A. J., & Bensman, J. (1958). *Small town in mass society: Class, power and religion in a rural community*. Princeton, NJ: Princeton University Press.

Wattenberg, M. (1984). *The decline of American political parties, 1952–1984*. Cambridge, MA: Harvard University Press.

Weaver, D. H., & McCombs, M. E. (1980). Journalism and social science: A new relationship? *Public Opinion Quarterly, 44*, 477–495.

Weber, M. (1915). Religious rejections of the world and their directions [From "Zwischen-betrachtung"]. Ch. 13, pp. 323–359 in *From Max Weber: Essays in Sociology*, trans. and ed. H. H. Gerth & C. W. Mills. New York: Oxford University Press, 1946.

Wheeler, D., & Jordan, H. (1929). Change of individual opinion to accord with group opinion. *Journal of Abnormal and Social Psychology, 24*, 203–206.

Whorf, B. L. (1956). *Language, thought and reality: Selected writings*, ed. J. B. Carroll. Cambridge, MA: MIT Press and Wiley.

Wilson, E. (1987). *Adorned in dreams: Fashion and modernity*. Berkeley: University of California Press.

Worth, S. & Gross, L. (1974). Symbolic strategies. *Journal of Communication, 24*, 27–39.

Wright, C. R. (1986). *Mass communication: A sociological perspective* (3rd ed.). New York: Random House.

CHAPTER ELEVEN

Things Fall Apart
Americans and Their Political Institutions, 1960–1988

RUY A. TEIXEIRA

INTRODUCTION

The 1950s in America were a quiet time. The country was absorbed in a march forward to ever-higher levels of prosperity, and most Americans happily participated in that forward march. The results, on an economic level, were quite impressive. Between 1949 and 1959, real median family income grew by 42.5%, whereas the percentage of the population in poverty declined by 10 points (Levy, 1987, p. 47).

The economic march forward was generally unmarred by political protest and turmoil. On the contrary, Americans were relatively stable and predictable in their political behavior during this period. This stability and predictability was extensively documented in a series of famous studies including, most prominently, *The American Voter* (Campbell, Converse, Miller, & Stokes, 1960) and *The Civic Culture* (Almond & Verba, 1963).

These studies allow us to draw a fairly detailed portrait of how Americans in the 1950s felt and thought about the political world (see Nie, Verba, & Petrocik, 1976, pp. 14–42 for an excellent summary along these lines). The most salient aspects of this portrait are as follows.

First, *the average citizen was involved in political life but not all that involved.* For most citizens, politics was not central to their everyday concerns. Their concerns focused around jobs, families, health, and other

---

RUY A. TEIXEIRA ● Economic Research Service–ARED, 1301 New York Avenue, NW, Washington, DC 20005-4788.

aspects of their family and daily lives. Their political involvement, such as it was, centered around the act of voting and following election campaigns in the mass media.

Second, *citizens tended to have strong, long-term commitments to one of the major political parties, and this commitment served as a guide to their political behavior.* Beyond party commitments, the political views of most Americans tended to be inconsistent and unsophisticated. It was really this partisan attachment that defined their relationship to the political world, in general, and to the electoral process, in particular.

Finally, *citizens tended to act politically in ways that reflected their membership in groups defined by various social characteristics.* That is, a good deal of citizens' political behavior, including partisan attachment, was linked to their social position, as defined by race, class, union membership, ethnicity, religion, and region.

These political attributes are key parts of what I have termed elsewhere the *system of the fifties* (Teixeira, 1987). It was a political system whose structure promoted stability and predictability. Citizens worked their way through a fairly orderly routine of group interests, partisan loyalty and turning out to vote (the three presidential elections, 1952–1960, had the highest average turnout of any three contiguous elections since 1912). There were few surprises.

American political society, after 1960, took on quite a different look. The 1960s were *not* a quiet time, and political turmoil and protest became commonplace. The stability and predictability of the earlier era quickly became lost amid a plethora of new issues, new social movements, and deviant voting behavior. In fact, political behavior became so unstable and unpredictable that many observers began to speak of a "dealignment" of the party system, where the old political guideposts had drastically declined in relevance, without being replaced by anything new.

If political affairs have quieted down since the 1960s, it is not because the political society of the 1950s has returned. There is no longer an orderly routine of group interests, partisan loyalty, and turning out to vote (the 1988 presidential election had the lowest turnout since 1924, down 13 points since 1960). Voters' loyalties seem almost permanently divided, and a large assortment of interest groups compete to claim voters' attention. Cynicism and apathy toward the political system is widespread, feelings only accentuated by the dramatic changes in the conduct of political campaigns. This is not a particularly stable, predictable, or coherent form of political society.

What happened? How did the system of the 1950s, with its relatively stable political institutions, change into the radically different political society of 1988? The reasons are many, but one of the most crucial lies in the dramatic erosion of the most basic level of support for American political institutions—that is, the ties of individual Americans to the political sys-

tem. This erosion has been manifest in three ways: (1) the decline of political participation; (2) the decline of political parties; and (3) the decline of
traditional forms of political consciousness.

In what follows, I discuss each of these changes individually and show
how they are interrelated, with decline in one sphere tending to promote
decline in others. I conclude with a discussion of the underlying basis of
these changes—the exhaustion of New Deal institutional arrangements
under the stress of economic, demographic, and generational change—
and the implications of this for the future of American politics.

DECLINE OF POLITICAL PARTICIPATION

One of the most critical aspects of any political system is the participation of its citizens. It provides the direct link between the individual citizen
and governmental actions. This link serves to legitimate the government
and, to the extent the system is democratic, shapes policy outputs so they
accord with popular interests and wishes.

In a parliamentary democracy such as the United States, the easiest
and most elementary form of political participation is voting. And yet,
between 1960 and 1988, U.S. voter turnout fell from an already low level of
62.8% of the voting age population (VAP) to just 50.2%—almost a 13-
percentage point drop. What caused such a dramatic weakening of this
link between citizens and the electoral system?

To understand this, it is first necessary to understand the basic dynamic of voting as a form of political participation. Specifically, it is necessary to understand why voting is a common, but not universal, form of
political participation. After all, from one perspective, it is amazing that
everyone doesn't vote. Voting is certainly a very low-cost activity, requiring
little more than fulfilling some minor bureaucratic requirements and travel-
ing to the polling place. On the plus side, the voter helps determine the
nature of policies affecting his or her life by participating in the selection of
policymakers.

Yet everyone does not vote. Even at the beginning of the 1960–1988
period, more than one in three members of the VAP didn't bother to cast a
ballot. And in European countries, where turnout has traditionally been
higher (see Teixeira, 1987, pp. 6–8, and Teixeira, 1988, for discussions of
cross-national differences), turnout rates are by no means 100% but vary
widely between 70% and a little over 90%.

There are two good reasons why the notion that everyone should vote
does not tally with the facts. The first is that voting, although a low-cost
activity, is not a zero-cost activity. The costs of registering, finding out
where the polling place is, and taking the time and effort to travel to it on
election day are tangible, nonzero ones. In addition, there may be informa-

tion costs, because not everyone will have easy access to the minimal amount of facts necessary to distinguish between candidates. For some people, this set of costs may seem large and not worth the trouble of absorbing.

The second reason has to do with the benefits obtained from balloting. Although it is true that the outcome of an election may have a substantial impact on a person's life, the individual citizen does not have to participate in the election to obtain these benefits. They are available to everyone, voter and nonvoter alike. (This is an example of the "free rider" problem, with the outcome of the election as the "public good"—see Olson, 1965.)

Theorists of voting have therefore pointed out that the worth of a citizen's vote is not equal to the benefits derived from a given election outcome but to the product obtained from multiplying the value of these benefits by the probability that the citizen's individual vote will produce that outcome (Downs, 1957). This "expected value" is the real outcome-related benefit of voting, and in most elections, it will be small, because the probability of a lone individual's vote affecting an election outcome is miniscule.

This makes it clearer why everyone does not participate in elections. The costs are nonzero and the benefits, in the expected value sense, may be so small as to be indistinguishable from zero. By this logic, it becomes surprising that anyone bothers to vote.

This problem—the "paradox of voting"—has been duly noted by theorists of voting (Cyr, 1975; Riker & Ordeshook, 1968). The solution proposed by these theorists is simple and compelling: There are other benefits involved in voting besides its expected value. These benefits (formally termed *side payments* or *selective incentives*) are primarily expressive. The citizen, by voting, expresses his or her sense of duty toward society, responsibility toward a reference group, commitment to a candidate, party, or cause or any number of other feelings that are linked to the election or its outcome (see Aldrich & Simon, 1986, and Brady, Nie, Schlozman, & Verba, 1988, for useful discussions of different types of expressive benefits). It is these various ways of finding an election "meaningful" that motivate most people who vote to absorb the costs of balloting.

This theoretical framework suggests two basic reasons why voter turnout among a given population might go down. First, the costs of voting—bureaucratic requirements, information costs, and so forth—might go up. Second, the expressive benefits discussed above might go down. The question then becomes, when considering the roughly 13-point drop in U.S. voter turnout from 1960 to 1988: Which reason or weighted combination of these reasons is responsible for such a dramatic decline in participation?

The first possibility, higher costs, does not seem to fit well with the known facts about the 1960–1988 period. During this period, registration requirements, the chief bureaucratic cost associated with voting, became substantially easier throughout the United States. Moreover, there was a huge increase in educational attainment. Not only does education theoretically facilitate a citizen's ability to absorb voting costs, it is known empirically to be the single strong promoter of voter participation (Wolfinger & Rosenstone, 1980).

In fact, as I have demonstrated elsewhere (Teixeira, 1987), the increase in educational attainment, all other things being equal, should have substantially increased voter turnout during this period. Thus consideration of these cost factors not only does not explain the drop in voter participation, it makes the question more of a mystery than before.

This suggests that the explanation for declining turnout lies more in the second possibility, declining expressive benefits of voting, than in the first. This view is strongly confirmed by my own research, based on pooled cross-sectional data from the American National Election Studies (ANES). Results from this research, covering the 1960–1980 period, are summarized in Table 1.

These results are based on a probit model relating voter turnout between 1960 and 1980 to a series of demographic and attitudinal predictors (see Teixeira, 1987, pp. 37–80, for details on model construction). They decompose decline in turnout in this period into the respective contributions made by different independent variables in the model. These contributions estimate the effects of compositional shifts in these independent variables over time.

The results in Table 1 show that there was an upward push on turnout, not just from increasing educational attainment but also from an increase in real family income and an upgrading of the occupational structure in the direction of white-collar work. The next part of the table, however, shows that this upward push from "socioeconomic upgrading" was roughly counterbalanced by another series of demographic changes.

These changes, the product of the rise of the baby-boom generation and of a society in cultural and economic flux, produced an electorate that was less rooted in the social fabric. Specifically, voters were younger, more likely to be single, and more likely to have moved recently. These characteristics are all generally viewed as making the act of voting harder for individuals, so the effect of these changes was to depress turnout levels.

Taken together, then, the effects of demographic change on turnout levels roughly canceled one another out. This implies that the act of voting became neither substantially harder nor substantially easier for citizens over this time period. Instead, as the next part of the table shows, it became less meaningful.

Three variables are listed, all of which tap different dimensions of the expressive benefits linked to voting. These are partisanship, campaign involvement (through the medium of campaign newspaper reading), and political efficacy (a variable that taps the extent to which individuals feel

TABLE 1. Explaining the Turnout Differential between 1960 and 1980

Variable	Predicted decline	Percentage of predicted decline
Socioeconomic characteristics		
Education	−.127	−50.3
Occupation, income	−.039	−15.4
All SES	−.166	−65.7
Non-SES demographic characteristics		
Age	.066	26.2
Marital status	.045	17.2
Residential mobility	.033	13.0
Race, region, sex	.014	5.5
All non-SES demographic	.158	62.5
Political characteristics		
Partisanship	.046	18.2
Campaign newspaper reading	.104	41.1
Political efficacy	.111	43.9
All political	.261	103.2
Total probit drop	.253	100.0

Percentage point decline in turnout predicted by probit model: 7.0
Percentage point decline in turnout reported in ANES survey: 8.0
Percentage of turnout differential explained by model: 87.5

they have any power over governmental actions). The levels of all of these characteristics declined substantially in the 1960–1980 period, and, once demographic changes are controlled for, these decreases appear to be the driving force behind turnout decline.

The story after 1980 becomes somewhat more complicated. To begin with, there was actually an increase in turnout in the 1984 election, the first one in 24 years. However, it was a rather small increase, only half a percentage point.

In fact, the interesting thing about turnout in the 1984 election was not that it went up but rather that it went up so little. This is because of all the factors favorable to increased voter turnout in this election. These factors included high levels of registration activity, another increase in educational attainment, aging of the voting-age population, declining residential mobility, and a reversal of the downward trend in the three political characteristics discussed (partisanship, campaign involvement, and efficacy). Thus a combination of favorable demographic trends and a modest revival of enthusiasm for politics, traceable perhaps to the popularity of Reagan and his leadership style, augured very well for increased turnout.

My analysis of the 1984 ANES data confirmed that, given these changes, voter turnout should have gone up more than it did (Teixeira, 1987, pp. 116–123). In fact, my analysis indicated that turnout should have gone up almost 80% more than the 2.3 percentage point increase reported in the 1984 data (see Abramson, Aldrich, & Rohde, 1987, pp. 116–119, for a similar analysis with virtually identical results). This suggests that some other factor (or factors) not included in my model was operative during this period, acting to retard the increase in turnout.

Although I was not able to identify this additional turnout-depressing factor, the logic of my overall argument led me to believe that this factor was probably related to the expressive benefits of voting—that is, to some way in which Americans are finding elections less intelligible and meaningful. And, because it seemed unlikely that the favorable trends affecting the 1984 election would be as strong in 1988, this led me to speculate, writing before the 1988 election, that "there appears to be little reason to expect substantial turnout increases and some reason for fearing further decreases" (Teixeira, 1987, p. 125).

This somewhat gloomy assessment was borne out by the 1988 election results. Turnout went down almost three percentage points, sinking to a level where barely half (50.2%) of the VAP bothered to cast their ballots (see Teixeira, 1989, for a discussion of the basic results). There are currently no indications of substantial reversals in the trends discussed, so the best guess is that an unknown turnout-depressing factor will also be implicated in these turnout results (unfortunately, the actual 1988 data were not available at the time this article was prepared).

If this is true, it would suggest that Americans are having an increasingly difficult time finding elections intelligible and meaningful—perhaps on a level deeper than that tapped by such variables as partisanship and efficacy. And this problem shows no signs of going away. Indeed, results from my research and that of others (Abramson & Aldrich, 1982; Teixeira, 1987, pp. 81–91) indicate that the problem may go all the way back to the period after 1968, because it is in this period that models start underpredicting turnout decline.

What might be causing such a long-term erosion in the meaningfulness of elections for Americans? One possible explanation may lie in the rhythms of American electoral history. An influential school of thought about American politics believes there is a periodicity to American electoral history, a periodicity that calls forth a "critical realignment" of the party system every 32 to 36 years (Burnham, 1970). These critical realignments are supposed to result in a renewal of the party system and reforging of citizens' political identities.

Now, in 1968, there was no critical realignment, at least of the sort typical in the past. Instead there was more of a "dealignment," where old voting patterns and political identities broke down without being replaced by new ones. It is possible that this lack of a traditional critical realignment, with its consequent restructuring of citizens' orientation to the political world, may be providing the additional downward push on turnout levels after 1968 that changes in other political characteristics cannot account for.

This suggests that dealignment may be playing an important role in the ongoing erosion of Americans' ties to their governmental system. The old political identities defined by the New Deal party system (now 56 years old) have been weakened by time and other factors, and, because of this, Americans now lack a firm basis for interpreting the political world around them. Because they lack a firm basis for interpreting the political world, the elections are less meaningful, and the electorate vote less often.

Overall, the evidence presented here suggests that declining voter turnout is rooted in the declining expressive benefits of voting for Americans, rather than in any cost-related factor linked to the voting process. These declining expressive benefits of voting can be linked to decreased partisanship, efficacy, and campaign involvement among the electorate, as well as to the general effects of dealignment on Americans' ability to meaningfully interpret elections.

This line of analysis also suggests an interrelationship between weakening ties to different aspects of the political system. First, declining partisanship, a key aspect of the decline of political parties, has been directly implicated in declining turnout. Second, the declines of political parties and traditional forms of political consciousness are usually considered to be integral parts of the dealignment process, which has been indirectly linked to declining voter turnout. Thus decline in other spheres of the political system has contributed to decline in the realm of political participation.

DECLINE OF POLITICAL PARTIES

The preceding section dealt with Americans' ties to the electoral system, as manifest in the act of voting. Another way in which Americans are typically linked to the political system is through one or another of the political parties. As touched on previously, the strength and durability of this partisan attachment was one of the key aspects of American political society in the 1950s.

Partisan attachment is generally measured by party identification — that is, the extent to which individuals categorize themselves as Democrats or Republicans (or neither). Those who explicitly identify with a given party are further categorized as "strong" or "weak" partisans. Those who say they are independents are further categorized by whether they "lean" toward one of the political parties or whether they are "pure" independents. The distinction between independent leaners and pure independents is an important one, because, in many ways, independent leaners' political behavior is more similar to weak partisans than it is to pure independents.

The most common view of party identification is that it is a loyalty, not unlike the ones individuals have to a church or sports team (Abramson *et al.*, 1987; Campbell, Converse, Miller, & Stokes, 1960). This loyalty may, and frequently is, passed on across generations and, once formed, tends to endure throughout an individual's lifetime. It forms the core orientation of an individual toward electoral politics and provides the prism through which the individual views the political world.

An alternative viewpoint sees party identification as being dependent on an individual's summary assessment of a party's past political positions and performance in office (Fiorina, 1981). This assessment is expressed in the individual's party identification, which tends, once formed, to be rather stable, because parties' general policy orientations change slowly. Because evidence favorable to this alternative viewpoint is generally also consistent with the traditional viewpoint, there is no good way of discriminating between the two. In any event, both viewpoints conceptualize an individual's party identification as central to his/her political behavior, especially voting decisions, so it is in this spirit that partisan attachment will be discussed.

The year after 1960 witnessed substantial changes in the party identification of Americans. To begin with, as mentioned briefly in the previous section, partisanship levels—the strength of individuals' party IDs—declined. We will now take a closer look at this decline of partisanship, so that the most salient aspects of this decline can be discerned.

Table 2 shows the distribution of partisanship among white Americans in the years 1960 to 1984 (it was among whites that the decline of partisanship really took place—partisanship among blacks actually increased). As the table makes clear, the key change is the decline in strong partisanship, down 8 points between 1960 and 1984. On the other end of the scale, pure independents were up 3 points and independent leaners up

TABLE 2. Party Identification among Whites, 1960–1984

Party identification	1960	1964	1968	1972	1976	1980	1984
Strong Democrat	20	24	16	12	13	14	15
Weak Democrat	25	25	25	25	23	23	18
Independent, leans Democratic	6	9	10	12	11	12	11
Independent, no partisan leanings	9	8	11	13	15	14	11
Independent, leans Republican	7	6	10	11	11	11	13
Weak Republican	14	14	16	14	16	16	17
Strong Republican	17	12	11	11	10	9	14

From *Change and Continuity in the 1984 Elections* by P. R. Abramson, J. H. Aldrich, and D. W. Rohde. Copyright 1987 by Congressional Quarterly Press.

11 points, for a total increase in the broad independent category of 14 points. (All of these figures are higher if 1980 is used as the endpoint of the interval, reflecting the modest revival of partisanship between 1980 and 1984).

Thus Americans were less and less inclined after 1960 to view their attachment to one of the political parties as a particularly strong one. This meant they putting less reliance on the traditional prism of party identification in viewing the political world. But the changes in American party identification were not limited to this. Not only were Americans putting less reliance on the prism of party identification, but, when they did use it, the view was noticeably less clear than before. This is illustrated in Table 3, where the party identification of white Americans is related to their propensity to vote Democratic in Congressional elections.

Clearly the salience of party ID to voting decisions has declined substantially over time. To take one of the most dramatic examples in 1960, 85% of weak Democrats voted for Democratic Congressional candidates, but only 66% in 1984. Conversely, only 14% of weak Republicans voted Democratic in 1960 but fully one-third did in 1984. In such a situation, it is easy to see why volatility and ticket splitting in voting behavior have become institutionalized.

In general, then, the role of partisan attachment in Americans' political behavior has undergone a double weakening. Not only has there been a decline in the general strength of Americans' party IDs, but the role this partisan attachment, of whatever strength, plays in forming voting decisions has also declined. Thus, for example, it is not just that there are fewer strong Democrats than before but that these strong Democrats are themselves less likely to vote Democratic.

These data make clear that there has been substantial erosion in the main way in which Americans are linked to political parties—their sense of partisan identification. In addition, although hard data on this are spotty, it is broadly accepted that the way parties themselves interact with individ-

TABLE 3. Percentage of White Major Party Voters Who Voted Democratic for the House, by Party Identification, 1960–1984

Party identification	1960	1964	1968	1972	1976	1980	1984
Strong Democrat	92	92	88	91	86	82	87
Weak Democrat	85	84	72	79	76	66	66
Independent, leans Democratic	86	78	60	78	76	69	76
Independent, no partisan leanings	52	70	48	54	55	57	59
Independent, leans Republican	26	28	18	27	32	32	39
Weak Republican	14	34	21	24	28	26	33
Strong Republican	8	8	8	15	15	22	15

From *Change and Continuity in the 1984 Elections* by P. R. Abramson, J. H. Aldrich, and D. W. Rohde. Copyright 1987 by Congressional Quarterly Press.

ual citizens has undergone a fundamental change since 1960 (Blumenthal, 1980; Hunt, 1987; Sabato, 1981; Schneider & Baron, 1986). This is usually attributed to the dramatically expanded role of television in communicating parties' positions in the public, replacing more "grass roots" methods of party interaction. This is especially true of campaigns, where televised advertising and the placement of "sound bites" on the television news now dominate the process.

It seems plausible that this transformation in the way parties interact with citizens has contributed to the ongoing decline in the strength and salience of partisanship, as well as eroding the link between citizen and political party in other, less measurable ways. In any event, the combined weight of declining partisanship and this transformation in party–citizen interaction strongly suggests a substantial erosion of the ties between citizens and political parties in the 1960–1988 period.

In addition, there is clearly a relationship between these eroding ties to political parties and eroding ties to the electoral system. First, as we saw earlier, declining partisanship played a direct role in declining voter turnout. Second, declining strength and salience of partisanship is undoubtedly an important aspect of dealignment, which was also implicated, if less directly, in decreased turnout. Finally, the reliance on television in party–citizen interactions may have contributed to declining campaign involvement, especially through newspaper reading, which is, in turn, another cause of decreased voter turnout. All this serves to illustrate how, as citizens' ties to one aspect of the political system weaken, it tends to promote weakened ties to other aspects of the system.

DECLINE OF TRADITIONAL FORMS OF POLITICAL CONSCIOUSNESS

The third way in which Americans' ties to the political system eroded between 1960 and 1988 was the weakening of traditional forms of political consciousness. These traditional forms of consciousness were a legacy of the New Deal era and were based upon the perception of shared political interests among certain social groups.

Besides similarities in social structural position, the perception of shared interests among group members can be based upon common historical experience, generational links, and interaction of group members with one another (Abramson et al., 1987). All of these are believed to have been strong among groups whose political identities were forged during the New Deal era.

Because of this perception of shared interests, members of these social groups tended to view the political world and evaluate the political parties in similar ways. Thus this shared political consciousness defined a common relationship to the political system among members of a given group, resulting in marked similarities in voting behavior.

This group voting behavior was most salient for the Democrats, who based their New Deal coalition upon it. The coalition depended on members of certain social groups casting their ballots for the Democrats at higher rates than the rest of the population. The groups making up this coalition can be more or less finely specified, but generally included blacks, southerners, union members, manual workers, and Catholics in various guises (Abramson et al., 1987; Axelrod, 1972; Petrocik, 1981). It was the eroding loyalty of these groups (except blacks) that broke down the New Deal and led to the decline of the Democratic Party after 1964. These changes are illustrated in Table 4, which shows, for whites, the relationship between social characteristics and Democratic voting for the years 1960–1984.

These data show a general weakening trend in the special relationship between the Democratic party and key group members of its coalition. The clearest example of this is with class voting. In 1964, class voting was at the 19-point level—that is, the Democratic voting rate among white manual workers was 19 points higher than among white nonmanual jobholders. By 1984, this had declined to the 8-point level, a drop of 11 percentage points.

The decreases in the salience of social characteristics were not as clear-cut among other groups but still suggest an overall weakening in group members' perceptions that their political interests were specially linked to the Democratic party. What caused this change in the way group members viewed their relationship to the political system?

The simplest answer is that the politics of the Democratic party ceased to correspond very well to the way group members conceptualized their political interests. This idea is consistent with the evolution of the Democratic party since 1964. It is broadly accepted that the Democratic party

TABLE 4. Relationship of Social Characteristics to Presidential
Voting among White Major Party Voters, 1960–1984

Type of voting	1960	1964	1968	1972	1976	1980	1984
Regional voting[a]	6	−11	− 4	−13	1	1	− 9
Union voting[b]	21	23	13	11	18	15	20
Class voting[c]	12	19	10	2	17	9	8
Religious voting[d]	48	21	30	13	15	10	16

[a]Percentage of southerners who voted Democratic minus the percentage of voters outside the South who voted Democratic.
[b]Percentage of members of union households who voted Democratic minus the percentage of members of households with no union members who voted Democratic.
[c]Percentage of manual workers who voted Democratic minus the percentage of nonmanual jobholders who voted Democratic.
[d]Percentage of Catholics who voted Democratic minus the percentage of Protestants who voted Democratic.
From *Change and Continuity in the 1984 Elections* by P. R. Abramson, J. H. Aldrich, and D. W. Rohde. Copyright 1987 by Congressional Quarterly Press.

after 1964 became identified with political views, on social, racial, and international issues that lie considerably to the left of the views of many manual workers, union members, Catholics, southerners, and so forth (Cavanaugh & Sundquist, 1985; Kuttner, 1987; Schneider & Baron, 1986). This undoubtedly made an important contribution to the erosion of traditional forms of political consciousness among these groups.

Beyond this, however, it seems likely that group members themselves changed in how they viewed their political interests. Specifically, it is possible that they no longer saw their identity as group members as being bound to a given set of common interests. Suggestive evidence along these lines is contained in a recent study of political consciousness among white men between 1960 and 1976 (Bloomquist, 1986).

This study used LISREL models to estimate the relationship between class identity (self-placement in the working class) and "class-interest consciousness" (measured by support for broad social programs guaranteeing jobs and medical care to all). Essentially, results of the study show that, although class identity and class-interest consciousness were strongly related to one another in 1960 and formed a coherent attitude structure, this attitude structure had eroded by 1976, as the relationship between class identity and class-interest consciousness became substantially weaker.

Bloomquist attributes the erosion of this attitude structure among white men to two factors. First, there was an increase in the salience of economic self-interest to these individuals' social consciousness. Second, there was an increased belief among these individuals that social programs were primarily of benefit to minorities. Both of these factors would tend to militate against a perception of group-based interests.

To the extent these results are generalizable, it suggests that, not only has the Democratic party become identified with policies group members view as inimical to their interests but also group members no longer view these interests as linked to a common group identity. The result has been an erosion in the traditional forms of political consciousness that linked group members to the political system. This has led, most directly, to a serious deterioration in the political fortunes of the Democratic party (five losses in the six presidential elections since 1964).

Because one of the most salient aspects of these traditional forms of political consciousness was the link between common interests and a political party, it seems likely that decline in these forms of consciousness has contributed to the overall erosion of citizens' ties to political parties. It also seems likely that this weakening group consciousness, as a constituent part of dealignment, has had a negative effect on group members' sense of the meaningfulness of elections, thereby contributing to declining voter turnout. Again, these connections illustrate how decline in one sphere of the political system can promote decline in other spheres.

CONCLUSION

The years between 1960 and 1988 witnessed substantial changes in American political society. At the beginning of the period, the system of the fifties was in place, a set of political arrangements based on group interests, partisan commitment, and moderately high levels of turnout. This set of arrangements led to relatively stable and predictable political behavior. By the end of the period, the stability and predictability of American political society was more a memory than a reality.

It has been shown that political change between 1960 and 1988 included dramatic erosion in the most basic level of support for American political institutions—the ties of individual Americans to the political system. This erosion consisted of three key changes in the way Americans related to the political world: (1) the decline of political participation; (2) the decline of political parties; and (3) the decline of traditional forms of political consciousness. Further, it has been shown that these changes were interdependent, with decline in one area typically promoting decline in the other areas.

What was the underlying basis of all these changes? What caused Americans' ties to their political system to become so much weaker over this time period? In my view, the reason lies in the inevitable tendency of political arrangements in a democracy to erode under the onslaught of structural change ("things fall apart"). There are at least three types of structural change that are relevant here: economic, demographic, and generational.

All of these changes tend to undermine the meaningfulness of old political paradigms for individuals. Economic change, for example, typically reduces the ability of a party to deliver the same benefits with the same policies. Yet the individuals who form the social base of the party understand the political world in this way and are confused when the party shifts policies. They are especially confused when the party not only shifts policies but also fails to deliver some semblance of the old benefits (for example, the Democrats in the post-1973 economic world).

Demographic change, on the other hand, alters the nature and relative weight of the types of individuals that make up (or should make up) a party's coalition. Again, this obliges the party to shift policies, confusing old members of its coalition, without necessarily clarifying matters for new and prospective members of the coalition (for example, the Democrats' attempt to please both blue-collar and white-collar workers after 1964).

Finally, generational change simply replaced older individuals, whose loyalty to a party or political viewpoint is rooted in historical experience, with younger individuals who lack such roots. Not surprisingly, these younger individuals have a harder time seeing the relevance of traditional party positions and political viewpoints to their lives (for example, class voting among whites in 1984 was at the 19-point level for those entering the electorate before or during World War II; only 2 points for whites entering the electorate after 1972 (Abramson et al., 1987)).

Thus all of these changes tend to reduce the meaningfulness of old political paradigms for individuals and, as a result, the political world becomes increasingly unintelligible to larger numbers of people. Lacking a firm basis for interpreting the political world, individuals' ties to the political system erode because political actions and commitments lose personal meaning. After all, the "natural" state of individuals is probably to be *disconnected* to politics, rather than connected, because individuals can "free ride" on election outcomes but not on outcomes in their family and daily lives.

This further suggests that the natural tendency of political systems is toward dealignment, not realignment on a regular basis. The logic seems compelling that old political arrangements and ties tend to fall apart under the stress of structural change, since they were designed for the old structure, not the new. The logic seems less compelling that new political arrangements will necessarily replace the old on a regular basis, so as to produce a better fit to the new structure. It seems more reasonable to assert that the natural tendency toward dealignment creates the opportunity for realignment but does not guarantee that this will happen at a specific time.

Of course, in the past, these opportunities did translate into regularly occurring major realignments (the last of which took place in the 1930s) so the confusion around this point is understandable. But today the situation is different. The opportunity for a major realignment has been present for 20 years without producing one. This is not to say that there have not been shifts in voting support between the two major parties—clearly, there have—but that there has been no reconstruction of political identities and loyalties such as has accompanied realignments in the past.

Why such a reconstruction of loyalties has not actually taken place remains a mystery to be solved. Solving the puzzle may depend on developing a better understanding of how individual ties to the political system are formed and how these ties (or the lack of them) enter into political decision making. In this regard, the work of Brady and his collaborators (Brady et al., 1988; Brady & Ansolabehere, 1989) seems promising because they are attempting to link appropriately nuanced rational choice theory (i.e., theory that takes into account the affective stance of the individual, from intense commitment to indifference and/or confusion) to data on actual participation and voting decisions.

Regardless, however, of the exact micromechanisms that govern the formation of political ties and their role in decision making, it appears that further erosion of these ties is quite likely. On the one hand, there appear to be natural tendencies for these ties to weaken over time and, moreover, for the weakening of one tie to promote the weakening of others. On the other hand, a major realignment of the political system, which could conceivably reforge these ties, does not appear to be in the offing. Just how long this erosion of political ties will continue is difficult to say. By the argument presented here, it depends on the emergence of new issues and political approaches capable of galvanizing the electorate toward a major realignment. Based on the conduct of the parties and level of excitement among the voters in the 1988 election, there seems little reason to expect this to happen any time soon.

REFERENCES

Abramson, P. R., & Aldrich, J. H. (1982). The decline of electoral participation in America. *American Political Science Review, 76,* 502–521.

Abramson, P. R., Aldrich, J. H., & Rohde, D. W. (1987). *Change and continuity in the 1984 elections.* Washington, DC: Congressional Quarterly Press.

Aldrich, J. H., & Simon, D. (1986). Turnout in American national elections. *Research in Micropolitics, 1,* 271–301.

Almond, G., & Verba, S. (1963). *The civic culture.* Princeton, NJ: Princeton University Press.

Axelrod, R. (1972). Where the votes come from: An analysis of electoral coalitions, 1952–1968. *American Political Science Review, 66,* 11–20.

Bloomquist, L. E. (1986). *Erosion of working-class consciousness in postwar America: The case of white men.* Unpublished doctoral dissertation, Madison, WI: University of Wisconsin.

Blumenthal, S. (1980). *The permanent campaign.* Boston: Beacon Press.

Brady, H., & Ansolabehere, S. (1989). The nature of utility functions in mass publics. *American Political Science Review, 83,* 143–163.

Brady, H., Nie, N., Schlozman, K., & Verba, S. (1988). *Participation in America revisited: A proposal.* Unpublished research proposal, University of Chicago.

Burnham, W. D. (1970). *Critical elections and the mainsprings of American politics.* New York: W. W. Norton.

Campbell, A., Converse, P., Miller, W., & Stokes, D. (1960). *The American voter.* New York: John Wiley & Sons.

Cavanagh, T. E., & Sundquist, J. L. (1985). The new two-party system. In J. E. Chubb & P. E. Peterson (Eds.), *The new direction in American politics* (pp. 33–67). Washington, DC: The Brookings Institution.

Cyr, A. B. (1975). The calculus of voting reconsidered. *Public Opinion Quarterly, 39,* 19–38.

Downs, A. (1957). *Economic theory of democracy.* New York: Harper & Bros.

Fiorina, M. P. (1981). *Retrospective voting in American national elections.* New Haven, CT: Yale University Press.

Hunt, A. R. (1987). The media and presidential campaigns. In A. J. Reichley (Ed.), *Elections American style* (pp. 52–74). Washington, DC: The Brookings Institution.

Kuttner, R. (1987). *The life of the party: Democratic prospects in 1988 and beyond.* New York: Penguin.

Levy, F. (1987). *Dollars and dreams: The changing American income distribution.* New York: Russell Sage Foundation.

Nie, N., Verba, S., & Petrocik, J. (1976). *The changing American voter.* Cambridge, MA: Harvard University Press.

Olson, M. (1965). *Logic of collective action.* Cambridge, MA: Harvard University Press.

Petrocik, J. R. (1981). *Party coalitions: Realignment and the decline of the New Deal party system.* Chicago: University of Chicago Press.

Riker, W., & Ordeshook, P. (1968). A theory of the calculus of voting. *American Political Science Review, 62*, 25–42.

Sabato, L. (1981). *The rise of political consultants*. New York: Basic Books.

Schneider, W., & Baron, A. (1986). *The radical center: New directions in American politics*. Unpublished manuscript, Washington, DC: American Enterprise Institution.

Teixeira, R. A. (1987). *Why Americans don't vote: Turnout decline in the United States, 1960–1984*. Westport, CT: Greenwood Press.

Teixeira, R. A. (1988). Will the real nonvoter please stand up? *Public Opinion, 11*(2), 41–44, 59.

Teixeira, R. A. (1989). Election '88: Registration and turnout. *Public Opinion, 11*(5), 12–13, 56–58.

Wolfinger, R., & Rosenstone, S. (1980). *Who votes?* New Haven, CT: Yale University Press.

CHAPTER TWELVE

Institutional Analysis

An Organizational Approach

WILLIAM FORM

Sociologists sometimes do not agree on the meaning and on the application of their most basic concepts. This clearly applies to *social institutions*. A science cannot accumulate systematic knowledge when it fails to agree on the meaning and operationalization of its basic concepts. Sociologists often blame this lack of consensus on the comparative youth of the discipline. Yet, we have taught courses on social institutions in American universities for over a century. This surely is enough time to develop consensus on the meaning and application of basic concepts. In trying to confront this problem, this chapter does five things. First, I select four representative experts on social institutions, examine how they define institutions and how they put that definition into practice. Second, I repeat the exercise for authors of some widely used introductory textbooks. Third, I elaborate the inadequacies and blindspots in institutional analysis. Fourth, I propose an operational conception of institutions that can be applied to all of them. Finally, I speculate on the future of institutional analysis.

EARLY CONCEPTIONS

I arbitrarily select four sociological apostles of institutions to demonstrate how they confronted the problem of defining institutions. An early writer, Hertzler (1929) thought that the study of institutions was a ne-

---

WILLIAM FORM • Department of Sociology, Ohio State University, Columbus, Ohio 43210.

glected area, and he proposed to repair this condition. He defined a social institution as "a complex of concepts and attitudes regarding the ordering of a particular class of unavoidable or indispensable human relationships that are involved in satisfying certain elemental desirable social ends. The concepts and attitudes are condensed into mores, customs, traditions and codes" (p. 67). Every activity in society takes place through institutions; on the individual level, through habits, and on the social level, through associations and organizations. The number of institutions are endless, but they can be classified arbitrarily into certain fields: family, economic, political, religious and ethical, educational and scientific, communicative, aesthetic and expressional, health and recreational. Typical of his time, Hertzler reviewed primitive institutions, how they evolved into modern ones, and how modern institutions protect values with authority and sanctions.

Twenty years later, MacIver and Page (1949) tried in their magisterial text to bring order into the field of institutions. Objecting to Barnes's (1942) definition of institutions as anything that is socially established, they defined institutions as rules and procedures to be distinguished from groups and organizations. Thus monogamy is an institution, whereas the family is a primary group; collective bargaining, an institution, and labor unions, an association. Confronted with the bewildering variety of groups all of which have institutions, they classified the institutions of groups according to their type of bond: territorial, ethnic, intimacy, rank, duration, or formality. All associations (groups) were also classified according to their *interests* that are either unspecialized or specialized. Groups with unspecialized interests include tribes, classes, age and sex groups, and the patriarchal family. Groups with specialized interests may be primary (i.e., cultural, as in clubs, families, churches), intermediate (educational, as in schools and reformatories), or secondary (economic, political, and technological, as in business, the state, and research organizations) (p. 447). The state, the economic system, and churches comprise the great associations. Thus, institutional analysis, as with Hertzler, has no boundaries. It applies to all groups in society.

Robin Williams's *American Society* (1970) has endured almost as the sole but certainly the dominant text since 1951. For Williams, cultural normative structure as a body of rules is basic to society. Norms vary according to the severity of their sanctions. Consensual norms to which society applies severe sanctions are institutional norms. These are classified according to the major "needs' or value centers to which they are most closely associated (kinship, economic, political, religious, and others). Institutions, then, refer not to concrete social organizations, as other sociologists claim, but to a set of institutional norms that cohere around distinct and socially important complexes of values (p. 31). Williams includes in his institutional chapters the following: family and kinship, social stratification, economy, polity, education, and religion. In a chapter on social organizations, he separately examined primary, secondary, formal, and other organizations wherever they appear—in and out of institutions.

Finally, Eisenstadt (1968) in the *International Encyclopedia of the Social Sciences* defined institutions as regulative principles that organize individual behavior in society into organizational patterns that deal with basic problems of ordered social life. Regulations are upheld by norms and sanctions that are legitimized. The major institutional spheres in all societies include family and kinship, education, economy, polity, cultural institutions, and stratification. Institutions are close to, but not identical to, groups or roles organized around special societal goals or functions. Apparently, the principles regulate group activities in the various spheres. But the principles and their modes of regulation are not made clear.

This brief overview of how four major theorists deal with institutions reveals persistent and unresolved problems. In Table 1, I distinguish four main areas of institutional analysis: (1) the substance or composition of institutions, (2) their purposes or functions, (3) classification of institutions, and (4) types of social formations that institutions cover.

My comments follow the historical appearance of the four publications. In terms of identifying characteristics, Hertzler's institutions are made up of concepts and attitudes; MacIver and Page's, group procedures; Williams's, sanctioned consensual norms; and Eisenstadt, regulative principles. As functionalists, the authors split on the purpose of institutions; they either satisfy certain individual or social needs or ends or they are supposed to control individual and group life. Only MacIver and Page stress that institutions serve as instruments to achieve group ends. All the authors exhibit ambiguity in how they classify institutions. Hertzler offers

TABLE 1. Bases of Institutions

Author	Substance	Purpose	Classification	Range
Hertzler	Concepts and attitudes	Satisfying needs and ends	Institutional fields	All groups
McIver and Page	Group procedures and rules	To achieve group ends	Types of interests	All groups and great associations
Williams	Consensual norms	Social control	Needs or value centers	Major social formations
Eisenstadt	Regulative principles	Achieve ordered social life	Institutional spheres	All groups and roles

no basis and classifies them according to their "fields." Similarly, Williams does not indicate how major "needs or value-centers" bear on the range of social formations he selects to analyze. Eisenstadt simply indicates the presence of certain "institutional fields" without indicating how to identify the fields. Only MacIver and Page present a rationale for classifying institutions according to their underlying interests and the size of their groups. Finally, three authors agree that institutions cover the entire range of groups or social formations. Indeed, Hertzler and Eisenstadt even include individuals and roles. Only Williams insists that institutions include only formations that satisfy major social needs or value centers. But he does not reveal how to determine which needs or values are major or basic.

In practice, whatever their theoretical rationales, all the authors devote most attention to four major social formations: family and kinship, what MacIver and Page call the *great associations, social stratification,* and *other groups.* The authors devote little systematic coverage to "other groups," such as communities, neighborhoods, voluntary organizations, friendships, crowds, and publics, even though they presumably contain institutions. When the authors do discuss these "other groups," institutional concepts, as they define them, rarely appear. But most important, whatever social formations they do discuss, the substance and purposes of the institutions, as proposed in the definitions are given short shrift. Thus, Columns 1 and 2 of Table 1 deserve detailed empirical analysis if the authors would apply their institutional theories. For example, because, according to MacIver and Page, institutions are procedures, in analyzing the economy they should devote most attention to the procedures of collective bargaining, modes of organizing production and services, banking regulations, the formal organization of corporations and labor unions, and so on. This is not done. Similarly, if sanctioned norms, regulative principles, social control, and regulations are central to institutions, these deserve most attention in analyzing the behavior of all kinds of groups, including cities, fraternal societies, jails, the military, schools, status groups, families, and government bureaus. Thus, for Williams, consensual norms or controls should be classified and then applied systematically across the entire range of social formations. This could be a worthy enterprise, a task that earlier sociologists undertook in their texts on social control. Indeed, Gibbs (1989) has recently demonstrated the utility of organizing all of sociology around the area of social control. Although contemporary institutional analysts do not systematically apply institutional theory, their empirical analyses often are useful because they do what sociologists do best, analyze organizations. Yet, as I indicate later, they do not engage in systematic organizational analysis. Finally, although all the authors stress the importance of interinstitutional relationships, they do not analyze them systematically with their theoretical frameworks.

Introductory Textbooks

I examined a dozen popular introductory textbooks for the type of institutional analysis they offer to introductory students today. Some of these texts are authored by distinguished sociologists. As others have noted, with rare exceptions, most of the texts are remarkably alike. I offer a general sketch of how they treat institutions.

Three texts did not list the concept in their indexes although they devoted several chapters to "the institutions." One text avoided using the term altogether, preferring to use *social system*. When authors defined institutions, contrary to the theorists, all of them indicated that institutions included groups and roles as well as norms and values that have purposes or functions: maintaining order, meeting social needs, social control, and so on. All texts but one contained a large section that typically included at least five chapters labeled *institutions*: family, economy, politics, education, and religion. What is important is that, despite statements on the theoretical importance of control for institutions, the authors generally did not include chapters in the institution sections that dealt formally with control, bureaucracy, the military, or social stratification. Typically, institutional rhetoric and analysis were completely absent in chapters dealing with groups, formal organizations, work, race, and ethnicity, collective behavior, deviance, social change, and the community.

None of the authors applied a consistent or common framework to analyze the different institutions. Neither did they agree on the order of the chapters, provide a rationale for the order, or attempt to relate all the institution chapters to each other. Institutional change should logically be considered in chapters dealing with deviancy, social change, technological change, alternative norms and values, changing technology, and interorganizational interactions. Without exception, these topics were treated separately. What is important is that all of the texts referred to and compared functional and conflict theories, and they sometimes applied them to the institutions they examined. Almost without exception, the authors preferred conflict to functional theory even though they offered functional explanations for the appearance of institutions and used functional analysis to explain social conflict. Finally, the authors did not provide a systematic inventory of the norms, values, procedures, or roles of the institutions they examined. The fact that a unique framework was provided for each institution meant that institutional structures could not be compared within or among societies.

Although introductory texts are not intended as serious theoretical works, they allegedly reflect the basic theory of the discipline. My analysis suggests that they do not adequately reflect dominant theories, which to be sure, are somewhat incoherent and divergent. Clearly, the time is ripe for a fresh start in institutional analysis. After a critique of institutional theory, I offer suggestions for such a start.

CRITIQUE OF INSTITUTIONAL THEORY

Sociology does not have a viable theory of institutions independent of general theories of society as those proposed by Marx, Durkheim, and Weber. If a nascent institutional theory exists, it is a cultural one that deals with the development of norms, values, and culture (Parsons, 1966). Such theories do not have a propositional structure similar, for example, to ecological theory of community growth (Hawley, 1986), the evolution of stratification systems (Lenski, 1966), and the demographic transition. True, the discipline is blessed with good general theories of specific institutions, as the economy, polity, religion, and education. Sociologists have also written good research monographs on such specific institutions as education, welfare, health, and government. But we do not have a general theory of institutions that is historical, comparative, and that can be applied to contemporary societies.

One important reason why sociology has not developed a theory of institutions derives from unsatisfactory conceptions or definitions of institutions. Whichever definition of institution scholars use (norms, value centers, procedures, orientations, control, or regulative principles), they are supposed to apply to all social formations: society, community, stratification systems, crowds, social movements, primary groups, associations, roles, and so on. But because the authors do not fulfill the task, they do not highlight the distinguishing institutional features of the social formations. Moreover, most writers tend to intuit the presence and operation of norms, rules, values, and regulative principles. Norms, for example, are rarely derived from systematic empirical research because they are difficult to operationalize. Moreover, scholars usually describe norms in very general terms. The extent that different populations embrace and apply the norms in different situations is typically not revealed. The problem here resembles that of the relation between the attitude and the act. The relationship is fuzzy, and it might be explained if factors external to both are brought to bear. The problem, as I explain later, is even more complex for institutional behavior. The idea that norms are abstractions and may not be applicable to specific situations and organizations is not a satisfactory research solution. Sociologists should be able to determine which norms are violated, the extent of the violation, the situation of the violation, and the conditions when one norm is substituted for another.

Norms, ends, goals, and value centers are very general concepts. They can be embraced by individuals, role encumbents, and even organizations under widely varying conditions and situations. For example, the institution of monogamy may persist in a society where marital stability is the exception rather than the rule. Of course, the writer may find an escape hatch by then positing the institution of serial monogamy or something else. Little is explained by such inventions. Again, the inability of institutionalized values to explain social organization has been massively documented in stratification studies. Thus the norm of equal opportunity is violated in the breach, making it an ideological legitimation of the system rather than an explanation of stratification as an institution (see Huber & Form, 1973; Kluegel & Smith, 1986). Even when researchers successfully operationalize normative beliefs and norm adherence, they learn little about institutional behavior. This suggests that general institutional theory operates with a faulty causal premise. The problem may not be one of demonstrating the relevance and importance of institutions (norms, values, ends, etc.) to explain individual or social behavior. It may be more fruitful to explain norms as dependent variables rather than as independent or causal variables. One of my colleagues suggested in a conversation that Sumner may have conceived the idea of institutions to justify stability and support for social order. The study of norms as ideology to stabilize the social order can be an important research undertaking, but the task of institutional analysis should be to explain how institutions affect social organization and behavior.

This raises the question of where institutions reside and how they get implemented. The traditional answer is that they reside in the person and they get there through role socialization. Moreover, roles are generally thought of as building blocks of individual behavior and all social organization. I take the position that, although role analysis may be fruitful for understanding behavior in small groups, it is not useful and certainly not parsimonious to explain large-scale structures such as the economy, polity, and stratification system. The implementation of norms and roles may get so involved with organizational concerns that the most appropriate unit of analysis may be the organizations themselves. Thus traditional institutional theory has a small group and anthropological bias that hinders its utility for analyzing large-scale organizations in contemporary societies. Attempting to study such societies in terms of norms and roles has many of the difficulties of individual reductionism in sociology (see Blau, 1987, p. 75).

Finally, traditional institutional theory has difficulty accounting for institutional change. From its earliest inception, the theory has been used to account for tradition, social control, and social order. To be sure, traditional theory does consider two possible sources of change: human needs and the interdependence of institutions. However, the persistent attacks on functional theory have proved, if nothing else, the disutility of changing needs to account for social structure and social change. Although interinstitutional interdependence seems a more promising explanation of social change, it too suffers from several limitations. Even a brief examination of research in this area reveals that the analysis of change moves from what institutions are (norms, values, principles) to interorganizational dynamics. That is, theorists do not attack the problem of how norms or values interact to produce changing norms or values. They cannot do this without referring to concrete problems, situations, and organizations. Thus theorists face two almost insurmountable problems. First, individual norms, values, and roles are difficult to translate directly into group or organizational norms, goals, and ends. Second, sociologists have not satisfactorily resolved the question of whether organizations have norms or ends and, if they do, how can they explain organizational and interorganizational behavior. Different positions, subgroups, echelons, and divisions of organizations, for example, have different ends, goals, and objectives that get redefined and changed in interaction (Perrow, 1970). Recent organizational research suggests that it may be more profitable to assume that change is endemic or normal rather than to embrace the stability assumptions built into the concepts of norms, values, and ends.

If the foregoing line of reasoning is correct, the study of institutions (as norms, values, principles) should proceed in a direction almost opposite to our historical practice. Such study would involve embracing four major principles. (1) Research should move from micro- to macrounits of analysis. This places institutional analysis directly into the arena of organizational and especially interorganizational research. This strategy is promising for two reasons. Institutions (norms, values) are abstract if not meaningless outside of their organizational contexts. Only in concrete situations and organizational settings can institutions acquire behavioral significance and be explained. Moreover, when organizations change, their institutions also change. Because organizations and institutions are linked and organizations typically change in response to external forces and influences, interorganizational relations become the central object of institutional study. (2) Researchers should posit that institutional and organizational change are standard and ubiquitous rather than assume the stability of norms, values, and ends. (3) Researchers should try to explain how institutions (norms, etc.) appear, get defined, and operate rather than using institutions to explain social order and behavior. That is, institutions should become dependent variables in research. Sociologists will be tempted to the view that organizations and institutions are mutually interdependent. I suggest that this is a research problem that should not be resolved *a priori*. It is possible that the study of institutions should be abandoned in organizational and societal analysis. (4) Although traditional institutional theory is static and conservative, strangely enough it is not historical. Therefore, institutional analysis should be historical in the sense it should address how institutions get changed in the vortex of associational life. Good historical analysis typically provides clues to the forces that produce change.

ORGANIZATIONAL INSTITUTIONAL ANALYSIS

The basic premise of this chapter is that advanced industrial societies are organizational societies and their analyses should proceed in organizational terms. In this orientation, the units of analysis are organizations and organizational relations. To minimize confusion, I will use the terms *norms, values,* or *procedures* to refer to the traditional meanings of institution and the term *institutional complex* to refer to what traditional theorists referred to as institutional fields, spheres, great associations, or major social institutions. Because I have taken the position that institutionalized norms and the like are embedded in organizations, analyses of institutional complexes deal primarily with the task of identifying the network of organizations in the complexes and how these complexes emerge, stabilize, and change. Contrary to the traditional analysis of norms and values, the proposed approach is dynamic in the sense that both stability and change are built into interorganizational analysis. That is, stability and change are both structural elements of interorganizational analysis. I will elaborate on this later, but it suffices here to note that this approach does not require a separate theory of change.

Two important caveats must be entered immediately. First, analysis of institutional complexes is not equivalent to societal analysis. The complexes represent only societal segments. Simply accumulating observations of all of the complexes is not equivalent to wholistic societal analysis. The approach taken is a partial one that probably should precede social analysis. Second, my approach does not replace a societal analysis of norms, values, beliefs, and ideologies. Clearly, it is possible and legitimate to study changing societal values, norms, beliefs, and ideologies on their own level as Williams (1970) has done. I have not solved the problem of how such studies can be integrated into analysis of institutional complexes.

A basic procedural tenet of my approach to institutional complexes is that no predetermined set of them exists. They have to be empirically established. It would be surprising if the methodology I propose to identify the complexes did not turn up clusters of political, economic, religious, family, and other organizations. By first identifying organizations that cluster rather than seeking to identify which organizations sustain certain norms, for example, we avoid making norms and organizations coterminous. Thus monogamy is practiced not only in the family but in economic, political, religious, and other organizations. Education is carried on in schools, but probably more of it occurs in work settings, for example. And schools and colleges may be run on profit norms as much as any business. The linkages of norms, functions, and organizations vary within and between societies, and the linkages should be determined empirically in institutional analysis.

How do we identify institutional complexes and how does the methodology we use produce useful knowledge about institutional complexes? Although I have not worked out the methodology in detail, I offer some suggestions. One can begin almost anywhere by identifying an organization and observing over time its routine and nonroutine interactions with other organizations. As in network analysis, dense networks of organizations will be distinguished from less dense ones. The boundaries of networks may not be readily discernible, but this in itself is an important finding about the relative integration or autonomy of institutional complexes. Obviously, the researcher cannot rely solely on a density measure of networks to identify institutional complexes because some interorganizational relations are more important or significant than others. Drawing the boundaries of organizational networks must be informed by direct knowledge about the quality and importance of interorganizational contacts. But a quantitative approach to identifying organizational linkages is a necessary first step in identifying institutional complexes.

Even a crude beginning would reveal that some networks are denser than others. For example, business firms, labor unions, and occupational associations probably form a tight internal cluster and share some external ties to selected government agencies. Of course, organizations rarely interact as wholes because they are themselves clusters of suborganizations that may themselves have independent relations with organizations in the external environment. I will consider this complication later. The utility of organizational density comparisons becomes quickly evident when we contrast the economic complex with a religious or cultural one. Thus individual churches may exhibit relatively few linkages to other religious bodies and more linkages to families and businesses. In the "cultural" arena, musical, art, literary, and related organizations are probably more loosely coupled than organizations in the economic complex but more tightly coupled than those in the religious complex. Although these speculations on the density of organizational interactions may not be accurate, the implications of density analysis for understanding collective action in various institutional complexes should be obvious.

It may be easier to conduct this type of analysis for a community than for a society because a community study could conceivably include all organizations (Reynolds, Knoke, & Kaufman, 1988). But researchers can sample and have successfully sampled organizations on a state or even national level (Spaeth, 1988). Both community and societal studies should produce two important types of findings. The first is a map of the organizational ties within each institutional complex. Obviously, some complexes are interactionally dense (economic), whereas others (religious) may be quite segmented. Conceivably, some organizations may have few or no ties, and this would raise questions about the pertinence and "coverage" of institutional analysis. The second type of finding should reveal information about ties among the institutional complexes. Sociologists have long speculated about interinstitutional relations but have provided relatively little systematic data on the subject.

The linkage of the educational institutional complex to other complexes is a case in point. Sociologists have observed that education has stratification, political, and economic functions. It is unlikely that these functions get realized without interinstitutional contact. What are the actual interactions of educational organizations to governmental, economic, and family (stratification) organizations? Who initiates them, and how do they work? Neither have the interactions of family to economic, educational, and religious organizations been systematically examined. Determining the number and strength of linkages among the institutional complexes will reveal important sources of tension and change within the complexes. The dynamic quality and dominance of the economic complex in American society, for example, probably reflects its more numerous ties to other complexes. On the other hand, in this era, religious complexes may be both internally more segmented and display fewer ties to other complexes. Finally, some organizations may not be part of a complex, yet they might be linked equally to two or more complexes. For example, ethnic organizations might link equally to political and religious complexes. Such a sociometric location would provide important clues to social and political movements. In short, the type of approach suggested here would stimulate bundles of research questions and hypotheses.

THE STRUCTURE OF INSTITUTIONAL COMPLEXES

I have suggested that a shortcoming of traditional institutional analysis is the differentiated approach to the study of each institution. Although certain advantages accrue to this strategy, comparing institutional complexes is also desirable, and it is difficult to achieve without applying a common methodology and frame of reference to all institutional complexes. Even a crude start toward this goal should yield immediate rewards. Form and Miller (1960) provided some suggestions in a monograph that probed the links of business and labor union to other institutional complexes in the community. The authors investigated the links of each institution (political, religious, family, mass communication, education, and welfare) with the same methodology and frame of reference.

The structural analysis of institutional complexes involved four tasks: (1) an inventory of major organizations in the complex and their patterns of interactions with each other and with organizations in other institutional complexes, (2) a brief history of the interactions' pattern so identified, (3) an analysis of how tensions and power relations changed among the organizations, and (4) an analysis of the future direction or flow of conflicts within the complex and its external environment. I will amplify each of these tasks and use the economic institutional complex to illustrate them.

1. The organizations in the institutional complex may be identified on three levels. In the local community, for example, they first include firms, labor union locals, professional, and other organized groups that interact in the workplace. On the second level, they include organizations external to the workplace but connected to it: community, state, and national organizations such as trade associations for particular industries, organizations for all businesses, and occupational associations, for example, chamber of commerce, National Association of Manufacturers, labor union federations, and professional associations. Organizations on the third level include those spawned by second-level associations to achieve particular goals in other institutional complexes; for example, political action committees of business and labor to achieve political goals. These third-level ties partly expose relationships among the institutional complexes.

The next task is to uncover the typical pattern of relationships among the organizations in the institutional complex. This first calls for a standard organizational study that exposes integration and cleavages among subgroups in representative organizations. In the economic arena, for example, this produces a general profile of labor–management relations within typical work plants. Of course, relations among other groups in the workplace (e.g., racial and ethnic groups) are also profiled. The primary objective of this analysis is to uncover the general pattern of tensions and cooperation and also to find the extent to which local disputes involve organizations on the second and third levels and how first-level disputes affect the external organizations. For the economic arena, such an analysis exposes the influence of politics and government in local disputes and the influence of economic interests at all levels on government policies. This research strategy produces a general picture of the way that intergroup tensions are structured in the institutional complex. In other words, the analysis produces a general picture of the power structure in the institutional complex.

In any power analysis of intergroup relations, the researcher must include the concerns of traditional institutional theorists, i.e., the ends, goals, norms, and values of the organizations. However, the advantage of the approach being forwarded here is that these institutional elements are not intuited beforehand but are derived from an analysis of intergroup relations. That is, they are tested for their appearance, persistence, and transformation in the context of intergroup relationships (informal and formal bargaining). The ends, values, and norms of an organization are examined for their influence on intergroup behavior where other organizations also have ends, values, and norms. The interaction of these elements (norms, values, and goals) in the context of intergroup bargaining may supplement the picture of interorganizational behavior, but the extent that is so needs to be determined. That is, traditional institutional theory can be tested by the strategy of analysis proposed here.

2. A brief history of the structure of the institutional complex is a necessary part of institutional analysis. The main purpose of the history is to provide a context for analyzing the changing power relations within the complex and to help predict their future course. The historical literature is a useful source for a broad historical profile, but it typically does not provide sufficient detail for sociological institutional analysis. Therefore, the researcher must obtain data on recent changes in interorganizational relationships by consulting the participants in major segments of the institutional complex. In addition, some documentary evidence may be available from organizational records and newspapers. Insofar as possible, the outline of the historical profile should follow elements as outlined in the present structural requirements.

3. The third requirement of institutional analysis is to examine the durability of the pattern of power in the institutional complex and the possible changes in it. The present structure of power will have been derived by fulfilling in the first objective of institutional analysis outlined above. This pattern is then compared directly to the structure of power obtained in the historical sketch of the structure, as determined in Point 2. Certain trends may be then noted.

4. Although predicting the future of institutions is hazardous, some things can be done to decrease the risk. The trends reported in Point 3 above will suggest alternative directions in the structuring of power within the institutional complex. The task then is to propose alternative power models and weigh the evidence whether present trends will stabilize the structure or introduce changes in it favorable to one of the alternative models. In the case of the economic institutional complex, the historical analysis will reveal that the power balance between labor and management at the local and national level is strongly influenced by the stance that government takes in industrial relations. Thus, outlining alternative power models involves considering other possible arrangements between labor and management and whether future political parties will change legislation that affects labor and management. The task then becomes one of analyzing the relations between the economic and political institutional complexes. Three likely alternative power models in a two-party system are (1) a management-dominated party versus a party with a management-dominated coalition, (2) a management-dominated party versus a coalition party in which management and labor have influence equal to other groups in the coalition, and (3) a management-dominated party versus a coalition party in which labor has a dominant influence.

An analysis of recent history will show that the present power arrangement follows the script in (1), a management-dominated Republican party and a coalition Democratic party in which business has dominant influence. This accounts largely for the weakening influence of labor nationally and in the Democratic party. The question then becomes whether power Model 2 or 3 will displace the present Model 1 in the near future. Although the limited space here does not permit an extended analysis, I (1990) have shown that certain organizational relationships of organized labor must change before Models 2 or 3 can be realized in a Democratic party victory. Labor would have to make stronger alliances with what I called the *passionate lobbies* of blacks, Chicanos, women's groups, and others. The strategy would call for changing labor's national priorities to give primacy emphasis to the priorities of the passionate lobbies. In addition, this might require labor to withhold support from the Democratic party until it changes its priorities and present commitments. This outcome will not likely be achieved for about 10 years. At that time the minorities will grow and exercise a more dominant influence in national politics. In short, ascertaining whether alternative power models will be realized calls for a systematic interinstitutional analysis.

CONCLUSIONS

This chapter has tried to expose the present confusion in sociological theories of institutions. Understandably, introductory textbooks reflect this confusion and tend to perpetuate it. I have suggested that norms, values, ends, and related concepts basic to traditional institutional theory should not be used as independent variables in institutional analysis. Rather, their effect, if any, should be determined in the crucible of interorganizational politics. To do this, sociology must launch a fresh approach to institutional analysis that begins by first determining how organizations cluster into recognizable networks, systems, or complexes. The structure of institutional clusters should be determined by a common methodology that identifies the organizations, their typical relationship, the history of the relationship, and possible future changes in them.

Critical to the new institutional analysis is the determination of power relations among the component organizations of the institutional complex. An exchange or bargaining framework to understand interorganizational behavior should be fruitful to expose the internal structure of power. Because changes in the institutional complex often arise from exchanges with other complexes, interinstitutional analysis is a necessary part of institutional analysis. The sociological literature reveals an overly simple approach to explain institutional change by applying either functional or conflict theories. Social processes are too varied to be fitted into a procrustean dichotomy, and functional and conflict theories are ill adapted to study the crosscutting cooperative, competitive, accommodative, and conflictful relationship within and between institutional complexes. Although the interorganizational approach to institutional analysis proposed here suffers from some obvious limitations, sociologists can advance this area by doing what they do best: study institutional life in largely organizational terms.

REFERENCES

Alexander, J. C., Geisen, B., Munch, R., & Smelser, N. S. (Eds.). (1987). *The micro-macro link.* Berkeley: University of California Press.

Barnes, H. E. (1942). *Social institutions.* New York: McGraw-Hill.

Blau, P. M. (1987). Contrasting theoretical types. In J. C. Alexander, B. Giesen, R. Munch, & N. J. Smelser (Eds.), *The micro-macro link* (pp. 71–85). Berkeley: University of California Press.

Eisenstadt, S. N. (1968). Social institutions: The concept. In *International encyclopedia of the social sciences* (pp. 409–421). New York: Free Press and Macmillan.

Form, W. (1990). Organized labor and the welfare state. In K. Erickson & S. Vallas (Eds.), *The nature of work: Sociological perspectives.* New Haven: Yale University Press.

Form, W., & Miller, D. C. (1960). *Industry, labor and community.* New York: Harper.

Gibbs, J. P. (1989). *Social control: Central concept of sociology.* Urbana: University of Illinois Press.

Hawley, A. H. (1986). *Human ecology: A theoretical essay.* Chicago: University of Chicago Press.

Hertzler, J. O. (1929). *Social institutions.* New York: McGraw-Hill.

Huber, J., & Form, W. (1973). *Income and ideology.* New York: Free Press.

Kluegel, J. R., & Smith, E. R. (1986). *Beliefs about inequality.* New York: Aldine-DeGruyter.

Lenski, G. E. (1966). *Power and privilege.* New York: McGraw-Hill.

MacIver, R. M., & Page, C. H. (1949). *Society: An introductory analysis.* New York: Rinehart.

Parsons, T. (1966). *Societies.* Englewood Cliffs, NJ: Prentice-Hall.

Perrow, C. (1970). *Organizational analysis.* Belmont, CA: Wadsworth.

Reynolds, P. D., Knoke, D., & Kaufman, N. (1988). *Estimating organizational populations.* Unpublished manuscript. Sociology Department. University of Minnesota, Minneapolis.

Spaeth, J. L. (1988). *Survey respondents as informants on the establishments for which they work.* Unpublished manuscripts, Sociology Department, University of Illinois, Urbana.

Williams, R. M. (1970). *American society.* New York: Knopf.

Index

American progressives, 200
American Bar Association, 54, 57

Baby boom, 54
Bioethics, 205–206
  organizations of, 207
"Black Monday," 13–14

Catholic church, 146–147
  growth in, 162, 163
  population change, 148–150
  Spanish diocese, 154–155
    projections, 160
  United States diocese, 154–155
Child care
  availability of, 43–44
  father's participation in, 41–42
  stress related to, 40–41
Class trajectories, 63
Clergy
  active, 156–158
  age distribution, 158–160
  decline in, 162
  population
    estimates, 155
    U.S. and Spanish, 152
  projections, 156–157
  retirement, 153

Democratic party, 252, 253
Demographic transition, 148–149
  stages of, 160–161
Depression, 37, 39

Depression (*Cont.*)
  related to child care, 43–44
  "Deskilling," 14
  Dictionary of Occupational Titles (DOT), 18, 19, 29
  Downturn period, 173, 175, 180, 183, 185
  Dropout rate, 73

Education, 25–26
  "loosely coupled systems," 76–77
  of women, 44–45
Employment
  income, 23
  incompatibilities, 40
  women workers, 23–25, 35–36, 44–45, 112
  effects of children on, 39–43
Ethics
  medical, 207

Fabian Socialists, 200
Family
  blended, 117
  "deficit theory," 94
  low-income, 94
  race, 101, 107, 117
  school connections, 105
  "strengths model," 94
Firms
  complexity of, 22
  levels of, 21–22
  workers, 21

Gallup poll, 221
Gender roles
    changing, 33, 43
    household labor, 35
    stress, 34–35

Health care expenditures
    inflation in, 203–204
    tables of, 203, 210
Health Maintenance Organization (HMO), 208
Hispanic students, 71
Household labor
    division of, 35
    economic influence on, 39

Income, 23
Industrial composition, 179
Industry and firm, 4, 27–29. *See also* Organization
Inflation, 176, 182, 186
Institutional analysis, 261, 265
    organizational
        change, 266
        concerns, 265
        meanings, 267
        patterns, 270–271
        power of, 272
Institutional complex, 267, 271
    educational, 269
    networks, 268
    structure of, 269
Institutionalized altruism, 199–200
Institutions, 263
    concepts of, 264, 266
    definitions of, 260–261
    textbooks on, 263

Job descriptions
    reclassifying, 22
"Job ladders," 55

Labor force
    developments, 10–25
        products, 19–20
    distribution of, 20
    job enlargement, 21
    in technology, 16
    women's participation, 23–25, 35
        lower earnings, 44–45
        supply and demand, 36
    worker supply, 23
Labor movement, 178–179

Labor strike, 179, 182, 186, 188, 190
    militancy, 189
Learning at home, 106
Legal firms
    corporate, 55
    expansion of, 54–55
    partnership, 57
    sectors, 55
    solo practice, 55
    subordinate levels of, 62–63
Legal profession
    class structure, 60–61
    comparison of U.S. to Canada, 50
    competition in, 58
    earnings, 57
    growth tables, 51, 53, 63
    power structure in, 58–59, 64
    transformation of, 64–65
    women in, 52–54, 56
        earnings of, 57
        job dissatisfaction, 58
        lower ranks, 63–64

Market research, 223
Marriages, 35
    depression in, 36–37
    survey of, 36
    transition of, 40, 43
    types of, 37–38
Marxian theory, 64
Mass mailing, 224
Mass media
    conflicts
        with education, 227
        with polity, 222–223, 229, 231
        with religion, 228
    convergence with public opinion, 218, 222, 233
    feedback, 220, 222
    influence of, 216
    link to economy, 228
    manipulation of society, 222–223
    new technology in, 223
    television, 226
Mechanical solidarity, 76
Medicaid and Medicare, 201–202, 204, 210
Medical-industrial complex, 209
Medical professionalism, 197, 209–210
Medical schools
    decline in, 199
Medicine
    controls of government, 204
    high status of, 200

Medicine (*Cont.*)
  laws of licensing, 198
  market forces, 199–200, 202
  professional authority, 210
  professional dominance, 204
  self-regulating, 199
  as welfare state, 210
    government-funded, 201–202
Megalawyering, 54
Minority students, 72–74, 81
  increase of, 71
  from low-income families, 72
Mothers in work force, 112. *See also* Labor
  force

National Assessment of Educational
  Progress, 72
National Commission on Excellence in
  Education, 73
Networks
  community, 80–82
"New Deal," 251
  erosion of, 248, 252
Nielsen ratings, 221

Occupational codes, 27
  of Census Bureau, 18, 19, 29
Occupational prestige, 26, 27
Occupations, 13–19
  boundaries of, 14
  changes of, 16, 28–29
  demands for, 21
  groups, 14
  measures of, 28–29
  retraining, 16–17
  segregation in, 23, 25
  service production, 19
  significance of, 15
  social class, 17
  social problems of, 16–17
  technology's effects, 21
  titles of, 16, 22, 27
  See also Labor force
Opportunity structure, 17
Organic solidarity, 76
Organization
  environments, 22
Organization of schools, 76–77
Organizational innovation, 22

Parents' reports, 95, 99, 111, 112
Parents
  characteristics of, 98

Parents (*Cont.*)
  education of, 94, 100, 111
  education of mother, 98–99
  married, 113
  See also Single parent
Partisanship, 249–250
  "critical realignment," 247
Peer influence, 81, 83
Political consciousness, 253
  decline in, 251
  identification, 248–250
Political participation
  dealignment, 248, 255
  decline in, 243, 246, 248
  of the educated, 245
  in the fifties, 241, 242
  turnout, 245, 253
  voting, 243, 252
    benefits of, 244
Political parties
  changing patterns in, 254–255
  decline of, 248–250
  renewal, 247, 256
Political socialization, 230
Postindustrial theory, 64
Precision journalism, 221
"Professional project," 197–199
Professionalization
  power of, 18
Proletarianization, 62
Proprietary medicine, 207
Psychological well-being, 36
  effect of children, 39–40
Public opinion, 216–217
  journalism, 221
  measured by elections, 218
  media control of, 217, 221
  polls, 221–222
  survey, 219, 221
  See also Mass media
Public relations, 220

Religion
  social change in, 146–147, 163
Research bias, 94

Scholastic Aptitude Test (SAT), 73
School research
  analytic studies, 115
  descriptive reports, 114
  integrative, ecological studies, 115
Schools
  administration in, 77

Schools (*Cont.*)
  cultural system, 79
  culture, 86
  discipline in, 85
  effectiveness in, 74–75
  future of, 87
  inner-city, 78, 81, 85
  interaction with family, 117
  interpersonal relationship, 79, 82, 84
  network, 80-81, 84, 86
  overlapping versus separate influences,
    92–93, 107
  parental involvement, 95, 97, 99, 104,
    113
    marital status, 100, 103, 114, 117
  private, 84–85
  urban, 101
Sectoral transformation, 14
Sex segregation
  in law, 56
Single parent, 113–115
  black, 101
  home, 97
  teacher bias, 111
Social capital, 84–85
Social democratic government, 177
Social institutions, 214
  language, 214
  mass media, 221–222
  new paradigm, 232–233
Social networks, 82–84
Stratification system, 17–18
Structuration, 214, 232
Student achievement, 104–105
Student behavior, 110–111, 114
  homework, 108–109

Teacher
  career table, 128
  evaluation of parental involvement, 100–
    101
  leadership, 99–100, 103–104, 108, 113, 116
  practices, 102–103, 115, 117
  of primary school, 130, 135
  qualifications, 132–133
  reserve pool, 124, 127, 134
  SAT scores, 133, 134
  single parents, 93–95
  training of, 132–133
  work load, 138

Teacher (*Cont.*)
  working with parents, 93
Teacher attrition, 132–133
  in high schools, 130, 135–136
  in inner-city schools, 135
  at private schools, 136
  and quality educators, 132–133, 135
  rates, 127
  school-related, 135, 137
  trends in, 125
Teacher shortage, 78
Teachers' report, 95, 103, 107, 111–112
  of parental involvement, 104, 107
  parents' status, 113
  on homework, 108–109
Teaching profession
  changes in, 123–139
  class size, 138
  dissatisfaction, 135, 138
  entering, 127
  exiting, 128
  reentry, 129–130, 132
  satisfaction in, 130, 137
  survival rates, 129
  women in, 127, 130, 132
Technology
  demand for, 20
Teenage parents, 88
Tertiarization, 19–20
Theoretical perspectives
  of teachers, 93
Trade dependence, 177
Traditional roles
  in family, 42–43
  of housewife, 39, 42

Unemployment, 176, 182, 186, 188
Union
  analysis of, 181
  decline in, 173–175, 180–181, 186
    explanation of, 176–177
    factors of, 176–180
  level of density, 179, 181–183, 185, 188
  militancy, 189–190
Unionization
  power of, 18

Values, 35

Wall Street, 13–14
White-collar jobs
    increase of, 17
    technicians as, 20
Women workers, 23–25, 35–36, 44–45, 112
    lawyers, 52, 54, 56
        earnings of, 57

Women workers (*Cont.*)
    lawyers (*Cont.*)
        job dissatisfaction, 58
        in lower ranks, 63–64
    teachers, 127, 130, 132
    See also Labor force; Occupations